In the Shadow of Nelson

By the same author

Nelson's Mediterranean Command

In the Shadow of Nelson

Denis Orde

Pen & Sword
MARITIME

For my wife Jane and
daughters Georgina and Philippa

First published in Great Britain in 2008 by
Pen & Sword Military
an imprint of
Pen & Sword Books Ltd
47 Church Street
Barnsley
South Yorkshire
S70 2AS

Typeset in Sabon by
Lamorna Publishing Services

Printed and bound in England by Biddles Ltd

For a complete list of Pen & Sword titles please contact
PEN & SWORD BOOKS LIMITED
47 Church Street, Barnsley, South Yorkshire, S70 2AS, England
E-mail: enquiries@pen-and-sword.co.uk
Website: www.pen-and-sword.co.uk

Contents

Maps and Diagrams

Preface and Acknowledgements

Although Vice-Admiral Lord Collingwood played a pivotal role in three of the greatest sea battles of the Napoleonic wars and was a close and lifelong friend of Horatio Nelson, the hero of the nation from whom he inherited the command at Trafalgar, very little has ever been written about him, either then or now. There was, for instance, little mention of him in the *Evening Chronicle* or the *Newcastle Courant*, the newspapers of the time which were local to his home town of Newcastle upon Tyne. It is true that he was essentially a quiet, modest, rather withdrawn man which may explain, to some extent, his relative anonymity, but the better and more obvious explanation is that throughout his naval career, which was really his entire life, he served in the shadow of the more flamboyant and inspirational Nelson who had captured the imagination of the general public and upon whom it wished to lavish its attention. But it remains the case that Collingwood was a significant factor in the meteoric rise of Nelson to national fame, and a distinguished servant of the British nation.

Fortunately many of Collingwood's own letters, many written in majestic prose, have survived, thanks to Newnham, the barrister who married his elder daughter after the Admiral's death and took the surname Collingwood, for he assembled, published and so preserved many of Collingswood's letters home. But some he obviously doctored and there is no doubt that his introductory narrative is unreliably selective with an eye to public approval and possibly also in the hope of royal patronage. This collection, to which further letters were added in later editions, was augmented in 1957 by the Edward Hughes publication and, in more recent times, by the Naval Miscellany VI, chapter IV, edited by Captain Owen under the aegis of the Navy Records Society. But inevitably no letter from his earlier days in the service has survived for the family was not, of course, to know then that the correspondence of a midshipman or junior lieutenant would be much worth saving for posterity. And, of those many letters written later which have been preserved, although they provide a very valuable insight into the character of the man, it has to be allowed that an author of letters written home from distant parts reporting events of national significance may himself have written with an eye to posterity. It is clear that, when writing many of these letters, Collingwood hoped, anticipated and indeed intended that they would achieve a wider circulation, as was the case. I have drawn several of the letters cited from the Newnham Collingwood and Hughes collections accordingly but in large part I have gone, in large part to those manuscripts written by his contemporaries which I have listed in the bibliography to see how he was judged by others with whom he served in order the better to know the true man.

I am grateful to the National Maritime Museum, London, and its staff for their assistance, in particular to David Turner of the Picture Library; to Stephen Courtney, Curator of Photographs at The Royal Naval Museum, Portsmouth; to the Laing Art Gallery in Newcastle upon Tyne; to the Newcastle upon Tyne City Library; to Mark Benjamin and his always helpful staff at the Hexham Library and, as ever, to the Bodleian Library in Oxford of which I have been a member ever since my student days at the university there, and which lies at such a convenient distance from our Oxford abode..

I owe my thanks to Edgar Vincent, author of *Nelson, Love and Fame*, to Rear-Admiral Richard Hill, naval historian, to Colin White, deputy Director of the Royal Naval Museum at Portsmouth, to Hew Strachan, Chichele Professor of the History of War at All Souls College, Oxford University and to Timothy Norton of Whalton for their helpful general advice early on, and to Dr Vernon Armitage, formerly Master of Hild and Bede College, Durham University, the Hon. Matthew Beaumont and Tommy Bates of Langley for their constant support of my interest in the naval history of the Napoleonic years. Lord and Lady Digby of Minterne provided much valuable information surrounding the lives of Admirals Robert and Sir Henry Digby, together with generous hospitality, coupled with enthusiastic support for the work, which was much appreciated. Lord Stevens of Kirkwhelpington helpfully suggested the title for the book and Commander Jeremy Pett RN, Dr David Harte of Newcastle University, Professor Roger Ainsworth MA, D.Phil., FRAeS, Master of St Catherine's College, at Oxford University, Mrs Susan Collingwood Cameron and His Honour Judge Guy Whitburn QC, a fellow judge, gave me help in certain specific areas. Sir Hugh Blackett Bt very kindly allowed me the run of his Blackett pictures at his home near to mine in Northumberland, as did the Master and Deputy Master of Trinity House in Newcastle, Captains Shipley and Healey, for which I am grateful.

Several friends of many years provided welcome encouragement, assistance and/or contributions, amongst them, as ever, the Viscount Dilhorne, always very hospitable; Tom Bowles, at one time a barrister colleague of mine in chambers, owner of the *Lady* magazine and grandson of 'Captain' Tommy Bowles; Lord Elliott DL of Morpeth who knew well the Matheson descendants of Collingwood's neighbour and friend in Morpeth; Sir Patrick Nairne MC, PC, formerly a master of a college at Oxford who had helped so much with my earlier book, *Nelson's Mediterranean Command*, Lord Howe of Aberavon CH QC, Sir John Campbell Orde Bt, Peter Campbell-Orde, Dr the Hon Matt Ridley and the Rt Hon Lord Justice Schiemann, a judge of the Court of Justice of the European Communities, a fellow Master of the Bench of mine at the Inner Temple Inn of Court, and a much more distinguished judge than I ever was.

An arrangement made several years ago to meet again, whilst sitting at the nearby Law Courts in the Strand, with the Dean of St Paul's Cathedral the Very Reverend Eric Evans, a friend made in student days at university, so that I could see what there was of Nelson in both the library and the crypt, was aborted by his sudden and tragic death. In contrast, my return there in recent months to photograph Collingwood's tomb was made very easy, for which I thank the Press Office at the Chapter House, the registrar and, as on so many occasions before and as ever, the Rt. Hon. The Baroness Butler-Sloss GBE, who now holds, amongst many other positions, the office of Chairman of the Advisory Council at St Paul's.

In writing again of the momentous events of 1805, my memory goes back also to an evening spent at dinner on board *Victory* on Trafalgar night at that same time, thanks to Admiral Sir John, then Admiral of the Home Fleet, and Lady Kerr, for Collingwood too dined in that same small cabin with Nelson in those very tense days before the battle.

And I here record my grateful thanks to my wife Jane and to my elder daughter Georgina, not only for their patient endurance but also for assistance given researching the provenance of some of the illustrations used.

Finally, to the publishing manager of my publishers, Pen & Sword Books Ltd, Brigadier Henry Wilson, I owe much for the support and encouragement he has given with such great courtesy and consummate professional skill. So too I was very fortunate to have the considerable expertise of a very understanding editor in Susan Econicoff to help me.

As ever it has been a labour of love and, in the early days, a welcome respite and escape from the ocean solitude of a judicial existence. If there be faults in the text, the faults are my own, save that if those are to be found in a description of Collingwood's gunnery, I lay the blame there on those instructors of gunnery who attempted to teach me, when a young artillery officer, the rudiments of their craft .

Denis Orde,
Chollerton, Hexham, Northumberland,
July 2007

Chapter 1

Of Collingwood and Nelson

> My friendship for him was unlike anything I have left in the navy –
> a brotherhood of more than thirty years.

So Collingwood wrote after the death of Nelson.[1]
And then:

> ...since the year '73 we have been on the terms of the greatest
> intimacy; chance has thrown us very much together in service, and
> on many occasions we have acted in concert.[2]

They were both fledgling midshipmen when they first met in the year
1773. But there the similarity ended for Horatio Nelson was then but a
boy of fifteen years, diminutive, spare, volatile, outgoing and with all
the confidence and enthusiasm of youth, where Cuthbert Collingwood,
ten years his senior, was by then a fully-grown man, tall, well-built,
dignified, handsome, intensely reserved and not a little austere. And yet
they took to each other immediately. Perhaps the one recognized in the
other a devotion to duty and a strong patriotism, for both were pas-
sionately dedicated to the service of their King, Country and the
Almighty. Both too were united in their hatred of the French, and,
coupled with this was a determination to achieve complete mastery of
their chosen profession. But whatever it was, and despite the disparity
in their ages, they truly delighted in each other's company and remained
the closest of friends for the rest of their lives. Almost forty-four of
Collingwood's sixty-one years of life and fifty years of service were to be
spent at sea in ocean solitude far from home, most of them in the
isolation of command. This, given his natural reserve, meant that
Collingwood made very few friends who were at all close to him. Only
Nelson, of those with whom he served, was ever able to penetrate that
reserve, and so it remained.

1

Clearly it was a friendship and a competence fully recognized and indeed encouraged by those set in command over them for with almost every advance made by the young Nelson in his inexorable and meteoric rise to fame, so Collingwood was appointed to succeed him in the command he relinquished. Their careers marched hand in hand. It was so when Collingwood took over as Master of the *Lowestoffe* in the year 1777/8 and it remained so until the death of Nelson twenty-eight years on at Trafalgar. And so to know the one is to know the other.

Yet, until Trafalgar, at no time did Collingwood in fact occupy a role which was subordinate to that of Nelson. Indeed there can be no doubt but that by his presence and participation and by the interventions he made in many of the engagements in which his friend was involved, he was, when in equal command, in no small part responsible for that success which was Nelson's. This undoubted fact has seldom been recognized in the wealth of literature which the life of Nelson has generated over the years. Indeed even public opinion of the day was largely silent about the contribution made by Cuthbert Collingwood and very little has ever been written of him.

It was, for instance, no coincidence that when Nelson played such a dramatic role at the Battle of Cape St Vincent which first brought him to the attention of the general public and propelled him to fame in the year 1797, his success was due in no small part to the timely arrival and considerable support of Collingwood. And in the final moments of Nelson's life on 21 October 1805, Collingwood was still there at his side, then as his second in command, executing the plan of campaign Nelson had devised, leading the attack and, after Nelson had fallen, carrying the fleet through to victory. Here again, for one last time, Vice-Admiral Cuthbert Collingwood stepped into the shoes vacated by Vice-Admiral Horatio Nelson, not simply as an interregnum but as full Commander-in-Chief of the Mediterranean Fleet, and there he remained until his own untimely death off the coast of Port Mahon, Minorca, five years on.

Many of those to whom the nation's affairs were entrusted in these momentous years no more than walked in the shadow of those giants who strode the national stage at the turn of the eighteenth century, those few men who so dominated the life of the nation at one of the most dangerous periods of its history, amongst them Pitt, St Vincent, Nelson and, later, Wellington; all men of magisterial greatness. So much so that little is ever written of others who also had a role to play. But at least those who fought at sea could count themselves fortunate to have served in the British Royal Navy through what undoubtedly were some of the most glorious years of its long and distinguished history, crowned as they were by Nelson's three great and epic victories at the Nile,

Copenhagen and off Cape Trafalgar. Collingwood was one such. But, unquestionably, he too was a warrior of outstanding distinction and one of the foundation stones of the modern British Navy.

Although the appetite of Napoleon Bonaparte for territorial expansion continued unabated for another decade or so, it was in the years 1803, 1804 and 1805 that Great Britain had been most at risk of invasion. Nelson appreciated this well enough, as did William Pitt, the Prime Minister. His relief was great indeed, therefore, when he was woken at 3 a.m. on the morning of 5 November of the year 1805 to be told of the great victory off Cape Trafalgar, but also of the sad death of Horatio Nelson, intelligence delivered to the Admiralty by the captain of the frigate *Pickle.*

The King too recognized full well that a great danger had passed when he was woken from his bed with news of the triumph, four hours later and, with tears in his eyes, read aloud the masterful and elegant dispatch written by Cuthbert Collingwood in majestic prose, yet modest of the part he himself had played in the battle.

Yet he himself had been responsible in no small part for his friend's success, both when Nelson stepped on to the public stage and again when he left it. And such had been their friendship that despite the younger Nelson's more rapid promotion in the service, and even though much greater attention had been given to Nelson for his different escapades, at no time on his journey through life did Collingwood ever resent it.

It was fitting, therefore, that after valedictory tribute and due homage had been paid and Collingwood was finally laid to rest five years on, it was alongside his friend Nelson in St Paul's Cathedral, buried in a plain stone tomb which had been constructed to receive the body of Cardinal Lord Wolsey and donated by the Duke of Clarence. And there he rests at peace, nestling in the shadow of his friend Nelson's larger and more flamboyant sarcophagus. As in life so in death.

Although less trumpeted than many, he was a just, humane and Christian man of immense courage, determination and professional skill. Indeed, he was an ornament to his profession and probably the noblest sailor of them all.

Chapter 2

Character

Effingham, Grenville, Raleigh, Drake,
Here's to the bold and free!
Benbow, Collingwood, Byron, Blake,
Hail to the Kings of the sea!
Admirals all for England's sake.
Honour be yours and fame!
And honour, as long as waves shall break,
To Nelson's peerless name.

Henry Newbolt's poem *Admirals All*.

Although not an inspirational, innovative or daring commander in the way of Horatio Nelson, and whilst he did not hold the chief command at any of the great sea battles of the French war, Collingwood became, above all else, the supreme and dedicated professional. His mastery of navigation and gunnery was prodigious and the firepower of three broadsides in five minutes achieved on every ship which ever fell under his command, was legendary. Indeed, it seems that at one point during the year 1805, even one broadside a minute was achieved, albeit the eminent naval historian Dr N.A.M. Rodger considered that so exceptional was that by any possible standard that it is unlikely that it could have been sustained for long. It was this pre-eminence which was the key to Collingwood's personal success at the three great Battles of the Glorious First of June, off Cape St Vincent and at Trafalgar. So much so that, many years on, a naval gunnery base at Portsmouth, now a shore training establishment, was named HMS *Excellent* after the ship commanded by him to such effect at St Vincent. Seldom can a ship have been named more aptly, for it was indeed a ship of proven excellence.
As William Davies was to write in the year 1875:

...[he] had an intimate and exact knowledge of all the technicalities of his profession...He insisted on everything being done rightly, and could himself splice a rope or perform any other office of the ship with as much dexterity as a common seaman.

He was not a man to set his men to carry out a task which he could not himself perform. Here then was a man of whom it could truly be said that he had advanced on merit and on merit alone. At no time in his career was he carried forward on the back of friendship or blood relation, as sadly is too often the case, nor could it, in justice, be said of Collingwood that he ever sought favour by expressing opinions deliberately manufactured to be supportive of those who enjoyed the gift of patronage and promotion.

In later years when in supreme command in the Mediterranean with all the powers of a plenipotentiary, responsible for the direction of naval affairs from Cadiz to Constantinople, such was his integrity, his devotion to duty and his sound judgment coupled with an instinctive diplomatic skill, that the Government found it impossible to replace him. Negotiating with a plethora of ruling autocrats of disparate ambition, each with his own agenda to pursue, to which policy would inevitably be subordinated, called for supreme patience and great tact. Fortunately Collingwood possessed both of these qualities in abundance and it was as well that he did for the responsibility for decision-making was often his and his alone without any prospect of support or guidance from the distant home government given the slowness of communication. And so his domination in that theatre of war became total and by his suppression of French naval activity in the Mediterranean in the years following Trafalgar and by maintaining vital supplies of food and ammunition for the forces in the Peninsula, the balance sheet will show that Collingwood's contribution towards the success of the Spanish uprising against Napoleon was massive.

Although he acquired a reputation as a stern disciplinarian throughout his years in the service, this was never achieved by brutal repression or excessive use of the cat, for he hated the degradation of flogging.

'I cannot for the life of me', he would say, 'comprehend the religion of an officer who prays all one day and flogs his men all the next.'

On those rare occasions when he did allow it, he would himself fall silent for many a long hour after the punishment had been inflicted. The records of punishment meted out on board flagships in the Mediterranean before Trafalgar show a marked contrast between those sanctioned under Collingwood's command, which were sparing, and those permitted on board, for instance, *Victory* when under the command of Horatio Nelson. It is of course so often the curious failing of the historian that he is tempted to judge the conduct of great men of yesteryear by the standards of today. But even if that approach was adopted with Collingwood he would still emerge as a merciful man, a man of humanity in an age of brutality, and it is this which stands as his true and lasting monument.

Rather, from 1793 onwards, he preferred to subject the drunkard, the thief, the disobedient, the neglectful and the violent offender to the performance of menial tasks, extra duty, watering of grog and exclusion from his own mess which made him the butt and object of ridicule and contempt, for, as a punishment, embarrassment was always reckoned to be the most effective weapon. At the same time he would often suggest to a young midshipman at the point of punishment of a man for disobedience to the young man's orders, which Collingwood would not allow, that the offender be spared if it was at all possible that the insubordination had been no more than a reaction to the midshipman's own failure of command.

So perhaps life at sea became more tolerable under Collingwood than under many another captain, some of whom were notorious for their abuse of power. And yet good order was renowned in the ships under his command. Indeed they became models of discipline. This was all the more impressive given that a ship's company was invariably composed of not only those genuine volunteers from Great Britain and elsewhere in the world who had been attracted to the service by the prospect of bounty, which in fact attracted but few recruits, but also those many violent and potentially mutinous convicted felons who had been sent from city gaols under the quota system, choosing service rather than the hangman's noose. With them came those many discontented individuals who had been press-ganged into the service and so were there very much against their will. Such men brought with them simmering discontent and every permutation of vice and base behaviour. Yet such was Collingwood's reputation that even that awesome and stern disciplinarian Lord St Vincent, and indeed Nelson too, spoke often enough of sending miscreants they could not tame over to Collingwood's ship so that they might be brought under control. 'Send them to Collingwood. He will tame them if no-one can', they would say.

In establishing methods for the maintenance of discipline at sea which were less brutalizing and less cruel than flogging, Collingwood was something of a pioneer and far ahead of his time. But it was to be another seven decades before the cat, as an accepted form of punishment in Her Majesty's Royal Navy, was finally outlawed.

Coupled with this was a constant and paternal concern for the welfare of his men which earned him, in the eyes of most, their gratitude, respect and affection. And so, behind his back, they knew him as 'Father'. To his friend Nelson he was always 'Coll', but to his fellow officers he was

'Old Cuddy', inappropriately, for this is the Northumbrian name for a donkey whereas Collingwood was endowed with the gift of high intelligence .

This concern for the wellbeing of those placed under his command was undoubtedly genuine and instinctive although it has to be allowed that he realized too, well enough, with an eye to battle conditions, that a man healthy in body and healthy in mind was much more likely to perform adequately than one who was sick and demoralized. He knew from experience that it is so often good morale which wins battles. And so, with a crew often separated from home for many a long and tedious year with little hope of leave, either because they were on blockade duty, the service most required of them, or because they were serving in ships deliberately kept offshore lest men who had been pressed were minded to depart, Collingwood constantly exercised his ingenuity to keep the ordinary sailor busy or amused and away from mischief. The only other break in the monotony to which a man could look forward was the prospect of enemy action in which, for all he knew, he might well perish.. And so, to relieve the tedium, maintenance tasks were ordained, home-made theatricals were encouraged and training schedules were devised to hone their skills for those very few days in the year when they would actually be required to face the enemy in battle.

A close watch was kept on the health of his crew for Collingwood was ever concerned with a lack of variety in the diet available, especially during those long weeks of blockade when he was denied provision of the usual victuals. At such times the reliable ship's biscuit, always in plentiful supply, became the centrepiece of every meal, although fresh fruit and vegetables were purchased whenever a relaxation of the blockade allowed. Every morning in life, Collingwood, even when an admiral, would leave his own more comfortable quarters and do an Orderly Officer's round of the sick bay, so concerned was he for the health of his crew. Many a time he would supplement the rations of a sick man with offerings from his own more well-stocked table, and, to combat disease and sickness, he organized constant ventilation throughout the ship, ordering the circulation of air and dryness in the cramped and crowded areas below and between decks. He was to write to Captain Clavell from the *Ocean* on 14 January 1807,

'Cherish your men, and take care of your stores, and then your ship will be serviceable.'

It has been written that sea life in the days of Nelson meant, 'Barbarous floggings [which] went side by side with bad pay, bad food and bad company.' If so, there can be no doubt but that Collingwood did much to mitigate the evil of at least two of these four cankers.

Like Nelson, the pastoral nurture and education of young midshipmen entrusted to his care, described by Collingwood as his 'Young Monkeys', was his particular concern, although he was not slow to let a sponsor know if, in his opinion, a young man was not destined to become a good officer.

In a letter to Walter Spencer-Stanhope MP, son-in-law of Winifred Collingwood who was a distant cousin of his, he wrote:

I shall be very glad to see your son William, and will take good care of him and give him the best introduction to the service that I can...do not burden him with luggage; if he takes care of it, it is but a miserable occupation, and if he does not it will be lost...a comfortable bed – that his health requires; two or three blue jackets and waistcoats; his navigation books that he has been taught from - whether it is Robertson's Elements or Hamilton Moore; a quadrant and a case of instruments...a history of England, of Rome, and Greece...But his luggage must be light – for the moment he enters a ship he must have no personal cares. All that relates to himself must be secondary – or nothing.

With respect to his supply of money or anything else, when he comes to me he shall want for nothing. I will take care he is sufficiently provided and whatever expenses he has, I will tell you that you may repay me.[1]

He was as good as his word, later reporting that:

...it is a great pleasure to me that I have nothing to say of him but what is good. His health has improved astonishingly, his body, which was puny and delicate, is become strong, he is grown much in stature, and is as diligent in his learning as can reasonably be expected.[2]

And then, later:

Of William everything I can say is good and such as must give you and Mrs Stanhope much satisfaction. He is the best tempered boy that can be, has a superior understanding which makes everything easy to him.[3]

And to his sister in October of 1808:

Stanhope breakfasts with me every day and is a signal midshipman – has sense and can take care of himself.

Yet he was to write of him later:

He will be a useful officer, a good one, but never a great one.

He also wrote:

I advance a great many who have not a friend to speak for them. Those who are diligent and promise to be useful officers never miscarry.

In another of his letters he said:

My business is to look for officers capable of doing the duty of the Service. When I find them, and find them gentlemen, I do not care who they belong to.

But one Currell he dismissed as 'Odd':

It is a pity that [his mother] had not put him apprentice to Jno. Wilson, the apothecary; he might have gone on very wisely. His gravity would have established his reputation as a learned doctor, and if it did poison an old woman now and then, better do that than drown a ship's company at a dash by running on the rocks.

Of another he reported to his wife that he should be:

...very sorry to put the safety of a ship and the lives of the men into such hands. He is of no more use here as an officer than Bounce is, and not near so entertaining. He is living on the navy, not serving in it.

Like Alexander Pope before him, Collingwood had named his dog 'Bounce'.

Yet he was diligent nonetheless in his attempt to impart to those midshipmen placed in his charge the secrets of his own navigational and gunnery skills, after which he would examine them weekly on what of it they had absorbed. In this way he unravelled the mysteries of seamanship to countless of the uninitiated, planting in their minds a basic understanding of the underlying techniques and principles of the sea, so very essential if an officer was to have any success when in command. There were lessons too in mathematics and literature, particularly the classics, in the hope that they, like him, might gain as good a grounding in these subjects as he had done himself thanks to his old headmaster, the Reverend Hugh Moises, to whom he was eternally grateful. Books were his favourite companions and became his salvation through many a long and lonely hour spent at sea. All of this and the sailor's *obiter dicta* gave him undisguised pleasure, surrounded as he was by the

9

product and flower of his own careful tuition.

Robert Hay, who served as a Boy Third Class in the *Culloden* with Collingwood in the year before Trafalgar, was to write in his memoirs:

How attentive he was to the health and comfort and happiness of his crew! A man who could not be happy under him could have been happy nowhere; a look of displeasure from him was as bad as a dozen at the gangway from another man.

In his *Anecdote Book*, Lord Chancellor Eldon was to write of finding Collingwood in the Strand with tears flowing down his cheeks. When asked what had so affected him, Collingwood explained that his ship's company had just been paid off which meant that he had lost his children, all his family, so dear were they to him. Small wonder that Eldon should write, 'He was an excellent man.'

It has been well said of Collingwood's management of men, that:

He shared their dangers, suffered their privations, and wore himself out in their service. By these different concerns his became in many ways the model ship of the fleet.

But it was perhaps a failing that, like Lord St Vincent, he should have been so obsessed with economy for he hated to see even the smallest wastage of fleet supplies or ship's equipment. At times he took this frugality to absurd and unnecessary lengths. The sails of his ship were literally worn to rags before he suffered them to be condemned,[4] and stray rope-yarns had to be picked up and saved instead of being thrown overboard. On formal occasions he dressed plainly, wearing a small cocked hat, a square-cut blue coat with tarnished epaulettes, a blue waistcoat and boots occasionally greased.[5] In tempestuous weather or when the enemy were in the offing his habit was to sleep on his sofa in a flannel gown, taking off no more than his epauletted coat. On such occasions he was to be seen on deck without his hat, his grey hair floating in the wind as torrents of rain descended – his eye, like an eagle's, alert and on the watch. 'Personal exposure, colds, rheumatisms, ague, all nothing seemed to him when duty called.'[6] It was rumoured that he became known by some senior officers as 'Salt Junk and Sixpenny' because he was apt to tell his guests at dinner that he had obtained the wine served at meal with the salt junk, at sixpence a gallon,[7] but there was probably little truth in that for he spared nothing for his guests on those increasingly rare occasions when time could be taken from his duties to entertain. For himself he was abstemious at table. The *Naval Chronicle* was to describe him as:

...extremely thin and temperate in his general habits; ate always with an appetite, drank moderately after dinner...whilst his personal attention to the lowest guest at his table was always universally observed.

At the same time, thrifty though he was by nature, through much of his life he continued to give financial support to hospitals in his native Newcastle upon Tyne, which was generous, and with each uplift in his salary increased the allowance he made to his spinster sisters back at home, wanting nothing for himself. And this concern for others extended to the financial wellbeing of the tenants on the estate left to him in the last years of his life, a legacy from which he had no wish to benefit at the expense of others.

But it was without doubt another failing, and a serious one, that he should have so concerned himself with detail, trivia and desk work, to which he was inextricably tied, that he found it impossible to delegate. He had become such a master of his craft that he could not bear to see a subordinate making a mistake in the handling of a ship which he, Collingwood, would not have made himself. Indeed he was to admit as much himself shortly before his death when confessing that 'I have an anxious mind from nature, and cannot leave to any what is possible for me to do myself.'[8] This was to cost him dear when he acquired the burden of supreme command in the Mediterranean after Trafalgar. A slave to diplomatic correspondence and the minutia of administrative duties, his cabin became his workplace and his ship became his home. It was a big mistake and it was to take its toll.

But perhaps the greatest of his handicaps was an inability to unbend or fraternize with officers under his command in a way which made Nelson such an attractive and magical commander. Although invariably cheerful, calm and under control, Collingwood was by nature a quiet, unbending, reserved, stern, religious, extremely dignified and intensely private and almost lonely man who was not addicted to the ordinary pleasures of life. He disliked theatrical flamboyance, pomp, frivolity, over-indulgence, lavish entertaining or debauchery and was never heard to swear or use coarse language when addressing his men. Although he did not condemn these things in others, and entertained at dinner as often as his duties would allow, this part of his role he found difficult to perform and it led some, such as Captain, later Admiral, the Hon Sir George Elliot, one of Nelson's pupils, to label him cold[9] and even austere and puritan in his ways, a man who made life a bore for those unfortunate enough to fall under his command. Some thought, unkindly, that he even preferred the company of his loyal dog Bounce to that of his officers. Certainly he liked to have quiet and thoughtful men around him such as Clavell, his first lieutenant at Trafalgar, Thomson, his Flag Captain in the Mediterranean, Scott, his gardener at home, and Smith, his personal attendant in the closing years of his life. It is true also that he cared nothing for popularity, notoriety or fame. Duty was his watchword and professional honour the only prize he cherished. An upright man of spotless integrity with a very acute mind, he could not bear to see an officer promoted unless it was on merit, for he would say, 'I like a man to get in at the port-hole, not at the cabin window.'[10]

Not surprisingly William Hoste was to say of Collingwood shortly after Trafalgar, 'He is a very different man from Lord Nelson, but as brave an old boy as ever stood.'

It was not that he lacked normal human emotion, for he was, in truth, a markedly warm-hearted and tender man who felt deeply. Rather it was a difficulty in communicating and expressing his innermost feelings to other than the nearest of his family and the closest of his friends, save in the written word.

It is all the more surprising, therefore, that his friendship with Nelson should have been quite so close and strong for although both were consummate, loyal and dependable fighting sailors of prodigious courage and determination, the small but flamboyant, vainglorious and mercurial Nelson, a man of burning ambition who was never slow to display his emotions, and a southerner who was ten years his junior, seemed almost a contrast to the older, taller, slimmer and more dignified Collingwood with an honesty, solidity, determination and quietness typical of one brought up in the northern Celtic fringes. But to Nelson and those others able to penetrate Collingwood's natural reserve, they were able to see the real man; just, highly intelligent and attractively modest as all knew him to be, but also warm, kindly, generous and possessed of a considerable wit which perhaps was not so apparent to those who did not know him well. During those long months and years of blockade, distanced as he was from home and family, letter writing had been his industry, pleasure and escape, and it is in his correspondence that the true Collingwood really emerges. His letters were for the most part works of elegant, sublime and exquisite prose written by a very well-read and well-educated, scholarly and thoughtful man, producing polished diction which was a delight to read and admired by all who saw it, including King George III who expressed wonder and admiration at the felicity and polish of his diction when he read Collingwood's dispatch sent home soon after Trafalgar which spoke of Nelson as an 'immortal memory', a phrase by which Nelson is remembered to this day. Such mastery of language was unusual in a sea officer, most of whom had been taken out of school at an early age and sent to sea. The result was usually poor grammar, bad spelling and amateur composition. Not so with Collingwood.

In many of his letters he wrote warmly, lovingly and longingly of his wife, his two small daughters and his garden back at home at Morpeth in Northumberland. But such were his absences at sea which stretched over most of his married life, they must have been all but strangers to him. Plainly very close to his heart they seem to have been present in his thoughts most of every day, but it is unlikely that, given the opportunity, he could have endured for long the humdrum inactivity of life at home in a small provincial market town. His real interest lay at sea where he could practise and deploy those skills which were his life's work and which he had so completely mastered, and where there was always a promise of action and excitement. The sailor dominated the man. Perhaps, at a distance, his family became for Collingwood a nostalgic and unreal vision mounted on a pedestal standing impossibly high above the harsh realities of normal everyday life. And so, in search of perfection, he constantly proffered advice to his daughters which was puritan in the extreme and would have been extremely difficult to follow. Above all else he exhorted them never to waste time on frivolities. Indeed, his advice to all was to plant acorns on the land, writing that:

> If the country gentlemen do not make it a point to plant oaks, the time will not be very distant when, to keep our Navy, we must depend entirely on captures from the enemy – I wish everybody thought on this subject as I do; they would not walk through their farms without a pocketful of acorns to drop in the hedge-sides, and then let them take their chance.

Alison was to write of Collingwood:

> If required to specify the hero whose life most completely embodied the great principles for which England contended in the war...the historian would, without hesitation, fix upon Collingwood.

Small wonder that, fifty years on, Thackeray should write of Collingwood in *The Four Georges*:

> I think since Heaven made gentlemen, there is no record of a better one than that. Of brighter deeds, I grant you, we may read performed by others; but where of a nobler, kinder, more beautiful life of duty, of gentler truer heart?...There are no words to tell what the heart feels in reading the simple phrases of such a hero, here is victory and courage, but love sublimer and superior.

Algernon Charles Swinburne, proud of his Capheaton, Northumbrian ancestry, was to end his poem *Northumberland*, which began with:

> Between our eastward and our westward sea
> The narrowing strand
> Clasps close the noblest shore fame holds in fee
> Even here where English birth seals all men free-
> Northumberland,

With:

> Our Collingwood, though Nelson be not ours,
> By him shall stand
> Immortal, till those waifs of old world hours
> Forgotten, leave uncrowned with bays and flowers –
> Northumberland.

This then was the man the gifted Nelson took to immediately when he was but fifteen years of age and they were to remain close friends for the rest of their lives. Nelson knew Collingwood as a man he could always trust and upon he could ever rely, whilst Collingwood recognized in the affectionate Nelson a sailor with a precocious talent and a magical touch who could stimulate in all who met him, including Collingwood himself, the ambition to achieve great things at sea. They complemented one another exactly and the result was complete harmony and to the end of their days the one took a genuine delight in the successes of the other. From the early years of their friendship in the West Indies there survive the portraits of Nelson drawn by Collingwood and Collingwood drawn by Nelson as a testimony to their close friendship. And when they were parted Nelson would write of Collingwood's departure as:

> ...a great loss to me; for there is nobody that I can make a confidant of.

And then in another letter:

> What an amiable, good man he is! All the rest are geese.

Whilst Collingwood would respond with:

> My regard for you, my dear Nelson, my respect and veneration for your character, I hope will never lessen.'

To his wife's uncle, Dr Alexander Carlyle, Collingwood wrote of Nelson that:

> [he] is an incomparable man,...his successes in most of his under-takings are the best proofs of his genius and his talents; without

14

much previous preparation or planning he has the faculty of discovering advantages as they arise, and the good judgment to turn them to his use.

In the last hours of his life at Trafalgar, Nelson could not resist crying out, on sight of Collingwood sailing headlong for the enemy line:

'Look at that noble fellow Collingwood, how he leads his Division into action!' whilst, for his part, Collingwood, when almost within pistol-shot of the Spanish fleet, touched his Captain (Rotherham) on the shoulder with, 'What would Nelson give to be here!'[11]

This afterwards led the *Naval Chronicle* to write of Collingwood:

The land we live in shall still be free, proudly defended by its wooden walls, and those brave warriors... .

Although lacking the genius of his friend, Collingwood was no poorer version of Nelson as some commentators of the late nineteenth century would have us believe. Indeed, for more than 200 years now the great victory at Trafalgar has been credited to Nelson and to him alone. Without doubt his reputation as a winner, his confidence which knew no bounds, his enthusiasm and his sure drive which was so infectious in the fleet, were crucial to the outcome. But the kernel of his battle plan, the tactic of breaking the enemy line, drive a wedge and then 'divide and conquer', was a model which had by then been recognized and adopted by most commanders – Jervis at St Vincent, albeit by accident rather than by design, Nelson himself at the Nile, and Napoleon on countless occasions on land. The constant truth of warfare is that even the best-laid plans are left behind in the heat and confusion of battle and are seldom adhered to. And that was especially so before the arrival of modern communication technology. Invariably the outcome lies in the hands of an individual unit and ship commanders who can, in the circumstances, but act on their own initiative. And in this regard Nelson at Trafalgar was blessed with captains, like himself, of very high navigational and gunnery skills. And pre-eminent amongst these was Cuthbert Collingwood. It was they, and the men they commanded, who also won the battle.

Nelson and Collingwood were both great sea captains in an age of great sailors when giants strode the national stage, and each in his own and different ways gave majestic and incomparable service to the homeland. Indeed both really sacrificed their lives upon the altar of the needs of their country as, hopefully, the pages which follow will serve to demonstrate.

Chapter 3

Collingwood and Nelson and The American War of Independence

When Horatio Nelson sailed onto the Jamaican Station of the West Indies in the year 1777 his arrival was greeted with delight by Cuthbert Collingwood after all that had gone before, for Collingwood felt both comfortable and liberated in his company. The opportunity now presented itself to indulge a friendship to the full which chance and the location of postings had prevented over the four years since they had first come to know each other

Both now sat securely in the rank of lieutenant although Nelson had achieved this through examination and following an impressive record of service spanning almost six years spent in the East Indies and on expeditions to the Arctic and to other distant parts of the world. In contrast, Collingwood's promotion had been won in the field of battle some two years before, so that, for the moment, he now stood senior to Nelson in the list of officers. It was not to remain so for long.

It was on 9 April of that same year that Nelson had presented himself to the Board of Examiners for a viva voce examination. Presiding that day was Captain Maurice Suckling, MP for Portsmouth and Comptroller of the Navy, although to Nelson he was his uncle and the sponsor of his service career. The other two captains who made up the Board that morning claimed afterwards that they knew nothing of this at the hearing or until Nelson had passed with flying colours. It was only then, they said, that Suckling revealed all. But it is clear that they did at least know before the hearing ever began that Nelson was well known to Suckling for one of the testimonials and records of service supplied to the Board by the five or six captains under whom he had previously served, bore the name of Captain Maurice Suckling, as a captain who had taken Nelson under his wing at the very outset of his career at sea. But he passed on merit, nonetheless, for his record of service was

16

impressive and he coped with the questions posed without undue difficulty, although, certain it is, the connection afterwards served him well enough for he was then appointed unusually quickly to an enviable post as second lieutenant of the *Lowestoffe*, a posting which had been secured for him by Suckling some little time before. Many an officer, newly promoted, had to wait months or even years before employment could be found. Although the deployment of ships and the disposition of officers was strictly in the gift of the Admiralty and its First Lord, still then the likeable and competent but possibly corrupt gambler Lord Sandwich, Suckling, as Comptroller and head of the Navy Board with responsibility for the supply of ships and men, stood high in seniority and there is no doubt that he exercised a great deal of influence in all matters naval. Many a flag officer would have been keen to cultivate his support.

In fact Nelson at eighteen years of age was strictly too young for promotion to the rank of lieutenant but a certificate produced falsely represented that he was two years older than in truth he was. Although the Admiralty insisted that records of naval service should be meticulous in their accuracy, it seems that it was commonplace for documents recording dates of birth to be manufactured or doctored in order to enable promotion from midshipman to lieutenant before due date, and whilst not actively condoning the practice, the Admiralty was but little concerned with such niceties. However, given the Suckling connection, it was no coincidence that the ship chosen for Nelson was the *Lowestoffe*, captained by William Locker, for she was then under orders for the Jamaican Station of the Caribbean where there was a clear promise of action, in this, the second year of the American War of Independence. Especially so when France came into the war ten months later in support of the American cause. Collingwood, meanwhile, had come to this same rank by a very different route.

Many years on, Collingwood was pressed repeatedly by the editor, Mr Joyce Gold, to pen a memoir of his life for publication in that important journal of naval affairs, *The Naval Chronicle*, which was published by Gold himself. The reluctant Collingwood had as often refused with the lame excuse that his life had been truly 'unremarkable' from start to finish and would have no interest for the average reader. Yet, in truth, Collingwood's service career had chanced to carry him to the scene of many of the very greatest events of the day, and often as an active participant, including three of the five greatest sea battles of the decade, ending with Trafalgar. Clearly this self-denigration was the product of a genuine modesty and a reluctance to advertise himself or court publicity in any way, By using the word 'unremarkable' he probably meant no more than that, compared with Nelson and some of the more flamboyant admirals and captains of that era, he was at that time really very little known to the general public outside the Royal Navy itself. But Trafalgar had changed all that whether Collingwood liked it or not, and so, eventually, he surrendered to Gold's request and reluctantly composed some sort of history in January of the year 1806.[1] But the result was no more than a short, perfunctory, summary account, shorn of any detail. Indeed it was little more than a catalogue of dates employed to identify the different stages of his career at sea. But he did at least in that narrative trouble to emphasize, with reference to the year 1777, that he 'had been long before in habits of great friendship' with Nelson. In fact they had met earlier in 1773 when both were midshipmen at Sheerness; Collingwood in the *Portland* and Nelson in the *Triumph*. In November of that year they were both serving at Portsmouth; Collingwood in *Lenox* and Nelson in *Seahorse*. And of his promotion to lieutenant he wrote the bare detail that:

In 1774 I went to Boston with Admiral Graves, and in 1775 was made a Lieutenant by him on the day the battle was fought at Bunker's Hill, where I was with a party of seamen, supplying the Army with what was necessary to them.

It was indeed the American War of Independence which eventually lifted Collingwood from the lowly rank of midshipman to the rank of lieutenant. And it lifted him too from obscurity and marked the turning point of his service career. From then on his life as a naval officer began to prosper. But not only that, for that same war also put his character and abilities to the test in five very hazardous situations in as many years, three of which placed his life in danger from combat, disease and drowning and the other two of which threatened his entire career. All of this was far from 'unremarkable'. It was this same campaign which truly brought Collingwood and Nelson together as friends and companions in arms when Nelson sailed into that theatre of war on board the *Lowestoffe*.

Battle of Bunker Hill

It is often supposed that this war was the culmination of a spontaneous protest against punitive and extortionate taxation levied by the home country and in no small part due to the blind obstinacy of King George III. Others judge that it was a war fought by ungrateful colonial leaders in search of riches, advantages and position for themselves and ever ready to enlist the help of the old enemy, France, to achieve their mercenary goal. But the simple truth is that most of the colonists led very independent lives in wide-open under-populated distant provinces where self-rule in their own assemblies was both a necessity and a reality. They felt that legislation enacted in Westminster, many hundreds of miles away and tailored for the more complex and populated areas of Britain, had little useful relevance to their way of life. The settlers had simply by this time come to regard themselves as Americans living in a country which was several thousand miles distant from the home government. As many of them saw it, their country had become a nation in its own right and they were anxious to have conduct of their own affairs. 'Colonies are the fruit which drops from the tree when ripe', said a French statesman at the time, and so, when the colonists came up against troops of the mother country they fought with dogged determination, as at Bunker Hill.

It is true that they accepted the assistance of France, a country which was all too ready to support almost any revolutionary movement which targeted the British nation as a country which at times during the eighteenth century, almost dominated the world. In the nature of things, as a dominant power, she had but few friends and many more enemies, all of whom sought her trade and coveted her Empire. France, with the intermittent support of Spain, was to challenge the supremacy of Britain as a world power for a century or more until their differences were finally resolved at the Battle of Waterloo. Under the Treaty of Utrecht in 1713, following the war of the Spanish Succession, Britain had been left with a presence in the New World which covered the eastern seaboard from Newfoundland in the north, which had been ceded in the treaty, down through the British New England colonies lying east of the Allegheny mountains, to Georgia in the south and extending also to the islands of the West Indies. But to the west of this line lay the threat of France, well established in control of the St. Lawrence River and the Great Lakes in the north, and in control of the Mississippi basin and Louisiana in the south. And in the year which followed she steadily consolidated this barrier to British territorial expansion westwards. Almost inevitably, war between the two nations came in 1756. After seven long years the French surrendered and under the terms of peace Britain gained the whole of Canada together with Nova Scotia and Cape Breton Island.

Clearly it was essential now to maintain a standing army of occupation in the New World to protect American as well as British interests. George III, an honest, well-meaning and straightforward man, now sought a contribution from the colonists, both for the cost of the war and for the expense of quartering a peacetime army. It was met with protest and proclamation by settlers who believed themselves already the subject of too much regulation, restraint and taxation at the hands of the home government. Allegiance to the government in Westminster

19

became even more lukewarm once the threat of French invasion abated. The colonists were then less ready to pay for a British military presence in their country or to accept terms of trade which had been imposed on them at a time when they had faced a common enemy. And so when the necessary legislation came forth to emphasize the right to raise revenue from the colonists by way of taxation, not least the Sugar Act, followed by the Currency Act, the Billeting Act and the Stamp Act which was replaced by Chancellor Townshend's Declaration Act, so the hostility grew. The Sons of Liberty Association was formed in opposition and the death of five Americans who had been shot when throwing snowballs at British soldiers in Boston in 1770, was dressed up as a massacre. As ever a handful of extremists exploited the situation to the full, led and orchestrated by the Bostonian Samuel Adams who had waited many a long year for just this opportunity. 'No Taxation without Representation' was the slogan borrowed from the writings of John Locke, the English writer long since dead.

But then, in the year 1773, in a moment of supreme foolishness, for most of the punitive acts had by then been repealed save for the Tea Act, which the Government had preserved in order to demonstrate its right to tax the colony, Lord North's Government, subservient to the King's wishes and sycophantic to his person, gave the East India Company a concession to protect them from the overwhelming competition of traders exporting tea to the American provinces on the black market which had brought the company to near bankruptcy. Since all tea had to be imported into Britain to be taxed at the point of entry before being exported to America ,the government allowed rebates of most of the tax paid by that company, thus making the price of tea imported from other traders less competitive. It gave the company a virtual monopoly and an unfair advantage, albeit one to the benefit of the American consumer. And yet, paradoxically, to prevent it being brought on shore, on 16 December 1773, and at the instigation of Samuel Adams, $75,000 worth of imported tea was tipped from the boats into the harbour by colonists, masquerading as Mohawk Indians. Although this was an act of criminal damage to private property which was wanton and illegal, the response of the British government to this 'Boston Tea Party' was heavy handed in the extreme. The port was closed to further business until full compensation had been paid and a number of punitive coercive measures were passed curtailing life in the province. At the same time it extended the French-speaking Catholic province of Quebec as far south as Ohio so that Puritan lands could be developed by the French papists. All of this gave momentum to the call for liberation and gave the radical minority the response it had been waiting for.

Anticipating trouble, the British eventually sent troops on 18 April

1775 to seize an armoury of weapons and ammunition which the colonists had assembled at Concord. But in the early morning mist on the way they were confronted at Lexington Green by rebel militiamen. In a twenty minute skirmish a shot was fired, it is not known by which side, and the war had begun. Ten Americans fell dead in that preliminary encounter but many more British troops fell to the bullets of snipers on the return journey to base that same day. There followed Thomas Paine's book *Common Sense* which presented a powerful argument for independence which led to the Declaration of Independence on 4 July 1776. The work of Thomas Jefferson, drawing heavily on the English work *Second Treatise On Government* by John Locke, it was a propagandist appeal to liberals the world over.

'We hold these truths to be self-evident that all men are created equal...Life, Liberty and the Pursuit of happiness.'

Yet, despite their differences, for most in America it was a war they did not want or need. And such were the ties of blood and kinship and the use of a common language, that those required to prosecute it had little stomach for the fight.

Cuthbert Collingwood was no exception. But like John Orde, his fellow Northumbrian, as a very junior officer he could but obey, and both were to gain by the experience of battle and to earn the commendation of those under whom they served. Promotion followed in its wake. In 1775 Collingwood sailed into the American war on board the diminutive fourth rate *Preston*, a midshipman of twenty-seven years but with little service in theatres of war. He was to emerge a captain in post rank with experience of warfare at sea. Orde had been a junior lieutenant. He was to emerge both married and blooded in battle as a post captain.

Bunker Hill lies above the town of Charlestown on the northernmost of two peninsulas between which lies Boston. In truth Boston had no real strategic importance to the British, the more so since the slender naval resources made available to General Thomas Gage, Governor of the Province of Massachusetts Bay, meant that they were quite unable to prevent the free flow of colonial shipping into its harbour which the British were there in 1775 to prevent, whilst at the same time the Army languished inactive in its streets, an easy target for any guerrilla attack. But after all that had happened, pride made evacuation impossible. It was only after months of procrastination, inactivity and inexcusable indecision on the part of the Governor and his staff, followed by the arrival of three British major generals in the shape of John Burgoyne, Sir Henry Clinton and Sir William Howe, who was the younger brother of Admiral Lord Richard Howe, that a decision was eventually taken to occupy the Charlestown Heights and the Heights of Dorchester on the most southern peninsula from which it was hoped it would be possible to control all entry to the harbour.

But, such had been the delay that when they woke on the morning of 17 June 1775 it was to find that 3,000 of the 9,000 rebel colonist militiamen who had previously surrounded the town, all part-time amateur soldiers who would come and go as the mood took them, had beaten them to it. Under cover of darkness the night before they had occupied the Breed Hill spur on the ridge of Bunker's Hill on the peninsula opposite.

Collingwood was at this time serving on board the *Preston*, then riding at anchor in the straits below, bearing the flag of Vice-Admiral Samuel Graves. When he came up on deck as dawn broke, he was as astonished as any to see the heights above now occupied by the rebels. At the same time, after weeks and indeed months of inactivity and uncertainty and not least boredom, he was not downcast unduly for he saw this threat as at last an opportunity for the active service which he craved. And he did indeed then play a crucial and enthusiastic role in storming the redoubt which the Yankees, led by one Colonel William Preston, had so skilfully fortified with trenches and obstacles which had made it almost impregnable to artillery fire from the British sloop *Lively*.

As on the first day of the Battle of the Somme 141 years later, it was assumed by the British, wrongly and tragically, that heavy bombardment from their artillery must have annihilated or, at the very least, dislodged the enemy in his entirety so that any advance would be a mere formality with little or no opposition. As it was the colonists, well dug in, had survived the onslaught more or less intact and unscathed and were more than ready to meet the advance when troops were landed at Moulton's Point. And so, although the unimaginative frontal attack on Breed's Hill devised by Gage and then launched by Howe did finally succeed and the Americans did eventually capitulate, it took three attempts to achieve that victory, the first two of which were repulsed. It involved wholesale slaughter on both sides. Here was the command first given to 'Fire when you see the whites of their eyes', upon which the colonists acted to such devastating effect when picking off British redcoats at close range as they struggled manfully uphill fully-laden. In fact it was only when ammunition supplies ran out and the British launched a bayonet attack in a third wave of the attack that all resistance finally collapsed.

Then, as the colonists retreated across Charlestown Neck, so artillery fire from His Majesty's ships *Glasgow* and *Symmetry*, supported by broadsides from floating batteries in the harbour below, decimated their numbers. Victory was indeed bought at a terrible price.

Collingwood was later to describe the fighting involved in this battle as the hottest he ever saw, and an obelisk still marks the spot where so many lives were lost. To complete the rout Howe afterwards ordered that the town of Charlestown, from which all but 200 of its citizens had fled, be fired. Shells then demolished the tall wooden buildings which soon caught fire and the town was quickly reduced to rubble.

Lord George Germain had written prophetically before the battle that:

> Gage...with all his good qualities, finds himself in a situation of too great importance for his talents. The conduct of such a war requires more than common abilities.

Not surprisingly Gage was recalled home in October of that year despite the opposition of the King. So ended for him more than twenty years of service on the American Station. He was replaced by General Howe, although he, too, was to be faced with a very comparable problem in the year following when George Washington successfully held his ground on the Dorchester heights until the British had evacuated the town.

But Collingwood had survived, and so impressed was Admiral Graves with the part he saw Collingwood play when commanding a party of seamen on shore at the foot of the hill, keeping the soldiers supplied with powder and shot throughout the advance, that he immediately promoted him fourth lieutenant of the *Somerset*. This was done on the day of the battle itself and the promotion was later confirmed the moment he returned to London in that same ship. Collingwood had before then languished in the ranks of midshipman and master's mate and without recognition for fourteen years or more – undoubtedly only because his abilities had never before been put to the test. It had not been want of ability so much as want of opportunity which had held him back, for he was a man of great seagoing efficiency. But now at last his career had been launched. This had been the first of the five trials he faced during the American War and he had passed with flying colours.

The Admiral who had finally recognized his talents and lifted him from obscurity and so rescued his career was Vice-Admiral Samuel Graves, first cousin of Thomas Graves, at that time a captain but soon to achieve flag rank and eventually the rank of admiral as Lord Thomas Graves. Samuel Graves on the other hand had in that year, unbeknown to him, reached the zenith of his career. When appointed Commander-in-Chief of the North American Station in 1774 at the age of sixty-one he had been given an almost impossible and extremely delicate assignment when ordered to implement the Boston Port Bill at Boston where the most ardent revolutionaries had assembled at the outset of the war when, if anything, diplomacy was probably what was required. He had but a handful of sloops of war at his disposal, none of which was armed or prepared on a war footing, and his instructions were brief to the point of obscurity. They simply required him to implement the provisions of the Boston Port Bill. When therefore the insurrection continued to gain momentum to the embarrassment of the home government, Graves took much of the blame for it and so was removed from his command in January of 1776. He was offered the port of Plymouth the following year but summarily refused it, angry that he had been made a scapegoat by a government anxious to obfuscate its own incompetence. At the same time he stated that he was ready to respond to any requirement for active service which may be made in the future. But none came and he was never offered employment again. In the general promotions Samuel Graves did finally rise to the rank of Admiral of the White. But then he died in the year 1787 at the age of seventy-four, not knowing that by the promotion of Cuthbert Collingwood to the rank of lieutenant he had launched a career which was to serve the British nation with considerable distinction for many a year to come.

In fact Collingwood's first baptism in his new rank was a distinctly unfortunate one for it was his misfortune to be appointed in the year 1776 to serve in the sloop *Hornet* in the West Indies under the command of one Captain Haswell. Haswell was a notoriously odious, unpopular and tyrannical man who had failed to reach post rank after many years in the service. He had very little appetite for any sort of action at sea, although it has to be allowed that, without a navy of any sorts, the colonists were seldom in conflict with the British navy in the early months of the war. Foolishly Collingwood was unable to conceal his dislike for the man. He was to write home:

I told him I was determined no longer to bear with his capricious humours... .He had not a word to say...but he kept out of my way.

Inevitably Haswell, when the opportunity arose when Collingwood was late in presenting himself as a witness at a court martial, retaliated by delivering an irrational and venomous attack on Collingwood's character. It took but a few questions by the tribunal to expose the outburst as entirely malicious and without foundation. But then, in 1777, Haswell brought Collingwood himself before a court martial as the accused, alleging want of enthusiasm, disobedience and neglect in the performance of his duties. It was a thin charge, but it was a charge of insubordination nonetheless. However, and fortunately, the tribunal again quickly saw through the character of Haswell and promptly acquitted Collingwood on all charges. But at the same time they seem to have reprimanded him for want of cheerfulness. Before that moment Collingwood had not realized that bonhomie was an attribute required of one of His Majesty's officers! His career in his new rank had been saved and he had survived the second of the five challenges which were to face him during this war.

Given his service with Haswell, it was with no little pleasure that he learned of his mercurial friend's arrival on the Jamaica Station of the West Indies in that same year, for with Nelson he felt he could unbend.

Both then fell under the command and spell of Rear-Admiral Sir Peter Parker, himself the son of a rear-admiral. At that time fifty-six years of age, Parker had been knighted in 1772 and promoted to flag rank on 28 April 1777 with command of the Jamaica Station. This he took up in the year 1778. From then on he was to take a paternal interest in the service careers of both Nelson and Collingwood. Indeed he was to become something of a father to them, yet lived long enough to see both off the stage at their respective funerals at St Paul's Cathedral, London, on each occasion as Admiral of the Fleet and chief mourner.

A man of considerable managerial skills, Parker soon recognized the worth of these two young officers at a time of greater naval activity with the arrival of France and then Spain in support of the colonists. Firstly, albeit on Locker's recommendation, he moved Nelson from the *Lowestoffe* into his own flagship, the *Bristol*, as third lieutenant and then, within three months, promoted him first lieutenant. Only three months later, in December of 1778, he posted Nelson commander of the 12-gun brig *Badger* and installed Collingwood in the *Lowestoffe*. And a mere six months on he appointed Nelson to the 28-gun frigate *Hinchinbroke* as its commander, in place of Captain Hooper who had been killed in action. Nelson, now with the coveted rank of post captain, had every prospect of reaching flag rank by the mere passing of time for, unless a post captain became disabled by illness or bad behaviour, promotion was automatic, inexorable and on seniority. And by this promotion at the tender age of twenty years, which brought with it gold lace on the cuffs and gold lace on the lapels of his blue frock coat, he now stood senior to the thirty year old Collingwood in the list of officers. He was entitled now to wear his cocked hat sideways. By then Collingwood was serving in the *Bristol* but then he too was given a further command on 20 June 1779, this time of the *Badger* in place of Nelson. And so once again he followed closely in Nelson's footsteps. Parker is therefore rightly credited with spotting Nelson's potential at an early stage of his career and then launching and advancing it with a number of appointments which were truly inspired. Although this was ultimately to the advantage of the British nation, it was not perhaps done solely for that reason for, newly climbing the ladder of promotion in flag rank, Parker would know full well that Nelson's uncle was at that time Comptroller of the Navy and therefore not without influence when the deployment of flag officers fell to be made. At the same time it has to be acknowledged that Collingwood, an officer without any sort of influence which was at all comparable, also received the support of Parker at this same time and events were of course to demonstrate that he was indeed absolutely right to regard both men as officers of enormous potential. When Captain Suckling died soon afterwards in July 1779, in the same year as that intrepid sailor from the north-east of England, Captain Cook, to his credit, Parker, and indeed his formidable and influential wife, Margaret, continued to shepherd the career of these two friends as best they could. And so Collingwood was able to write later that, 'Whenever Lord Nelson got a step in rank, I succeeded him.'

Parker himself was raised to the rank of vice-admiral on 19 March 1779 and on his return to England at the close of the American War in 1782, was rewarded with a baronetcy. Although he never went to sea again he was advanced to the rank of admiral in 1787 and then finally to the ultimate rank of Admiral of the Fleet in the year 1799. It was though his personal tragedy that his son, Vice-Admiral Christopher Parker, who had married the daughter of Admiral John Byron, the uncle of George Gordon Byron, sixth Lord Byron, the poet, was to die before his father. But then Parker lived to a great age, famous by then as the patron of Nelson.

Collingwood had served a difficult apprenticeship both at Bunker Hill and under the unpleasant Captain Haswell. But now that Spain had entered the war in June of 1779, a third and even more severe challenge faced both he and Nelson when they were appointed in April of the year 1780 to join the ill-fated expedition to the River San Juan and Lake Nicaragua in the Spanish overseas territory of Nicaragua, with Nelson placed in command of its naval force.

Encouragement for the campaign had come from the Colonial Office in London, and in particular from the formidable Colonial Secretary, Lord George Germain, who had long since rescued his career from oblivion after his dismissal from the Army at Minden some twenty years before. The hope in London was that by attacking Spanish territories in the way proposed, not only would the British be able to plunder the riches and bountiful natural resources which lay in Spanish Nicaragua, but that, and more importantly, Spanish troops sorely needed by the American rebels further north would be pinned down in that far away station in central America.

The plan was to land a task force of 500 or so troops at the mouth of the River San Juan on the Mosquito Coast of the Atlantic eastern seaboard of Nicaragua and then leave it to penetrate up river as far as Lake Nicaragua, a journey of more than 100 miles. This would involve the capture of a lookout battery and two forts which lay in its path protecting the river, after which the troops would capture and plunder both the capital, Leon, and the larger and richer city of Granada which lay on the shores of the lake itself, before striking west a further ten miles or so across the neck of the peninsula to the Pacific Ocean. In this way it was hoped that Spanish America, north and south would be split in two leaving a British Army in occupation of the middle ground with a gateway to the Pacific Ocean..

Hatched by the Governor and Commander-in-Chief of Jamaica, Major-General Dalling, a rotund and amiable but determined soldier from Suffolk, who had fought with Wolfe at Quebec and who saw in it a way of making as big a name for himself, it was an ambitious plan and it was doomed to fail. The force itself was too small and it was composed for the most part of a motley collection of ill-disciplined and inexperienced irregulars, volunteers, drunkards, gaolbirds and adventurers, stiffened by a core of 250 or so regular soldiers equipped with canoes, a gunboat, weapons, ammunition, provisions and medical supplies. But, although many were persuaded to support the plan upon Dalling's assurance that the dry, open Nicaraguan uplands surrounding the lake far from the Mosquito Coast would be better for the health of the soldiers than Jamaica, the greatest enemy proved to be not so much the enemy as tropical disease, sickness and death.

When asked to provide sloop transport to carry the troops to the mouth of the river, Sir Peter Parker hesitated long and hard for he could at that time ill afford to spare any ship of his fleet. He considered too that little was to be gained from such an expedition which, in any event, would probably end in disaster. But, eventually, he did give his consent and Nelson, twenty years of age and commanding the frigate *Hinchinbroke*, was the officer appointed to transport the small expedition to the Mosquito Coast.

On arrival there he soon discovered that supporting units of volunteers and Indians which the superintendent general of the British settlements on the Mosquito coast, James Lawrie, had promised, had failed to arrive, and the native population of Mosquito Indians which was to provide guides for the trek inland and to navigate the party up river had, for the most part, disappeared into the jungle, fearing that the visitors were simply there to abduct them as slaves. However, the commander of the expedition, Acting Colonel Polson, persuaded enough of them to creep back to the shore and act as guides by guaranteeing their liberty and promising financial reward and then, finally, Lawrie himself appeared. But it was with a very much smaller force than had been expected and, by this time, valuable days of what was left of the dry season had been wasted. Nelson then lost no time in transporting the expedition to the mouth of the San Juan and there the contingent

27

disembarked. But, almost inevitably, the moment they clambered into their boats and made for the mouth of the river in the small craft which had been provided, many of the boats capsized in the strong current, such was their lack of sailing skill and experience. Although Nelson had by now given all the support which the navy had been asked to provide and had dropped anchor offshore to guard the back of the force, ever enthusiastic and with the thought of adventure and possible glory and riches, he yet again came to the rescue. Not only did he then navigate the small craft safely into the estuary himself, he then undertook to accompany and supervise the ascent up river as well, taking with him several of his crew.

So began a lengthy and difficult journey through tropical rain forests in extremely hostile and dangerous jungle territory where a fall into the water meant death by alligator and where a brush with a tree invariably flushed out a snake. Several of the contingent were struck down by malaria or fever contracted from the mosquitoes on the coast and incubated over the previous several days. And many of those who went down lay dead where they fell, left to be devoured by the indigenous wild animal population. The more fortunate were accorded some sort of burial, most of them buried where they lay. But eventually, three weeks on, those who survived managed to reach the battery post which was the first of the obstacles to be overcome. This they found to be manned by a starving, badly equipped and thoroughly demoralized collection of fourteen or so soldiers. Here Nelson organized a bombardment followed by a frontal assault and the position was taken without much opposition and the soldiers who had manned it quickly surrendered. However Fort Juan, five miles further upstream and just short of the lake and grandly named the Castle of St John, presented a more formidable obstacle manned, as it was, by seventy or more troops supported by many more civilians. The more so when, despite Nelson's insistence that an attack be launched without delay, Polson ordered that it be suspended until ammunition and reinforcements being brought up river had had time to arrive.

In the meantime Nelson and one Lieutenant Despard organized an artillery bombardment until what remained of their ammunition had been spent, and then they waited. In the result, before the additional troops were able to reach the fort, the dry season gave way to torrential rain, which made further progress almost impossible. And by the time further supplies and reinforcements had arrived and the attack renewed, Nelson, its leader, like so many others before him, had fallen prostrate and dangerously ill, a prey to dysentery thought to have been contracted from water taken from a pool polluted by a poison tree. A few days later he finally succumbed to the deadly yellow fever, known as Yellow

28

Jack, or black vomit, or, as it is now thought, tropical sprue, probably caught on the Mosquito coast and all the while incubating, and he was quite unable to take a step further. It was then that Despard, a very capable and resourceful soldier, took over.

He had, on the journey up river assisted Nelson with efficient determination and, with the help of those reinforcements of men who had survived, he stepped into Nelson's shoes and continued the assault. And it was Nelson's great good fortune at that critical moment that a timely order from Parker should then have arrived delivered by the commander of another wave of reinforcements, for it directed that the ailing Nelson should relinquish command of the *Hinchinbroke* forthwith. Not knowing that Nelson had left the mouth of the river to accompany the expedition upstream, he ordered him to take command of the larger *Janus* after its captain, one Bonovier Glover, had succumbed to the plague and expired. Nelson was ordered to hand over command of the *Hinchinbroke* immediately to Cuthbert Collingwood . The probability is that this order saved Nelson's life, for he was brought back down river without delay, the return journey taking but three days to accomplish on the back of a now swollen river. But he remained too ill to take command of the *Janus* and so was billeted by a worried Captain the Hon Billy Blue Cornwallis with his emancipated Jamaican ex-housekeeper, and then with Sir Peter Parker before being shipped back to England to recuperate, this at the insistence of a concerned Sir Peter and his wife, both of whom had developed a considerable affection for the young Nelson.

In the meanwhile, soon after Nelson had withdrawn, the fort surrendered. It, too, was found to be occupied by starving soldiers whose water and ammunition had run out, together with a number of refugee civilians from nearby settlements who had found sanctuary within its walls.

The whole escapade had been something of a disaster, as Parker had predicted it would be. But Polson and Dalling saw it as success enough and were warm in their praise for the contribution to the outcome which had been made by Horatio Nelson. Without doubt, it would have failed altogether but for his initiative and determination. Indeed Dalling insisted that the trek to the Pacific Ocean should continue but, faced with mounting sickness and torrential rain, it was abandoned before it ever started and the fort itself was evacuated by Polson within a matter of days. He and his skeleton force retreated back down the river to its mouth, by now but a remnant of that which had set out. Not surprisingly a Board of Enquiry convened later in Jamaica, to which Collingwood gave evidence, acquitted Dalling of blame but found that had the expedition set off earlier and then attacked the fort of St Juan without delay, a trek to the lake and the healthy uplands would have been possible before the onset of the rains. Dalling was quickly recalled to London by a government angry at the futility of the whole venture and appalled at the number of lives which had been sacrificed in its cause. His plan had been badly planned and as badly executed. He suffered a reprimand and was never employed again.

As for Collingwood, once more in the shadow of Nelson, he was left to salvage what he could from the venture when he sailed as a passenger from Port Royal on the frigate *Resource* on 10 of April to take over command of the *Hinchinbroke*, still then lying at anchor at the mouth of the river. Here he received the news that Nelson had gone up river with the expedition and, again in the shadow of Nelson and with sickness all around, took control of the situation, washing down the lower decks with vinegar, fumigating all areas to keep the mosquitoes at bay and erecting structures on shore for the hospitalization of the sick. But even so, it was his report that such were the ravages of yellow fever that, of his ship's company which had comprised 200 men, he buried no less than 180 of them in the space of just four months. Dr Moseley, Surgeon-General of Jamaica, in his *Treatise on Tropical Diseases*, claimed that of some 1,800 men sent to different locations on the expedition, no more than 380 survived. The crews had been drenched by torrential rain in that ill-chosen season of the year and most had been decimated by disease. Indeed Collingwood had been so shocked at the sight of Nelson on his return to the *Hinchinbroke*, that he was to write, 'the climate was deadly. No constitution could resist its effects.' It was imperative that his friend Nelson be evacuated from the deadly Mosquito Coast without delay, whilst duty required that he, Collingwood, remain on guard at the mouth of the river, ready to shepherd away what was left of the expedition when it emerged.

Happily his own more robust north country constitution was better able to withstand the conditions and he was able to write calmly of this terrible experience that, 'My constitution resisted many attacks, and I survived most of my ship's company.'2

Although Collingwood had obviously endured this nightmare with fortitude and courage and afterwards made light of his experiences, it is not difficult to imagine the sure horror with which he must have been surrounded, as the dead piled up on the deck of his hearse of a ship, perhaps fearing all the while that he himself would at any moment succumb.

When he gave up his command in December of that year, it was something of a ghost ship. An old capture from the French it was now leaking and in need of repair and, in the year following, it sank. As for Despard, twenty-two years on he stood trial and was convicted of engaging in treasonable activities in London for which he suffered the supreme penalty, despite pleas entered on his behalf by Horatio Nelson, ever loyal to his friends and, by then a vice-admiral.

Command of the *Hinchinbrooke* had brought with it advance to the rank of post captain for Collingwood, as it had for Nelson, so that he too had now begun the ascent to flag rank. But although promotion for a post captain or flag officer was largely seniority driven, appointments to fleet commands remained within the discretion of the Admiralty which supposedly selected on merit and suitability. Many an admiral thought to be worn out or incompetent could find himself permanently unemployed and on half pay, consigned, it would be said, to the Yellow Squadron. Both Collingwood and Nelson now stood firmly in Parker's debt and, to their credit, they never forgot it. And so the careers of Collingwood, and Nelson now seven months his senior, blossomed and continued to march hand in hand.

Having survived a very real threat of extinction from tropical disease Collingwood was exposed in the very next year to an even greater danger of death, this time by drowning. In December 1780 he had taken command of the frigate *Pelican* of 24 guns. Eight months later, in August of 1781, the ship was caught in a hurricane so severe that it drove many ships into Port Royal harbour and dismasted two others.[3] A violent storm erupted overnight which cast his ship onto the rocks of the Morant Keys islets thirty to forty miles south-east of Morant Point in Jamaica. Fortunately, although the ship was wrecked, there was no loss of life and at first light Collingwood was able to rescue his crew by organizing the construction of wooden rafts from the broken yards of his ship. These proved sturdy enough to carry them to an island shore. And there they lay, marooned for ten days or more in the hostile territory of Sandy Hills with little water and no food, save for what they had been able to salvage from the wreck, supplemented by the meat of native monkeys.[4] Indeed this became their principal diet. Mercifully, Collingwood was eventually able to make a boat seaworthy enough to carry a distress signal to Jamaica. The frigate *Diamond* then quickly came to the rescue and carried them off. Although Collingwood was to report this incident too in language which was moderate, it is clear that he and his crew had been fortunate in the extreme to survive. He had emerged intact from yet another very testing experience.

Collingwood was now able to enjoy a short respite in London to which he returned at the beginning of 1782, although his time there was fully occupied bombarding the Admiralty with requests for further commissions, all of which seemed to fall on deaf ears. He was to write to his brother John of his frustration on 22 June adding, of one lady he had met:

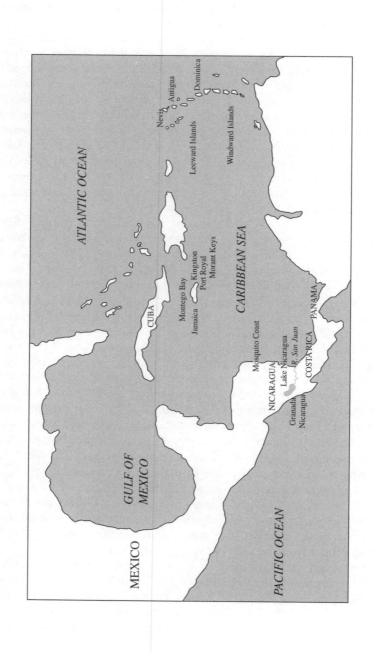

Let a woman alone for a good story. I begin, John, to think they are more dangerous to encounter than Hurricanes, as they do not give so fair a warning. Wou'd I was abroad again! Better be wrecked a thousand times at sea, than once ashore.

Eventually, in January 1783, his pleas were answered and he was appointed to the *Sampson* of 64 guns, but this was not to be for long for this ship was paid off that same year at the end of the American War. But he was then quickly transferred to the new frigate *Mediator* from which he wrote to his sister in August 1783 of another pain, this time in a tooth, which he said was 'so painful to me that I have had it taken out, the hollow part fill'd with caddee lead and put in again, and tomorrow I hope it will be as good as any I have.'

But his next posting was to carry him back to his friend Horatio Nelson in the West Indies so that all for the moment was again set fair.

Chapter 4

Nelson and Collingwood
in the West Indies

It is clear from the events which followed that Nelson and Collingwood had by now become the very closest of friends for Nelson was to write of their friendship whenever the call of duty chanced to separate them.

From the *Boreas* to Captain Locker on 24 September 1784, Nelson wrote:

Collingwood is at Granada, which is a great loss to me for there is nobody that I can make a confidant of.

To Captain Cornwallis that same year he wrote, on 28 October:

...the others are ignoramus, except Collingwood who is a very good officer and an amiable character.

And, in a letter to another, dated 23 November Nelson wrote:

Collingwood desires me to say he will write you soon such a letter that you will think it a history of the West Indies. What an amiable good man he is! All the rest are geese.

And then again in a letter dated 16 March 1785 when at St Kitts Nelson wrote of Collingwood:

What a charming good man! He is a valuable member of society.

And on 5 March 1786 when at Martinique he wrote:

The station has not been over pleasant: had it not been for Collingwood, it would have been the most disagreeable I ever saw.[1]

34

For his part Collingwood was to write in 1792:

> My regard for you, my dear Nelson, my respect and veneration for
> your character, I hope will never lessen.

The strength of this friendship was to be tested and demonstrated during
these years in a very tangible way, for with the end of the American War
in the year 1783 it was Nelson's decision and determination to uphold
and enforce the Navigation Acts in the West Indies, and to do so in the
teeth of considerable opposition from both the settlers and the merchant
traders.

For a century or more it had been the policy of the British government
to keep foreign trade out of the Empire and to legislate for reciprocity
between the two economies of America and Britain for the advantage of
both, although undoubtedly for the greater advantage of Britain.
Accordingly the colonists had been obliged to purchase those commodi-
ties they were unable to produce for themselves, from the mother
country at prices favourable to the London merchants fixed in London,
all of this to be transported for reward by the British mercantile fleet or
other colonial transporters. And it had been ordained that any foreign
commodity which was imported by the colonists had to be channelled
through a British port where it would attract levies and create business
for the home country. The instruments for such policy were the
Navigation Acts, the first of which had been passed 100 years before in
1651. It was an arrangement which had been of advantage to both
countries, and of immense advantage to Great Britain in particular, but
it had amounted nonetheless to a distortion of the terms of trade and a
restriction on the New England merchants which they came to resent.
Although they had enjoyed the advantage of a guaranteed market for
their produce in Britain, it had not been on their own terms. In the
outcome they sought to compensate for this by engaging in the illicit
export of goods to foreign countries despite the embargo.

Nelson, Collingwood and Collingwood's younger brother Wilfred
were all at this time serving as young captains on the station; Nelson as
commander of the *Boreas*, Collingwood as commander of the frigate
Mediator, and the shy but very astute Wilfred Collingwood in the
Rattler as its commander.

Wilfred was to be described by Admiral Byam Martin as, 'slender like
his brother but of delicate constitution'.[2]

For many years there had been a heavy traffic of American traders
conducting a brisk and legitimate trade in these waters with all the pref-
erential advantages which the Navigation Laws had conferred upon
them as British subjects, sailing ships registered as British. The Acts

together with legislation enacted in 1783 ordained that all carriage by sea should be conducted in British-owned ships manned by crews which were substantially British. But now, with the declaration of independence, they were strictly foreigners and therefore no longer entitled in law to enjoy the privileges and advantages which the Acts had previously given them. However, with the cessation of hostilities, customs officials on most of the islands as well as British commanders on the station, including the Commander-in-Chief, Rear-Admiral Sir Richard Hughes, effectively turned a blind eye to this fact and allowed the Americans to trade very much as before.

Only Nelson, probably inspired by the well-informed and upright Wilfred, who had studied the Acts closely, saw it otherwise, taking the view that if America wanted to be a foreign country then they must be treated as foreigners. Whether it all mattered very much is open to question, for it was to the advantage of the West Indies as well as the American traders that they should be allowed to trade as before since goods imported from the new American nation cost a good deal less and were more readily available than those brought out from Britain or shipped down from a thinly populated Canada.[3]

However that may be, on his arrival at Barbados on 26 June 1784 Nelson sought to uphold and enforce the letter of the law by attempting to stop this illicit trade, which he thought to be unfair to British traders. And, as in all things, he set about it with gusto, careless of the possibility that he could, by so doing, place his whole career in jeopardy. It took considerable courage. His friend Collingwood, with the strong support of his brother, Wilfred, decided to stand by him, thus taking the same risk. They were the only officers to do so of the seven captains on the station.

Indeed, by failing to take any steps to stop this trade, Sir Richard Hughes, as Commander-in-Chief, implicitly condoned it. Quite why he should have taken this view is difficult to understand, for he came from a family steeped in naval tradition. His grandfather, Captain Richard Hughes, and his father Sir Richard Hughes, the first baronet, had both been commissioners of the Navy at Portsmouth. He himself had entered the Royal Academy at Portsmouth at the age of ten in 1739 and so had forty-four years of naval service behind him. He had succeeded to the baronetcy and been promoted to the rank of rear-admiral in the year 1780 and then in 1782 had been sent out to the West Indies to take over from Admiral Pigot as Commander-in-Chief. With such a background and with such experience he must have known well enough where his duty lay. But he was an easy-going and amiable enough man despite gout and a significant disability after losing the sight of one eye back in 1752 when a table-fork had accidentally sprung into and impaled it when trying to kill a cockroach, and the true explanation may be that, after listening to representations from the merchants and traders, he had hoped, by suspending the full rigour of these laws, to promote harmony and peace. Or perhaps the truth was that he simply lacked the energy or determination to take any more positive action. It is probable too that he was not prepared to have an officer considerably junior in both rank and age telling him where his duty lay. Clearly Nelson thought laziness to be the truth of the matter for he wrote:

> Sir Richard Hughes is a fiddler; therefore, as his time is taken up tuning that instrument...the squadron is cursedly out of tune. He lives in a boarding-house at Barbados, not much in the style of a British Admiral. He has not that opinion of his own sense that he ought to have; he does not give himself that weight that I think an English Admiral ought to do.

Collingwood's part in all this was brought to the attention of the local authorities early on, for in December 1784 he intercepted an American trader heading for harbour on the pretext, oft advanced, that his ship was in need of running repairs which, when done, could only be paid for if he was allowed to unload and sell the cargo he was carrying. But Collingwood soon had the measure of him. He quickly surveyed the reported fault, had his carpenter repair it in short time and so prevented the trader from offloading his cargo on shore. In many other cases an offending trader would purchase false registration documents from customs officials, all too ready to earn a little money on the side, which would allow the trader to masquerade as an English vessel and so circumvent the rigour of the law.

His brother Wilfred, and Nelson too, were active in policing the harbours and local seas for suspected offenders, but it was only when their attempt to prevent pirate ships from entering harbour failed, that they resorted to actual seizures. But then, over the ensuing months, those vessels taken by Nelson ran into double figures whilst Wilfred's tally was four or five and Collingwood's two. In fact it is doubtful whether their activities did very much to prevent this illicit trade from going on, but they did make enough of an impact for the matter to be the subject of protest. It was Collingwood's enforcement of the law which was the first to be brought to the attention of the authorities and the matter was duly reported to the Governor, General Sir Thomas Shirley who, in turn, complained to the Admiralty. He had been advised by his law officers, wrongly, that the traders had the law on their side. Indeed a judge of the Vice-Admiralty Court in Barbados had actually held, again wrongly, that only customs officials had the right to arrest or seize merchant vessels, and that Collingwood, as captain of a man-of-war, had no authority to do so. Hughes, at the insistence of Shirley, then tamely directed that although the Navy had every right to intercept and interrogate foreign shipping for possible breaches of the Navigation laws, it should be allowed to come ashore where the final decision in each case was to rest with the local civil governor. Suspecting all civil authorities, Nelson expressly refused to recognize that order, arguing that he would not be a party to illegality. Fortunately for him, Hughes chose to ignore what amounted to rank insubordination, probably for the sake of peace.

But the traders themselves not only sought to defend at court all claims for seizure, but also set about launching an action for damages naming Nelson as defendant. The claim was for the sum of £4,000 to compensate for false imprisonment and direct assault when under arrest. For Collingwood and Nelson this was the last straw and they now referred the matter to the Colonial Office and Lord Sydney, after whom the Australian city was later named.

A decision by a judge on the island of Barbados that Collingwood had had no right to seize the *Dolphin* caused further outrage but, after due consideration, Sydney took Collingwood's view that the law be upheld and the Governor was informed accordingly in a letter which stated that, 'the same suspicions exist among the King's servants here, as are entertained by Captain Collingwood.'4

Nelson too had bombarded Sydney with letters of complaint but, in his case, these drew no response at all. In the meantime, and with great skill and determination, he argued in support of the arrests at the court hearings and won judgments before two different courts that the Navy did indeed have the right of seizure. This won many doubters over to his side, but the suit filed against him personally for damages still remained, as did the real danger of suffering arrest himself pending trial.

But then, by letter dated September 1785, Sydney eventually wrote that the King had directed that the Crown be instructed to defend Nelson against any action which the traders may bring against him for any activity of his when only doing his duty and enforcing the laws of England. He then made the hollow excuse that he would have written sooner had he not heard on good authority that Nelson was dead! The action brought against Nelson was then quickly dismissed.

So, when Nelson made it clear to Hughes again that he really had no authority at all to waive enforcement of the law, citing the view from London, Hughes saw the error of his ways and thenceforth ordered compliance. The authorities then gradually came into line. The victory for the determined Nelson had been total, but the irony of the whole episode was that it was Hughes who then received the official thanks of the Treasury in a letter which recorded that:

...the Commander-in-Chief of the Leeward Islands and officers under him have shown a considerable zeal in endeavouring to put a stop to the illicit practices which were carrying on in the Islands, in open violation of the law.

Understandably Nelson considered that such thanks were more properly due to him and a further irony was that within but a few years the home government was forced to relax those same laws somewhat in the face of mounting hardship to the islanders. But it remained true that Nelson had, throughout this whole episode, demonstrated those qualities of determination and perseverance as a combatant of illegality which were to mark him out from others and bring him many more, and more important, victories in the years to come.

Collingwood had thus survived this fifth stern test of his character while serving on this station and now moved off to Granada.

In these less demanding years of fragile peace Nelson and Collingwood had been able to indulge their friendship on the West Indies Station to the full. Indeed, in 1784 both had developed something of an infatuation for the wife of the resident commissioner of the Naval Dockyard at English Harbour, Antigua, one Mary Moutray.

Collingwood had brought Captain and Mrs Moutray and their two children out to Antigua to take up the appointment as commissioner in the spring of 1783, just before the peace, and on the long voyage out he had come to know and like both of them. These feelings were reciprocated and indeed were extended to his friend Nelson to whom he introduced them.

Their friendship with the Moutrays was even strong enough to survive yet a further protest to the Admiralty by Nelson, this time about the appointment of John Moutray himself to act as Commander-in-Chief of all shipping in Antigua in the absence of a senior officer. This had been made by Sir Richard Hughes who had ordered Moutray to hoist a commodore's broad pennant in the absence of a flag. In a second brush with Hughes, Nelson, as the senior captain and therefore second in command, refused to recognize or obey the authority which had thus been vested in Moutray, protesting that the office of Dockyard Commissioner was a civil one and that Moutray was at that time only on half-pay from the Navy with no executive authority granted him by the Admiralty to exercise a commodore's power over the other captains. In this Collingwood supported him, albeit he was more open to compromise. Nelson had no high regard for the command of Hughes, and still less for the prattling of his wife whom he had earlier brought out from England in the *Boreas*, 'with her plain daughter and with all her clack' he afterwards complained. It was a trivial matter and for his protest Nelson received an official admonition for not taking such a minor complaint to his commanding officer first rather than going over his head to the Admiralty, although, when it *was* referred to the Admiralty, Moutray's authority, which it seems he *had* in fact been given, was then withdrawn and he was later recalled home since the expense of the post could no longer be justified. In any case he was, by then, a dying man.[5]

The way in which Nelson pursued these complaints perhaps made little allowance for the age and infirmity of these two very senior officers, although it did show a courage and perhaps a naivety, for a more circumspect and devious officer would probably have gone to great lengths to avoid such confrontations knowing that those set in authority over him probably had power or influence enough to damage his career.

At the same time an officer more capable than Hughes would probably have dealt with Nelson's outbursts with much greater tact than he was able to employ.

In fact John Moutray, a son of Fife, had been fortunate to hold the position of commissioner at all for only two years before he had been court-martialled and dismissed his command as captain of the *Ramilles* for conduct judged to have been 'reprehensible' when a convoy had been lost. His ship had been part of a squadron escorting merchant shipping carrying valuable cargo out to the West Indies and North America. For some reason never explained, once clear of the English Channel and the Channel Fleet, the escort had been reduced to but three ships when the authorities knew full well that the combined Franco-Spanish Fleet was at that time blockading Gibraltar and could be met with at any stage of the voyage. Moutray must have been alert to this possibility too yet when shipping was spotted at a distance great enough to be avoided he foolishly dismissed it as of no significance and continued to run on collision course for some hours, until, towards midnight, when lights were seen to be much closer ahead than he had anticipated, he eventually gave the night signal to alter course and steer to the westward. But at that late hour and, in the darkness of the night, most of the merchant ships failed to respond to the signal and sailed on and into the enemy fleet and into inevitable captivity.

The loss borne by the underwriters was upwards of 1½ million pounds and the loss to the fleet in the West Indies was of much needed supplies. Indeed the whole episode gave considerable encouragement to the Spanish demand for the surrender of Gibraltar. Moutray was fortunate therefore to have been appointed to two further commands and then to the commissionership. But he was to die prematurely at home in Bath shortly after his return from the West Indies in 1785 at the age of sixty-two.

At thirty-two years of age Mary Moutray was thirty years younger than her husband and much more of Collingwood's age, which had made it an easy relationship for Collingwood and Nelson to form and the door of her house, Windsor, above the harbour, had ever been open to them. She was an attractive woman, and a cheerful woman, and the prospect of an escape from the rigours of life on board ship to all the comforts of a home on shore in Antigua meant that they were often visitors at her house. When describing Collingwood as she remembered him to be from these days, Mary Moutray, who seems to have preferred the tall, well-built Collingwood to the diminutive Nelson, wrote in a letter to his daughter Sarah long after Collingwood's death, of the vigour of his mind. But she remembered above all else his great diffidence and reserve, 'which prevented the playfulness of his imagination and his powers of adding charms to private society from being duly appreciated.'

Clearly the long voyage out had allowed the Moutrays to come to know Collingwood's true self in a way not given to many, for she recalled that, 'whenever he was at St John's or in English Harbour, he was a beloved brother in our house.' Perhaps it was that they both were of northern stock, for Mary Moutray, formerly Mary Pemble, had been born a Northumbrian in Berwick-on-Tweed to a mother from Belford in Northumberland and a naval officer father from Newcastle upon Tyne, not many miles from Collingwood's Tyneside home, and it was from Berwick that she had married Captain Moutray, then a widower. But whatever it was, it seems that she allowed him into her boudoir to help her curl her fair hair for a ball, had him turn the pages of her music when she entertained them on the piano and welcomed his assistance in countless other ways of which he was later to write, which suggests that a close familiarity existed between them although it clearly fell short of intimacy. For his part Collingwood responded with compositions of romantic poetry dedicated to her. And Nelson, even more besotted, came to regard these months on the island as amongst the happiest of his life.

Tangible evidence survives of this interlude in their lives in the shape of drawings made at the time by Collingwood of Nelson and by Nelson of Collingwood. This descent into the world of art was triggered off by the temporary need for Nelson to wear a wig following a bout of fever which had required that his head be shaved.. But the only wig available was an ill fitting, bizarre and discoloured animal which gave rise to good-humoured ribaldry in the Moutray household which prompted Collingwood to capture the scene with a coloured portrait of his bewigged friend. Nelson then took his revenge with a serious and accomplished pencil drawing of Collingwood, his long hair down to his shoulders and tied in a queue. Mrs Moutray ever after preserved and treasured these reminders of those happy carefree days until, close to death, she gave them into the care of Collingwood's daughter, Sarah. They were to end up in the National Maritime Museum at Greenwich. It says something for the Moutrays that they had not allowed the issue of the flag to damage their friendship with Nelson and Collingwood.

Indeed their friendship with Mrs Moutray was such that when the moment came for her departure home she presented Collingwood with a purse she had netted for him as a memento of their friendship, to which he responded with a verse of thanks:

> Your net shall be my care, my dear,
> For length of time to come,
> While I am faint and scorching here,
> And you rejoice at home.
> To you belongs the wondrous art
> To shed around your pleasure;
> New worth to best of things impart,
> And make of trifles – treasure.[6]

Her friendship with both Nelson and Collingwood survived the death of her husband by many years. Indeed it was kept up for the rest of their short lives, although, with the arrival of Emma Hamilton in his life, Nelson's thoughts were then mostly elsewhere. Her daughter, Kate, died without issue twenty-five years before her, but Mary Moutray herself lived on until 1841, outliving both of her friends, although she never married again. The journey through life can be hard for those who travel alone, but she appears to have retained her cheerfulness to the end.

A small snapshot of life on board the *Mediator* when on the Jamaican Station under Collingwood's command, as seen through the eyes of a midshipman, was later provided by one Jeffrey Baron de Raigersfeld long after his career was over and at a stage in his life when he stood to gain nothing by writing untruths or flattery. Raigersfeld was a diligent and responsible man but lacked those leadership qualities which mark out an officer for promotion and so, although his father had the ear of Admirals Hood and Howe,[7] he never, in fact, had a seagoing command and really saw very little active service. But he did, in time, rise to the post list as the captain of service ships and was, in later life, raised in the general promotions to the rank of rear-admiral many years after he had last gone to sea.

Entered as captain's servant, a label given to those apprenticed to the

42

captain who enjoyed the same status as midshipmen, service in the *Mediator* had been Raigersfeld's first taste of life on board ship and so allowance has to be made for the tendency of the impressionable young to venerate and idolize those first set in authority over them. But even so, Collingwood, then still in his mid-thirties, was seen by Midshipman Raigersfeld on the lower deck as a humane and thoughtful commander who took a fatherly interest in both the welfare and the education of those midshipmen placed under his command. This was so almost from the first day of Raigersfeld's arrival on 28 April 1783 when he was but twelve or thirteen years of age and fresh out of his boarding school in Whitehaven.

Like the rest of the crew, midshipmen lived in conditions which were extremely cramped. They existed on a diet that was most unpleasant, the main constituent of which was the hard biscuit drawn from old stock and usually occupied by weevils and maggots. To Raigersfeld those interlopers were fat and, when swallowed, tasted cold. But it seems that he quite enjoyed a well-cooked rat from the many well-fed rats which infested all ships, and Collingwood was ever active in the purchase of milk, bread, fruit and vegetables whenever the opportunity arose. On one occasion he even donated eleven of his pigs for immediate con-sumption by the crew after they had been killed by lightning while living forward under the forecastle of the ship. Water casks were replenished with regularity from rivers flowing from the high hills on shore, such as those flowing into the magnificent Prince Rupert's bay of Dominica which, from the height of the surrounding hills, always has a sombre appearance and, on occasion, Collingwood sent his clerk on shore with the young Raigersfeld to purchase clothing to replace that which had worn through, although the frugal Collingwood preferred his young charges to make and mend their own clothing themselves whenever possible. Raigersfeld wrote of this that he was:

> ...thankful it did so happen that upon my first going to sea I was placed under so considerate a man as Captain Collingwood, necessity obliging me to do many things for myself.

Raigersfeld, along with all the midshipmen, was subjected by Collingwood to a weekly oral examination in mathematics, literature and seamanship. Success was sometimes met with an invitation to breakfast, but on one occasion Collingwood took his penknife to the hair of those who had failed the test and cut off their pigtails telling them to keep them in their pockets until they could show that they were able to work satisfactorily. Soon after that, pigtails for officers went out of fashion. There were, of course, the range of punishments usual to any ship in the Navy in those days but Raigersfeld wrote that Collingwood was sparing of the cat, and he was thankful that, when it was administered, this was done in the privacy of the cabin where the crew were not able to witness the humiliation. Collingwood's preference when an infringement occurred was to ban the offender from his mess for a given period, with all the labouring duties which that brought with it. And so Raigersfeld was to write that:

> During upwards of three years and a half that I was in this ship, I do not remember more than four or five men being punished at the gangway, and then so slightly that it scarcely deserved the name, for the Captain was a very humane man...he looked after the midshipmen of his ship with the eye of one who felt a duty to keep youth in constant employment, not only for the benefit of themselves, but for the service which he not only considered the bulwark of his country, but the root from whence its pre-eminence had struck.
> Captain Cuthbert Collingwood was a reserved man, a good seaman and navigator, and well read in the English classics; and most heartily do I thank him for the care and pains he took to make me a seaman.

In August 1786 Admiral Hughes returned to England. Since no other flag officer was sent out to replace him this left Nelson as senior captain in command of the squadron. And then, later that summer, Collingwood too quit the station for England in the *Mediator* and there made his way home to his native Northumberland where he was retired on half pay.[8] This was to be the first of only three leaves home of any length that ever came his way. This combination of events left Nelson in the West Indies happily free of superior officer authority but without his friends Collingwood and Mary Moutray. And so he turned his attention to the pursuit of his future bride, Frances Nisbet. Collingwood had told her of the impression she had made on Nelson. He busied himself also with the entertainment of His Royal Highness Prince William Henry, who had arrived on the station in November 1786 as commander of the frigate *Pegasus*, and so now fell under Nelson's command. According to one historian, the boisterous and plump extrovert Prince was born with a head shaped like a pineapple. He was to become a good friend to Nelson, gave Nelson's wife away at their wedding and became a regular correspondent of both Nelson and Collingwood.

In the month which followed, Nelson accompanied the Prince when he sailed for Dominica to witness work which was being done there to develop the harbour and fortify the island on the initiative of the governor, Captain John Orde. Nelson was hoping too to discuss with

Orde on behalf of his friend Captain William Locker the administration of an estate Locker owned on the island, a matter he had first raised with Orde back in 1784 when bearing gifts of wine, for he had taken delivery of four casks of wine at Madeira which had been given to Orde. But nothing came of it.[9]

Orde had accepted the appointment of governor of the island at the end of the American War on the clear understanding that should hostilities involving the Royal Navy ever be resumed, he would be allowed to return to active service. But there followed ten years of peace and so ten years of rule by Governor Orde culminating in the award of a baronetcy before he returned to his duties with the Royal Navy.

Prince William reported this visit favourably to the King[10] and Nelson was to write to his wife in a letter dated 12 December 1786:

> Some ladies seem very much charmed by him. He is volatile but always with great good nature. There were balls during his stay and some of the old ladies were mortified that His Royal Highness would not dance with them, but he says he is determined to enjoy the privilege of all other men, that of asking any lady he pleases. Mrs Parry dined at table the first day at the Government House, but afterwards never appeared at dinner nor were any ladies at Governor Orde's dinner.[11]

Unbeknown to either of them, both Collingwood and Nelson were to embark soon after this on the last third, albeit most glorious years, of their much too short lives.

Chapter 5

Collingwood's Marriage and Family

Save for one short expedition to the West Indies in command of the frigate *Mermaid*, Collingwood was to remain at home in Northumberland on half pay until the outbreak of war in the year 1793.

This was an unusual but welcome respite for Collingwood. In his fifty years of active service with the Royal Navy which had begun in the year 1761 when only twelve years of age, forty-four were to be spent at sea. The cabin was his workplace, the ship was his home. It is not at all surprising therefore that he was better known to Nelson at this stage of his life than to any member of his own family, except perhaps his younger brother Wilfred and perhaps also the dog he had acquired, which, he wrote, 'is a good dog, delights in the ship and swims after me when I go in the boat'.

Now, approaching his fortieth birthday, he resolved to take the opportunity to rediscover his blood relations to whom he was almost a stranger and to start a family of his own. He had been more or less absent for almost thirty years. But things had changed.

One of his older sisters, Eleanor, had died in the year 1772, aged just thirty-two years. His father Cuthbert was also long since dead. He had died aged sixty-four on 15 February 1775, the year Collingwood had sailed into the American War of Independence.

The Collingwood family had long been in the county of Northumberland. Indeed, Collingwood himself was later to refer in his letters to one of his kinsmen, one George Collingwood of Eslington in Northumberland, who had sided with the House of Stuart and the young Northumbrian, Lord Derwentwater, in the 1715 Jacobite Rebellion. It had been in the closing months of James II's reign, when James Radcliffe had been granted the Earldom of Derwentwater, that the Duke of Newcastle had raised a band of supporters for the cause from amongst the disaffected Northumberland gentry. Matters had then come to a head with the accession of George I in 1714 when the need to raise taxes to pay for the war with France had impoverished many a landed gentleman. There were many then who were ready and willing to answer the call in the hope of forcing a change in the Ruling House which would restore both their solvency and their status. But many a family was divided in both its religion and its support, and most were, in any case, anxious to retain a foot in both camps in the hope of preserving the family inheritance whatever the outcome should be. In Northumberland it was so with the Collingwoods, the Swinburnes of Capheaton, the Fenwicks, the Widdringtons, the Shaftoes, the Ordes of Weetwood who were cousins of the forbears of Admiral Sir John Orde, the Allgoods, the Forsters, the Blacketts, the Riddells of Swinburne Castle, the Crasters of Craster, the Erringtons of Beaufront and many another Northumbrian family, all of whom provided recruits for the cause. In fact Collingwood had joined somewhat reluctantly and then only at the insistence of his wife, Catherine Browne, the daughter of the Viscount Montagu.

So, after the rebels had been goaded into action by the issue of warrants targeted at them in 1715 by a government fearful of the declaration of the Highland clans for James III, there followed the rout at Preston and the total capitulation of the rebel force. George Collingwood, two Swinburnes and two Ordes were amongst those taken, many of whom were carried off to London to face trial, execution, imprisonment or transportation to plantations in America. One Orde brother had been killed, another was killed or executed,[1] a third was imprisoned but released along with most others two years later under the Act of Indemnity, whilst the fourth brother escaped to Boulogne where he continued to give active support to the cause. Their Weetwood estate had to be sold in 1719, although it was bought back a few years later by a protestant branch of the family.

In Collingwood's case it was reported that the onset of gout had made a journey to London impossible. Tragically it is probable that this benign malady cost him his life for it was considered by many at the time that had he been tried in London, his life would have been spared. As it was it was his fate to be tried, convicted, hung, drawn and quartered in the town of Liverpool in the presence of his wife who had travelled to be with him. His estate at Eslington in Northumberland had then stood forfeit to the Crown, to be sold later at a bargain price to a coal owner and government supporter in Newcastle, Sir Henry Liddell.[2] The money raised went to support Greenwich Hospital in London which was funded appreciably by the forfeited Derwentwater Estates in Northumberland. But then £6,000, which represented a third or so of the sum which had been raised by the sale of Eslington, was recovered by Collingwood's widow in 1724 as a maintenance payment for herself and her family; a claim sanctioned by Parliament.

The ballad *Derwentwater's Farewell* (otherwise known as *Good Night*), by Robert Surtees, which portrays the last days of Derwentwater on the banks of the Tyne in his native Northumberland, contains the verse,

> And fare thee well, George Collingwood,
> Since fate has put us down;
> If thou and I have lost our lives,
> King James has lost his crown.[3]

As for Collingwood's father, he was never a warm man financially although by the time of his death from apoplexy in 1775, while living at Rosemary Lane in Newcastle, he was in fairly comfortable circumstances. But at one point in his life it had been a very near run thing.

Collingwood's grandfather, Cuthbert Collingwood, had inherited from his uncle, Edward Collingwood, a life interest in Ditchburn, a small estate in the parish of Eglingham in the county of Northumberland. And when Edward's daughter Dorothy, his intended wife, died young she, too, had named Collingwood's grandfather a beneficiary, leaving him a share of the income from land and properties let out at both Shipley, which stands adjacent to Ditchburn, and North Dissington, which lies ten miles west of Newcastle. And so it was that Collingwood's father had been born into a home of comparative affluence in the early part of the century at Newburn, near Newcastle upon Tyne. It was there that he was baptized on 14 January 1711 or 1712.

But then, for some reason never disclosed, Collingwood's father had moved into Newcastle itself in the year 1728 to bind himself apprentice to a merchant adventurer and booth man or corn merchant, one Christopher Dawson. This then became Collingwood, the father's occupation, albeit by then in business on his own account. He was so employed when he married Milcah, daughter of Reginald Dobson of Barwise in Westmorland.[4] In 1737 he was admitted free of the coveted Company of Merchant Adventurers of Newcastle. When Collingwood was born his father's business was therefore stated to be that of supply merchant for it was so recorded in the register reporting Collingwood's baptism. But it was a business which all but failed and Collingwood's father then faced demands from many an angry creditor who remained unpaid. But, fortunately for him, his great uncle Edward Collingwood had come to the rescue. A barrister, an alderman and an honorary recorder of Newcastle upon Tyne, Edward had acquired an estate at Chirton near North Shields by marriage to a Roddam of Hethpool. and his will, proved on 21 January 1792, gives that as his address and John Orde of Weetwood, his sisters and his cousin Shafto, as some of the beneficiaries. Indeed, in the course of time a life interest in the Chirton estate was to be left to Cuthbert Collingwood by Edward's son when he died a bachelor in 1806. But, back in 1744, Edward Collingwood had agreed to become one of two trustees charged with the duty of winding up Collingwood's father's affairs and, in so doing, they had, by 1747, managed to save his home in Newcastle, retain his wife's estate in Barwise[5] and repay his creditors sixteen shillings and sixpence in the pound. It had been enough to secure a discharge for Collingwood's father which had enabled him to carry on trading.

The Reverend 'Jupiter' Carlyle was to write in his autobiography that Archibald, 1st Duke of Argyll had died in one of two houses which lay on the Chirton estate which had been acquired by him at the end of the seventeenth century as a convenient staging post on his long journeys from Inverary to London.[6]

But there had been yet further change before Collingwood returned home, for his boyhood home in Newcastle upon Tyne had gone, sold by his mother, Milcah. A commodious three storey building of ample proportions, it stood at the head of the Side, a very steep and narrow lane which spills out onto the banks of the River Tyne, to be demolished in 1904 to make way for a purpose-built block of offices named Milburn House. From the sale she had raised the princely sum of £900.[7]

Now, sadly, Collingwood was also to lose the two remaining members of the family who were closest to him.

Firstly his younger brother Wilfred went down with consumption and inflammation of the bowels while Collingwood was far away at home. He died at sea on 20 April 1787. He was thirty-seven years of age and unmarried. In Collingwood's absence it was left to Nelson to bury him.

He was interred on the island of St Vincent with full military honours. Fittingly it was Nelson who conveyed the sad news to his friend. In a letter dated May 1787 he wrote:

To be the messenger of bad news is my misfortune, but still it is a tribute which friends owe each other. I have lost my friend, you an affectionate brother...The esteem he stood in with his Royal Highness was great [there referring to the Duke of Clarence, later William IV]. His letter to me on his death is the strongest testimony of it. I send you an extract of it. 'Collingwood, poor fellow, is no more. I have cried for him, and most sincerely do I console with you on his loss. In him, His Majesty has lost a faithful Servant, and the Service a most excellent Officer.'[8]

Then, in the following year, in the month of April 1788, Collingwood buried his mother Milcah. She had given her husband seven daughters, Mary, then forty-nine years of age, Elizabeth, forty-seven, Dorothy, forty-six, Philadelphia, forty-five; all of them spinsters, Eleanor, by then deceased, Barbara who had died as a child and the first Elizabeth who had died in infancy, followed by three sons of whom Wilfred was the second. Cuthbert, the eldest, was now thirty-nine years of age having been born on 26 September 1748. His baptism on 24 October 1748 is recorded in the register of the Church, now the Cathedral Church of St Nicholas, which stands 100 or so yards up the hill from the Collingwood home. All of these survivors were to outlive Collingwood. Indeed, John, the third son and youngest of the family, who had been born on 1 June 1750, carved out a career in Customs, became 'deputy customer' at Newcastle, married one Sarah Fenwicke of Earsdon, when he was sixty-two years of age, and lived on until 2 January 1841 when he died at the ripe old age of ninety. He had, by then, outlived all of his brothers and sisters, even Elizabeth who had died at the age of ninety-five.

Now Collingwood decided to establish a family of his own and so embarked on a courtship with Sarah Blackett, daughter of John Erasmus Blackett, Mayor of Newcastle upon Tyne. It was to end in marriage in the church of his baptism, the Church of St Nicholas, on 16 June 1791, two days before her twenty-ninth birthday. Collingwood was by then forty-two years of age so that neither was exactly on the nursery slopes of life! In a sense they complemented each other for, where Collingwood was serious, industrious and not a little austere, his wife, although also a quiet person, was fond of dancing, dress and the usual pleasures of life. A placid and contented woman she seldom complained or spoke ill of others.

Coincidentally this tie brought with it not only a settlement of £6,250, but also a very distant relative by marriage who held senior rank in the naval service, Vice-Admiral Robert Roddam. Roddam was distantly related to Collingwood's wife's maternal grandfather and was a distinguished member of a prominent Northumbrian naval family.[9] It brought too friendship with her uncle Sir Edward Blackett Bt and indeed with the celebrated Reverend Dr Alexander 'Jupiter' Carlyle, who had married Mary Roddam, sister of his wife's mother, back in 1760. Collingwood was to address much of his personal correspondence to his father-in-law and to both Edward Blackett and Carlyle over the twenty years which remained to him, no doubt confident that it would then be circulated amongst family and friends and would probably also survive for posterity, as indeed was the case.

John Erasmus Blackett had been born on New Year's Day 1728,[10] the youngest of five sons of John Blackett of the stately Newby in the West Riding of Yorkshire, a Merchant Adventurer in Newcastle. The Company of Merchant Adventurers was an exclusive body which commanded a near monopoly of the import and export trade, just as the host man controlled the coal trade. Membership was much valued. The Blacketts had originated in Hoppyland in County Durham but one of them had later acquired and rebuilt Newby. Blackett's father had died prematurely after which his elder brother Edward had inherited a baronetcy from his uncle, Sir Edward Blackett of Newby and Hexham Abbey, who had married the daughter and heiress of Oley Douglas of West Matfen near Hexham. Newby Hall had been sold by Edward's father two years before his death, after which the new Sir Edward made his home at West Matfen in Northumberland, although he had a second home at Thorpe Lea, Egham, Surrey.[11]

Of the other brothers, one became a soldier, another a rector whilst a third died when young.

In Carlyle's autobiography he makes mention of the John Erasmus Blackett of years before as:

...a very handsome young man of about thirty, who had been bred at Liverpool with Sir – Cunliffe, and was now settled partner with Alderman John Simpson, an eminent coal dealer in Newcastle who lived in Broad Chare and became Mayor of the City.

John Blackett was called Erasmus after Erasmus Lewis, who was secretary to Lord Oxford in Queen Anne's time and his father's close friend.[12] Carlyle also wrote Blackett down in his autobiography as, 'a man so imperfectly educated...and of ordinary talents' which was not at all the case although, undoubtedly, he was an extravagant and improvident man. Blackett had met Sarah Roddam of Hethpool, Northumberland, described by Carlyle as 'a beautiful highland place', while serving as a captain in the Northumberland Militia at Berwick upon Tweed in north Northumberland. She was, by then, an orphan since both her father Robert Roddam and her mother Sarah, the niece of Alexander Collingwood, had died of smallpox in the year 1744-1745. Sarah was then five years old and so had been brought up by her uncle, Alexander Collingwood, until his death in 1758. The younger daughter Mary, then aged two, had been raised in less affluent circumstances by one William Hume, a minister at Polwarth. Blackett and Sarah Roddam had been married in 1761 at the Episcopal Chapel in Edinburgh by the Reverend George Carr, who, according to 'Jupiter ' Carlyle in his autobiography, had been an under-usher (assistant master) at Collingwood's old school, whilst Carlyle himself was to marry the younger sister Mary, a lady twenty-one years his junior.

Blackett and his wife had set up house after their marriage in a small but pleasant abode in Pilgrim Street in the town of Newcastle, from which he could follow his trade as merchant adventurer and boothman.[13] Then, in 1764, the year in which the *Newcastle Chronicle*, which still survives, was founded, Blackett had become an alderman of the town. The following year he had succeeded a relative, Sir Walter Blackett, as mayor, and a street in the city was named after him. But then, sadly, his wife Sarah died prematurely in 1775 and his son died in the year following. In 1782 Blackett moved to Charlotte Square in the town and it was there that his daughter Sarah often stayed and kept house while her husband pursued the French at sea, and it was to this address that Collingwood so often wrote. It was a correspondence much welcomed and cherished by the lonely Blackett in his widowhood and in his admiration for his famous son-in-law.

The Collingwood connection suggests that Cuthbert Collingwood's marriage was clearly not the product of a chance encounter.

Vice-Admiral Roddam had been born in 1720, the second son of Edward Roddam of Roddam and Littlehoughton Hall. Roddam had gone to sea in the *Lowestoffe* as a midshipman in 1735 and afterwards served with the celebrated Admiral Vernon. But his promotion to the post list as captain came in 1746 as a reward for distinguished service while commanding the *Viper* when it successfully destroyed a fleet of thirty transports laden with naval stores at Cederia Bay, Cape Ortugal, Spain, while under bombardment from the guns of two batteries on shore. The action had captured the public's imagination and on his return to England, he had been hailed a hero.[14]

In fact Collingwood was already well acquainted with Roddam since both he and his brother Wilfred had served with him in 1772 when they had moved into the *Lenox* guard-ship at Portsmouth when Roddam, then aged fifty-three years, was its captain. And there they had remained until Roddam was relieved in December the following year. By then the three of them had become firm friends, despite the difference in rank and age, no doubt due in part to the fact that all three were natives and products of the same remote county bordering the distant lowlands of Scotland. Roddam had, by then, accumulated thirty-seven years of service, and so had many a tale to tell his eager young friends. On the death of his elder brother in 1776 he had succeeded to the family estates at Roddam and Little Houghton Hall in north Northumberland but had continued to devote his life to naval service, becoming a Rear-Admiral of the White in 1778, a Vice-Admiral of the White in 1787, a Vice-Admiral of the Blue in 1779 and an Admiral of the Blue in 1793, although by then retired from active service. After the glory of Trafalgar Roddam wrote in the *Naval Chronicle* of Collingwood:

His private worth equals the splendour of his well-known public value. He is in every respect a great and good man: and in every circumstance, both professionally and otherwise, he has finally proved himself deserving of the high opinion I early formed of him, and which I always hoped would in time render him as much approved by his country as he was valued by me.

When Roddam died on 31 March 1808 he too was at Morpeth. He was by then the senior Admiral of the Red and stood highest on the list of officers. But despite his career success there had been disappointment for, notwithstanding the opportunity which three marriages had afforded him, he died childless, and so left the Roddam estates to one William Spencer Stanhope, his godson and the great-grandson of his first cousin Mary, the wife of Edward Collingwood. This was the Stanhope who had served as a midshipman with Collingwood. But he too was to die without leaving heirs so that the estate then passed to the Falder family, one of whom had married a descendant of a Roddam.

'Jupiter' Carlyle, a graduate of Edinburgh University, had been ordained minister of Inveresk, near Edinburgh, and so lived with his wife in Musselburgh, a place Collingwood found dismal whenever he was required to stay there. He acquired the nickname 'Jupiter' because of striking good looks, and had won fame as a poet and pamphleteer who stood on terms of close friendship with many of the literary celebrities of the age, including Adam Smith, David Hume and Tobias Smollett. A man much caricatured in his day, he was, in truth, a wise, liberal-minded, genial and portly character sporting an aquiline nose who won justified praise from Smollett in his description of Edinburgh life in his novel *Humphry Clinker*. Sir Walter Scott, on the other hand, must have thought nothing of his poetry for Lockhart, in his *Life of Scott*, records that Scott said of him, 'The grandest demi-God I ever saw was Dr Carlyle...commonly called 'Jupiter' Carlyle...and a shrewd old carle was he no doubt, but no more a poet than his precentor'.

Carlyle, on the strength of the doctorate he had obtained as a student, liked to pose as a man of superior intellect and tended to dismiss as stupid or ignorant those who did not show him the respect or consideration which he considered was his due. His visits to Newcastle upon Tyne to stay with his brother-in-law, John Erasmus Blackett, were many and long, and he was to write of the town:

At this period there were not many conversable gentlemen in Newcastle, which made one value Mr [Recorder] Collingwood the more; for the men were in general very ill educated, while the ladies who were bred in the south, by their appearance and manners, seemed to be very unequally yoked. The clergy at the time were almost all underbred, there being only one vicar in the town, and the rest only curates or lecturers...had it not been for the ladies, the state of society would have then been disagreeable. For many years past it has been totally different... At a grand dancing assembly our ladies were gratified as much as they could be, for Mrs Blackett had the honour of dancing with the Duke of Portland, and her sister with Viscount Torrington.[15]

Carlyle's autobiography nevertheless provides a good insight into Edinburgh life in the eighteenth century, although it did not achieve publication until the year 1860, long after his death, for he died at eighty-three years of age on 25 August 1805 without knowing of the fame which his friend and relative Collingwood was to win at Trafalgar only fifty-seven days later.

In the two years left to Collingwood before the onset of the French war and his return to sea, his wife bore him two daughters, Sarah, born in May 1792, and Mary Patience, born in 1793. After marriage they lived in a rather forbidding brick-built rented house on the banks of the River Wansbeck with a prospect looking out over open country in what is now Oldgate Street in the town of Morpeth. Morpeth was then but a small village in Northumberland and a pocket borough of the Earl of Carlisle, run by his agent Robert Fenwick. But in the eighteen years of life which were to remain to Collingwood he was to spend not much more than a year at home and so saw his wife and daughters but seldom, such were the demands made of him by his naval overlords during the war with France. It is a record of duty without compare. But they, and that same house, which he later purchased when it came on the market in 1802 and which he loved very much even though not built in the traditional and more attractive Northumbrian stone, were ever in his heart and mind and the subject of constant mention in his correspondence. Indeed, before he returned to sea he lavished much time on the gardens surrounding the house with the assistance of his gardeners, Scott and William, and even persuaded a neighbour living opposite, one Matheson, to plant trees along the banks of the river between his house and the grounds of Morpeth Castle. It remains wooded to this day, thanks to Collingwood's industry and foresight. Although there very little, apart from his childhood home, this was the only house he ever lived in. He was to inherit another which his wife then occupied, but not Collingwood who remained at sea. And he did spend the occasional night on shore in both the West Indies and in the Mediterranean, but otherwise his ship was his home.

It is difficult to know quite what had caused Cuthbert to decide in the year 1761 to make his career at sea when only twelve years of age. But it is certain that he joined as a volunteer. There had been no tradition of naval service in his family, although by marriage he was related to a seagoing captain who had, before this time, married his mother's sister. Born in 1725 Captain Braithwaite had entered the navy in 1743 under the wing of a relative, Sir Chaloner Ogle and was, in 1761, commander of the frigate *Shannon*. And it is of note that Collingwood himself paid tribute to this uncle when penning the memoir of his own career dated 7 January 1806, when he wrote:

> I went into the Navy at a very early period of my life, in the year 1761, in the *Shannon*, under the protection and care of a kind friend and relation, the late Admiral Braithwaite, to whose regard for me, and to the interest which he took in whatever related to my improvement in nautical knowledge, I owe great obligations.

His uncle was to die at Greenwich, an Admiral of the White, on 28 June 1805 aged eighty years, only six months before this was written. And so he too was not to know of the fame which Collingwood was to win at Trafalgar, a little more than four months on.

Significantly, in Collingwood's account there is no mention of sobbing for home and family in those first days on board ship or of sharing a plum cake which his mother had packed in his sea chest with a kindly lieutenant who had taken pity on him, as his son-in-law, the barrister Newnham who adopted the name Collingwood, afterwards claimed had been the case. Indeed he had the advantage of an uncle's protection at that crucial stage of his career, which many a boy had not, and since he had been rated midshipman and moved into the frigate *Gibraltar* with Braithwaite in 1766 and then again went with him as a master's mate into the *Liverpool* in 1767, where he remained until 1772, that protection continued for eleven of his most formative years.

It may be that the example and encouragement of this uncle had prompted him to seek a naval career. Or perhaps it was the proximity of commercial and port activity in the River Tyne no more than 500 yards from his front door which had fired his imagination. Certainly he lived in a county which was a breeding ground for many a distinguished sailor. But whatever the reason, the decision must have brought welcome financial relief to his hard-pressed father, then struggling to support and care for a wife and seven children, the eldest of whom had only just reached the age of twenty-one years. And so it is probable that the suggestion when made that his son should sign on at the tender age of twelve years, had the backing of his father. It is probable too that it had the enthusiastic cooperation of Collingwood himself since he no doubt saw enlistment as an avenue of escape from the routine and discipline of school where his limited academic ability and failure to learn, had brought him so much reprimand, punishment and detention. He no doubt realized that schooling had little more to offer him.

At the same time both he and his King were to pay homage in later years to the remarkable skill and success of his famous headmaster, the Reverend Hugh Moises, who had nurtured in Collingwood, in those few early formative years, such a love of classical literature and composition that he was ever after able to correspond in such sublime and exquisite language and choice of phrase that his letters and reports and written observations were always a delight to read. In this he was the envy of his colleagues, not least Nelson who, although an impressive writer, often wrote in a clumsy and at times ungrammatical style and had difficulty in expressing himself on paper. Collingwood's love of books and reading carried him through many a long and lonely hour at sea. They were his favourite companions and his constant joy. This advantage he owed in no small part to the teaching of his headmaster, Hugh Moises.

Joseph Cowan, member of Parliament for Newcastle upon Tyne, wrote of him:

...he was a man of great influence, and engaged a large share of public attention...Mr Moises was a born teacher...He had the faculty of constituting himself the companion as well as the master of his pupils. He was a strong disciplinarian, and, when in school, was supreme. He took his seat at his desk with as much dignity as a Judge takes his seat upon the Bench. Every one bowed to him. But when their tasks were over, his relations with his scholars were of the most cordial character. He invited them to his house, assisted them with their lessons, walked with them in the country, and counselled them not only as to the work of the day, but as to the work of their lives. He advised his pupils to read only the works of great authors as much with the view of learning their style as their doctrines. He had himself a passion for the classics, but he always strove to ascertain the special aptitude of his scholars, and urged them to pursue only such studies as they were likely to excel in.[16]

Clearly he was greatly loved by his pupils who venerated him.

Moises was a graduate of Trinity College, Cambridge and a classical fellow of Peterhouse, Cambridge, who had succeeded one Richard Dawes as headmaster of that small school in 1749 on the recommendation of Edmund Keane, Master of Peterhouse and later Bishop of Chester and Ely, and there he remained until his nephew, the Reverend Edward Moises, succeeded him in the year 1787. He lived on long enough to marry three wives and to know of Collingwood's fame at Trafalgar but died soon afterwards at his house in Northumberland Street, Newcastle, on 5 July 1806 at the age of eighty four.

A boy is fortunate if his years at school chance to coincide with the tenure of a great and gifted teacher for he cannot choose the date of his birth, still less the choice of his school. These decisions are in the gift of his parents. It was Collingwood's good fortune as a boy to live no more than 900 yards or so from the school where Moises did his teaching but also to do so at a time when Moises was in post there, for his parents had not the wherewithal to experiment with schools more distant

It has to be remembered that Collingwood's school at Newcastle upon Tyne over which Moises presided, was at that time but a very small academy located discreetly beyond what is now Collingwood Street at the junction of Neville Street and Westgate Road and close to St John's Church, with playing fields on grounds on which the Central Railway Station now stands.

It is true, as the records of that school show, that it had produced scholars such as the Reverend Henry Bourne, a scholar and graduate of Christ's College, Cambridge, who had won national fame as an antiquary earlier in the century for works such as *Antiquitates Vulgares*. And there had been the poet and doctor Mark Akenside. The King had learned a little of that distant academy many years before since Akenside had become physician to Queen Charlotte in the early years of his reign, and he seldom lacked employment, for the King fathered fifteen children, six of them born before Akenside died of fever in 1770 when lying in a bed donated by a friend in which Milton was said to have died. And so, while Akenside tended to the King's family, that originally more humble man of Northumberland, Capability Brown, tended to his gardens as His Majesty's royal gardener

In fact Akenside had started life from a similarly modest background and had acquired a further handicap when partially crippled at the age of seven when a meat cleaver had fallen on his foot while playing in his father's butchers shop near the quayside in Newcastle. But happily a brother Puritan dissenter of his father's had arranged financial support which paid for his fees at the school and also at William Wilson's academy in the town and this was followed by a degree in medicine from the University of Edinburgh, a doctorate from Leyden University, a large, fashionable and very lucrative practice in London, fellowships of the Royal Society and of the Royal College of Physicians, an appointment as chief physician at St Thomas's Hospital in London and a street named after him in Newcastle. It was in his early years that he had written some of his more celebrated poetry, including the famous *Pleasures of Imagination* which was translated into many languages and which he afterwards said had been inspired on a visit to Morpeth 'by solitary Wansbeck's limpid stream'.[17] But he ended life an arrogant, humourless, difficult man who seldom referred to his more humble origins. It is probably true that where Newcastle was proud of Mark Akenside, the pride of Mark Akenside hindered him from being proud of Newcastle.

Collingwood's school was not the very large, independent, fee-paying Royal Grammar School of such high academic performance which it seems to have become in the nineteenth and twentieth centuries, set in acres of grounds on the outskirts of the city with, according to the *History of the Royal Grammar School* by Mains and Tuck, a production line of scholars to three or four particular colleges at Cambridge and, less strongly, to the University of Oxford. A perusal of the alumni list shows it to have been the nursery of many a distinguished judge, academic or doctor.

It is all the more remarkable therefore that the good and gentle Moises should in his day have produced from his tiny school, Brand the antiquarian, Burdon the philosopher, Sir Robert Chalmers the Indian judge, Sir William Scott, later Lord Stowell who was for many years the senior Maritime Judge, his younger brother Lord Eldon the longstanding Lord Chancellor to both George III and George IV and High Steward of Oxford University, both of whom had lived in their father's house in Love Lane on the quayside, as well as Cuthbert Collingwood and many others. His achievement was immense and was fully recognized by very many of his former pupils. So much so that they came together after his death to erect a mural monument in his memory in the porch of the Cathedral Church of St Nicholas which appropriately carries an inscription in Latin written by Sir William Scott as he then was. To his regret Collingwood was unable to be present at the dedication, tied as he was to duty in the Mediterranean in the service of his country.

Eldon later spoke of Collingwood, who was three years older than him, as a 'pretty boy' and as a 'mild boy' who 'did not then give promise of being the great man he afterwards became; he did not show any remarkable talents then.'[18] It is not known with certainty how long Collingwood spent at that school, but it is sure that he was there for at least four years and long enough for Stowell, who was three years senior to him although in the same class according to Eldon, and Eldon who was three years junior to him, to remember and speak of him as they did, and for Collingwood himself to receive the education that he did for which he so often gave thanks to his old headmaster.

Certainly he was not of the academic calibre of another pupil, John Brand who, after graduation from Lincoln College, Oxford followed by ordination and a domestic chaplaincy with his friend and patron, the Duke of Northumberland, became resident secretary of the Society of Antiquaries, an office to which he was re-elected annually for the rest of his life during which his poem *On illicit Love* written among the ruins of Godstow Nunnery, Oxford, his *History and Antiquities of the Town and County of Newcastle-upon-Tyne* and his massive *Observations on Popular Antiquities* were published; the latter containing a re-publication with additions of Bourne's earlier work upon which Sir Henry Ellis and W. C. Hazlitt later built.

Nor would he have been able to compete with the business and literary skills of the Yorkshire man William Burdon who, after graduating as a classical scholar from Emmanuel College, Cambridge of which college he became a fellow, made a fortune from his ownership of coal mines, built Hartford Hall in Plessey Woods near Morpeth, married the daughter of Lieutenant General Dickson and was the author of a wealth of literature, including a *Life of Napoleon*, and *Materials for Thinking*, a publication which ran to several editions.

It is true also that John Scott, Lord Eldon, and his brother William, Lord Stowell, known as Harry, were in a different league intellectually which allowed them to go on to scale the very highest echelons of the English judiciary.

Although Eldon was fond of broadcasting his supposedly modest origins, in fact their father had prospered substantially as a coal fitter, keel owner, keeper of a public house, shipping and marine insurance broker, owner of a sugar-house and supplier of timber, wagon wheels and rails to the collieries around Newcastle upon Tyne. Hence the nickname 'Old Coal Bags' mischievously attached to Eldon by the Prince of Wales. At his death in 1776 his father left to his family property valued at between 30, and 40,000 pounds.

Although Eldon himself, a product of University College, Oxford, and the Inner Temple in London, drew no income from his office as High Steward of the University, with his earnings at the Bar travelling the Northern Circuit to Newcastle and Durham, the stamping ground of many a fledgling barrister and the scene too of an infamous prison sentence imposed by the notorious Judge Jeffreys in the year 1684 upon two defaulters for failing to attend church for three years past, he soon acquired a respectable income. Added to that were fees earned as a tenant of Chancery chambers in London, as Temporal Chancellor of Durham, and then as Solicitor-General followed by Attorney-General. And so he earned a considerable income while still in practice. He then drew a not inconsiderable stipend as Chief Justice of the Common Pleas with the title Baron Eldon of Eldon in the County of Durham, and then as Lord Chancellor and Keeper of the Great Seal over more years than any before or since, so that, with this accumulation of riches augmented by a legacy from his father and very judicious investment, he left almost 1 million pounds when he died an earl in 1838. He lies buried in an unpretentious grave at Kingston Chapel not far removed from his estate at Encombe in Dorset.

His older brother, Lord Stowell of Stowell Park in the county of Gloucester, although living mainly at Earley Court in Berkshire was, if anything, blessed with an even more powerful intellect, and continued to preside over the Admiralty Court, dispensing judgments until the ripe old age of eighty-two. He was truly an outstanding judge in an age of naval warfare when so much of international complexity was brought before the Admiralty Court for adjudication.

Born in 1745 across the river from Newcastle at his father's country house in Heworth, so that his mother in labour should avoid the army of the Pretender which threatened to march on the city, his grounding had been in academia. After winning a Durham scholarship to Corpus Christi College, Oxford in 1761 for which he was eligible because of birth at Heworth which lies across the border in County Durham, he had stayed on at the university sampling the delights of Oxford as a tutor, lecturer, reader, fellow of University College and Camden Professor of Ancient History[19] until called to the Bar by the Middle Temple in 1780, after which, although no orator, his rise had been meteoric. Knighted in 1788 as King's Advocate-General, he had been raised to the High Court Bench as the Admiralty Judge in 1798, became the Member of Parliament for Oxford University in the year 1802, and was raised to the peerage in 1821.

But his judgment failed him in the year 1812 when he had occasion to pass sentence upon the Marquis of Sligo for enticing two seamen to desert their ship, for he afterwards embarked on a second marriage with Sligo's mother, the Dowager Marchioness, daughter of old Admiral Lord Howe. It proved to be a very stormy alliance which only ended with her death five years on.

A dishevelled man with a serious appetite for food, drink and conversation, he was a lifelong friend of Dr Johnson and one of his executors.[20] He was to die in 1836, almost as wealthy as his younger brother. Indeed, Viscount Sidmouth, the former Prime Minister Henry Addington, profited greatly from his will for he had married Stowell's daughter. So much so that he resigned a Crown pension which had been granted him in the year 1817.

Campbell described him as:

The great scholar who had been the boast of Oxford...the great Judge, or rather legislator – the author of a code of international law, which defines the rights and duties of belligerents and neutrals, and which is respected over the whole civilised world.

Lord Brougham wrote of his 'vast superiority', whilst it was the judgment of Twiss, in his biography of Eldon, that 'He stamped his own mind on the international jurisprudence of the world'.

Although Collingwood may have lacked the intellect of those gifted pupils and had not the equipment to take full advantage of the teaching which Moises laid before him, he had much to thank that school and Moises for, and ever stood in their debt, since, at the age of twelve years, he departed that school equipped for life.

It is not surprising therefore that after reading Collingwood's Trafalgar dispatch with tears in his eyes on the morning of 5 November 1805, the King should have said: 'Where did this sea captain get his admirable English? Oh I remember, he was educated by Moises', recalling what his Lord Chancellor and schoolfellow Lord Eldon had earlier told him.

It is probable that Nelson and many other of Collingwood's colleagues had not such an educational advantage for their correspondence for the most part fails to match the style and perfection of his. Although inspired, clear and always fascinating, even many of the writings of the prolific Nelson lack punctuation, grammar and good spelling. But then, the son of the rector of Burnham Thorpe and born on 29 September 1758, his mother had died when he was nine and he had been shuffled from one school to the next in his early years, including the High School at Norwich which was his first school and the Paston School at North Walsham to which he then moved. Like Collingwood he had been lured to sea at an early age by the offer of a place from a seagoing uncle, in his case Captain Maurice Suckling.

In these years of comparative idleness before the onset of the French war in 1793 when both he and Collingwood were languishing at their respective homes, waiting the recall to duty, their friendship remained alive and was not forgotten. By letter from Morpeth dated 14 November 1792, Collingwood wrote to his friend:

You must not be displeased that I was so long without writing to you. I was very anxiously engaged a great part of the time, and perhaps sometimes a little lazy; but my regard for you, my dear Nelson, my respect and veneration for your character, I hope and believe will never be lessened. God knows when we may meet again, unless some chance should draw us to the seashore.

That chance was to occur sooner than perhaps they thought or Collingwood wished, for storm clouds were, at that very time, looming over the continent of Europe which were to draw him away from his home and from his family in the service of his country for almost the rest of his life.

Chapter 6

Collingwood at the Battle of the Glorious First of June 1794

On 21 January 1793 revolutionary France beheaded their King, Louis XVI, and the French Ambassador at London, Chauvelin, was ordered out. On 1 February the National Convention, already at war with Prussia, Austria and Sardinia, declared war on Great Britain and the United Netherlands. This was then extended, in quick succession, to Spain, Portugal and the Kingdom of the Two Sicilies. So the whole of the continent was very soon locked into a war which was to continue, on and off, for almost twenty-two years until matters were finally resolved at the Battle of Waterloo.

'These were the machinations', Collingwood was to write, 'of a mad people, who, under the mask of freedom, would stamp their tyranny in every country in Europe'.

The history of the British nation in the 200 years or so leading up to Waterloo could so easily be written through the eyes of the developing Royal Navy for the two marched hand in hand. For the last 100 of these 200 years, France, as the most populated and the most powerful nation in the world, had been the common enemy. Rivalry between the two for trade with the emerging countries across the globe was intense. The threat posed to British commercial interests abroad, and indeed at home, was correspondingly great for France appreciated well enough that invasion of British territory would very quickly stifle all competition. And so, as trade routes opened up in distant parts, so did competition for them amongst the great nations of western Europe. This stark reality dictated the basic need. If these island shores, and British territory and commercial interests around the world, were to be protected from predators and armies of invasion, a strong and commanding naval presence was required to guard these many highways, playing a defensive role, for Great Britain really stood alone. And, rather than concentrate British ships in home waters in immediate defence of the island, it became the central policy of the Admiralty to seek to dominate the Channel by blockading France's Atlantic ports twenty-four hours a day, principally that of Brest, and so prevent the French Fleet putting to sea, confident that if British ships were blown off station by winds of gale force, that same circumstance would prevent the French Fleet from setting sail. Likewise, exploiting the geography of France's divided coastline, a blockade would be mounted at Toulon to prevent the French Mediterranean Fleet from being able to combine with any fleet which may have succeeded in breaking out into the Atlantic. The same strategy was to be applied off Cadiz should Spain rally to the support of France. Other ships, meanwhile, would be deployed in protection of British convoys and territories across the world, but in three main areas, North America, the West Indies and India, as the British Empire proceeded to grow.

So the year 1793 found Great Britain at war with France yet again. Across the channel, a few years before, Frenchmen had become preoccupied with revolution, the seeds of which had been sown when fighting with the rebels in the American war against the British King, thus undermining the authority of Louis XVI. Finally Louis delegated the responsibility for government to a Parliament of the Estates General which had then turned on him, looking for its support to the Committee of Public Safety, Robespierre, Danton, the hard-pressed and overtaxed majority of ordinary Frenchmen and a starving Paris mob which had been unable to meet the exorbitant price which the sale of bread commanded in the market. In its wake came the uprising, triggered by the storming of the Bastille in 1789 after which the country was in the grip of revolution. It was the hope of new France that the revolutionary idea and spirit could be exported, and that, encouraged by infiltrators and agitators, it would quickly and spontaneously spread across the channel and capture there the hearts and minds of ordinary Englishmen and so overthrow all established order and peace. But the mood of the average Englishman had been badly misread. As the terror, ordered by the National Assembly and later by the Convention, gathered momentum, so it rapidly escalated beyond the control of its creators. And as it did so, the ordinary decent Englishman, sickened by the atrocities, bloodletting and butchery, and the drunken thirst for more, and finally the executions of Louis and his wife Marie Antoinette, quickly lost all interest in the French solution. Indeed such was the revulsion for the whole spectacle that it set back proper movement for reform in Great Britain for a generation or more. In the result the French Republican Army marched into Belgium and Holland and occupied the Flemish coast, the Scheldt estuary and the water highways across Europe in violation of all treaties of neutrality and now threatened to use those territories as a springboard to cross the English Channel.

Under William Pitt the Younger as Prime Minister the country had enjoyed ten years of peace, prosperity and consolidation. But ships and manpower had been scaled down to a dangerously low level. The Navy had for many years operated as a mercantile fleet, ill-equipped to wage war and with little or no experience of battle conditions. Many trained officers such as Collingwood and Nelson had been languishing at home unemployed without a command and on half pay. But now officers of experience were rapidly brought back into service and all the great admirals of the day were given fleet commands. Admiral Lord Hood, First Sea Lord and much admired by Nelson, if not Collingwood, as a modern professional officer who owed nothing to birth or influence, was given command of the Mediterranean Fleet. He was now almost seventy years of age. And Admiral Lord Howe, claimed by George III to be a blood relation through his aristocratic Hanoverian mother, an illegitimate daughter of George I – although this was refuted in Trowbridge's *Seven Splendid Sinners* – was now recalled at the age of sixty-eight at the insistence of the King. A dapper, inaccessible and apparently cold man he was, in truth, kindly and compassionate and much loved by the ordinary sailor for the concern he showed for the welfare of those who served under him, although Collingwood was to be disappointed with him in the matter of honours following the Battle of the Glorious First of June. Although he was the product of a highly privileged background with an awesome reputation in the service as a professional sailor who had gone to sea at the age of fourteen, he was at the same time entirely without ambition and very much the darling of the service.

Howe was now brought back as Commander-in Chief of the Channel Fleet. Officers were recalled to the colours, amongst them Captain Horatio Nelson, Captain Sir John Orde and Captain Cuthbert Collingwood.

The Admiralty now appointed Collingwood to join Lord Howe's Fleet in the Channel with command of the Second Rate *Prince*, a sluggish ship of 90 guns which carried the flag of his friend Rear-Admiral George Bowyer. Bowyer was then in his early fifties and had only been appointed to that rank on the day war was declared. However, like Collingwood, he had fought in the American War of Independence when serving as a post captain under both Byron and Rodney, and so had experience of warfare at first hand. Indeed it had been at the end of the American War that Collingwood had first met Bowyer in London and had come to know him quite well.[1]

As ever the declaration of war in 1793 caught the government unprepared and, despite the urgency of the situation, great difficulty was encountered in recruiting enough men to man those ships which were ready for sea, and then in training them to be of use. The *Prince* was no exception but, eventually, Collingwood was ready to sail.

At a count there were probably about 300 ships available, 120 of them ships of the line, but less than half were then in commission and ready for sea, and less than 50,000 officers and men were on hand to sail them. Sixty-four of these were admirals, 400 by then post captains and up to 1,500 stood in the rank of lieutenant. It seemed that Great Britain now lay at the mercy of the French invader.

Yet, although it involved dissipating the fruits of ten years of peace and consolidation, ships were rapidly brought into commission, shipbuilding in the dockyards was stepped up, volunteer forces were hurriedly put together and an amateur attempt was made at coastal defence. It now remained to be seen whether the patriotic and revolutionary fervour of the recently emancipated Frenchman, which was to be the winning ingredient for so many victories on land when harnessed and directed by the military genius of the Corsican Bonaparte, would be sufficient to produce a like result at sea where the trained and experienced pre-Revolution officer class had been all but decimated or dispersed in the turmoil. The French had at their disposal recently and well-built ships of some size, but the use to which they put them now depended almost entirely upon the courage and patriotic spirit of those who sailed them. And here, what was lacking was seamanship and experience. Supplies too were short, for French seamen were kept on meagre rations and issued with the barest minimum of clothing which did nothing for their morale. In 1794 the French Convention added to the problem by dismissing the 6,000 trained seamen gunners it still had at its disposal upon the ground that 'it savoured of aristocracy that any body of men should have an exclusive right to fight at sea'.

Collingwood was happy to be serving in a line of battle ship. Writing to his eldest sister on 17 February 1793, he said:

> ...it gives me a claim in future to a line of battle ship in preference to a frigate, into which I will never go again if I can help it...I will never command a two-decked ship when I can get one with three.

Although it is perhaps inevitable that the lives of warriors who achieve fame should be told in terms of the battles in which they have fought, the truth of any soldier or sailor's career is that he will be engaged in battle and exposed to danger on but very few days of his service. For the rest it is training for conflict, watching and waiting and perhaps striving in the meantime to present a threat and a deterrent. So it was for Collingwood and the British Navy throughout the year 1793 and well into the spring of 1794.

Patrolling the blockade was laborious and tedious work, although, to Collingwood's great relief, in 1794 Bowyer was given the more agile Second Rate *Barfleur* in place of the *Prince* and shifted his flag into her in March of that year, taking Collingwood with him.

But, despite one or two peripheral skirmishes with the enemy, there was no real success to report. Indeed there had been one reverse.

In those early days of un-preparedness it is not surprising that the British government found itself unable to send reinforcements to assist the fleet at Toulon in support of the French Royalists who had seized the town at the start of the war and opened the port and harbour to Lord Hood's ships, placing themselves under his protection. It was not possible therefore to exploit the advantage. And so it was that it was soon recaptured by French Republican forces, thanks in no small part to the crucial intervention of Napoleon Bonaparte, then a humble lieutenant colonel of artillery, courageously disobeying the written orders of the Committee of Public Safety sitting in far-off Paris. Thus was Fort L'Aigulette, which commanded the entrance to the harbour, recaptured and the British Fleet forced to withdraw, abandoning behind them all but three of the French Fleet which had previously been captured, together with those local Royalist supporters it had not been possible to evacuate. They were left to their fate as the incoming Jacobins and their guillotine moved closer. Nelson had played his part dancing attendance on the King of Naples at Hood's instruction which, with the help of Sir William and Lady Hamilton, had produced military assistance for Toulon. But alas the Neapolitan contingent, dispatched in support, took fright under attack and could do nothing to save the town or to stop the wholesale slaughter of its citizens; a massacre which left an indelible mark on the mind of the young Napoleon who saw it.

In a letter to Sir Edward Blackett dated 2 March 1794, Collingwood, who could now write as an officer who knew something of the art of warfare at sea, wrote of his regret at what he described as the 'mismanagement' at Toulon:

> No preparation was made for the destruction either of ships or arsenal; and at last perhaps it was put into as bad hands as could be found – Sir Sidney Smith, who arrived there a few days before, and had no public situation either in the fleet or Army, but was wandering to gratify his curiosity...The ships should have been prepared for sinking as soon as he got possessed of them...

At the same time, Collingwood made no allowance in that report for the undoubted fact that Smith, acting at Hood's specific request, did what he did while all the while under bombardment from the Republicans who were then advancing on the town.

There was, at this time, no Nelson available to relieve Collingwood's boredom. However in the summer of that year, 1794, the British tasted some success off Ushant and Collingwood played an active role in achieving it, although to his dismay and disappointment, and to the great surprise of many of his colleagues, when campaign medals were awarded the outstanding contribution he had made went unrecognized.

Howe had put to sea in his flagship the *Queen Charlotte* with a fleet of ships with orders to blockade the port of Brest when he found, to both his astonishment and his delight, that the French under Villaret-Joyeuse had already broken out and were at sea. Their mission was to escort into port a large convoy of ships carrying vital supplies of grain from the Chesapeake in America for the starving and desperate blockaded citizens of France. Ship for ship they were evenly matched and the French were confident.

'Never before did there exist in Brest a fleet so formidable' wrote the Moniteur before the battle. After two days of searching followed by peripheral skirmishing in poor visibility and fog, Howe managed to bring the French to battle off Ushant and there he scored a decisive victory on what came to be known as 'The Glorious First of June' from the date of the encounter, for it was fought so far out into the ocean that no geographical point was available to identify the exact location.

Six ships were captured, one was sunk, twelve were dismasted and no less than 7,000 Frenchmen were killed, wounded or taken prisoner. Eight of Howe's ships suffered severe damage, eleven were dismasted and there were 1,500 British casualties. The cost in human life had therefore been great. A commemorative panel was afterwards designed around the simple message, 'England expects every man to do his duty',[2] advice later employed by Nelson in his Trafalgar signal. It is sure that every man had done his duty that day and those many who died had given much more! Indeed victory could, to some extent, be attributed to good fortune which had favoured the British, for the battle had not gone according to Howe's plan which had been to pass through the French line from leeward. Despite the advantage by this time of a signalling system of flags of different shapes which had been devised by Admiral Kempenfelt and later codified by Howe himself [3] (who had introduced numbers) for the use of Home Fleets (Popham's more efficient solution was still many years away), some of Howe's captains found themselves unable to conform. Very few ships had followed Howe through the enemy line as planned. The rest had hauled up to windward and fired at

68

a distance. In the result, the attack went in from all sides which threw the French into confusion, disarray and, ultimately, defeat.

Thackeray was later to draw on a letter which Collingwood afterwards wrote to his father-in-law on 5 June in which he described how:

> The night was spent in watching and preparation for the succeeding day; and many a blessing did I send forth to my Sarah, lest I should never bless her more... .

And of the day itself, a Sunday morning:

> It was then near ten o'clock. I observed to the Admiral that about that time our rivals were going to church, but that the peal we should ring about the Frenchman's ears would outdo the parish bells.

Thackeray wrote:

> There are no words to tell what the heart feels in reading the simple phrases of such a hero. Here is victory and courage, but love sublime and superior. Here is a Christian soldier spending the night before battle in watching and preparing for the succeeding day, thinking of his dearest home, and sending many blessings forth to his Sarah, lest he should never bless her more.

Perhaps Collingwood was conscious of Howe's failure to give his commanders licence to pursue the enemy, because his letter continued:

> Our condition did not admit of a further pursuit; indeed to take possession of what we had got required exertion. Two of our ships were totally dismasted, and many of us very much crippled. We left off in admirable good plight, having sustained less loss than could be expected, considering the fire we had so long on us. We had nine men killed, and twenty-two with severe wounds, a few others slightly hurt; our masts etc all in their places, though much wounded.
>
> We have not obtained this victory without losses that must long be lamented. Admiral Bowyer and Admiral Palsey have each lost a leg; Admiral Graves is severely wounded in the arm, and as he is seventy years of age, or nearly, it is hard to say what will be the consequence. Captain Montague was killed; and Captain Hutt, of the *Queen*, lost his leg. Several Lieutenants are killed and wounded: and this, altogether, has been the severest action that has been fought in our time, or perhaps ever...

The *Barfleur* had indeed come under heavy fire that day and so close was the engagement that an enemy sniper had been near enough to Rear-Admiral Bowyer to hit him with a shot as he stood within range on deck. It cost him his leg. Indeed he had fallen wounded into the arms of Collingwood who had been standing with him. And it had left Collingwood in sole command of the *Barfleur* early on, and so any tribute for the significant role then played by the *Barfleur* when engaging French ships at close quarters was rightly due to him. But none came.

Yet medals enough were awarded, for many, including Collingwood himself, saw it as a great victory. He was to write to Sir Edward Blackett on 15 June: 'We have, with God's blessing, obtained as complete a victory as ever was won at sea...'

Yet in fact Howe's plan for the destruction of the French merchantmen under escort had failed. This can probably be attributed to the cunning of the French Commander, Villaret-Joyeuse, who had lured Howe away from the convoy and into battle, but his neglect to pursue the French all the way back to Brest after they took flight was, in part, to blame. And so the French achieved their aim which had been to land their vast cargo of grain on the shores of France for consumption by a starved and very desperate population. There was therefore much rejoicing in that quarter for it had been a matter of life and death.

Nonetheless, when the victorious fleet docked at Spithead on 17 June, Lord Howe stepped on shore in the presence of a great crowd and was greeted with the music of *See the Conquering Hero Comes*, *Rule Britannia* and *God Save The King*, and that night he and Lady Howe were dined by the Port Admiral, Sir Peter Parker, in great splendour.

King George saw it as victory enough to persuade him, contrary to all previous custom, to visit Lord Howe on his flagship which he did on 26 June. That day he and Queen Charlotte descended on Portsmouth and there went on board Lord Howe's flagship, the *Queen Charlotte*, where the King presented the Admiral with a diamond-hilted sword. It was a royal occasion without precedent, as much appreciated by the ships' captains as by Lord Howe himself, for they recognized that their Commander had played a cool, courageous and skilful role in carrying them through to victory, so they rejoiced in the honour done to him. But, regrettably, the arrangements made for the royal visit generated appreciable complaint and bitterness amongst the captains when they discovered that they had been excluded from much of the ceremony itself even though it was they who had delivered the victory for their commander and for their country.

Collingwood, in a letter to Sir Edward Blackett dated 30 June, records that they all attended in their barges to provide an escort for the royal party to Lord Howe's flagship but were then not allowed to be present at the ceremony itself, yet the King, by his visit, had sought to honour not just the Commander but the fleet as a whole. Meanwhile they sat in their barges on the water brooding for four hours or more waiting for the ceremony to end. This, according to Collingwood, had brought a sour note to the occasion. Lord Hugh Seymour was to report this to Howe the following day when the captains lined up on shore at the Governor's residence to be presented to their Majesties and to kiss hands, after which the admirals were presented with gold chains. Yet that same evening a dinner was then given by the King to which only the admirals were invited. However it seems that peace was restored to a certain extent on the Sunday following, when all dined with the King on what turned out to be a very happy occasion.

Amongst a small number of honours bestowed after the battle on a fortunate few, Collingwood's now disabled flag officer and friend, Rear-Admiral Bowyer, was granted a pension of £1,000 a year, a baronetcy and a gold medal suspended from an admiral's chain. These were perhaps small compensations for the loss of a leg which had ended his career at sea, but in the general promotions on 4 July 1794 he was advanced to the rank of vice-admiral. In November of that year, when his wound had healed sufficiently, he made his way back home to Abingdon and was there welcomed by the townsfolk as a local hero. A troop of the Abingdon Independent Cavalry then mounted an escort to see him safely and in triumph back to Radley Hall and his own front door, and there he lived on long enough to see in the new century. He had, by then, succeeded to a baronetcy held by his brother which had merged with the baronetcy which had been awarded to him after the battle, and he had been promoted also to the rank of full admiral in the general promotions of 14 February 1799. Edward Lloyd's coffee house in London had before then presented him with the Bowyer silver vase which is now in the possession of the town of Abingdon. But he died on 6 December 1800. He lies buried in Radley Church where his death is suitably recorded. A portrait of him hangs in the council chamber of Abingdon Town Hall, and Radley College, which now occupies Radley Hall, flies the Union flag on 4 June every year in his memory.[4]

It is said too that the privileged few can at times hear his one-legged walk stumping up the main staircase of the main house, although Sir Patrick Nairne, who spent many of his formative years at the college as a boy in Kenneth Boyd's house, certainly never heard it in his time, and he has the qualifying ancestry as a descendant of Alexander Nairne, a sixteen year old midshipman from Fife who served on the *Polyphemus* at the Battle of Copenhagen with Hyde Parker and Nelson before joining the sea service of the East India Company as a very popular and respected captain, during the temporary cessation of hostilities after the Peace of Amiens in 1802.[5] The ship he there commanded was named the *General Kyd*, after General Alexander Kyd, his maternal uncle and part owner, and in that command he was to make many a voyage to the East Indies until retirement brought him directorships of the Peninsular and Oriental Steam Navigation Company and the Marine Insurance Company.[6]

The current archivist and a master at Radley College, Tony Money, to whom Sir Patrick kindly spoke, gives no credence to the Bowyer rumour either and he spent forty years of his life in and about the school. Rather he attributes it to the fanciful imagination of a former long-serving master and chaplain at the school, for it seems the rumour died with the death of that master.

Bowyer, of Denham Court, near Uxbridge, had inherited the brick built Radley Hall in 1794 from his mother who was the daughter of Sir John Stonehouse, member of parliament for Berkshire, who had built it in 1725 in place of an old house which had stood there before. Two sketches of the hall, painted by J.M.W. Turner in 1789 when he was fourteen years of age, now hang in the Tate Gallery. It was a house well known to Collingwood who had stayed there for appreciable periods of time. Indeed as early as 1782, Collingwood wrote to his brother on 22 June that:

Captain Bowyer with whom I was a good deal when in town, is I believe now married to Miss Brett, the daughter of the late S. Peircy, [Admiral Sir Peircy Brett] and gone into the country. He has given me a very civil invitation to come down with him, and as it is little more than thirty miles from town I propose going down on Monday next, and if there is good company and I like the place, I shall probably stay there a few weeks, unless my good fortune calls me thence to a ship.

He had, in that letter, somewhat underestimated the distance from town as, no doubt, he was to discover.

But the award of the campaign medal to Bowyer for the performance of his ship makes it all the more surprising that no such medal was granted to Collingwood, since he had had the handling of her from the moment he had been left in sole command. This was the first time medals were granted for a large fleet action and they were clearly much treasured by those officers who received them since only those who had fought in a battle and who had fought in it with distinction were eligible to receive and wear them. They were an exclusive body of men.

Such honours were, of course, in the gift of the sovereign acting on the recommendation of the Admiralty which in turn acted upon the advice of the local commander and, in his report dated 2 June, Lord Howe had indeed singled out certain names for mention. But because those mentioned were so few in number, he was bombarded with requests to add to the list, and under pressure he eventually agreed to do so. He then had his First Captain, Sir Roger Curtis, compose a supplementary letter[7] in which several admirals and many captains who had not been mentioned in the first report, were then included, and these officers were in due course awarded the medal. But those not mentioned still included Collingwood, which made his omission all the more pointed. Collingwood was to write to Sir Edward Blackett on 30 June:

> Lord Howe's supplementary letter threw the fleet into the utmost consternation and astonishment...the appearance of the letter near broke my heart...[8]

To Dr Carlyle he wrote that he was: '...Sick with mortification...'. In his dispatch Lord Howe sought to explain his actions, implicitly, where he wrote that:

> ...the commander of a fleet is unavoidably so confined in his view of the occurrences in the time of battle as to be little capable of rendering personal testimony to the service of officers who distinguish themselves. To discharge this part of my public duty reports were called for from the flag-officers of the fleet for supplying the defects of my observance.

It may, therefore, be that Bowyer, who after all had been on close and friendly terms with Collingwood for twelve years or more, had just been in no condition to make any detailed report at all when Howe had called upon his flag officers to make their recommendations, for he was afterwards, in a letter to Roddam dated 11 October of that year to write of Collingwood that he did not know:

> ...a more brave, capable or a better officer in all respects than Captain Collingwood. I think him a very fine character; and I told Lord Chatham when he was at Portsmouth, that if ever he had to look for a first captain to a commander-in-chief, he would not find a better than our friend Collingwood.

Captain Pakenham of the *Invincible*, who did receive a medal, was heard to say: 'If Collingwood has not deserved a medal neither do I, for we were together the whole day.'

But whatever the reason for the omission, it hurt and wounded

Collingwood deeply. He took it as a reflection on his own personal conduct during the battle which had in fact been truly heroic. This was made clear in his letter of 30 June to Sir Edward Blackett in which he described how he had gone immediately to see Howe's captain, Sir Roger Curtis, to tell him that:

> ...the conduct of the *Barfleur* had merited commendation when commendation was given to zeal and activity; and that an insinuation that either had been wanting was injurious and unjust. Nor do I believe that any ship was more warmly or effectively engaged than the *Barfleur* from the beginning of the action to the end of it...He assured me that no disapprobation was meant to be implied, but that in the selections the Admiral was pleased to make he must stop somewhere...

Collingwood did in fact try to see Howe himself but he had been granted an audience with Curtis instead. Collingwood obviously suspected that the hand of Curtis lay behind the report which Howe had submitted to the Admiralty for he went on in his letter to Sir Edward Blackett that:

> Lord Howe is less blamed for his letter than his Captain, who has ever been an artful, sneaking creature, whose fawning, insinuating manner creeps into the confidence of whoever he attacks, and whose rapacity would grasp all honours and all profits that come within his view.

Collingwood considered that the report was:

> ...an attempt upon the credulity of the world to make them believe the *Queen Charlotte* with very little help defeated the French Fleet. It may be considered a libel on the fleet.

Curtis was little more than two years older than Collingwood and had, by then, had a distinguished career in the service. He had also by this time established a longstanding bond with Lord Howe, having served with him in the American War. Indeed for part of the time he had acted as captain of Howe's flagship, and such had been his contribution in that war that he had emerged from it with a knighthood for his services. And then in 1790 he was again appointed Howe's Flag Captain, and after a spell in command of a ship of his own, had returned to Howe in 1793 on the *Queen Charlotte* as his first captain or captain of the fleet. It is probable therefore that by the year 1794 he did have great influence with Howe. Indeed the failure of the fleet to pursue the broken enemy in its flight on 1 June was widely attributed to the hold Curtis had over the Admiral and the advice which he had no doubt given him to proceed with caution.

For his own contribution to the battle as captain of the fleet, the Queen presented him with a gold chain on the Royal visit to Portsmouth and he was then promoted rear-admiral and granted a baronetcy on 4 July. He was to be much named in the dispute concerning Rear-Admiral Sir John Orde in the Mediterranean in 1798, and was promoted vice-admiral in February 1799 and full admiral in April 1803. He died in 1816 at the age of seventy and was then succeeded in the baronetcy by his second son, who ended up an Admiral of the Fleet.

Whether therefore, given such career success, there was substance in Collingwood's suspicion is difficult to know but the wrong done to Collingwood was not repaired until 1797 following the action off St Vincent when medals for both battles were granted him, the earlier one retrospectively.

In fact and in truth Collingwood can have been very little deprived by all this for the medal was not ready for issue until November 1796, only three months before he was awarded it after the Battle of St Vincent.[9]

In the meantime Lord Chatham had investigated the complaint and then notified Collingwood to the effect that he would soon be employed in a ship proper to his rank. He was as good as his word and soon afterwards offered Collingwood any 74 that was ready for active service. Of the two then available, Collingwood chose the *Hector*. In the few days it took for the ship's incumbent, Admiral Montagu, to move out, Collingwood was able to spend a few precious hours in his beloved Northumberland with his long-suffering wife and family before the recall to duty summoned him back to Portsmouth, where Lord Howe spoke with him in cordial terms.

Lord Chatham then transferred Collingwood to the 74-gun *Excellent* which allowed him a further short leave back in Northumberland. A further small compensation for his part in the battle off Ushant came his way when he was notified that his share of prize money would amount to £1,400, which was not a trivial sum in those days.

It is difficult to imagine an officer in the armed services of today daring to voice a complaint of the sort which Collingwood had made and still retaining the respect of his colleagues but, in Collingwood's time these officers came of independent and opinionated stock. And there was not then the array of decorations which are now available to enable commanders to reward and recognize the various degrees of meritorious and gallant service. Campaign medals did not exist. Titles there were and these were granted liberally to flag officers in particular, when victorious, but the First of June medal was the first medal of its kind and it had only been struck at the suggestion of the King. It was an innovation. After the next battle of significance, off St Vincent, a medal was again awarded, but this time it was issued to all captains and flag officers without distinction or omission. So too at Camperdown, the Nile and Trafalgar, although none at all were awarded after Copenhagen. But gold chains for the admirals did not survive.[10] Indeed in future years the naval gold medal was only awarded for fleet actions and then not at all after 1815.

For those below the rank of captain there were no rewards at all except perhaps that of promotion. The mistake of course had been to issue a supplemental list, as Howe himself had foreseen when he wrote:

> I am so assailed to name those officers who had opportunity of particularly distinguishing themselves, that I shall proceed with the earliest preparation of it, though I fear it may be followed by disagreeable consequences.

The power of patronage is indeed a mixed blessing if it causes resentment in those who merit inclusion yet are omitted. And it may simply be that Howe had so wearied of the task himself that he had delegated it to another, for he was to write to Chatham:

> ...I beg you will allow me to refer you to Sir Roger Curtis for any particulars you may desire to be informed of which are unnoticed respecting the late operations.

Happily, it seems that although Collingwood felt the hurt greatly, he refused to let the disappointment sour him.

As for Lord Howe, older brother of General Sir William Howe and already a viscount in the Irish peerage by inheritance, and both a baron and an earl in the English peerage by creation, he was appointed a Knight of the Garter and then, the following year, raised to the rank of Admiral of the Fleet on the death of Admiral Forbes. But he was to live for only four years more. On his death the titles created became extinct and the titles inherited passed to General Howe who later died without issue. But to one of Admiral Howe's daughters a barony descended and her son, the Viscount Curzon, assumed the name Howe in 1821 and was then created Earl Howe from whom the present earl is descended. It is a confused ancestry and the islanders can perhaps be forgiven who assumed, mistakenly but in all good faith, that Lord Howe of Aberavon, CH, PC, QC, was of that stock, when, as a former British Foreign Secretary, he made a private visit to Lord Howe island, a haven for birds off the east coast of New South Wales, in 1995.

The island had been named after the Admiral by some of the first arrivals from Britain in the 1780s. At a welcoming party Lord Howe of

Aberavon thought it right to explain that he was not the real but only a bogus Lord Howe, which brought the comment from one bold resident, 'Yeah – but at least you earned yours, mate!'. Fortunately Lord Howe of Aberavon is not only a man of great distinction but also a man of understanding with a well developed sense of humour and so the mistake was quickly forgiven. Indeed Lord Howe told me this story against himself.

In truth the victory in 1794 had not been as decisive as it was at that time thought to be, but the King had been overjoyed at the news, so much so that it was his suggestion that the word 'Glorious' be used to describe it. It had, nonetheless, restored confidence in the mind of the British sailor who from then on firmly believed that he could always beat a Frenchman at sea. The enemy seems to have thought so too for the French Navy ever afterwards demonstrated a marked reluctance to join battle with the British Navy.

Chapter 7

Nelson and Collingwood at the Battle of Cape St Vincent, 1797

In the two years following the Glorious First of June, events in the Mediterranean began to escalate. They culminated in the emergence of Nelson as a hero in the eyes of the nation. These were years too which brought Nelson and Collingwood together again in the service of their country and, without doubt, Nelson's dramatic success in 1797 at the Battle of St Vincent was due in no small part to the active support given him by his friend Cuthbert Collingwood in his hour of need.

The turn of the year 1794 brought several changes for, at its close, Chatham was replaced at the Admiralty by Earl Spencer. In the summer of 1795, Howe, overtaken by ill health, began to bow out as Commander-in Chief of the all-important Mediterranean Fleet which was placed in the hands of Alexander Hood, now Lord Bridport and a Nelson supporter.

Collingwood that summer was employed on convoy duties in command of the *Excellent* escorting Indian merchantmen through those hazardous waters. These ships with their valuable cargoes were constantly the prey of independent privateers as well as of enemy warships, all of which followed the convoys like vultures awaiting their chance to pounce on any ship which might stray off course in the darkness of the night. And so, alert to the dangers which these predators presented, there was ever the need for vigilance, a duty which Collingwood found exhausting. But his mission was successful and, once accomplished in August of that year with all of his charges safely delivered and intact, he signed off at St Fiorenzo and rejoined the fleet at Leghorn. Here he found that Hood had relinquished his command in favour of Admiral Hotham.

Nelson had written to Collingwood of Hotham in August of that year that: 'Our Admiral, *entre nous*, has no political courage whatever, and is alarmed at the mention of any strong measure.'

In fact Nelson in the *Agamemnon* was far away on blockade duties off Toulon in the Mediterranean when Collingwood returned, but a letter from him was waiting for Collingwood. It read:

> My dear Coll, I cannot allow a Ship to leave me without a line for my old friend, who I shall rejoice to see; but I am afraid the Admiral will not give me that pleasure at present...I hope, my dear friend, you left Mrs Collingwood well. How many children have you? Did you see Mrs Moutray lately? Her dear, amiable son was lost by serving under me. I have a stone on board, which is to be erected in the church of St. Fiorenzo in his memory. I hardly ever knew so amiable a young man. Believe me, ever, my dear Collingwood,
> Your most affectionate friend,
> Horatio Nelson.
> Tell me a great deal.

Like many others Lieutenant James Moutray, when serving with Nelson, had gone down with Calvi fever whilst taking part in the costly campaign to occupy Corsica in order to secure it as a base in the Mediterranean after the loss of Toulon in 1793. The object too had been to assist General Pauli who had asked the British to help him drive the French invader from the island. The town of Bastia in the north had earlier been captured successfully by a small force under Nelson's command, but it was in June 1794 at Calvi, further to the west on the island, that James Moutray had met his end. He died soon after Nelson had himself suffered an injury in that same campaign which caused some disability for it cost him much of the useful sight in his right eye. An enemy shell had exploded dangerously close to him as it struck a sandbag on the parapet of a battery which he had established on shore as he supervised an artillery bombardment, throwing up sand and debris some of which had entered his right eye. Fortunately it was to leave little in the way of cosmetic blemish, but he did occasionally thereafter wear an eyeshade attached to the brim of his service hat to protect his left eye from the sun, but not the mythical black patch so often assumed by popular artists of the day since the eye had remained in its socket and there was little physical disfigurement.

Indeed there can be seen in old ledgers still retained by Locks the hatters of St James's Street, London, an entry recording that Nelson had required, on 20 August 1805, that a green eye shade be attached to a hat he had left with them for renovation, another dated 11 February 1803 which states that he had ordered the supply of a cocked hat with a green shade and a third dated 20 August 1805 when a like order was placed by him for a cocked hat with cockade and green shade.[1] Any who patronize that establishment for their headwear will see too a hat of Nelson's on display there which appears to have a black patch inside the brim which can be lowered as required.[2] This may account for the portrayal of him in the well-known late nineteenth century painting now in the Victoria Art Gallery, Bath which shows Nelson walking through the streets of Portsmouth wearing a black patch over his right eye.

The ambiguity here which has lasted over many years is perhaps not dissimilar to that concerning Nelson's height. For instance, whereas the naval historian Oliver Warner thought it must have been 5 feet 4 inches, judging it from the size of his uniforms, Christopher Hibbert, in his engaging biography of Nelson, points to an effigy of Nelson in Westminster Abbey, which, he states, stands 5 feet 5 inches high and is believed to be life size. In fact this figure, done in wax and standing in the Islip Chapel, although indeed thoroughly lifelike, was rushed out in a hurry in an attempt by the Dean and Chapter to win back some of the crowds who had deserted the Abbey and were flocking to St Paul's to see Nelson's tomb and the funeral car which had been put on show there, and it was modelled from a smaller one already in existence for which Nelson had sat in life. The height of the figure may not therefore be accurate, although it is to be noted that the clothes, except for the coat, were clothes actually worn by him in battle. Indeed on the inner lining of the hat is a mark where an eye patch must have been.[3] But then Colin White, respected Nelson historian and director of Trafalgar 200 at the National Maritime Museum, thinks he must have stood nearer 5 feet 6 inches high once his undress uniform coat is measured and other evidence is considered, and he cites an estimate made by one James Bagley, a marine who had fought at Trafalgar, who had thought him nearer 5 feet 7 inches.

The death of James Moutray was a sad reminder of that very precious friendship Collingwood and Nelson had forged with Mary Moutray in their earlier years in the West Indies, and it left her all alone in the world, for she was never to remarry. and her daughter predeceased her.

Surprisingly Collingwood had given vent to a dislike of Corsica back in August 1795, when he had written to Sir Edward Blackett:

A more miserable prospect than that island presents is scarce to be conceived of, the most savage country, barren brown mountains rearing their rugged, wrinkled, heads to the skies; the valleys produce a little corn, bad wine and olives, but the barbarians who inhabit there have not industry to cultivate any of them. Their manners are savage, their ignorance is gross, but the part of their

80

character of most consequence to us is the inveterate hatred they on all occasions express to the English. Every man of them travels in the country with a rifle, gun and a dagger, with which he kills with admirable dexterity such game or Englishmen as he may chance to meet in his way...and do it with the same composure that an old butcher kills a pig.

Certainly, although for the moment the Corsicans could be regarded as British, Nelson too formed the view that they were not to be relied upon, whilst Collingwood considered that the island had produced no more than 'wild hogs, assassins and generals like Napoleon Bonaparte'.

It was towards the end of that year that dramatic change came to the Mediterranean with the arrival on the station of the awesome Sir John Jervis who had succeeded to the Mediterranean command. Hotham had struck his flag and returned to England at the beginning of November to be succeeded in command by Vice-Admiral Sir Hyde Parker who held the command until the arrival of Sir John. Once in post Jervis had shifted his flag to the *Victory* and the protection of Corsica and the blockade of Toulon then began in earnest, the more so when, in October 1796, Spain declared war on England and placed her ships at the disposal of France. Jervis now watched and waited for his opportunity should the now stronger Franco-Spanish Fleet ever be brave enough to put to sea. No port of call was left to him in the Mediterranean after 26 September 1796 which was when he had been ordered by Spencer, because of stretched resources, the entry of Spain into the war and the domination of Italy by the French, to withdraw from Corsica. Nelson, now a commodore, who had given everything and suffered injury in taking the island for the British not many months before, was now required to organize its evacuation, which he thought ignominious and humiliating. But it was accomplished nonetheless with masterful efficiency in the face of aggressive hostility from Corsican troops and residents alike who saw it as prudent to transfer their allegiances to the incoming French, the more so as an advance unit of French soldiers had landed and was marching on Bastia. Nelson held all at bay with strong ultimatums until all 2,000 or so British troops, merchants, residents and loyalists had been embarked safely, together with their baggage, supplies and equipment. Again, Collingwood was on hand in the *Excellent* which provided assistance, although his mission to retake the small Genoese island of Capraia was quickly abandoned. And so, abandoning the Mediterranean, Sir John's Fleet was now necessarily based at Lisbon where Portugal had remained loyal to the British flag, albeit reluctantly. Gibraltar could provide no more than an anchorage.

The threat posed by a France torn by revolution daily grew more menacing now that she had the military genius of the fast-emerging Napoleon Bonaparte at her disposal. Once the Terror had abated and the Directory had taken control, his contribution at Toulon was remembered and he was given command of the forces of Paris. And there, with the skilful and determined use of cannonade, he quickly scattered and repulsed an attempt on the legislature. It was but the beginning of a dramatic rise to the very summit of power. A year or so later, given command of the Army of Italy, he force-marched his Army across the Alps and down onto the plains of Lombardy with the promise of riches and glory plundered from the conquered lands. And there, despite the overwhelming odds stacked against him, he routed the Austrian Army in a series of lightning and brilliant strikes and became, overnight, the sword and hero of the Revolution. One by one the armies of western Europe were defeated in battle and the whole of Europe now lay at the feet of France. Yet, with Bonaparte's territorial ambitions no more than whetted and an insatiable appetite for conquest in battle still not assuaged, France looked for fresh fields to conquer. Accordingly, in 1797, Bonaparte was ordered by the Directory to the shores of northern France to review the progress of plans for the invasion of Britain, possibly through the back door of Ireland where there was great rebellious unrest, although if the French were ever allowed to break out of Toulon where they lay at harbour and link up with the fleet at Brest, the aim would more probably be to gain command of the Channel long enough to cover a crossing to England. Britain now feared the worst.

It was in the climate of this emergency that Sir John Jervis, later to become Earl St Vincent, had begun his command of the Mediterranean Fleet, with the rank of full admiral. He was then sixty-one years of age.

Within months of his arrival on the station Jervis stamped his formidably stern character on the ships and men under his command by imposing a regime of iron discipline and round-the-clock devotion to duty which produced seamanship and gunnery of a prodigious standard which had never before been equalled. And so in no time at all a previously ill-disciplined and largely mercantile marine had been transformed into an efficient blockading and fighting machine which was to serve both Nelson and the British nation so well in its domination of the French in the perilous decade which followed. Indeed this was without doubt the greatest contribution Jervis ever made in the service of his country during his long and distinguished career with the British Royal Navy for there is no denying that the supreme fighting efficiency of the Royal Navy in the closing years of the eighteenth century was very much due to his work. In the ten years which followed his assumption of command in the Mediterranean it achieved a position of pre-eminence in the waters of the world. Those ten years were to be the most glorious in the long history of the British Navy, crowned as they were by Nelson's three great victories at the Nile, Copenhagen and off Cape Trafalgar, all won in the last seven years of Nelson's life.

But not surprisingly his arrival had been greeted by some officers who were fearful of the fierce and rigid discipline which they knew would be imposed, with consternation. And there did indeed follow a close and watchful eye on every ship, and on every officer in every ship, with frequent inspections of performance in all its detail, and any insubordination, however trivial, would be met with condign punishment. Mutinous elements faced death by hanging, the insubordinate suffered flogging. So, too, the need to eradicate waste in the use of government supplies became an obsession. Yet at the same time he introduced many reforms which undoubtedly did much to improve the service conditions of the ordinary sailor, and he insisted that the highest standards of hygiene be observed. For the first time a hospital ship was established where the sick and the wounded could be ministered to with a modicum of privacy and comfort, and many other reforms were introduced by him which were to stand the test of time.

All of this was but a reflection of the character of the man. Born a second son to a barrister father many miles from the sea at Melford Hall in Staffordshire, John Jervis had attended the local grammar school at Burton-on-Trent. But then his father, Swynfen Jervis, had readily exchanged the all too modest court practice he had built up in Staffordshire for a paid position further south as a rather inefficient solicitor and a very casually attending treasurer of Greenwich hospital, since this brought in a regular income which was secure. It brought too his son John within sight and sound of the naval presence which so dominated Greenwich village. Very soon this fired the boy's imagination when still in his formative years and at a very impressionable age. So at the tender age of fourteen and when still on the very nursery slopes of life as a pupil at the Reverend Samuel Swinden's academy, along with James, later Major-General, Wolfe, he was entered for the Navy with the rating able seaman and with a donation of twenty pounds from his father to launch him in his career. Jervis was to claim in old age that this was the last donation he ever received and so, at the age of fourteen, he was signed off by his father and left to make his own way in the world. It left its mark and was to cloud his outlook on life for ever more. It bred in him a complete independence of others and an ability to survive on his own resources. This prevented much in the way of friendships for the future but it taught him too the need for extreme frugality which he came to expect also from all who were placed under his command and until he married his cousin, when forty-seven years of age, he turned his back on life outside the service. Indeed all the leave to which he was entitled and all the ordinary pleasures of life were subordinated to naval duty so that he could devote all his waking hours and the whole of his energy to his chosen profession. In so doing he became a complete master of it and a supreme professional. Advancement and promotion followed inexorably in its wake and without interruption through the whole of his career. He was remembered as a lieutenant during the Seven Years War, upon whom Wolfe relied to return to Kathleen Lowther a miniature of her which hung around his neck, since he had a premonition of death. As it turned out, in this Jervis failed for it fell into the hands of Mrs Wolfe. After a brief spell in parliament as the Whig member for Launceston and then Yarmouth, he had arrived at the rank of rear-admiral in 1787 and then vice-admiral in 1793 with command of an expedition to the West Indies.

Therefore, before Jervis ever arrived to take up the Mediterranean command with the rank of full admiral, he was a flag officer of considerable stature, much feared and much respected. Yet his command of the fleet, because of his method of it, was to generate much discontent amongst the officers on the station in the years which followed, not least Sir William Parker and Sir John Orde, but including also Cuthbert Collingwood. But not so Nelson for, from the moment when he had sailed into St Fiorenza in the *Agamemnon* and joined his command on 19 January 1796, the two had taken to each other immediately. So much so that Jervis very soon offered Nelson not only the choice of another ship, but also the rank of commodore. Not surprisingly Nelson had immediately warmed to the man. And by making sure the following year that Nelson was appointed to the command of the Mediterranean Squadron which was to hunt down Napoleon and lead to the Battle of the Nile, Jervis made a further contribution of paramount significance to naval history, for in so doing he unleashed the brilliance of Horatio Nelson as a naval commander for the everlasting benefit of the British nation.

Although both were determined, energetic and egocentric men, qualities which so often mark out those who are destined to advance in life, beyond that and their undoubted qualities of courage, integrity, patriotism and duty, they really had little in common, which makes the mutual attraction even more difficult to understand. For whereas the diminutive and supposedly delicate Nelson was a vain, romantic and slightly effeminate and theatrical extrovert, desperate for fame and glory who sought flattery and attention almost to the point of undignified vulgarity, Jervis was a cold, austere, reserved, secretive, monosyllabic and dogmatic autocrat. Of medium height, thickset and strong with head sunk into his shoulders and eyes sitting low in their sockets, he resembled nothing so much as an ageing bassett hound. Often difficult, hot-tempered and, at times, gratuitously offensive, he hated any show of any sort. In contrast, such was Nelson's flamboyance that it probably cost him his life at Trafalgar where he was determined to parade on the deck of *Victory* medalled up like a Christmas tree, thus presenting an easy and identifiable target for a sniper nestling in the tops. Nelson was an inspirational and magical commander, with a charm, magnetism, humanity, warmth, tender-heartedness and gift for friendship, coupled with a genuine concern for the welfare of others which brought out the very best in those hard-bitten men placed under his command. By his own example, he always won the respect and indeed love and adoration of those officers and men who served under him, many of whom would, if necessary, have followed him to the ends of the earth and have laid down their lives for him. Jervis, on the other hand, never obtained more than a grudging and mechanical obedience to his commands, and that only wrung from his subordinates by the imposition of an iron discipline which was at times both harsh and unnecessary.

It is not difficult to credit the rumour which circulated after Trafalgar that his crew of sailors not only insisted that it should be they who brought home the body of Nelson on the battered *Victory*, but also that, so much did they worship him, they drank the brandy which had preserved his body as far as Gibraltar, almost as an act of communion.

But perhaps the greatest contrast lay in their respective intellectual resources for whereas the highly strung Nelson had a markedly restless, inspirational and innovative mind which made him a ball of nervous energy and something of a genius as a tactical commander who was always on the attack in his campaigns of war, Jervis was utterly reliable as a conventional, predictable, unimaginative, cautious, calculating and very hardworking officer, but with a somewhat pedestrian intellect.

Yet, although in many ways complete opposites, they undoubtedly took to each other in 1796. Perhaps it was simply a mutual respect, for Nelson recognized in Jervis the dedicated professional like himself. He saw too an officer, like Hood, who had a reputation for success in fleet command with which he wanted to be associated, whilst Jervis saw in Nelson a sea captain of daring and inspiration who could be relied upon to take on the enemy whenever the opportunity arose, thus serving at one and the same time Jervis on the one hand and the British nation on the other. But whatever the reason it was as well that it was so, for both were much needed by their country at that dangerous time.

Sadly much of Jervis's distinguished career at sea was later to be tarnished by a disastrous term of office as First Lord of the Admiralty when he pursued such economy in naval affairs that it seriously damaged the fighting strength of the British Navy at a very critical time in the run up to Trafalgar. And long before then he had fallen out with pretty well every officer in the fleet, including Nelson. But Collingwood was to retain his support, and it is of note that Jervis made a point of finding his way down to St Paul's to be at the funeral of Collingwood where he had found it inconvenient to attend that of Nelson.

At all events it had been two years since the British had tasted the fruits of any victory and the government were now desperate for a battle won to revive flagging spirits at home. And this Jervis and Nelson, with the help of an appreciable contribution from his friend Cuthbert Collingwood, were to provide on St Valentine's Day 1797.

Jervis received intelligence that the Spanish Fleet had assembled and were at anchor in the port of Cartagena. And so, sensing that his opportunity may now have arrived, he lost no time in sailing for the Tagus, a friendly haven, in the hope of bringing the enemy fleet to battle. In this location he was well placed to observe and, if possible, intercept any movement of the Spanish Fleet which was gingerly hugging its way up the coast in an attempt, unbeknown to Jervis, to give safe conduct to a merchant convoy carrying a valuable cargo of mercury as far as Cadiz and then to run for Brest to reinforce the fleet there assembled and raise the blockade for an attempt on England. A serious threat was therefore in the offing.

Sir John's force was by now somewhat depleted since the ravages of the winter gales had taken their toll. Some ships had been destroyed and others had been damaged, leaving him with but eleven ships of the line. The plan was for a junction there with a squadron of five sail of the line and one frigate which had been detached by Lord Bridport from the fleet watching Brest and placed under the command of Rear-Admiral Sir William Parker. But it still meant that he would be outnumbered almost two to one by the Spaniards, should they choose to emerge, the more so when he then lost the services of another ship of the line, thus reducing the totality of his force to a bare fifteen ships of the line as against the Spanish twenty-seven. These were sailing under the command of Admiral, Teniente General, Josef de Cordoba y Ramos, in his mighty flagship, the 132-gun *Santissima Trinidad*, the only four-decker afloat.

It was on 13 February that the Spanish Fleet was spotted at sea standing fifty miles off the imposing and sheer mass of rock known as Cape St Vincent. It was drifting hopelessly thanks to a wind which had blown it out into the Atlantic as it struggled for the shelter of Cadiz and the prospect of watering and provisioning. Like a cat stalking its prey Jervis now waited his moment to pounce.

Although outnumbered by a fleet containing some of the largest ships in the world, many of them newly commissioned and well constructed and manned by Spaniards of undoubted courage, Jervis would not hesitate to bring them to battle the moment the opportunity arose for he knew full well that his well-ordered fleet of ships-of-the-line, crewed as they were by highly trained and experienced officers and men, many of whom had already known warfare at sea, were more than a match for the untried Spaniards who had been cooped up in harbour during the weeks and months of the blockade, unable to acquire any sort of operational seagoing experience. And, unlike the French, these were not men driven on by the revolutionary spirit. For the most part they were sons of noblemen, soldiers, tradesmen and fishermen who had been conscripted to serve, and then only for the duration of hostilities.

Although Jervis knew he would be outgunned, for these vast oak structures were but floating wooden platforms for arsenals of guns alongside which many of the crews lived, slept and, in many cases, died, he knew too that the ships under his command had the enormous advantage of much greater manoeuvrability. They were lighter and they were crewed by professionals and, ever since the disastrous loss of the *Royal George* at Spithead in 1782 which had gone to the bottom taking Rear Admiral Kempenfelt with her trapped in his cabin, they were now copper-bottomed. It was the presence of honeycomb decay in the bottom timbers of that ship caused by the dreadful teredo worm which had persuaded the Admiralty to require that thenceforth the hulls of all ships should be bottomed with copper sheathing which would not only resist the teredo worm, but also the accumulation of weeds and barnacles, thus improving movement and speed.

He knew also that he had some very accomplished gunners in his squadron who had made themselves masters of the art, and in Cuthbert Collingwood he had perhaps the hardest hitter in the fleet. Indeed such had been Collingwood's gunnery training of his ship, the *Excellent*, that it was in this battle able to fire one broadside every ninety seconds to every one fired by the enemy in five minutes. In later tribute to his firepower, the gunnery school was to be given the name HMS *Excellent*.

The inexperience and poor seamanship of the Spaniards very soon became apparent as Cordova struggled ineffectively in difficult weather conditions to bring the loose columns of his fleet, scattered as they were into three separate columns for escort duties, back into linear formation ready for battle on sight of the British.

Watching the Spaniards in disarray Jervis saw that his moment had come and so at first light on the morning following, the morning of St Valentine's Day, the order was given for decks to be cleared for action, for magazines and gun ports to be opened and for cannon to be run out ready for fire.

If J.S. Tucker was correct and factual in the oft-repeated account he gave of this moment in his *Memoir of St Vincent* published in 1844, his cautious and diffident captain of the fleet known as the First Captain, Robert Calder, receiving signals reporting the disposition of the Spanish ships, relayed this intelligence to Jervis as it came in, with:

'There are eight sail of the line, Sir John.'

'Very well, Sir.'

'There are twenty sail of the line, Sir John.'

'Very well, Sir'

'There are twenty-five sail of the line, Sir John.'

'Very well, Sir.'

'There are twenty-seven sail of the line, Sir John. Near twice our own number.'

'Enough Sir. The die is cast and if there are fifty sail I will go through them!'

In telling this story it has to be remembered that Tucker's father, Benjamin, was a keen supporter of Jervis and had been so for many years as his personal secretary. His regard for Jervis almost amounted to idolatry. At the same time he had certainly been present on Sir John's flagship that day and had therefore been in a position to overhear the exchange, if it took place. But, whether it has truth or not, there can be no doubt that Jervis was indeed a man of great determination and immense courage.

The order to fall into line and prepare to intercept the enemy fleet was signalled shortly after 11 a.m., with Collingwood in the *Excellent* bringing up the rear of thirteen. But it was not until 11.12 a.m. that Jervis hoisted the signal to engage and, at 11.26 a.m., he ran up the signal to pass through the enemy line which was now in two separate formations composed of eighteen ships in the rear and nine in the van.[4]

It was the conventional naval wisdom of the day, of which Jervis was an exponent, that ships of the line should stay in line when in battle so that each component ship, in a war of attrition, could engage the vessel which lay alongside her firing broadsides with no possibility of another allied vessel being caught in friendly crossfire. Indeed the *Fighting Instructions* of the time decreed that ships should always keep in the sacred line of battle unless a signal was received which ordered otherwise. However it came to be accepted in the years following the Battle of St Vincent that use of the most heavily gunned ships to break the enemy line, usually at the rear, could be more effective, for it then gave the attacker a numerical advantage when concentrating on the destruction of the ships so detached before the real engagement began, and then again, if successful, when turning to the main fleet. This tactic of divide and conquer was to serve Nelson well and to such devastating effect at the Battles of the Nile and Trafalgar when used deliberately, and it was a manoeuvre which could compensate for a disadvantage in

Battle of Cape St Vincent

N

Spanish Weather Division

Salvador del Mundo

San Nicolas

San Josef

Santissima Trinidad

Culloden

Prince George

Victory
(Jervis flagship)

British Fleet

Excellent
(Collingwood)

Captain
(Nelson)

Spanish Lee Division

numbers which would otherwise tell against the smaller fleet when formed in line of battle. To divide and then pick off the detached portion could restore the balance, and to a limited extent this is what occurred at the Battle of St Vincent. But it was not the tactic which Jervis had ordained that day.

It was a few minutes before midday when fire broke out on both sides as the armada of British ships passed menacingly through the gap in the Spanish lines in an impeccable single line of battle, thus driving a wedge between the two rapidly closing groups of Spaniards, with Collingwood in the rear. There followed an hour or more of hard pounding. Those not familiar with heavy artillery bombardment will find it difficult to know and appreciate the mighty and deafening roar and terrifying clap of thunder which heavy and persistent gunfire raises as it hits the ear and fills the skies. Still less will they be able to picture the confusion which the smoke and ferocious noise of battle generate amongst combatants caught up in the carnage and destruction.

In a letter to his wife, Collingwood described it thus:

We flew to them as a hawk to his prey, passed through them in the disordered state in which they were, separated them into two distinct parts, and then tacked upon their largest division.

In another letter to Dr Carlyle he said:

...We dashed at them like griffins spouting fire...[5]

Nonetheless, despite the confusion of battle, these well-ordered ships dutifully obeyed the signals which Jervis then raised at eight minutes past twelve for each ship in the column to tack about in succession as it reached the turning point, rather than altogether. This notwithstanding that the time taken for ships in the column to move in a direction away from the enemy to reach the turning point, gave the detached Spanish ships, which had got ahead, time to follow an obvious avenue of escape by tacking north around the rear of the British ships in the hope of engaging the rearmost in battle before hauling to the wind east to rejoin the other detached division. The tactics of Jervis had allowed that other division to get away unmolested with no order to chase. And so, in an attempt to accelerate matters for those ships in a position to engage the escaping Spaniards, at ten minutes to one he hoisted another signal for the leading ship of the rear division to tack first, rather than waiting for those ahead to do so first. However, to this there was no response, perhaps because it had gone unseen.

But Nelson, now a commodore and in command of the *Captain* of 74 guns, with Captain Miller his Flag Captain, sailing two ahead of Collingwood, third from the rear in the line of battle in the flotilla proceeding through the two divisions, read the situation in a flash and quickly came to the rescue. Blatantly disregarding the express, and indeed the standing battle orders which Jervis had so recently issued to stay in formation and tack in succession, and throwing caution to the winds, now suddenly, and not in succession, broke from the line, and wore his ship round by turning the bow fore-end away from the wind so that the stern came into the wind, rather than tacking about which involved turning the bow into and then past the source of the wind; usually a slower manoeuvre. Then, with all press of sail, he swung away back across the bows of *Excellent* towards the leading Spanish ships in the van as they circled round towards the leeward or downwind division as opposed to the windward, or nearer to the source of wind, squadron of ships. There he courageously laid the *Captain* across the path of the leading enemy ships and so cut off their retreat, and his was the only ship to do so. In so doing he confronted all the might of the largest and most heavily gunned galleons afloat, including the *Santissima Trinidad* which packed 132 guns, and the *Mexicana* and *Salvador del Mundo* each of which carried 112 guns, although it has to be remembered that the British van of ships, including the *Culloden*, with all their superior gunnery skills were, by then, hard on his heels. In this way Nelson's action halted Cordoba's escape in its tracks.

It could perhaps be argued that in leaving the line, he was acting within the general intent of Sir John's plan for individual captains to act to some extent on their own initiative, and some maintain that further signals from Jervis, which were undoubtedly logged, had changed and revised the earlier order to tack in succession by ordering that the rear division should tack back towards the Spanish first, an order that had been missed by all. But if that is the correct interpretation to be given to signals which were, to say the least, ambiguous, it is surprising that Nelson should not have mentioned it afterwards in his own defence, and that Jervis did not claim it. The truth must be that it was an act of insubordination at once audacious and daring by which Nelson risked, not only loss of his ship and the wrath and indignation of his commander, but also the loss of his entire career at sea, for the probability is that he had received no signal which could possibly have been taken to authorize his move.

After an hour of skirmishing and murderous fire, and as he watched in wonderment, Jervis did eventually signal others in the rear to move in support. Nelson then laid his heavily damaged ship alongside the *San Nicolas* which had by then drifted into collision with the 112-gun *San Josef*, the flagship of Rear Admiral Winthuysen. He fastened to her as

91

much to keep the *Captain* afloat as for any other reason and the two ships became entangled.

Ammunition stocks on the *Captain* had by this stage been all but expended, and such was the damage to her foretopmast and rigging that the crew had lost all control of the ship. However, and mercifully, Collingwood was on hand in the *Excellent* and it was at this moment that he, in turn, came to the rescue and so enabled what followed. Collingwood had before then tacked out of the line, but in his case in compliance with Sir John's later signal to wear out of line to reinforce the van, and so had been leading the centre. It was Sir John's signal at five minutes past two to Close Action, and then at fifteen minutes past two for the *Excellent* to break the Spanish line from the windward, which brought him to a position from which he could help Nelson. After joining battle with the *Salvador del Mundo* of 112 guns when '...not farther from her than the length of our garden...', he was later to report to his wife, with what Nelson was later to describe as 'masterly fire', and after that ship appeared to have hauled down her colours, Collingwood transferred his attention to the 74-gun *San Ysidro* and engaged her in devastating heavy fire for twenty minutes or more until she too hauled down her colours. The gunnery skills of his crew were now dominant. It was at this point that Collingwood caught sight of the *Captain* and the *San Nicolas* towering over her. At the mercy of several Spanish ships, her predicament was obvious and desperate and so, rather than boarding the *San Ysidro* to take the prize, and without a moment's hesitation, Collingwood hauled his ship within a few feet of the starboard side of the *San Nicolas* and from there poured into her a deadly and withering fire until she was rendered impotent. He later wrote:

> ...we did not touch sides, but you could not put a bodkin between us...My good friend, the Commodore, had been long engaged with these ships, and I happily came to his relief, for he was dreadfully mauled...

The modern golfer would describe the distance as less than a mashie shot away.

Nelson was later to describe this action by Collingwood as:

> ...disdaining the parade of taking possession of beaten enemies, most gallantly pushed up with every sail set, to save his old friend and mess-mate, who was to appearance in a critical state...

Small wonder that Nelson held his friendship of Collingwood so dear. Mission accomplished, Collingwood then turned his attention to the mighty *Santissima Trinidad*, as the *Prince George* moved in to assist further.

Witnessing the carnage which Collingwood's broadsides had caused, Nelson now saw and seized his opportunity. And so, yet again, Collingwood had come to the support of his friend and paved the way for what was to follow, for Nelson now ran his ship against the *San Nicolas* and sailors, armed with cutlasses, accompanied by soldiers with fixed bayonets, then used the ship's bowsprit as a bridge and boarded the *San Nicolas*. Nelson then followed with a second contingent, forcing a quarter gallery window and then entering the Captain's cabin which lay beyond. This act too flouted all convention which was that captains, and certainly flag officers, should remain with their ships, come what may. A skirmish followed after which the Spaniards capitulated and laid down their arms and the ship surrendered.

But now, despite the battering their ship had received from Collingwood and other British ships, sailors on the *San Josef* opened up with a heavy fire and several mariners fell dead or wounded. However, nothing daunted, Nelson was determined to carry on and with, according to a contemporary commentator in 1806, the cry 'Westminster Abbey or Victory', which most have dismissed as apocryphal, he then rapidly led a boarding party up onto the quarterdeck of the *San Josef* which lay entangled alongside. By then her Admiral, Don Xavier Winthuysen, lay wounded and dying in a cabin below, with both of his legs shot away. The moment his Flag Captain caught sight of this cutthroat party of marauders advancing towards him, he rushed over to Nelson, offered up his sword on bended knee and so surrendered without resistance. The officers of his crew then followed suit handing over their swords one by one which were gathered up by William Fearney, one of Nelson's coxswains or bargemen. Collingwood was later to describe this in a letter home to Dr Carlyle, as: '...Fearney making a bundle of them with as much composure as he would tie a bundle of faggots', a description later quoted by Southey in his *Life of Nelson*. It was an episode without precedent or parallel in the long and distinguished history of the British Royal Navy. So much so that it gave rise to a number of opportunist paintings and prints, not least the colourful and famous version quickly put out by Daniel Orme.

In the last hour of the battle the *Excellent*, under the fearless Collingwood, still not done, engaged in a punishing exchange of fire with the towering *Santissima Trinidad*, the largest ship afloat, until that vast ship too had been reduced to impotence with 500 of her crew killed or wounded.

By half past three in the afternoon the *del Mundo* and the *San Ysidro* had also been captured. The bombardment then subsided, calm was

93

restored and by four thirty the battle was won. The British Fleet slowly extricated itself and stood for Lagos whilst the remainder of the crippled Spanish Fleet ran for the shelter and sanctuary of Cadiz but also the opprobrium of the outraged Spanish public, which was followed by courts martial for the Commander-in-Chief and several of his officers.

Nelson wrote his thanks to Collingwood the day after the battle with:

> My dearest friend, a friend in need is a friend indeed was never more truly verified than by your most noble and gallant conduct yesterday in sparing the *Captain* from further loss.

And to the Duke of Clarence Nelson wrote:

> Captain Collingwood, disdaining the parade of taking possession of beaten enemies, most gallantly pushed up with every sail set to save his old friend and messmate, who was, to all appearance, in a critical situation, the *Captain* being actually fired upon by three first-rates and the *San Nicolas*. The *Blenheim* being ahead, and the *Culloden* crippled and astern, the *Excellent* ranged up, and hauling up her mainsail just astern, passed within ten feet of the *San Nicolas*, giving her a most awful and tremendous fire.

Collingwood himself was to write of this later:

> After I had driven the *San Nicolas* on board the *San Josef*, and left them on their fire ceasing to be taken possession of by somebody behind, they fell on board my good friend the Commodore, and as they had not surrendered, he, in his own little active person (for he could almost go through an Alderman's thumb ring), at the head of his ship's company, boarded them, driving the Spaniards from deck to deck at the point of their swords; and they at last both surrendered, and the Commodore, on the deck of the Spanish first-rate *San Josef*, received the swords of the officers of the two ships; while a Johnny, one of the sailors, bundled them up with the same composure he would have made a faggot, and twenty two of their line still within gunshot...I have given St Ysidro a good berth in my cabin – the least I could do for his holiness after he had consigned his charge to me. It is a good picture, as you will see, when he comes to Morpeth.

In his reply to Nelson's letter of thanks, Collingwood wrote:

> ...let me congratulate my dear Commodore on the distinguished part which he ever takes when the honour and interests of his

Country are at stake. It added very much to the satisfaction I felt in thumping the Spaniards, that I released you a little.

The highest rewards are due to you and *Culloden*: you formed the plan of attack, we were only accessories to the Dons' ruin; for, had they got on the other tack, they would have been sooner joined, and the business would have been less complete.

And to Sir Edward Blackett, his wife's uncle, he wrote: '...brave, honest Nelson with his little crew did wonders.'[6] To Dr Carlyle he wrote of Nelson in this action as possessed of,'...judgment supported by a most angelic spirit...'[7]

Fortunately no more than seventy-three British lives had been lost as against 200 or 300 Spanish, so that this had not been as bloody a battle as most. However, although the failure to order a chase had allowed all but four captured Spanish ships to reach the safety of Cadiz harbour intact, albeit they remained there blockaded for many months to come, it had been a modest victory of sorts and it had succeeded in opening up the Mediterranean to the British once more and for the rest of the war That was thanks largely to the initiative of Horatio Nelson who was rewarded with spontaneous and loud hurrahs from the fleet as he made his way over to the *Victory* and his commanding officer to make his report, hatless, battle scarred and dishevelled. Because it had succeeded Jervis forgave him his disobedience immediately and welcomed him on board his flagship with open arms. Had he failed Jervis would probably have court-martialled him. According to Benjamin Tucker, Calder later suggested to him that Nelson's escapade had been an act of insubordination, to which Jervis had replied: 'It certainly was, and if ever you commit such a breach of your orders, I will forgive you also.'[8]

It had indeed been an episode unique and without parallel in the long history of the British Navy.

Jervis had narrowly escaped death himself in the battle when a marine standing next to him was felled by a cannon shot which took off his head and splattered blood and tissue all over the Admiral's body and uniform. Astonishingly Jervis lost nothing of his composure at that terrifying moment but stood his ground seemingly unmoved, calmly asking George, the Northumbrian Captain George Grey, to get him an orange to quench his thirst and clear his mouth, which he then proceeded to suck.[9] In the eyes of the British public, desperate for news of a victory, the threat of invasion had been averted and he was now hailed as the hero. Although he had but a few weeks before then been gazetted a peer for his service in the Mediterranean, he was now granted an annuity of £3,000 by a grateful nation and raised a further step in the peerage to an earldom, taking his title from the scene of the battle. It was to be the highest honour bestowed on any naval officer during the whole of the war.[10]

The flag officers too received their reward. As second in command Vice-Admiral Thompson was made a baronet, despite St Vincent's disappointment with the contribution he made, as was the fourth in command, Rear-Admiral Sir William Parker, who was also given the freedom of the City of London. But Vice-Admiral William Waldegrave, who had fought with great distinction, declined that same honour when it was offered, with the explanation that as the second son of an Earl, the third Earl Waldegrave, he already stood higher than a baronet in the order of precedence. But he was then given command and governorship of the Newfoundland Station, and then, three years on, was raised to the Irish Peerage as the first Baron Radstock of Castletown. He was to die a full Admiral of the Red.

As for Nelson, the true author of the victory, he was promoted to the rank of Rear-Admiral of the Blue, although this had in fact occurred some days before as a matter of seniority. It had been gazetted before the battle had ever begun.[11] But he received too the Knighthood of the Bath he so coveted and, as a flag officer at the time of the engagement, he was entitled also to his share, which was appreciable, of whatever money the Spanish prizes would fetch. But his fragile body had been struck yet again, although not, on this occasion, seriously. A flying splinter had caught him in the midriff and may have caused a rupture, although it was not so diagnosed until after his death.[12]

But his reward did not end there for he very soon became the nation's true hero over and above the Earl St Vincent. In fact Jervis had made no mention of Nelson in his official report. A charitable view might be that this had been done to avoid drawing attention to his act of insubordination, or perhaps, and more probably, because he wished to avoid the trouble Howe had run into when naming some officers for commendation whilst omitting mention of others after the Battle of the Glorious First of June, for he certainly reported later in a private letter to Lord Spencer that: 'Nelson had contributed very much to the fortune of the day as did Captain Collingwood,'[13] which was something of an understatement. At the same time he made mention also of Captains Berry, Hallowell, and Troubridge. But whatever the reason for the omission in his official report, Nelson's contribution to the victory would have gone unnoticed but for his own unquenchable thirst for fame and glory, for he lost no time after the battle was over in planting his own version of events in the minds of those he knew would very quickly give it circulation in the streets of London.

The very morning after the battle had been won Nelson hastened on board the frigate *Lively* hoping there to find his friend Sir Gilbert Elliot who had transferred there for the duration of the battle from the *Minerve* which had carried him from Corsica on his way back to England.

Born at Minto in the county of Roxburghshire, across the border from Northumberland, Elliot had been educated alongside Mirabeau in the Pension Militaire, Fontainebleau, and afterwards at Edinburgh University and Christ Church College, Oxford. He had been called to the Bar at Lincoln's Inn in May 1774 and had then travelled the Northern Circuit, pleading his cases in Northumberland, Durham and the north of England generally, his stamping ground, while at the same time serving as Whig Member of Parliament for the town of Morpeth in Northumberland from 1774 until 1784. That seat he lost but he was then returned for the Northumberland constituency of Berwick upon Tweed and, later, for a constituency in Cornwall. Appointed Commissioner at Toulon in 1793 he had supervised the evacuation to Florence of refugees when the revolutionary forces recaptured that town, and so was well placed for appointment as Viceroy of the island of Corsica when it was taken by the British in 1794. It was then that he and Nelson had became such friends and he had come to admire Nelson greatly. And so when the French retook the island in October 1796 it was Nelson who evacuated him from the island, which made Elliot a lifelong friend and supporter of Horatio Nelson. He was later to be raised to the peerage as Lord Minto before serving as British Minister in Vienna and then as Governor-General of India.

And so, on the morning of 15 February, Nelson judged that Elliot would be a suitable receptacle to receive and then disseminate his own version of events, especially since he must have had a grandstand view of the most dramatic moments of Nelson's exploit, for Jervis had ordered the *Lively* to move in and take possession of the *San Ysidro* after she had surrendered to Collingwood.

But in fact Nelson's first encounter when he stepped on board the *Lively* that morning was not with Gilbert Elliot but with Colonel John Drinkwater, the thirty-five year old son of a Manchester general practitioner, for he too was making his way back to London after the evacuation of Corsica. Drinkwater had been secretary for the military department and Deputy Judge Advocate during the British occupation of Corsica under the Viceroyalty of Gilbert Elliott and he, too, had become a firm friend of Horatio Nelson. But more than this he had achieved some fame as an author, for his *History of the Siege of Gibraltar* during the American War of Independence in which he had himself taken part as an officer in the Manchester Regiment. It was to become something of a popular military classic. He was later to take the name Bethune when his wife inherited her brother's estate in Fife.

From Drinkwater Nelson learned that Elliot had gone but a few minutes before with the Captain of the *Lively*, Lord Garlies, to call on Jervis. And so to John Drinkwater Nelson spoke of his deeds, confident that his account would very quickly achieve the wider circulation he hoped for on Drinkwater's return to London. His confidence was well placed, for Drinkwater later published, anonymously, a pamphlet entitled *A Narrative* of the battle which did not understate Nelson's contribution to the outcome. Many years later it was to be expanded into a book with the proceeds donated to a fund established to finance the erection of the Nelson monument in Trafalgar Square.

Not done, Nelson also in his official dispatch to Captain Sir William Locker, repeated the account of his exploits not unfavourable to himself, ending with the note that:

> There is a saying in the Fleet, too flattering for me to omit telling, viz., Nelson's Patent Bridge for Boarding First Rates, alluding to my passing over an enemy's eighty gun ship. If you approve…you are at liberty to insert the account in the newspapers, inserting the name of the Commodore instead of 'I'.

Accordingly and within a matter of weeks of the battle, Nelson's version of events, unedited, duly appeared in the *Sun* newspaper in London, long before Drinkwater's account could be published.

The government, the Duke of Clarence, his family and his friends were also supplied with his account of the battle under the title *Remarks Relative to Myself* …, which, as he intended it should, then found its way into the other organs of the press. That version of events made mention of the strong involvement of *Captain, Excellent* and *Culloden* but little credit was given to any other ship.

And so, Sir William Parker, as commander of the van sailing in the *Prince George*, raised a public note of dissent when he learned of Nelson's claims on his return to Spithead in July of that year, stating that the *San Josef*, crippled by bombardment from the *Prince George* assisted by the *Culloden* and the *Blenheim,* had already fallen against the *San Nicolas* and had surrendered long before Nelson ever boarded her. Many others were to confirm Parker's version of events as correct, but there was, in truth, room for both of these two apparently contrasting accounts. And, in any event, Nelson was, by then, too firmly established as a hero in the eyes of the British public to be dislodged from that pedestal, and so Parker's protestations fell on deaf ears. And if there was room for a second view, then the role played by Collingwood in the *Excellent* in support of his friend should have had a place in it, for it had been heavy fire from his ship which had been more instrumental in the demise of the *San Nicolas* than that from any other. But it had been Nelson, essentially, who had come to the rescue of not only John Jervis, but also the British nation and both now stood firmly in his debt.

The reward received by Collingwood was a Battle of St Vincent gold medal. Although on the face of it this was seemingly but small recognition for such exposure to danger, the award of a campaign or battle gold medal was in fact the honour most treasured by a sailor or soldier, for self-evidently, unlike the grant of a title or rank, only those who have been engaged in a battle are eligible to wear the coveted medal. It could then be worn with pride as evidence of participation. However, when told by St Vincent that he was to receive the medal, Collingwood, still nursing a sense of injustice over his omission from the medal list three years before, at the Battle of the First of June, announced that he would refuse it for, to accept it, would be to condone the earlier injustice. But Lord Spencer met this difficulty by awarding him medals for both occasions, writing that in any event it had been decided before St Vincent had ever begun that he was to be awarded a medal for the 1794 victory. In the circumstances Collingwood accepted both medals, although it is unlikely that he fully swallowed the explanation which came with it.

Edgar Vincent, in his fascinating *Life of Nelson*, was to write of all this:

> Then, as now, justice in the matter of honours was not to be hoped for. If there had been justice, neither Thompson, the ignorer of critical signals, nor Calder, the hidebound defeatist, would have received anything; Troubridge, Collingwood and Frederick would have been made baronets, or at least knighted; and Nelson, in spite of his wishes, would have been elevated to the peerage with a very substantial pension, as the true begetter of Jervis's earldom.

Although modest of the part he had played, Collingwood did send home to his wife some of the letters he had received from fellow officers after the battle, which had paid tribute to his conduct, amongst them letters from Captain Dacres who had written his 'congratulations upon the immortal honour gained by the *Excellent* yesterday...God bless you, and may we all imitate you'. Admiral, William Waldegrave, wrote endorsing those views and added:

> ...nothing in my opinion could exceed the spirit and true officership which you so happily displayed yesterday. Both the Admiral and Nelson join with me in this opinion...God bless you, my good

friend; and may England long possess such men as yourself – it is saying everything for her glory.

Although Collingwood asked his wife not to pass them on to others, she could not resist showing them to Sir Edward Blackett as she explained in a letter dated 14 March 1797. In a letter to Dr Carlyle, Collingwood begged that his letters home about the action at St Vincent should not be circulated generally, for: 'It has too much the appearance of trumpeting, which I detest.'

In his letter to his wife on 17 February Collingwood had added:

I have got a Spanish doubled-headed shot, fired from the *Santissima Trinidad*, which I intend as a present to your father, to put among his curiosities; it weighs 50 lbs. These are no jokes when they fly about one's head.

This strange object is now in the possession of Sir Hugh Blackett at his home in Northumberland and it takes some lifting.

Further tribute came from another officer, too, for when Sir Robert Calder was introduced to the King after his arrival home with the dispatches and His Majesty spoke to him of the spectacular part Nelson had played in the battle, after agreeing that that was so, Calder added that however great that may have been there had been no one who had distinguished himself more than Cuthbert Collingwood.[14]

And Nelson was to write:

I beg you will thank all our friends for their kind congratulations; and I must be delighted, when from the King to the peasant, all are willing to do me honour. But I will partake of nothing but what shall include Collingwood and Troubridge. We are the only three glorious ships who made great exertions on that glorious day: the others did their duty, some not exactly to my satisfaction...

Certainly the battle had proved the legend of Collingwood's gunnery prowess. The achievement of three broadsides in five minutes was truly remarkable when it is remembered what was involved – running out the gun after the violent recoil of the previous shot, albeit held to some extent by restraining ropes, thrusting a wet sponge into the muzzle with a rammer and rotating it to dampen any heat or sparks from the earlier explosion, inserting the gunpowder brought up by the powder monkeys, ramming home the shot itself which was then compressed with rags to generate pressure and produce velocity, driving a further trail or fuse of gunpowder to the explosive through a vent at the breach end, aiming the gun to the order of the chief gunner and then, finally, the equivalent of lighting the touch paper using a flintlock or taper to spark and so ignite the fuse and detonate the explosion. Each gun on the side of the ship exposed to the enemy could then only fire in succession rather than in unison, such was the violence of the recoil. It all, therefore, called for tight discipline and strong coordination.

In the public's concentration on the remarkable role played by Nelson at St Vincent, Collingwood's appreciable contribution, and that made by Parker and the other captains, had largely gone unnoticed. Collingwood was truly in the shadow of his friend Nelson. But his fellow officers, and not least Nelson himself, obviously valued his support greatly and it further consolidated their lifelong friendship and the very high regard in which they held each other.

Chapter 8

Discord in the Mediterranean
1798-1799

In a letter to the Duke of Clarence dated 26 May 1797, Nelson had made mention of his friend, writing: 'The Good and Brave Collingwood has at last received a 1 June Medal. I believe no man in that fleet deserved it better.'

But Nelson and Collingwood saw nothing of each other over the winter of 1797-8 while Nelson languished at home, nursing the stump of his right arm which had been amputated. He had been sent to Tenerife in the Canary islands in July 1797 by a reluctant St Vincent, in command of 900 or more men. Their mission had been the capture of a Spanish treasure ship which lay at Santa Cruz. During the attempt his right arm had been injured beyond repair by a shot from a gun fired as he jumped out of his boat, with the intention of scrambling onto the quay, and not, as he was later to suggest himself, while advancing towards the enemy. The attack had failed with the sacrifice of many lives but, thanks it was said, to the prompt attention of his stepson Josiah in applying a tourniquet, Nelson had survived. Collingwood had reproached himself for actively encouraging Nelson to volunteer for that ill-fated expedition for, when it had been reported that a convoy of ships carrying Spanish gold had sought the safety of Santa Cruz rather than Cadiz off which stood the British Fleet, this had led Collingwood to write to Nelson in a letter dated 13 April 1797:

When I heard the Spanish American Convoy was arrived at Teneriffe [sic] I thought it a probable thing that the Admiral would make a detachment to that quarter – to try how far they were vulnerable there – and if he did who could he send but one whose name is poison to a Spaniard?[1]

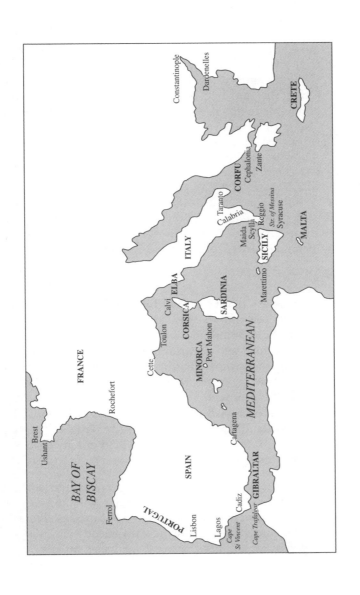

But in truth it is probable that no encouragement was needed to persuade Nelson to take part in that pointless episode. To this day the Spanish commemorate this victory over Nelson, yet at the bicentenary celebrations held in Tenerife in 1997, the Royal Navy generously presented the governor with a Stilton cheese as a gesture of goodwill, repeating a similar gift which had been made by Nelson at the time to his opponent, General Gutierrez, who had invited the British officers to dine with him after the raid had been repulsed; an invitation which Nelson had been unable to accept while his wound was being dressed.

In any event Nelson had recovered enough to sit for Lemuel Abbott, albeit, as the portrait itself reveals, he was by then aged by disability. By 19 December he was able to join a royal procession to St Paul's Cathedral for a *Te Deum* and service of thanksgiving for victories at sea, mainly those of St Vincent and Camperdown, recently won, and then, on 29 March 1798, wound healed and health restored, the crippled, disabled and now left-handed Nelson rejoined his new ship, the *Vanguard*, now in the rank of Rear Admiral of the Blue. Collingwood lost no time in penning a letter to him dated 13 April.

My dear friend,

I hope you are not angry that I have not been on board the *Captain* – but consider how little you are with us; only just long enough to communicate with the Admiral and away again; and generally our movements are so sudden and uncertain that I have got a habit of staying on board, perhaps more than is required of me. But I am satisfied that you know my heart, that there are none in the fleet, few in the world that I meet with more pleasure than yourself…Mrs Moutray is in Ireland on a visit to O'Burne, who is a bishop – he was the Duke of Portland's private secretary. My darlings (heaven bless them) are all well, and very glad to hear I have got my head on. Sarah says you are a most excellent creature…

They met again soon afterwards when Nelson delivered letters which he had brought out from England from Collingwood's wife and from his father-in-law, and the two were able to talk over old times. Collingwood afterwards wrote of this meeting: 'I never saw my friend Nelson look so well, he is really grown fat and not the worse for losing an arm.'

Sadly in the early summer of that year, 1798, they were separated again when Nelson was appointed to command a newly formed squadron of ships to hunt down Napoleon in the Mediterranean, which culminated in the Battle of the Nile.

Collingwood was still serving with Nelson in the Mediterranean Fleet under the command of St Vincent throughout this period, and yet, although still on the station and serving there with distinction, he was not chosen to accompany Nelson. Without doubt he was bitterly disappointed at being left behind and felt aggrieved at this separation from his friend when such an obvious opportunity for action and glory had presented itself. And he held St Vincent responsible, although in truth the *Excellent* was in need now of overhaul back in England and would not have been able to respond to the demands of such an expedition.

In fact Collingwood, as a trusted and loyal servant of his commanding officer, was on fleet and blockade duties of some importance in the Mediterranean throughout this time, albeit extremely monotonous and very tedious work. Indeed for a time St Vincent granted him the rank of commodore, although he was to write home:

> My wits are ever at work to keep my people employed, both for health's sake, and to save them from mischief. We have lately been making musical instruments, and have now a very good band. Every moonlight night the sailors dance; and there seems as much mirth and festivity as if we were in Wapping itself. One night the rats destroyed the bagpipes we had made, by eating up the bellows; but they suffer for it, for in revenge we have made traps of all constructions, and have declared a war of extermination against them.

It was essential to invent distractions to occupy young minds in moments of idleness for Collingwood was all too mindful of the recent 1797 mutinies at Spithead and at the Nore.

Indeed such was his success in maintaining a tight discipline and in setting his men to specified tasks that St Vincent would make a point of placing any potentially mutinous elements under his command.

'Send them to Collingwood, he will bring them to order' he would say. Then, later, he wrote of one Collingwood's ships: 'They have always preserved the order of a regulated family, rather than of men kept in subjection by discipline; their duty seemed to be what most interested them; they have done it faithfully and well...'.

This was praise indeed from one who himself preferred the use of harsh punishments, imposed without mercy, to win obedience, although it has to be conceded that whilst Collingwood was without doubt a humane commander by the standards of the day, and certainly so when compared with St Vincent, he did to some extent model himself on St Vincent for he, too, believed in maintaining a tight discipline and did not spare the lash if and when the occasion demanded.

But at bottom this was a low moment in Collingwood's seagoing career and he was not alone in his unhappiness for he was but one of many officers serving with St Vincent in the Mediterranean Fleet that summer who were much disgruntled and discontented, and the result was much dissension.

In a letter home dated 22 July, which was private and therefore not an act of insubordination, Collingwood confided in his father-in-law:

> This appointment of Nelson for a service where so much honour was to be acquired, has given great offence to the senior Admiral of the Fleet, Sir William Parker, who is a very excellent officer, and as gallant a man as any in the navy, and Sir John Orde, who on all occasions of service has acquitted himself with great honour, both are feeling much hurt at a junior officer of the same fleet having so marked a preference over them, and have written to Lord Spencer, complaining of the neglect of them. The fleet is, in consequence, in a most unpleasant state; and now all that intercourse of friendship, which was the only thing like comfort which was left to us, is forbidden; for the Admirals and Captains are desired not to entertain, even at dinner, any who do not belong to their ships. They all complain that they are appointed to many unworthy services, and I have my share with the rest. But I place myself beyond the reach of such matters; for I do them with all the exactness in my power, as if they were things of the utmost importance; Though I do conceal what I think of them. In short, I do what everybody else does – wish myself at home very much.[2]

In fairness, Collingwood had perhaps, in that criticism, overlooked the fact that any dinner engagement attended by officers from different ships involved also seamen on escort duties waiting alongside the host ship which provided every opportunity for mutinous discussion with opposite numbers in those difficult and inflammatory times. But his complaint of unhappiness amongst the officers in the fleet, including himself and, in particular, the two flag officers to whom he referred was, sadly, no more than the harsh truth.

In the spring of 1798 intelligence reports had told the British government that Lisbon could soon be lost to the British as a key friendly haven, but also that the French had massed an expeditionary force at Toulon and at other ports in the Mediterranean ready for embarkation. Its destination was unknown but it was feared that they were headed for these shores and that England could be the target, now that Bonaparte had become all but master of continental Europe. Accordingly, alarm bells had begun to ring in the corridors of Whitehall. Clearly what was needed now was a flying column of ships to re-enter the Mediterranean, hunt down the French armada and destroy it, or, at the very least, keep it contained and at bay. Command of such a squadron would, therefore, and very obviously, carry with it immense responsibility and the possibility of great prestige, and it called for an officer of outstanding determination and skill.

Although promotion in the service for post captains and above was largely a matter of seniority and many officers of indifferent ability, therefore, simply rose on the conveyor belt of advancement to swell the already extensive list of flag officers, fleet commands and appointments of significance, it still remained in the gift and discretion of the Admiralty which attempted to choose on merit and suitability.

Even so there were, at the time, many contenders for this post, not least those actually serving in the Mediterranean Fleet who were senior in rank, including those named by Collingwood, namely Sir William Parker Bt., a Rear-Admiral of the Red and second in command to St Vincent, Sir John Orde Bt, a Rear-Admiral of the White and third in command, and also, of course, Sir Horatio Nelson, a Rear-Admiral of the Blue. All three were officers of distinction with a lifetime of naval service behind them. The disparity in their ages was quite marked for whereas Parker was by then fifty-five years of age, Orde was forty-seven and Nelson forty-one.

Parker was distantly related to Collingwood by marriage having married Jane, the daughter of Edward Collingwood, and therefore Collingwood's cousin. Born in Kent in or about the year 1743 he had been a commodore in command of the Leeward Islands Station from 1787 until 1790, succeeding Nelson there and then, at the onset of the Battle of the Glorious First of June in 1794, commanding the *Audacious* of 74 guns, he had almost single-handedly put the French *Revolutionnaire* of 120 guns out of the war. In July of that year he was rewarded with promotion to the rank of rear-admiral and awarded the coveted gold medal which had been denied Collingwood. The following February he was given command of the Jamaica station, flying his flag in the *Raisonnable*, and there he remained until illness interrupted that service. But, health restored, he had joined Jervis in the *Prince George* two days before the Battle of St Vincent in 1797 where, with five sail of the line under his command, he had made a telling contribution to the victory. Hence his fury at Nelson's one-sided account of the part he himself had played which had not allowed that others may have done as much. After the battle, as a newly created baronet, he had stayed on as third in command of the fleet until the recall of the unfortunate Vice-Admiral Thompson which had raised him to second in command. He therefore had a strong claim to be chosen to command the squadron to hunt down Napoleon. After all, his quarrel had not been with the Earl St Vincent, but rather with Nelson, although, two years on, in the Court of Common Pleas, he was to bring an action against St Vincent in which he claimed for himself, and for the junior admirals under St Vincent, their share of the admirals' third of freight money which St Vincent had received from Captain Masefield of the frigate *Andromeda*, and then kept for himself. The claim was founded on common usage in the Navy, which St Vincent steadfastly refused to recognize but, in the result, a verdict was given for Parker by the judge and jury empanelled to try the case.[3]

Sir John Orde was a very different man. A much fuller account of his career is to be found in the author's *Nelson's Mediterranean Command* (1998). Born at Nunnykirk near Morpeth three days before Christmas 1751, he was the third son of a Northumberland landowner. Although he was not, as Collingwood was, the offspring of a large family which had fallen on hard times or, like Nelson, the fourth of eight surviving children of an impoverished clergyman or, as was the case with St Vincent, the son of an unsuccessful barrister struggling to make ends meet, at the same time he had no blood relative in the service to shepherd and protect him in his teenage years below deck, as Collingwood had in his uncle Braithwaite or as Nelson had in his seagoing post captain uncle who was later to become the influential Comptroller of the Navy.[4]

He was descended from the Ordes of Tweedmouth who, according to the historian Welford:

> ...were established at Orde on the southern bank of the Tweed as early as the twelfth century. The whole township of that name, including East, Middle and West Orde with Murton and Unthank constitutes their patrimonial estate...They owned property in almost every hamlet of that wide-spreading district which...was known as Norhamshire and islandshire...Descended from this old and honourable family came Admiral Sir John Orde.

Raine was to write that:

> The Ords of Fenham have, I believe, no connection with this ancient stock or name; an aged lady of the true family designated them, with great indignation, as the usurpers of the name and arms.

But then those without an 'e' would no doubt have responded in like manner.

Although therefore the *News Chronicle* was right when it reported that: '...the family Orde appears to be of great antiquity', the truth in fact is that few, if any of them, had made any mark at all outside the

108

boundaries of Northumberland county, until the arrival of John Orde and his brother Thomas.

It was at Nunnykirk, nine miles west of Morpeth and some twenty miles from the Scottish border at its nearest point, that Orde was born; a house and estate which had been acquired by his family but a few years before through marriage. And so, thirty-nine years later, when granted a baronetcy, it was Sir John of Morpeth that was chosen.

Born the third son of John Orde, the estate and house were certainly large enough to accommodate and support Orde and both of his two older brothers who lived there, had they so wished. .Built in the early 1700s on the site of an old Cistercian chapel and tower, it is set in parkland in the wooded and sparsely populated valley of the River Font which was a convenient stopping place for the Cistercians on the road from Newminster Abbey to the Abbey of Hexham in the rich, gentle, lush and beautiful rolling pastures of the upper and north Tyne valleys some thirty miles distant to the west. At a later time, in the year 1829, it was to be set in the larger Greek classical style, fronted with Ionic columns and a pillared porch, by the celebrated Georgian architect, John Dobson, but that was five years after Sir John Orde had died. The author's own smaller Dobson-built Georgian house in the valley of the North Tyne north of Hexham, noted as 1830 and 1847 by Pevsner, bears witness to the beauty and soundness of Dobson's work.

It is difficult to know why Orde should have chosen a career at sea, although the order of his birth may have been a contributory factor given that he was the third of three sons with no hope of inheriting the estate to which William, the eldest son who had been born to his father's first wife and therefore Orde's half-brother, was certain to succeed. But to sea he went in 1766 at the tender age of fourteen years, thus separating himself from his home and from his family, although the muster roll of his ship, the *Jersey*, records, wrongly, that he was then sixteen. And without any sort of influence upon which he could draw, he was required to endure exactly the same hardships and privation below deck as any other midshipman in the service, thrown together as he was with several hundred others. The contrast between that apprenticeship and the education of his talented older brother Thomas Orde, the future first Lord Bolton, could not have been more marked, for in those same years that John Orde was subjected to the tough disciplines of duty and practical seamanship in the hard school of life on board ship in a floating wooden world all of its own, so his brother Thomas moved easily from Eton College to the cloistered magnificence of King's College, Cambridge, followed by a fellowship, a call to the Bar at Lincoln's Inn and the promise of a glittering and more comfortable career in public life.

But Orde survived and, after service in the Mediterranean and on the Newfoundland and Jamaica stations, he was promoted lieutenant by the celebrated Sir George (later Lord) Rodney in 1774. After taking well-earned leave he was recalled to the colours two years later and then, like Collingwood, sailed into the American War of Independence and a baptism of fire. He was to emerge six years on a post captain, a married man and a man blooded in battle with a considerable experience of warfare at sea.

The assistance which he had given the Earl of Dunmore, Governor of the colony of New York, in the evacuation from Norfolk to Gwynn Island in the Chesapeake, before his camp there was decimated with smallpox, had been considerable.[5] But it was a combined offensive, with New York the target, which had brought him promotion to first lieutenant. A flotilla of ships, including the *Roebuck*, had been deployed in a supporting role and had advanced on New York by way of the Hudson River. Not surprisingly they had been met with a heavy bombardment from batteries of artillery strategically placed on shore. In running the gauntlet of this sustained barrage of fire, nine men and one officer lost their lives on the *Roebuck*, that officer being the first lieutenant. Orde had then been promoted to take his place before the vessel reached New York. And then, only a few months later, he had been appointed by Lord Howe to the post of first lieutenant of his flagship, the *Eagle*, and then master of the sloop *Zebra* with the rank of commander, all in the year 1777 when he was twenty-six years of age.

In that same year he had assisted in the reduction of Philadelphia and the forts of Delaware and, for his part in that campaign, he had been advanced to the rank of post captain with command of the captured American frigate, the *Virginia*, which gave him the prospect of a flag in the fullness of time.

Ralfe's *Naval Biography* written a few years later was to report of his service at that time:

> The ardour, activity and undaunted firmness manifested by Captain Orde when the French Fleet appeared off the Bar of New York, were not exceeded by that of any individual in the fleet, great as were the exertions made on that occasion.

The following summer Orde and the *Virginia* distinguished themselves in pursuit of the American Fleet in the Bay of Penobscot which lies between Boston and the St Lawrence Gateway in the north.

Then, in the spring of 1780, Orde was to win the commendation of Vice-Admiral Arbuthnot, who had succeeded Howe and Collier on the American Station. This was for his part in the capture of Charleston in South Carolina which was seen by many as the largest of many defeats suffered by the American Army during the eight years of conflict. Up river lay the heavily fortified Fort Moultrie on Sullivan's Island, an obstacle which had thwarted a British attempt on Charleston four years earlier. However, nothing daunted, Arbuthnot had decided to force a passage through the gut, which was a distinctly bold and dangerous undertaking. Taking his flagship, the *Roebuck*, together with the *Virginia* commanded by Orde and six other ships, he had run the gauntlet of a punishing heavy artillery bombardment from the batteries on shore until they had emerged battered and bruised but more or less intact on the Charleston side of Sullivan's Island. It had been an act of remarkable daring and courage.[6] And then he took steps to occupy Mount Pleasant on the far side of the estuary by sending in a force of seamen at daybreak under the command of Captains Orde, Hudson and Gambier. There was little resistance for, in the face of the advancing British sailors, the opposition ran for the safety of Charleston abandoning their weaponry as they went. From there Arbuthnot then directed an attack on Fort Moultrie by both land and sea and the fort quickly capitulated. Lincoln then finally surrendered the town on 12 May. It had been a substantial victory and in the admiral's dispatch, Orde, amongst others, was singled out for mention as one who had distinguished himself in the naval operation.

Orde was to take three more warships from the Americans whilst on that station[7] before sailing out of the war in 1781, and indeed a wife, for he had by then bound himself in marriage to Margaret Emma, daughter and heiress of Richard Stevens of St. Helena, Charleston.

After further service in the North Sea, Orde, then commanding the *Roebuck*, had been appointed to join a squadron lying off Brest commanded by John Swinfen Jervis, then a captain commanding the *Foudroyant*, and so it was that he had met for the first time the man who was later to become his arch enemy. Their meeting was cordial enough but it was destined to be of short duration for the end of the war in America in that same year, 1783, caused a further twist to his career.

After the intervention of the French Fleet in the Chesapeake in 1781 which had forced Admiral Graves to withdraw, Cornwallis had capitulated at Yorktown. The war was now over, for the British public had no appetite to pursue it further. The intervention of the French Navy had been decisive. It had been a war in which the British had won almost every battle yet had lost the war. But in the peace treaty negotiated by Lord Shelbourne in the following year, the terms agreed had been favourable enough to the British, thanks in part to a victory won by Admiral Lord Rodney at the Battle of the Saintes a few weeks before. Although she was required to cede some of the territories in the West Indies which had been acquired in the Seven Years war, and Senegal and

Tobago and St Lucia were handed over to France, the rest of the islands were recovered by Great Britain, including the island of Dominica, for which a governor was then required.

After his consistent record of distinguished service over the previous eight years, that post was offered to John Orde and he had accepted it on the clear understanding that should hostilities involving the British Navy ever be resumed he would be allowed to return to active service. There followed ten years of peace.

For almost the whole of that period he presided over a thoroughly quarrelsome and truculent people of differing and mixed ancestry and conflicting objectives, who had been thrown together in an impossibly humid climate on an island barely fifteen miles wide and thirty miles long from its northern tip to its southern extremity. The oldest inhabitants, the fierce, war-like, hard-drinking Caribs, were as violent in those times as the hostile terrain itself; far removed from the gentle, peace-loving Carib people who still occupy part of the island to this day. Intrigued by their reputation for feeding on the flesh of man, but never of woman or child, Christopher Columbus had gone in search of the Caribs when he discovered the island in 1493. Landing on a Sunday (Domingo in Latin) he had named the island Dominica, pronounced 'Domineeca', not to be confused with the Dominican Republic. But he very soon beat a hasty retreat, never to return, preferring to leave the island to the domination of the Caribs with their dislike of foreigners and preference for the flesh of Frenchmen, which, according to the priest, de Rochefort, writing in 1658, they found more appetizing than that of Spaniards whom they found less digestible even when spliced with vegetables.[8]

Almost 200 years later, white settlers, mainly the French, had arrived with but one object in mind, the exploitation of the island's reserves of coffee, and later to grow sugar. In their wake came African black labour imported by the settlers and with them came political unrest, the more so as the size of the black population began to exceed by far that of the rest of the island put together, and those unfortunate people were condemned in those harsh and cruel days to live in cramped and often primitive conditions which they openly and understandably resented. Governor Orde's primary objectives in taking up office were to develop the harbour in Prince Rupert's Bay, restore law and order amongst the population and, above all, retain possession of the island for the British. Without doubt he tackled these objectives with a military efficiency which initially won him the praise of the settlers, the Assembly and the Council alike, and throughout he had the support of the home government and King George III who was, at the end of it, to grant him a baronetcy.[9]

And it was there, in Dominica, that he had first come to know Horatio Nelson when Nelson had visited the island in 1784[10] and then again when he had returned to accompany Prince William on his visit to the island in December 1786.[11] It was while still Governor of Dominica that his young wife had died in 1790 nine months after giving birth to a daughter who had died soon after birth.

But once war with France had been declared in 1793, the need had been for every trained and experienced officer to return to the colours which, in fact, had always been Sir John Orde's wish and intention. Happily, in December of that same year, he had married Jane, daughter of John Frere of Roydon in Norfolk who was to bear him five children, only two of whom were to survive, a daughter who never married, and a son, John Powlett Orde.

And so, once again a married man, he had sent in his application for a naval command. But, sadly it was his misfortune that he should have crossed the incoming First Lord of the Admiralty, the second Earl Spencer, and this was to tell against him in the years to come, and especially so when the Mediterranean command came up for consideration in 1798. The outgoing First Lord, the ineffective Lord Chatham, younger brother of William Pitt, had responded to Orde's application by giving him command of the 74-gun *Venerable*.[12] But then Lord Spencer, on taking up office, promptly withdrew that appointment with the explanation that it had been earmarked for Lord Duncan.[13] He then appointed Sir John to command the 98-gun *Prince George* instead. It is difficult to know why Sir John should then have raised a protest at this change of plan, but that is what he did and it was to cost him dear, for Spencer was slow to offer him much else in the future which was to please him. Spencer was to remain in that office for five or six years more, which were five or six of the most critical years of the nation's history.

Son of the first Earl Spencer, George Spencer was then thirty-six years of age and married to Lavinia, the celebrated daughter of the first Lord Lucan who was probably the most handsome lady in London society and certainly a very influential, astute and formidable one. A man of great literary interests, Spencer was to accumulate a large number of very rare books, building on a library at Althorp which had been started by his great-grandfather, the Earl of Sunderland, and organizing a collection which was later, in 1892, bought by a Mrs Rylands as the basis for what was to become the John Rylands library in Manchester.

He was an intelligent, scholarly, mild-mannered, amiable and just man who had little knowledge of ships or the sea. It was later said of Lord Goschen when he succeeded to that same office that 'Goschen has no notion of the motion of the ocean'. The same could be said of the second Lord Spencer. But for all that he was, on the whole, a successful First Lord with achievements which were never fully recognized. Perhaps this was because of an arrogance which some put down to his aristocratic birth and a constant reluctance to consult the opinion of others, coupled with an obstinacy which made him many enemies. But as a minister he was a good administrator who was both firm and fair and this extended too to his own affairs for he was ever concerned for the wellbeing of the tenants on his Althorp estate in Northamptonshire. Spencer left office in 1801 with the departure of Pitt's government and, apart from a brief spell as Home Secretary in 1806, he devoted the remainder of his life to intellectual pursuits.

As for Sir John Orde, he was, by all contemporary accounts, a man of integrity with a passion for fairness and justice quite apart from his reputation as a very efficient and courageous officer. Although a strict disciplinarian, he was undoubtedly a humane commander by the standards of that somewhat harsh and brutal age. Ralfe's *Naval Biography* was to describe him, *inter alia*, as:

> ...firm, strict, cool, decided, zealous, considerate, kind, indulgent...In commanding he had a dignity and clearness which always ensured that respect and prompt obedience...integrity...and though he had a dignity of manner and deportment, which, to a stranger or casual observer, savoured of hauteur, he was warm...and kindly...His purse was always open to relieve distress...He was endowed by nature with a noble prepossessing appearance, finished by high good breeding...a thorough gentleman... .

These were perhaps generous words for they were written soon after his death, no doubt in a spirit of charity, but one author has written of him since that he was:

> Not only a very nice man but a very fine one, who possessed in great degree that candour of soul called uprightness...he hated the routine of flogging...and if...he found it...he put a stop to it...far ahead of his day in notions of cleanliness, he hated dirt in any form... .[14]

A contemporary portrait of him written in 1795 by a midshipman then fifteen years of age who was serving on the *Prince George* and who was later to become Vice-Admiral William Dillon, wrote of his apprehension when he heard that Sir John had been appointed to the command, for he was not a popular officer. But then, after he had adjudicated a complaint which had been made against Dillon himself, he was impressed with his fairness and justice, writing that he: 'had made a favourable impression on Sir John Orde, to whom I was a perfect stranger.'

Whether his opinion would have been quite so generous to Orde had the decision gone against him, remains to be seen. In that same narrative he described Orde as:

> ...a tall, thin, well-limbed man...fond of walking the Quarter Deck in a gold laced cocked hat, with a long spy-glass which he generally poised over his shoulder, giving his orders with great precision, and rather pompously. He appeared to be much pleased with his command of such a fine ship. He took great interest in the fitting of her, making such improvements for those days...Sir John was fond of repeating, when in familiar conversation with some of his officers, that he was tall enough to be an Admiral... .

Those words probably capture the true character of the man for there can be no doubt that he was insufferably proud, and very sensitive in his pride. It presented as consciousness of rank, pomposity and, at times, arrogance. At one moment he would stand aloof, at another he would be foolishly and childishly outspoken in his protestations, however justified they may have been.

It was this which was to cause so much irritation to St Vincent in the Mediterranean three years on, of which his fellow Northumbrian Collingwood wrote, for, undoubtedly, there was there a clash of personalities. With others he could be remote, which was at times resented by Horatio Nelson, and it was clearly the foolishness of his petulant protest in 1794 which had so annoyed the second Lord Spencer.

Nonetheless, Dillon's words were prophetic for it was on 1 June of that same year, 1795, that Orde was promoted to the rank of Rear-Admiral of the White in a general promotion of flag officers, and the Admiralty required that he leave the *Prince George* for pastures new. It is clear from Dillon's narrative that this was much regretted by the crew who had by then come to know, like and respect him, for he wrote that:

> All the officers were annoyed at the circumstance. Sir John had taken a great deal of pains to fit the ship...in the evening we all assembled on the Quarter Deck out of respect for Sir John, who bid all his officers a friendly goodbye...he came over to the side of the ship where I was walking. There were at least 20 Mids, and, to my surprise he took me by the hand in a most cordial manner, saying, 'Farewell to you', then left the ship...I was the only Mid whom he noticed in that way...As Sir John was of a haughty disposition, his condescension to me made the greater impression on them... .

115

Dillon was to write that by placing that ship under the command of another at that moment, the opportunity of joining the French admiral's flagship in battle in the action close to the Ile de Groix off L'Orient, was lost, for the new commander gave way to the 98-gun *Queen* flying the flag of Vice-Admiral Sir Alan Gardner and allowed Gardner to overtake him in pursuit of the French, after which most of the enemy fleet escaped and ran for the safety of the Ile. Dillon's final word was:

> Had Sir John Orde been on board the *Prince George*, all his followers declared, he would have run alongside the French Admiral in spite of Sir Alan Gardner or any other superior officer, unless ordered by signal to act otherwise. They all deplored his absence.[15]

In the outcome Orde languished at home unemployed for a year or more before Spencer came up with another offer of active service which was acceptable to him, this time with the Mediterranean Fleet under St Vincent. This drew from Lord Lansdowne by letter dated 13 March 1797 a message of congratulations, whilst Lord Howe wrote that he was: 'glad you are now on a footing with Lord Spencer that promises a continuance of more satisfactory consequences.'[16]

But it was not to be for, although Orde jumped at the opportunity given him, before he was ever able to sail for the Mediterranean he was redirected instead to Plymouth where he was ordered to take command in the temporary absence of Admiral Sir Richard King.[17] And it was his ill-luck that mutinous elements there had begun to surface, taking their cue from the mutiny at Spithead. But then news of peace at Spithead caused the mutiny in Plymouth to abate there as well and on this occasion his success in suppressing the insurrection was quickly recognized by Spencer who, after a visit to Plymouth, was effusive in his praise,[18] after which he appointed Orde to preside over the courts martial of the more serious Nore mutineers, to be held at Portsmouth. His performance in that duty won further praise and thanks and the recommendations he made were accepted by both Spencer and the King.[19]

In the meantime, by letter dated 5 May St Vincent had written to Orde:

> I am very much hurt to learn from Sir Robert Calder that you have not received an answer to your obliging communication of the imperious treatment you had met with from a certain quarter, [referring here to Lord Spencer]; he will bear witness that I wrote to you immediately and expressed the strongest indignation on the occasion, and I greatly lament your just indignation on the occasion deprived me of the benefit of your gallant services – I am happy

however to find your flag is flying, and I hope soon to hear of your appointment to a Chief Command.[20]

That hope was soon realized in October of that year when Orde was ordered to proceed to the Mediterranean in the *Princess Royal* of 98 guns, taking with him a captain and officers of his own choice, and there to join the Fleet, standing off the Tagus as third in command to the Earl St. Vincent. And so, at last, Orde was able to return to active service and he went with not only the plaudits of Lord Spencer still ringing in his ears but also with an assurance from Lord Hugh Seymour, one of the Lords of the Admiralty, that he would in short time stand second in command of the Fleet.[21] In fact, ominously, St Vincent had before then urged Spencer not to send him any more flag officers for he found that most of them he could not trust. Spencer had replied that his request had come too late for two more were on their way, namely Orde and Frederick, to which St Vincent had responded on 14 September:

> I have no objection to any number of Admirals your lordship may think fit to employ in the Fleet provided they are firm men and obedient officers. I believe Sir John Orde to be of the sort above described, although I never served with him. Both he and Frederick will be acceptable, but should the war continue over the winter I beg Admiral Nelson may be sent to me.

Orde was to prove his worth in the ensuing six months of blockade duty at Cadiz, which St Vincent was quick to recognize. On arrival he was ordered to relieve Collingwood of his command of a squadron of eight of the line, standing off Cadiz in turbulent seas where he was outnumbered more than two to one by twenty Spanish ships lying in harbour and poised to break out at any moment. And there was the danger too that the French Fleet at Toulon may at any moment put to sea with no force in the Mediterranean to oppose it. Yet for three months or more Orde, with calm determination, held the Spaniards in port until relieved by Sir William Parker in January 1798. When, later, Parker was driven off the station by a superior force, Orde returned to the command and successfully mounted the blockade once more in extremely difficult circumstances until St Vincent himself resumed command off Cadiz in April. St Vincent then penned a letter to Sir John, writing: 'You have shown uncommon ability and exertion in preserving your position during the unpleasant weather, and I very much appreciate every step you have taken.'

Captain William Cathcart was to write home from his ship the *Alcmene* on Sunday, 6 May 1798:

117

...we have just left Gibraltar after a stay of about four days. Sir John Orde gave a grand chevaux [dance] to which he was so good as to invite me. He introduced me to General O'Hara and a Mrs Fryers ...I never saw anything neater in my life... .[22]

Nelson's rather priggish comment on this, when writing to his wife on 1 May was: 'Sir John Orde is here giving fetes etc., but I have no time for such things when we had better be alongside a Spaniard.'[23]

And so, when command of the Mediterranean Squadron came up for consideration, both Parker and Orde were eminently qualified for the appointment and their claims had been real. Indeed Orde's general prospects were about as good as those of any other flag officer on the list. He had an impeccable record of service behind him both in the Royal Navy and in colonial administration. Added to that he now stood third in command of the main combatant Fleet in the Navy with every hope of succeeding St Vincent as Commander-in-Chief in the course of time given that he was sixteen years his junior. And it seems he had the ear of the government for his brother Thomas was at that time close to William Pitt.

But then the claims of Horatio Nelson were by this time very strong indeed. Although junior to Orde in both rank and age, for he was seven years younger and eighteen below him in the list of admirals, and despite the fact that his frail and diminutive body was grossly disabled with the loss of his amputated right arm and all useful sight in his right eye, he had, by then, accumulated an impressive record of service in the West Indies and on other stations and his reputation stood high with his brother officers. In a supposedly more enlightened age such overall disability would have disqualified him from further active service, even as an admiral for whom the physical demands may not have been as great as those made of more junior officers, although the autopsy of his body seven years on was to reveal a man healthier than his years would suggest.

A more detailed analysis of the appointment of the man chosen has been discussed by the author in *Nelson's Mediterranean Command* in greater detail, but it seems clear that it lay ultimately in the gift of Lord Spencer as First Lord of the Admiralty. And he was to write: 'Upon its command...the fate of Europe may be stated to depend.' That being his belief it is probable that others too brought their influence to bear, not excepting the Prime Minister himself and even George III.

Certainly Nelson's friend from Corsica days, Sir Gilbert Elliot, later Lord Minto, was singing his praises in the drawing rooms of London while, at the same time, bombarding Spencer with his advice that Nelson be given the command. And the rumour was that the King himself had asked for Nelson to be appointed, perhaps in response to the pleas of his son, Prince William, the Duke of Clarence, who had struck up such a close friendship with Nelson in his West Indies days to which both were ever loyal. The Prince had insisted on giving away the bride at Nelson's wedding when he had married the widowed Mrs Frances Nisbet at President Herbert's house in Montpelier on 11 March 1787 and the two had corresponded on a regular basis ever since. Like the equally diminutive Napoleon Bonaparte, he had married a widow from the West Indies, and, curiously, the one portrait of a British commander Napoleon ever kept in his study was that of Nelson whose fighting qualities he so admired. This friendship was to last for the rest of Nelson's short life, except for a small hiccup when the Prince dared to pay attention to Nelson's Lady Hamilton at a later date, but the Prince was forced to continue his life as a naval officer vicariously through his correspondence with Nelson, Collingwood and others for he was rightly denied the seagoing appointment he sought by a government which felt that it could not employ him safely in a position which his rank would have dictated he occupy. And so, if consulted, it is probable that, of the three, George III gave his support to Nelson. Indeed Nelson had been careful to take his leave of his King before returning to the Mediterranean from sick leave in 1798.

It is true that the relationship between Spencer and Orde was now on a reasonable footing, but here again Nelson had the advantage for he had made several calls on Spencer during his convalescence. Lady Spencer's first impression of him had not been favourable, dismissing him as an uncouth simpleton determined to upset the seating arrangements at her dinner table by insisting that he sat next to his own wife. But she changed her opinion very quickly once the brilliance of his conversation was heard and when it became apparent too that sitting near his wife was not just a wish to be near that lady, but rather to meet a need for her assistance in transporting food from the plate to the mouth with but one hand to perform the operation. Indeed such was the formidable Lady Spencer's concern for Nelson's welfare that she later had an eating utensil specially designed and made for him which Nelson was to put to regular use.

But the probability too is that, of all the advice Spencer received from these and many other quarters, it was the opinion of St Vincent which carried the most weight as that of the commander on the spot and so the man in the best position to know. Here Nelson had the unwavering support of St Vincent, especially so since his exploits off Cape St Vincent the previous year had left the Commander-in-Chief firmly in his debt. And so, however much he may have denied it later, St Vincent made it clear to Spencer which of his subordinates he favoured for the command, advising that Nelson was the officer who would be best able to deliver what was required. Accordingly Spencer, ending a letter dated 29 April to St Vincent, added: 'If you determine to send a detachment into the Mediterranean, I think it almost unnecessary to suggest to you the propriety of putting it under the command of Sir H. Nelson.'[24]

St Vincent's prompt response to this was to detach ten 74s together with the 50-gun *Leander* to which would be added the three ships already under Nelson's command to form the new squadron. He then released eleven of his ablest captains for service in this new high-powered Mediterranean Fleet which he then placed under the command of Horatio Nelson. Perhaps imagining himself in the part of Shakespeare's Henry V, Nelson was to label them his 'Band of Brothers'. Only one of them had been at all critical of Nelson's talents and that was Sir James Saumarez. He had professed dislike of Nelson's naked ambition, once describing him as 'the desperate Commodore', but he too was soon won over by the Nelson charm.

The quarrel over this appointment was misunderstood at the time and has been misunderstood ever since. More than a century later, in July 1914, Lord Fisher, about to return to the Admiralty as First Sea Lord, found occasion to use the incident by way of analogy, incorrectly. Winston Churchill, then First Lord, was seeking to replace Sir George Callaghan as Commander-in-Chief of the Home Fleet before the outbreak of war, on the ground of old age. In fact he was but sixty-two and so two years younger than St Vincent had been in 1798 when commanding the Mediterranean Fleet. But Churchill's judgment, no doubt correct at the time, had been that Sir George would not be equal to the strain of war. On the advice of Fisher his replacement was to be the reluctant Jellicoe, even though Jellicoe himself objected most strongly to the arrangement. By letter to A. J. Balfour, former Prime Minister and later to become First Lord of the Admiralty in the coalition government, Fisher wrote:

> ...as to Winston scrapping the Admirals with a courageous stroke of the pen, I want to mention to you that since being a Midshipman I have adored the English principle of having civilian Lords of the Admiralty, because I read how Lord Spencer, then First Lord, on his own initiative and against the navy traditions sent Nelson to the Mediterranean over the head of Sir John Orde and others (who had their flags flying) and hence we got the battle of the Nile! the finest of all fights since the world began... .[25]

But what Fisher had there overlooked was that Parker in 1798 was fifty-five years of age and Orde forty-seven, and both were eminently well qualified as fighting commanders.

With hindsight, the choice of Nelson for command of the new fleet of ships was demonstrably correct and fully justified by subsequent events. Indeed it proved to be an inspired appointment for it unleashed for the first time the brilliance of Nelson as a fleet commander and placed it at the disposal of the British nation. But, at the time, it bred surprise and indignation, not just amongst those officers in the fleet left behind, including Parker, Orde and Collingwood, but also at home where it was greeted in many influential quarters with a mixture of incredulity, dismay and even hostility. This was after all the key appointment upon which the very survival of the British nation could depend, and here it was going to an officer of comparatively junior rank, and one untried as a fleet commander.

And so, as Nelson in the *Vanguard* sailed off up the Mediterranean in search of the French Fleet, with the enormity of that responsibility on his all too fatigued, battle worn and fragile shoulders, so the hopes of the Admiralty, and indeed, all England went with him, and not without some trepidation. And as the days slipped by and turned into weeks and the weeks then stretched into months and the French Fleet still eluded Nelson, so the fears of the people at home became more vocal. So too did criticism of the appointment gain momentum, not least in the British press. The fear was that he had been sent on something of a wild goose chase and that perhaps the French Fleet had been put up as a decoy to draw away British ships from the Channel. Even out in St Vincent's Fleet itself, a letter from one of the puisne Lords of the Admiralty was read out publicly on Sir William Parker's ship, the *Prince George*, denouncing St Vincent in round terms for having sent so young a flag officer on a mission of such crucial importance.[26]

And no one was prepared to admit or accept responsibility for the appointment of Nelson. The belief that St Vincent had been responsible was scotched by St Vincent himself, sheltering behind the assertion that he had simply had his orders from the Admiralty. Yet Lord Spencer, too, disowned responsibility, hinting that it had been the work of 10 Downing Street. For his part William Pitt maintained a dignified silence, making no attempt to deny a rumour then in circulation that the appointment of Nelson had been a royal command. George Rose, Treasurer of the Navy, was adamant in a letter to Orde that neither Lord Spencer nor Lord St Vincent was to blame. The author Russell argues that in that letter Rose was seeking to protect and shield none other than William Pitt, who had no wish to invite the opposition of Orde's friends.

But most despondent of all was Nelson himself. The burden of such a responsibility was beginning to tell and he had too few frigates at his disposal to be able to conduct much of a search. In fact, unbeknown to Nelson and the British government, Napoleon had before then travelled to the northern shores of France and, after seeing the position for himself, had decided that the plans entrusted to him by the Directory for the invasion of Britain were premature and unrealistic. The force was far from ready and, as ever, the Royal Navy stood in its way, dominating and controlling the waters of the Channel. In the light of this he had himself decided that British interests could best be damaged by striking at British trade routes to India, or indeed India itself, from a base which the French should seek to establish in Egypt. He had therefore turned his eyes east to the Middle Eastern states and the passage to India. His plan was to secure Malta as a strategic base on his way to Alexandria and then, after conquering Egypt, sweep through Turkey, then an ally of France, in the hope of promoting enough of a Christian revolt there to overthrow the Ottoman rulers. He would then return to Paris absolute master of the Mediterranean and all its surrounding territories with the riches of the Orient and British India within his grasp also. Then would be the moment to plan any invasion of Great Britain, the greatest and most obstinate of France's enemies.

And so his fleet managed to evade Nelson, slipping out of Toulon while Nelson was in dock in Sardinia for repairs to his flagship which had been dismasted in severe weather. In the outcome, he was to be separated from his frigates for many weeks to come as they conducted a fruitless search in the waters around Gibraltar, far from the route taken by the French armada. And it was to prove to be a severe handicap in the weeks which followed as he scanned the Mediterranean for the enemy without the advantage of frigate intelligence. On arrival in Alexandria he learned that the French had captured and plundered Malta, and then, setting sail for Sicily he missed the arrival of Napoleon and his fleet at Alexandria by no more than a few hours.

It was not until 1 August that his frigates spotted the French Fleet at anchor in a single crescent line of formation in Aboukir Bay, the men-of-war such as the *L'Orient* too big to be able to enter the shoal waters of the harbour at Alexandria itself. There followed the Battle of the Nile which was to provide Nelson with the first of his three great sea victories over the French.

And it was not until news of the victory reached London later that year, brought home by the brig *Mutine*, that wagging tongues were stilled. All criticism then abated, save from Spencer and Dundas who were concerned that Napoleon had been allowed to make good his landing and conquest of Egypt. Nelson was denied the Viscountcy he so richly deserved but he was raised to the peerage as Baron Nelson of the Nile and Burnham Thorpe. And the rejoicing at home was great.

Nelson's close friend and treasurer, Alexander Davison, even celebrated and marked the battle at his Swarland estate a few miles north of

Morpeth in Northumberland, which he had purchased three years before, by putting down a large plantation of trees in carefully located groups to represent the battle formation of the two fleets.

But back in 1798, when news of the victory at the Nile reached London, it brought several forward now falling over themselves to claim the credit for Nelson's appointment back in May. In a letter of congratulation to Nelson dated 27 September, St Vincent referred to allegations which had been made by Orde and Parker concerning the selection of Nelson for the command, and then wrote: 'the original sin was appointing you to command the detached squadron, the event of which has proved that my judgment was correct... .'[27]

And Sir Edward Berry, in a letter to Nelson dated London, 30 December 1798 wrote: 'The Duke of Clarence insisted I would tell you from him that it was the King that sent you with the squadron up the Mediterranean, and formed the whole plan. I believe it seriously.'[28]

Nelson's own word on the appointment was not received until the year 1801 when, in a letter dated 7 July, in reply to a letter from Orde, which he described as kindly and friendly, Nelson wrote:

I never did try to supplant anyone or ever pushed myself beyond a laudable ambition to try and get forward, and having no friends or connections to assist me, that I never thought any person would say a word against me, much less you an old and friendly acquaintance, who I never did, or would wish to do any injury to in my life... .[29]

Then in a further letter he added:

I can assure you on my word of honour, that neither Earl St Vincent nor Lord Spencer were the original cause of my being sent to the Mediterranean. the arrangement was made in April 1797, a year before I was sent... .[30]

This clearly suggests that Nelson knew with whom the responsibility lay and that it lay in high places, but it is a little difficult to accept that the decision had been made one year earlier before forces had begun to assemble at Toulon and before the emergency had ever arisen.

Certainly both Orde and Parker had been bitterly disappointed over the whole affair for they saw it, wrongly, as a reflection on their own talents and a setback to their hopes of further advancement. Both accepted that it was the absolute right of the Admiralty to install whomsoever they thought fit to such an important command, but having only a few months before chosen a chain of command in the Fleet, Nelson's appointment had suggested to them either that they had been lured out under false pretences or, more probably, that there had been a change of heart in high places. Either way it was resented and it was the opinion of Nicolas, Nelson's biographer, that this was only natural.

It was Parker who first gave vent to his feelings, as he had after the Battle of Cape St Vincent the year before. Going to St Vincent with his complaint, he was met with the somewhat disingenuous reply that he, St Vincent, had had no say in the appointment. Parker then bombarded the Admiralty about it for three months or more, writing that their decision 'must necessarily be considered a doubt of my abilities or worse...'[31]

Eventually, finding that he was getting nowhere, he asked for and was granted a transfer to another command rather than serve any longer under St Vincent, considering him guilty of duplicity, untruths and deception in the matter of Nelson's appointment. On New Year's Day 1802 he was to die in a fit of apoplexy.[32]

Orde meanwhile swallowed his disappointment and uttered no word of complaint. But then in the general climate of discontent which prevailed amongst officers in the fleet at that time of which Collingwood had written, a number of broadsides were fired in his direction which stung his pride and eventually caused him to break his silence. With hindsight they look trivial but at the time they loomed large in the mind of this proud man.

The first involved the arrival of the infamous Sir Roger Curtis of whom Collingwood had been so critical after the Battle of the Glorious First of June, four years before. Curtis joined the fleet on 24 May simply in order to deliver the reinforcements from the Channel Fleet which had been promised. But then, to the annoyance of both Parker and Orde, St Vincent retained him as second in command, thus at a stroke relegating Parker to third and Orde to fourth, and thus undermining too those appointments which had been made by the Admiralty.

This was the first of many causes of dissent which then followed which have been examined in detail by the author in *Nelson's Mediterranean Command* and are not germane to the present account, but suffice it to note that it was not simply the appointment of Nelson which caused the rift which was to develop between Orde and St Vincent out in the fleet of which Collingwood and the newspapers were to write.

The particular misunderstanding which was to poison their relationship irrevocably was childish in the extreme for it arose from an assumption made by St Vincent, wrongly and for some reason never explained, that a blunt letter written by one Lieutenant Colonel Desborough of Marines to St Vincent seeking to defend the conduct of one of his marines who had been reported by Captain Hardy, had been written by Orde.[33] Labouring under that misapprehension St Vincent wrote a severe letter of reprimand[34] to the astonished Orde who not unnaturally wrote back very promptly disowning all knowledge of the letter. And only when that drew no response from St Vincent did he go over to St Vincent's flagship to confront him with the truth. Yet still St Vincent refused to acknowledge his mistake and again accused Orde of impropriety until Orde insisted that he look again at the letter as tangible proof of his assertion. Thus put on the spot he eventually agreed to do just that. And it was only then, when St Vincent saw the signature of Desborough on it, that he was prepared to make an apology, but it was the gruff and half-hearted apology of a man obviously chastened and embarrassed and indeed livid, for he was not a man who liked to be crossed or shown up. And although Orde afterwards wrote to St Vincent to assure him of his continuing loyalty and St Vincent corresponded with him in courteous and amicable terms, even to the extent of acknowledging in writing that his letter of reprimand had been a thorough mistake, it is clear that this small event soured for evermore a relationship which had until then been cordial enough, and it was the precursor for much of the trouble which was to come. It is so often thus.

It was then that Orde very foolishly put pen to paper, and in a letter to Lord Spencer dated 16 June which he first showed to St Vincent, he complained of both the appointment of Lord Nelson to the independent command and also of the installation of Curtis as second in command, while at the same time reassuring Spencer of his wish to go on serving his country.[35] For his part St Vincent reassured Orde that he had had no part in the appointment of Nelson, asserting that it had been the work of the Admiralty, adding, ominously, that because Parker had been writing letters about it he would have to be recalled home. Certainly the storm clouds were looming.

There followed a reprimand from St Vincent for Orde's Flag Captain, Captain Draper, which was thought by Orde to be unjustified, although on this occasion he wisely decided not to take it up with St Vincent in Draper's best interests and after taking the advice of his fellow Northumbrian, Captain George Grey, in whom he felt he could confide. This was the third son of General Sir Charles Grey of Howick in Northumberland. Sir Charles was later raised to the peerage in 1801 and to an earldom in 1806, the year before he died, and it was George Grey's studious and eloquent elder brother Charles who became the celebrated Grey of the Reform Bill.

But then further criticism came from St Vincent, targeted at two lieutenants serving on Orde's flagship, the *Princess Royal*, judging that they, along with lieutenants from two other ships, had been guilty of insubordination when returning from a foray by rowing boat with cannonade to the mouth of the harbour of Cadiz to prevent the ship *La Vestale* from breaking out. But when Orde conducted his own enquiry into the allegation he found the two to have been innocent of the charge and acquitted them of all blame. Perhaps foolishly he then sent his report along with the two officers concerned, to confront St Vincent with it, only to be told that he should have sent Captain Draper since he was the person who had nominated the two for that duty in the first place, and that, in any event, he stood by his own decision. It was a further nail in the coffin of Sir John Orde.

It could be argued that this proud man was himself responsible for then bringing matters to a head for he wrote on 31 July a long and most imprudent letter to his commander, in which he reminded St Vincent that it was he who had asked for his services, that it was St Vincent's own written judgment that he had acquitted himself well, that word had reached him from members of the Admiralty Board that they had had nothing to do with Nelson's appointment despite St Vincent's insistence that they had, and setting out various further complaints. To this St Vincent replied by letter of that same date that:

> The moment you communicated to me the letter you sent Lord Spencer, I considered it impossible you could remain an hour longer in the fleet...Sir William Parker, to whom I communicated the letter I received from Lord Spencer, touching the employment of Sir H. Nelson, knows that I had no share in that transaction...at the same time I shall be glad of any opportunity to hear testimony to your merits as an officer.

The following day St Vincent wrote further:

> ...had you attended to the earnest wish I expressed, that you should not remonstrate against the measure of putting the detached squadron under the orders of Rear Admiral Sir H. Nelson, you must eventually have succeeded to the command of this fleet, for my health will not admit of my continuing in it many months longer.[36]

And so the squabble and the acrimony continued. By letter dated 18 July, Lord Spencer, in reply to Orde's earlier letter and not knowing then that St Vincent had since resolved to send Orde home, sought to placate Orde and calm ruffled feathers by diplomatically offering his regrets that Orde should have felt unhappy with decisions made out in the Mediterranean, ending:

...you cannot fail to deserve all the credit which is due to a zealous and active officer, and all the satisfaction that must infallibly attend on consciousness that you are performing your duty to the public....

But by then the die was cast.

In August, when addressing Parker while pacing the quarterdeck, St Vincent accused some of his officers of conspiracy in allowing certain mutineers to escape the death penalty, saying:

But I know the reason for all this; the members have entered into a conspiracy or combination against me for the orders I have given respecting the marines. By God! I will stay here no longer to be so served.[37]

Again Sir John foolishly put pen to paper, for he himself had been one of the members of the courts martial which had imposed the sentences concerned. In his letter to St Vincent he referred to the allegations of conspiracy which St Vincent had made and assured him that he was incapable of such unofficer-like proceeding or of any unworthy motive.

To that letter he received no reply, but he continued to receive further reprimands, for the quarrel was now far removed from any resentment Sir John may have felt over the appointment of Nelson back in May and St Vincent was clearly now using his greater rank to censure and humiliate him whenever the opportunity arose so to do.

Before sailing for home on 31 August Orde wrote a letter to Evan Nepean, secretary to the Admiralty, seeking a court martial so that the matter could be judged impartially and objectively. He then struck his flag in the *Princess Royal* and sailed for home in the *Blenheim*. Thus did Sir John Orde quit the fleet and crawl back to England, delivering a parting shot in the shape of a letter to St Vincent written at Lisbon to which St Vincent responded saying that it was expressed in terms of insubordination.

The judgment must be that St Vincent was wrong to take the draconian step of asking Orde to strike his flag. Rather he should have tactfully found him another role in the fleet to allow time for the hurt to his pride to subside. But then the correspondence foolishly generated by Orde may perhaps have made that impossible, for St Vincent had been sorely provoked, a thing very easily achieved. It is not at all surprising that St Vincent was, in time, to fall out with nearly every one of his contemporaries, not excepting Nelson himself, who at the time could do no wrong in his eyes, and who was, for the moment, oblivious to the storm which his appointment had created as he continued his search for Napoleon's Fleet in the eastern Mediterranean. Orde's petulant protest at his appointment had been wrong in a time of national emergency, especially since Nelson turned out to be so unusually and exceptionally qualified and suited for the difficult task which he was called upon to perform, as Orde himself came to recognize. It is doubtful that others, however courageous and accomplished they may have been, possessed the daring and initiative required and which Nelson displayed to such effect at the Battle of the Nile. And, in any event, Orde himself recognized and fully accepted that whilst promotion by seniority is one thing, selection for command is quite another.

But it is to be noted that, despite St Vincent's earlier claims that he had had no part in the appointment of Nelson, in a letter to St Vincent dated 9 October, enclosing notification of Nelson's peerage, Nepean, the secretary to the Admiralty wrote, 'you will hardly be questioned now, upon the propriety of your choice'.

Back at home Orde renewed his request for a court martial with first Nepean then Spencer but the reality of it was that his predicament was of but small account when set alongside the need to keep the Commander-in-Chief in post and at his station in this time of national emergency. And so both requests were refused. He then requested at least an enquiry for he had many in London who were on his side in the matter, and it was eventually in reply to this last plea that the Admiralty expressly recognized the injustice of what had been done and wrote on 2 November, through Nepean, that their lordships did

'not consider the reasons his Lordship had assigned for sending you home, sufficient to justify the measure'.

A reprimand was then sent to St Vincent stating that:

> Their Lordships...can by no means approve of your sending home Sir John Orde...they...therefore direct that you do not in future send home any flag officers without receiving instructions from their lordships to do so unless some very strong and some very peculiar circumstances should make it absolutely necessary... .[38]

It was not made public but, needless to say, St Vincent did not receive that reprimand kindly, writing to the Admiralty:

> my pride is very much wounded by the censure...I desire that you will state to their lordships...the extreme injury my reputation suffers by a sentence passed upon me without my defence being heard.

Lord Spencer then offered Orde a command with the Channel Fleet but this he foolishly declined, preferring instead to concentrate his efforts on clearing his name when he should perhaps have subordinated his feelings to the national interest in a time of such national emergency. He then put out his own version of events in a private pamphlet which he had published and then circulated amongst his influential friends. This drew from St Vincent a vitriolic response and amongst several letters written to the Admiralty in bad temper he wrote:

> with the exception of Sir Roger Curtis and perhaps Collingwood, I do not believe there was an officer of any standing who did not in some sort, enter into cabals to pull down my authority and level all distinctions. I saw this clearly, and had no other card to play but to get rid of Sir John...and if your Board has half an eye...instead of a rebuke, my conduct merited silent approbation... .

It was the letter of a man in temper who had begun to see enemies all around him and, in particular, in Sir John, a man who had earlier received his fulsome praise.

In the general promotions which followed on 14 February 1799 Orde became a Vice Admiral of the Blue, although when further commands fell vacant none of these were offered to him. Finally, after he had exhausted all the normal avenues of complaint, he decided that only one course was now left open to him. He would await the return home of St Vincent and then obtain satisfaction from him for he felt that St Vincent alone was the author of his fall from grace. And so after St Vincent returned to these shores, and after allowing him time to recover from an illness diagnosed as dropsical, Sir John and his second set out for St Vincent's country retreat at Rochetts near Brentwood in Essex, in search of revenge. What then occurred has been explored by the author in detail in *Nelson's Mediterranean Command*, but suffice it to note that *The Times* newspaper in London reported on 5 October 1799 that:

> The public will recollect with regret the serious misunderstanding which prevailed between some of our commanders on the Cadiz station, about the period when Lord Nelson was sent up the Mediterranean with a detached squadron. It was conceived by the senior Admirals that Lord St Vincent had treated them with some disrespect by appointing a junior officer to a separate command. Several distinguished officers were much disgusted on that occasion, which also laid the foundation of subsequent misunderstandings and quarrels of a very serious description. Sir John Orde, brother of Lord Bolton, was amongst those who felt themselves most insulted or aggrieved...and it was but too clearly understood...that he would seek...satisfaction...This unfortunate event has actually taken place. A challenge was sent to the noble Earl who was hastening up to

town yesterday in consequence. Happily the activity of the Magistrates of Bow Street has been able to frustrate an intention, which in every event would have proved fatal to their country. Sir John Orde was arrested about 4 o'clock yesterday morning at Durrant's Hotel in Jermyn Street by Townshend and Sayers, who waited with him till Mr Ford's arrival about 11 o'clock, when, entering into a proper security for keeping the peace, he was liberated. Mr Ford, attended by Townshend, then set off for Earl St Vincent's seat in Essex, and met the noble Lord on the road, on his way to town. On acquainting him with their purpose, his Lordship also gave bail to keep the peace, himself in £2000 and two sureties in £1000 each, being the same security as given by Admiral Orde. Earl Spencer and Mr Dundas were two of their sureties.

In fact Orde had travelled up to Durrant's Hotel from his then home at Tunbridge Wells on 30 September and then, sending his second and emissary, Captain Wellrond, round to Colonel Barre's house in Stanhope Street, where it was thought St Vincent was staying, the written challenge had been sent in. But St Vincent had before then departed for Rochetts, and so Orde took a room at the White Hart Hotel nearby, armed with the challenge in his pocket and with two duelling pistols in his bag. From there Wellrond had been sent up to the house to deliver the challenge, but St Vincent, safe indoors would not receive him, giving the explanation that he was too unwell to be seen. But the challenge had been delivered nonetheless and it drew from St Vincent a written refusal on the ground of indisposition. After sending a further note up to the house seeking redress[39] and after taking a much needed dinner at the inn, Orde had then returned to Durrant's Hotel in London to await St Vincent's reply. And there he waited for two more days but no reply came.

In the meantime Colonel Barre, one time Treasurer of the Navy, had reported these events to Lord Spencer who had lost no time in mobilizing the assistance of the law in the shape of Sir Richard Ford, to the result reported by *The Times*. There the two bailiffs found Orde in bed fast asleep;[40] such was the composure of a battle-hardened veteran of many a naval campaign. This proud Northumbrian, realizing then that nothing could now come of his challenge, abandoned the enterprise and left for Tunbridge Wells and the wife who was nervously waiting there for him, before going down to the place he had recently acquired in the then fashionable town of Bognor in Sussex. Before his departure he had urged the bailiffs to proceed with care if they went to St Vincent's home and to conceal their business from all but St Vincent, for his wife lay there dangerously ill and a knowledge of the affair might produce a harmful reaction. And the truth is that St Vincent was reached before he ever set out from home.

Lord Spencer, however, feared that the challenge had been no more than postponed and so he now sought the intervention of the King. In reply to Spencer's letter, the King wrote from Weymouth on 7 October expressing his approval:

> ...of the Earl of St Vincent being in the strongest manner acquainted by the Board of Admiralty, in my name, that I expect he will not accept any challenge from Sir John Orde, but I think Sir John should also be acquainted with the instructions I have given to the Board of Admiralty, that he may not offer any further insult to the Earl St. Vincent.[41]

And so there the matter had to rest. Sir John had been denied satisfaction and the challenge was never to be raised again.

On 8 October the editor of *The Times* pronounced that:

> Mr Ford and Townshend have accomplished a greater achievement than the united force of Spain could effect – they have taken two of our best Admirals prisoner!

And he wrote of the affair:

> Deeply as we enter into the high and honourable feelings of this distinguished officer, we cannot but congratulate the country at large upon his disappointment. The general voice of the British public bears ample testimony to his high character. Nothing can add to the opinion he has so well deserved; and the issue must have proved injurious to the kingdom, and to the service, of which these brave officers are ornament and support.

On 21 October Lady Nelson wrote to her husband:

> Sir John Orde has again made himself the subject of conversation. Matters are very properly set to rights by binding him over to keep the peace. Every man who refuses a challenge exalts himself in my opinion.[42]

But the squabble between them was destined to run on and on and to remain for ever unresolved. The following year, 1800, found Pitt a sick and tired man. A slave to a punishing schedule of work which was beginning to take its toll on his health, and at the mercy of port wine, he was slowly dying from exhaustion and alcoholic poisoning. At the turn of the year his government fell over the question of Catholic emancipation and he was succeeded by his friend and political opponent, Henry Addington, a man who worshipped the very ground Pitt walked on. For Sir John Orde, too, it marked the end for many a year of any hope he may have had of reinstatement in the fleet for, paradoxically, with Addington, a most cautious man, came radical change. Spencer departed as First Lord of the Admiralty to be succeeded by none other than the Lord St Vincent. Clearly any chance Orde had of further service with the fleet disappeared with the arrival of St Vincent, and so it was not until Pitt returned to government in 1804 that Dundas, then as Lord Melville, brought Orde back into fleet command in the months running up to the Battle of Trafalgar. And then, at Nelson's funeral, as the chief pall-bearer, he was to be the officer who stood closest to Nelson at the moment of his interment at St Paul's Cathedral.

It was to all of this trouble in the fleet that Collingwood had referred when writing to his father-in-law on 22 July 1798 in the letter already cited that:

> ...the appointment of Nelson had given great offence to Parker, who is a very excellent officer, and as gallant a man as any in the navy, and Sir John Orde, who on all occasions of service has acquitted himself with great honour...The fleet is, in consequence, in a most unpleasant state...the Admirals and Captains...all complain that they are appointed to many unworthy services...

But he was perhaps over-censorious of St Vincent when, after Nelson returned from the Nile triumphant, the scar of a wound on his forehead, Collingwood wrote to Captain Ball:

> Our good chief found employment for me; and to occupy my mind, sent me to cruise off San Luccars, to intercept the market boats of the poor cabbage carriers. Oh humiliation! But for the consciousness that I did not deserve degradation from any hand, and that my good estimation would not be depreciated in the minds of honourable men, by the caprice of power, I should have died with indignation.

To accuse St Vincent of caprice of power was to do him an injustice on this occasion for Collingwood had been sent to a spot, not far removed from the scene of the later Battle of Trafalgar, on perfectly legitimate business. And he did, in fact, encounter there enemy shipping which had to be dealt with. In any event his ship the *Excellent* was in serious need of overhaul and repair and was really not at that time up to campaign duties.

But by letter dated 3 December of that year, long after Orde had returned home, Collingwood was to write again to his father-in-law of unhappiness in the fleet, once he had returned to Spithead, saying that the station of late:

> ...has not latterly been very agreeable...The disagreement between the Chief and other flag officers, and his impetuous conduct towards several others on trifling occasions, shuts the door to the few comforts...to be found here...I could not help feeling disquietude at the many violences and innovations which I witnessed. The Admiralty, I find, have entirely disapproved of his sending Sir John Orde home; it seemed to everybody an unwarrantable stretch of power and...a hardy stroke at their authority in sending the officers of their appointment home...without even the slightest charge of misdemeanour...Sir John Orde is proud and carries himself very high...it needed not great sensibility to feel indignities. They were generally gross enough for the roughest minds...it would have been more judicious in him to have left the Board of Admiralty to defend themselves and their appointments...The only great mortification I suffered was not going with Admiral Nelson. He [St Vincent] knew our friendship...but my going would have interfered with the aggrandisement of a favourite to whom I was senior, and so he sent me out of the way...

These were not words of charity uttered simply because he was talking there of a fellow Northumbrian, for Collingwood always chose his words carefully and was an objectively fair man. Nelson was, after all, the closest friend he had in the service.

To his Chirton cousin, Collingwood wrote on 14 December that:

> very few escaped the asperity of his temper...His not sending me with the reinforcement to Lord Nelson when of right I ought to have gone if an Admiral did not, gave me so much dissatisfaction that from that day I looked to my return to England with very great impatience. The reason he would assign was the infirm state of my ship; the true reason was that my going would have interfered with the command of his great favourite Captain Troubridge...He treated Sir John Orde very ill...when two proud Dons meet, it is not difficult to find a cause of difference. I believe Sir John Orde is as zealous in the public service as himself, but in his manners and style of living there is a magnificence that the Chief was perhaps jealous of, and so in a very unprecedented way he sent him home.

Two days later he wrote to Jupiter Carlyle:

> The Chief...carried trifles with a high hand, took dislikes and prej-
> udices most capriciously, and in the instance of Sir John Orde, and
> some of the Captains, carried his resentment of, I could never under-
> stand what, to such extremity as to send them home. Those who did
> not feel the effect of his caprice could not witness it without feeling
> a certain degree of disgust... .

Indeed, long afterwards, in 1800, Collingwood was to return to this
same criticism when serving under St Vincent in the Channel Fleet lying
off the coast of Brest, when he wrote:

> I see disgust growing round me very fast. Instead of softening the
> rigours of a service, which must, from its nature, be attended with
> many anxieties, painful watchings and deprivations of anything like
> comfort...a contrary system is pursued...there is no exercise of the
> military part of our duties – no practice of those movements by a
> facility at which one fleet is made superior to another...whoever
> comes here ignorant in these points must remain so, for he will find
> other employment about blankets and pigsties, and tumbling provi-
> sions out of one ship into another.

Feeling amongst many officers continued to run against St Vincent for
some time to come, thus obscuring the massive contribution he had previously made to the fighting efficiency of the Royal Navy and indeed his
many acts of kindness to the offspring of sailors lost or wounded in
action, and to those who had served with him who had then fallen on
hard times. Chief command can be a lonely and difficult place, especially where mutinous elements have to be suppressed or contained.[43] Yet
when it became known that he was to take over the Channel Fleet in
1800, it was reported that an insubordinate toast was drunk by one of
the captains at Lord Bridport's table with the words, 'May the discipline
of the Mediterranean never be introduced into the Channel Fleet.' And,
as glasses were raised, there was apparently no murmur of dissent. It is
to be hoped that this was only because of the rivalry which existed
between the two fleets.

But throughout all this turbulence Collingwood had wisely kept his
own counsel and had confided his own thoughts to only his family at
home. There had therefore been no question of insubordination. That
was not in Collingwood's character. Newnham Collingwood, in assembling some of Collingwood's correspondence long after his death, was
to claim that he had, in fact, rounded on St Vincent on one occasion

when he had been summoned to his flagship only to discover that it was to take delivery of two bags of onions for the use of the sick, saying:

> Has the *Excellent*'s signal been made five or six times for two bags of onions? Man my boat, sir, and let us go on board again.

Newnham Collingwood went on to assert that although Collingwood was then pressed repeatedly by Lord St Vincent to stay for dinner, he refused to do so and withdrew. But it is difficult to credit this story as true, for it would have been totally out of character for Collingwood, and would, had it occurred, have been met with a severe reprimand, if not much more from the Lord St Vincent.

St Vincent was to take his revenge on Parker later. In October of 1798 he had reported of Parker that although he was 'a gallant man', he had a 'low, vulgar manner', and one who had been worked on by Calder. Five months later he wrote to Nepean, that his 'weakness [as] President of a Court Martial, exceeds that of Sir Roger Curtis, if possible'. That same month Parker escaped St Vincent's clutches when he was appointed commander-in-chief at Halifax, but the moment St Vincent became First Lord he recalled him. Parker was to die of apoplexy in 1802, a rich man.

It was in December 1798 that the *Excellent* was ordered home for refitting, which presented Collingwood with a prospect of home leave. The crew had, of course, to be discharged and paid off which kept him at Spithead and away from his family over the New Year. Without doubt Collingwood felt sad to have to bid farewell to the *Excellent* which had served him so well for so long and which had achieved a reputation for gunnery efficiency under his command which was really without equal in the fleet.

But the prospect of leave, the second of any duration during his long career at sea, was compensation enough for the sadness he felt as he made the long journey north to Northumberland and to the wife and two daughters who waited for him there in the cold month of January 1799. Command of the *Atlas* of 90 guns had been offered to him by Lord Spencer in place of the *Excellent* but this Collingwood had sensibly declined in favour of leave with his family after an absence of almost four years.

Chapter 9

With the Channel Fleet

On 14 February 1799, the anniversary of the Battle of St Vincent of two years before, Collingwood was raised to flag rank as a Rear-Admiral of the White, having leapfrogged the blue squadron in the general promotion of flag officers. He was now fifty years of age and a seagoing veteran.

It meant much to be able to fly a flag denoting occupation by an officer of flag rank. Indeed flags in general had enormous significance to ships of the line for, if lowered or struck, that would be seen as a signal of surrender. Because it was so the eighteen year old sailor from Sunderland in County Durham, Jack Crawford, had won a place in naval history at the Battle of Camperdown in 1797. There he had bravely climbed up and nailed his admiral's colours to the broken mast of his ship, the *Venerable*, as it sailed through the Dutch lines, lest the rest of the fleet mistook the fact that the flag was down as a signal of surrender after being shot away from the mast head. For this he was to return to London a hero where he was met by cheering crowds and a grateful King. Back home the citizens of his native Sunderland presented him with a silver medal, and an attractive engraving depicting his act was quickly got out by Daniel Orme. Hancock's Camperdown medal then commemorated the exploit further by showing his deed in its design on the face of the medal with the caption, 'Heroic Courage Protects The British Flag.'[1] And so it was that the expression 'nailing your colours to the mast' entered the English language.

It is clear from letters written to Sir Edward Blackett at the time that Collingwood had treasured every moment of that rare and brief visit home, devoting much of his time to his favourite pastime of gardening and to the education of his beloved small daughters who had been taken out of Mrs Wilson's school at Newcastle so that Collingwood could give them his undivided attention. He wrote, too, of planting acorns so that in the fullness of time there would be wood enough to satisfy the appetite of the builders of ships of the line which required enormous quantities of oak for their construction. And there was mention, too, of dining with his neighbour, William Burdon, the philosopher, although by neighbour he may have meant one who lived six miles or so away since Burdon lived at that time on his estate at Hartford. In fact Collingwood was related by marriage to Burdon, a man he described as strange and eccentric, perhaps because he hung portraits of the Revd Horne Tooke, the radical MP, and Tom Paine on his walls. This was the same Tom Paine who, bankrupt, had emigrated to America where he had involved himself in the Revolution both there and in France. He was to die in the New World in poverty.

In years to come Collingwood would repeat his belief in planting acorns in the national interest. To his father-in-law he later wrote: 'I wish everybody thought on this subject as I do; they would not walk through their farms without a pocket-full of acorns to drop in the hedge-sides, and then let them take their chance,' for it was reckoned that the construction of a 74-gun ship would consume 2,000 trees of fifty cubic feet. Certainly Collingwood planted oak trees on his wife's little estate at Hethpool in the College Burn of Glendale, which had so often in medieval times been the target of Scottish raiders from Kale Water. These he planted on slopes within sight of the house which had been built in 1687, but they failed to mature well in the shallow soil there, unlike the luxuriant oaks which grow naturally a mile or so further upstream at Harrow Bog. The old house was demolished in 1919 in favour of a more modern structure, but remnants of the tower and walls, now covered in ivy, remain part of the garden feature.

He was concerned too that his daughters should not be so provincial in their speech that it would prove a disadvantage to them. But at the same time he was to emphasize where his priorities lay, writing that: 'Their hearts, their minds, are of much more consequence than their tongues.'

However, although Collingwood's heart was obviously and always very much at home with his wife and two daughters, to whom he was clearly deeply devoted, as a sailor who had by now mastered his profession and achieved a rank of significance, it is clear too that, as the months went by, he was also at that time impatient to be back at sea. That, after all, was the only place where he could deploy the skills he had acquired and exercise the rank to which he had so recently been appointed and if there was to be action he wanted to be part of it. Indeed he admitted as much in a letter written to Sir Edward Blackett, for intelligence had reached him that the French were assembling troops and ships at the port of Brest for the invasion of Britain: 'There is a

137

nothingness in a sailor ashore at such a time that will, if it lasts long, weary me.'

Accordingly he travelled to London in March 1799 and there offered his services to Lord Spencer, in the hope that he might be given a seagoing appointment in home waters which would allow him to arrange accommodation nearby for his wife and daughters. He had no wish to command in port, except, he wrote to Dr Carlyle, 'at Morpeth, where I am only second'.

He wrote that whilst in London he attended a drawing room where: 'there were a great many people...and a good number of naval officers who kissed His Majesty's hand on the same occasion as I did.' Having lodged his application Collingwood then returned to Morpeth to await the summons. This came soon afterwards in early May.

He then returned to the Channel Fleet under Lord Bridport, hoisting his flag on 27 May in the *Triumph*, a slow two-decker ship of 74 guns, and later joined Lord Keith in his abortive hunt for the French Fleet in the Mediterranean. In private correspondence with Sir Edward Blackett Collingwood laid the blame for this failure at the door of St Vincent, still then Commander-in-Chief of the Mediterranean Fleet. He had retired ill to the Rock of Gibraltar yet still issued detailed instructions to Keith at sea as to how, when and where he was to conduct the search. This left the French Fleet under Bruix able to avoid Keith and move much as they wished. Indeed it is implicit from the words used in that letter that Collingwood was suggesting that his own view was that St Vincent had no real wish to see Keith succeed when he was not there himself to receive the accolades for any victory.

But a measure of good fortune did come his way in the autumn of that year when the frigate *Alcmene*, captained by one Henry Digby, and assisted by three others including the *Ethalion*,[2] captured two Spanish frigates from La Vera Cruz off Finisterre on 16 October, the *El Thetis* and the *S.Brigida*. One of these, the *El Thetis*, was found to be carrying a cargo of no less than 1,411,500 dollars on board, which raised two-thirds of a million pounds at the Bank of England. That was an enormous sum of money in 1799. By the rules of distribution which had applied since 1708, and which would continue to do so for many more years, although adjusted to some extent in 1808, the net product of prize money was divided into eight equal shares. The captains involved in a capture took the lion's share of the proceeds, namely three-eighths, divided between them, the remainder going to the other officers and to the seamen, which was rank driven. The intention here was to encourage the more enterprising and belligerent captains, who, after all, exercised great autonomy when patrolling the distant oceans of the world. But if the prize was taken when serving in fleet formation, then the distribution was one-quarter to the captains and one-eighth to the fleet commander, or one-sixteenth if there were flag officers serving with him, who would then have one-sixteenth shared between them. And so it was the captains and their commander who stood to gain most from a capture. Thus did St Vincent, far from the action, profit to the tune of £14,149-13s-0d from the Battle of the Nile according to a note made by Nelson's agent, Davison in 1801, where Nelson's share amounted to £2,358-4s-6d. So too, Sir John Orde, by then languishing at home waiting his moment to confront St Vincent, shared to a like extent in the sum of £2,358-4s-6d, from which, of course, his agent, Hulbert, would take his commission. And so, as one of seven flag officers serving in the fleet patrolling those waters at the time of the capture of the *Thetis*, Collingwood stood to gain a not insignificant share of the proceeds which he calculated should bring him more than £2,000, a not inconsiderable sum by the values of the day. He had Digby to thank for this bonanza. In reporting his luck in a letter to one of his sisters in late October, Collingwood wrote:

> ...the frigates are doing their duty to some purpose...What makes it particularly satisfactory is I shall probably share two thousand pounds...which, let me tell you, is no bad Michaelmas goose, considering how many are to share...

But Collingwood was careful in a further letter to put his windfall into perspective by noting that that same Captain Digby had already accumulated more than, 'four score thousand pounds by his prizes this war', to which would then be added a lion's share of the proceeds of this, his latest capture, which could have amounted to as much as 40,000 pounds.

However, unlike his friend Nelson who was to resent bitterly the riches acquired by Vice-Admiral Sir John Orde when in Spanish waters as Commander-in-Chief of the Cadiz squadron in the years 1804-1805, which he described as 'reaping the golden harvest' which was properly due to him, Collingwood in that same letter to his wife's uncle, Sir Edward Blackett, dated 12 January 1800, to whom Digby had recently been introduced, applauded Captain Digby as 'a fine young man, one of those active spirits that maintains the credit of the navy and he has been well paid for it...'. He did not for one moment begrudge him his good fortune.

To Collingwood, newly promoted to flag rank after serving as a captain in Sir John Orde's Larboard Squadron the year before, such a significant share in the proceeds of a capture not made by himself was a novel and welcome experience, although he was later to proclaim loftily that he really had little interest in the acquisition of riches, whether won on the high seas or indeed anywhere else. He maintained that all he needed was enough, 'to keep a good fire in the winter...' and that, 'I do not consider [being rich] ...has any relation to our happiness'.

Nonetheless the sum received no doubt went towards a purchase of the Morpeth property negotiated by his wife in the year following, and, nine years on, he was to be heard complaining that, 'I am treated shabbily on all hands about prize money'. This outburst was prompted by a decision to appeal a judgment which had gone in Collingwood's favour at first instance in the King's bench division, which meant that payment of the sum awarded as prize money, £5,000, for a share of a capture made by Duckworth when away from his station, but, according to the judgment, whilst still under Collingwood's command, would be further delayed until the appeal had been heard, and, hopefully, dismissed, as, in due course, it was.

In fact, although the payout on Digby's capture had been speedy, for the treasure had come in cash or bullion and was therefore already in a liquidated form, this payment was to be the subject of an action in the Court of King's Bench Common Pleas between Lord Nelson and Lord St Vincent three years on. St Vincent's secretary, Tucker, as his agent for the prizes taken by the Mediterranean Fleet in October of 1799, acted on St Vincent's behalf as defendant in name only. It was an action to recover £13,000, a one-eighth share of the prizes which had been taken by Captain Digby when serving in St Vincent's Squadron, on the ground that St Vincent had left the station and returned to England to recover his health – and, as it happened, to meet the allegations levelled at him by Sir John Orde. In his absence Nelson had held the command and so claimed the share of the prize money due to the commander in post which St Vincent had refused to disgorge. Judgment was given for St Vincent both in the court below, and, on appeal, by the judges of the Common Pleas who found that a flag officer returning home on account of his health ought not to be considered as having abdicated his command. But upon writ of error to the Court of King's Bench, Lord Chief Justice Ellenborough of Ellenborough in Cumberland, otherwise Edward Law, a son of the Bishop of Carlisle, delivered a judgment on 14 November 1803 which reversed the earlier decision and found for Nelson upon the ground that the moment a superior officer left his station, the rights of the flag officer commanding devolved upon he who then had conduct of the fleet. Accordingly it was held that Nelson was entitled to the commander's share in its entirety.[3] So much so that, ironically, the principle there established was to be used against Nelson himself, successfully, in the year following when he, in turn, claimed a commander's share of monies raised from prizes taken by Captain

140

Moore when serving with Sir John Orde's Squadron off Cadiz in 1804, at a time when Nelson was supposedly travelling home on a leave which he did not then in fact take.[4]

The naval historian Richard Hill, in his valuable work, *The Prizes of War*, calculated that such was Digby's activity on the high seas when commanding the frigates *Aurora* and *Alcmene* in the eastern Atlantic in the years 1797 and 1798, that no less than fifty vessels were taken by him in the space of twenty-one months, thirty-nine of which were Spanish.

The adventurous Captain Henry Digby was the son of William Digby, Dean of Durham from 1777 to 1788, younger brother of Edward, 6th Baron Digby of Geashill in the Irish peerage, and also younger brother of Henry, 7th Baron Digby of Geasehill, the politician who became a Lord of the Admiralty and for whom the title Baron Digby of Sherborne in the UK peerage was created. Captain Digby was also a nephew of Admiral Robert Digby, one of his father's older brothers, and he was to serve with distinction at Trafalgar. He died at the age of seventy-two in 1842, as Admiral Sir Henry Digby GCB. A memorial to his memory is to be found in the little church at Minterne Magna.

On the later death of the 7th Baron's unmarried son in 1856, Sir Henry's son succeeded to the title of his nephew, Baron Digby of Geashill, as the 9th Baron, and also to that of Baron Digby of Sherborne since this had been created for the 7th Baron Digby of Geashill with special remainder, failing male issue of his own, to male issue of his father, but a further title, that of Earl Digby and Viscount Coleshill which had been created in the year 1790 for the 7th Baron, died with the 7th Baron's son.

It is not clear quite how the riches made at sea by Sir Henry were applied, although Hill, in *The Prizes of War* is right to assert that the Digby home at Minterne Magna near Cerne Abbas owes much to the prize money won by naval officer members of the Digby family. But strictly, and sadly, it no longer stands as a memorial to Sir Henry's career for it was demolished in the year 1902 when extensive dry rot was discovered[5] and the present house was built in its place. In fact the estate and earlier house had been purchased because of its very dilapidated condition for a modest sum by Sir Henry's uncle, Admiral Robert Digby, in 1768, from the executors of General Charles Churchill, brother of the 1st Duke of Marlborough, who had inherited it from their father, Sir Winston Churchill. Charles had died there in 1714, without legitimate issue, but his executors had then done little to halt the decline. But the location was convenient, for the Admiral's paternal family lived nearby at Sherborne Castle which the Digbys had been allowed to purchase after the fall of Sir Walter Raleigh, despite the execution of Sir Everard

Digby for complicity in the Guy Fawkes conspiracy to blow up both the King and Parliament at the State Opening of 1605. And certain it is that much of Admiral Robert Digby's seagoing wealth was then lavished on the renovation and restoration of the original house and its grounds, no doubt augmented after his marriage in 1784 by contributions from his wife, the daughter of the wealthy Governor of New York whom he had met when serving as the commander of the North American station during the American War of Independence. The design of the present house, which copies that of the house demolished, and the layout of its delightful gardens, woodland valley walk and nearby lake, therefore owe much to the work and investment of Admiral Robert Digby. Indeed Lord Digby tells me that many of the curved garden and outbuilding walls owe their shape to the Admiral's devotion to ship curvature. And when he died in 1815, he died without issue, leaving the house and estate to his by then very affluent nephew, Admiral Sir Henry Digby, then living at Foston House. But it is not clear to what extent Sir Henry's riches were then applied to the maintenance and further development of Minterne, for Robert's wife lived on there until her death in 1830, and there were without doubt other calls on his income and wealth. Indeed the dalliances of his only daughter were in the course of time to cost his branch of the family much of the land which had been held by the 7th and 8th Barons Digby.

Sir Henry had, after Trafalgar, married the widow of the Viscount Andover, a daughter of Thomas Coke of Holkham Hall, later 1st Earl of Leicester and a descendant of the great Lord Chief Justice. One of their offspring was Jane, a beautiful, endearing, devoted but equally adventurous daughter who married the son of the same Lord Chief Justice Ellenborough, a man twice her age. A remote connection with the Navy was there, for Lord Ellenborough, as Edward Law, had also married the daughter of a naval officer, one Captain George Philip Lowry of Shipley in the County of Northumberland,[6] and his son, Jane's husband, a somewhat unpopular politician, was in due time to become First Lord of The Admiralty. It was a second marriage for the second Lord Ellenborough and it was doomed to fail. Indeed it ended dramatically and in scandal six years later with the celebrated and much-reported Ellenborough divorce case of 1830. But to the everlasting credit of Sir Henry he showed the same loyalty and devotion to his daughter as he had shown in his years of service to those men who had come under his command, at a time when the 8th Lord Digby and his family, the Cokes of Holkham Hall and, indeed all English society, turned their backs on her. And he stood by her not just at that difficult time but throughout her notorious affair with the co-respondent, Prince Felix Schwarzenberg, who was to become Chief Minister in Austria. It

142

was so, all through her other much publicized adulterous affairs and second marriage, although Sir Henry was to die before she had embarked on her final and most successful betrothal to Sheikh Medjuel al Mazrab. But even then he had made provision for her in his will, no doubt drawing on the fortune he had made from prize money won while serving on the high seas. But, because of the divorce case back in 1830 and the unwelcome publicity it had attracted, much of the land held in Dorset and Somerset passed to the son of the unmarried 8th Baron's sister, one George Wingfield-Baker, afterwards Wingfield-Digby, whose younger brother inherited in like manner the Coleshill estate in Warwickshire. Thus was the bulk of the land held detached from the title inherited by Sir Henry's son, leaving him with little more than 2,000 acres.

But the gardens and grounds and the present house, albeit rebuilt, do indeed stand as a lasting monument to the energy and efficiency of those two very successful naval commanders. And it is a legacy carefully maintained and lovingly preserved by its present owners.

The tradition of military and naval service continued through the years, for one Digby grandson of Henry Digby was to serve as a captain in the Royal Navy and to marry a daughter of Lord Ravensworth of Ravensworth in North Durham and of Eslington in Northumberland, a second cousin of the Alice Liddell of Ravensworth immortalized as *Alice in Wonderland* by the Reverend Charles Dodgson, writing as Lewis Carroll. Then a great grandson served with distinction as an officer in the Royal Artillery in the First World War, and the present Lord Digby's father served throughout the First World War as an officer in the Coldstream Guards, as did the present Lord Digby during and after the Second World War. A Lord Lieutenant of Dorset County and KCVO, he married Lady (Dione) Digby, now DBE for services to the arts, a daughter of Rear-Admiral Robert St Vincent Sherbrooke who had won a Victoria Cross for conspicuous bravery when on the Arctic Run in 1942.

And so the habit of military service has continued through the generations.

Tom G.A.Bowles, barrister-at-law and proprietor of the *Lady* magazine, helpfully brought to my notice two works of interest which were published in the early part of the last century. One, by his father, George Bowles, one-time naval officer, Member of Parliament and former proprietor of the *Lady* magazine, is aptly entitled *The Strength of England*, for it argues with clarity and force the importance to the nation in those now far-off days, of a strong naval presence. The other, *Sea Law and Sea Power* published in 1910, was one of three books written by his very energetic, extrovert and certainly most unusual grandfather, Thomas Gibson Bowles, founder and one-time editor and proprietor of *Vanity Fair*, the satirical magazine made famous by the spy cartoon caricatures it carried, the work of Sir Leslie Ward. Indeed Bowles, a close friend of the Reverend Charles Dodgson, was to be the subject of a spy cartoon himself in the 19 October 1905 issue of the magazine, sixteen years after he had sold it on. However, although founder and owner too of the *Lady* magazine, which survives to this day, and although perhaps better remembered now as the father of Sydney Bowles, wife of the second Baron Redesdale of Redesdale in Northumberland and mother of the Mitford sisters, his real, lifelong and more serious interest lay with ships and the sea, so much so that when thirty-three years of age in 1874, and shortly before his wife died, he troubled to study for and obtain a Master Mariner's Certificate and became something of an authority on maritime law. Indeed it was he, as a backbench MP and almost single-handed, who had persuaded the House of Lords to prevent the dangerous Naval Prize Bill of 1911 from becoming law at a time of growing national emergency in the years leading up to the First World War, in which both of his sons were to serve as naval officers. His book was written for that very purpose. Had the Bill passed into law it would have given Germany and the other major European nations the menacing power to override on appeal all prize law decisions made in London. For his efforts he was thanked publicly by Admiral of the Fleet, Sir Hedworth Meux, a younger son of the second Earl of Durham, and again at a dinner held in his honour over which his old friend Admiral Lord Charles Beresford presided. Known by *Punch* as Captain Tommy Bowles and often portrayed in that magazine in pirate dress, it was therefore no more than fitting when he died in 1922 while on holiday in Algeciras that the Navy should have come to the rescue, for the admiral commanding the Gibraltar station sent his barge over to bring the body back to Gibraltar where Bowles now lies buried.[7] And it brought forth from another naval officer, King George V, a letter of condolences, written to his elder son George Bowles at the King's request by his secretary, Lord Stamfordham of Stamfordham in Northumberland. It read:

> I write by order of the King to say with what regret His Majesty heard of the death of your father and to express His Majesty's true sympathy in your loss. The King fully appreciates the services rendered to the country by Mr Bowles during his long public career.[8]

Whether Winston S. Churchill wrote as well is not known, although he did pay tribute to Bowles ten years later in his book, *My Early Life*, as a fellow member who had thrown a lifeline to him in the House of Commons moments before he had risen to make his maiden speech. This had taken the form of a quip provided by Bowles which had enabled Churchill to deal effectively with a sudden and unexpected turn taken by the member who had spoken immediately before, one David Lloyd George, which had unnerved the young Churchill.

The judgment of Bowles in *Sea Law and Sea Power* had been that:

> The Prize Courts...were trustworthy. They constantly decided against the wishes of their own Governments, or the interests of their fellow-subjects; they were on the whole more just and impartial than any municipal courts administering municipal law.

Although written in the early twentieth century, there can be no doubt but that much of the credit for this must lie with the Newcastle-born Admiralty Judge, Lord Stowell, one-time school contemporary of Collingwood and already discussed, for he had presided over that court with such enormous distinction over very many years during what was perhaps the busiest period of its life, and it was he who had first won for the court such universal respect.

For his part Collingwood seems to have profited very little from prize money. Quite why that was so is difficult to know for it could never be said that he was ever wanting in his pursuit of the enemy, and his declared disinterest in money or riches, even if genuine, could hardly have led him to allow hostile warships or merchantmen to pass by unmolested. And even if that had been so, as a flag officer he must still have shared in the success of others, albeit the lion's share would go to the captains of those ships directly involved in a capture. However, the flag officers who must have profited most must have been those who held that rank on active service longest during the great harvest of the war years from 1793 to 1815, and it is to be noted that Collingwood stood in that rank for no more than eleven of those years. Yet at his death he was to leave an estate valued at £163,743 exclusive of an interest he held in two estates which had come to him by marriage and by legacy,[9] so that it is more than possible that this had been accumulated in part from money obtained from prizes.

But service for most officers in the Royal Navy in the years 1799 to 1805 meant blockade duty. It was a strategy to keep the French Fleet in harbour and also to deprive their nation of much-needed supplies. It was dull and monotonous work which tried and tested the most patient and long-suffering of men. And it continued relentlessly, week after week, month after month, year after year. The constant hope was for action or shore leave. But there was little opportunity for either. It meant too that there was little in the way of contact or fraternization between the officers and men of ships in a squadron, Collingwood and Nelson not excepted. These were tedious duties but they were of vital importance. As the naval historian Mahan so well described it in a much quoted and famous passage:

> Far away, Cornwallis off Brest, Collingwood off Rochefort, Pellew off Ferol...in that tremendous and sustained vigilance which reached its utmost in the years preceding Trafalgar, concerning which Collingwood wrote that admirals need to be made of iron...Further distant still...Nelson before Toulon....
>
> They were dull, weary, eventless months, those months of watching and waiting...Purposeless they surely seemed to many, but they saved England. The world has never seen a more impressive demonstration of the influence of sea power upon its history. Those far distant, storm-beaten ships, upon which the Grand Army never looked, stood between it and the dominion of the world.

Of his blockade duties, Collingwood who, after almost twelve years of it, had probably had more experience of blockading than any other officer in the navy, was later to write to Blackett from the *Dreadnought* on 4 February 1805 when off Ushant: 'Their idea is that we are like sentinels standing at a door, who must see and may intercept all who attempt to go into it.'

Lord Howe, too, was a harsh critic of the efficacy of blockading tactics, arguing that the elements took a severe toll of ships kept at sea in all weathers and all the year round while, at the same time, sapping the morale of those employed in manning them, and in the outcome very little in his judgment was achieved. He maintained that the Channel Fleet could as easily be harboured at strategic points ready to sail should an emergency arise. And it may be that a more agreeable tactic would have been to deploy frigates to watch the French while maintaining the men-of-war at base close to their supplies and sheltered from the elements yet ready to sail at a moment's notice. But the lesson of later events would seem to support the tactic of blockade, for not only did it restrict the flow of supplies to the French nation by sea, it prevented also the invasion force mounted by Bonaparte from ever crossing the Channel. And when the French did eventually put to sea such was their inexperience after years of inactivity dictated by the blockade, that they were no match for the disciplined, practised and experienced sailors of the British Royal Navy.

And so the contribution made by the blockade to eventual victory was as significant as any of the three great sea battles fought off the coasts of France and Spain.

Collingwood's birthplace on The Side, Newcastle upon Tyne. *Drawn by C.J. Spence.*

Entrance to Collingwood's school in the eighteenth century, drawn by T.M. Richardson senior. *From the author's collection.*

Chapel/hall of Collingwood's school 198
By permission of Taylor and Francis Books,
Professor Anthony Tuck and Dr Brian Mains

Sir William Scott, later Lord Stowell, an
outstanding Admiralty Judge, a great
intellect and a school contemporary of
Collingwood. *From the author's collection.*

John Scott, Lord Eldon, longstanding Lord Chancellor to both George III and George IV, High Steward of Oxford University and a school contemporary of Collingwood. *From the author's collection.*

Nelson by Collingwood. Drawn on the same occasion. Nelson is wearing a wig to cover his head which had been shaved following a bout of fever.
By permission of the National Maritime Museum.

Collingwood by Nelson. Drawn in 1784 at Windsor, Mrs Moutray's house at English Harbour, Antigua, and treasured by her. Collingwood was then a lieutenant.
By permission of the National Maritime Museum.

English Harbour, Antigua, from Great George Fort, Monks Hill by Johnson, published in 1817.
By permission of the National Maritime Museum.

Admiral Sir Peter Parker Bt, who was something of a father to Nelson and Collingwood in their early years of service in the West Indies.
By permission of the National Maritime Museum.

The Duke of Clarence (Prince
William Henry) serving as a
midshipman. He served with Nelson
and Collingwood in the West Indies.
*By permission of the National Maritime
Museum.*

Collingwood's wife and children
in 1800, artist unknown.

Collingwood's father-in-law, John Erasmus Blackett, at one time Mayor of Newcastle upon Tyne, to whom Collingwood often wrote when at sea. *By permission of Sir Hugh Blackett Bt.*

Collingwood's mother-in-law, Sarah Blackett, daughter of Robert Roddam. She had been dead for sixteen years when Collingwood married her daughter in 1791. *By permission of Sir Hugh Blackett Bt.*

The tallest house in the middle distance was Collingwood's house in Oldgate, Morpeth, in 1791. Pictured today, the road has changed very little since then. *Photograph in the author's possession.*

Admiral Richard, 1st Earl Howe, known as 'Black Dick', in Admiral's dress uniform showing three cuff rings of an Admiral, 1795. He comanded the fleet at the Battle of the Glorious First of June, 1794. By Henry Robinson after Thomas Gainsborough. *From the author's collection.*

Admiral Sir Roger Curtis when younger. He was Howe's First or Fleet Captain at the Battle of the Glorious First of June, 1794.
From the author's collection.

Double shot which nearly hit Collingwood at the Battle of Cape St Vincent, 1797, and was brought home as a memento. *By permission of Sir Hugh Blackett Bt.*

Admiral John Jervis, created Earl St Vincent after the Battle of St Vincent, from an engraving by Richard Cooper in 1809 after William Evans and Sir William Beechey.
From the author's collection.

Vice-Admiral Sir William Parker Bt in 1801, who was critical of Nelson after the 1797 battle.
From the author's collection.

Admiral Sir John Orde Bt. A mezzotint engraved by Samuel William Reynolds from a portrait by George Romney in 1811. He wears the uniform of a full Admiral with three stars on the epaulettes.
From the author's collection.

George John Spencer, 2nd Earl Spencer, who was First Lord of the Admiralty during much of the naval war with France. Engraving after J.S. Copley.
From the author's collection.

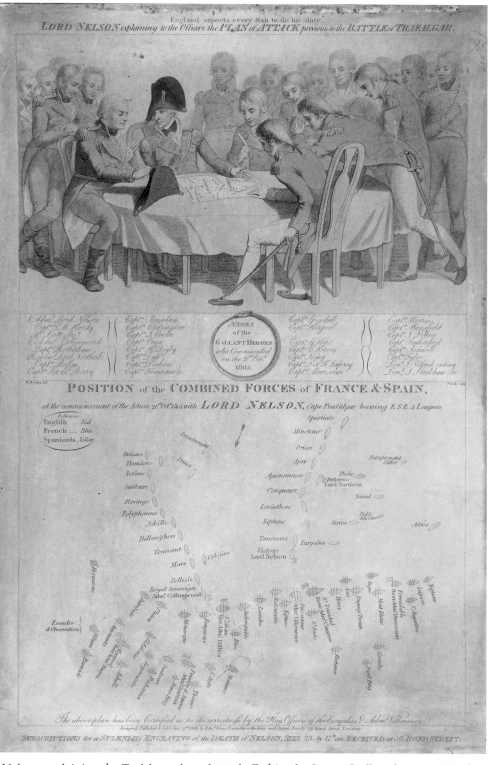

Nelson explaining the Trafalgar plan of attack. Etching by James Godby after an original by William Marshall Craig and published by Edward Orme on the day of Nelson's funeral. *By permission of the National Maritime Museum*

Nelson at prayer before Trafalgar by T.J. Barker from an engraving by F. Jouberi, 1854.

From the author's collectio

Battle of Trafalgar. 'Collingwood in the *Royal Sovereign* breaking the enemy line' by Eduardo de Martino. *By permission of the National Maritime Museum*

Hugh Percy, 2nd Duke of Northumberland, with whom Collingwood conducted an active correspondence in his final years. Drawn by H. Brown, engraved by W. Grainger, 1891. *From the author's collection.*

Collingwood's tomb in the foreground, in the shadow of Nelson tomb at St Paul's Cathedral. As in life so in death. *Photograph in the author's possession, reproduced by permission of the Registrar of St Paul's Cathedral.*

Statue of Collingwood at Tynemouth. The work of Northumbrian sculptor John Graham Lough, then living in London, it was shipped up in thirteen pieces and set in a monument designed by the celebrated architect, John Dobson. Unveiled in 1845, four 35-pounder guns salvaged from the *Royal Sovereign* were later placed around the plinth in 1848. *Photograph in the author's possession.*

Collingwood by J. Lonsdale. Painted in 1812 when it was presented to the Mayor and Corporation of Newcastle upon Tyne by the Newcastle Volunteers. It now hangs in the Laing Art Gallery. Portrayed in the regulation dress uniform of a Vice-Admiral, wearing the First of June, St Vincent and Trafalgar Gold Medals. *From the author's collection and by permission of Tyne and Wear Museums.*

The irony was that soon after Collingwood's move from the Mediterranean to the Channel Fleet, Lord Bridport resigned his command in April 1800 and was succeeded by a Lord St Vincent now fully restored to health. This meant that the harsh discipline he had imposed on the Mediterranean Fleet was soon transferred to the Channel Fleet and the same unease and unhappiness this had generated amongst the officers and men in the Mediterranean, followed in its wake. With obsessive but ill-founded fears of mutiny ever in his mind, fraternization was all but outlawed, an embargo was placed on unnecessary ship visits, shore leave in nearby England was drastically curtailed, and senseless duties were devised and to be observed on pain of condign punishment. Of this Collingwood was to write privately to his father-in-law, the letter already quoted:

> I see disgust growing round me very fast...deprivation of everything like comfort...[yet] no exercise of the military part of the duty, no practice of those movements by a facility in which one fleet is made superior to another...

Collingwood was in favour of a much more humane enforcement of discipline although, without doubt, there was need at that time for a stricter regime in the Channel Fleet, for things had been allowed to drift too far under the more relaxed command of Lord Bridport. Indeed Nelson was to write to St Vincent at the turn of the year, which marked the onset of the new century:

> I see much slackness that in the Mediterranean I have not been used to; and it requires a man of our friend Collingwood's firmness to keep some of them to their duty.[10]

Indeed Collingwood himself wrote several letters home complaining of the terrible inexperience, ignorance and inefficiency of many of those who had now swelled the numbers serving in the navy in these dangerous times. It clearly irritated him, and he even described his own Flag Captain on the *Triumph* as incompetent.

A transfer back to his old ship the *Barfleur* was therefore welcomed. This occurred in the spring of 1800 and it took him to Irish waters for a time, although he was to report home that he there found the contingent of Newcastle boys allocated to his command, disappointing in their enthusiasm for the work to be done.

It is clear that by the turn of the year the sure monotony of the blockade coupled with the need for constant vigilance had begun to undermine his health and wellbeing for he wrote then to one of his sisters complaining of 'weak nerves', reporting that:

147

I have been very poorly lately, weak in the greatest degree, and never sleep at nights. The only time I am free of this weight, this oppressive something, as if I bore a mountain on my shoulders, is the few hours that I am dispatching my business and at that time I know no ill, all is brisk with me then.

However he seems to have found that wearing a warm flannel waistcoat was the cure for many of his ills and despite his own problems he still took active steps to improve the lot of those less fortunate sailors condemned to occupy the lower decks by installing a ventilation flue to evacuate stale air. This produced a significant improvement in the health of the ship's company, so much so that it was recognized and credited by the Surgeon to the Fleet, Doctor Thomas Trotter, who wrote it up in his *Medicina Nautica* a few years later.[11] A great admirer of Collingwood, he later set up in successful practice in the city of Newcastle upon Tyne. During many long months at sea on blockade duty it was ever Collingwood's concern to promote the health of every member of his crew, and in this endeavour he was largely successful.

It was in September of 1800 that Nelson and his entourage made a long journey home which took them to many of Europe's major towns including Trieste, Vienna, Prague, Dresden and Hamburg, from which they sailed for Yarmouth. Joseph Haydn had recently returned to Vienna after his triumphant second tour of London. and had returned to his old position as Kapelmeister to the opulent and magnificent Esterhazy family at Eisenstadt with new patrons in Prince Nicholaus Esterhazy II and his wife Princess Martia Hermenegild.

Nelson's original intention had been to return from Naples direct to England for well-earned rest, recuperation, and no doubt adulation, taking with him Sir William and Lady Hamilton, who dwarfed Nelson with her height, generous proportions and theatrical flamboyance. But the insistence of some that they should return overland had persuaded him to accompany their friend, the Queen of Naples, Maria Carolina, sister of Marie Antoinette and grandmother of Marie-Louise, who was later to marry Napoleon Bonaparte, on a visit she had planned to Vienna to see her paternal Austrian Imperial family at the Schönbrunn Palace.

They set out on 1 August and, in Trieste and at all points on the journey to Vienna, the one-armed Nelson was greeted as a hero and a saviour and, once installed at an inn in Vienna close to the Esterhazy town palace, he was feted and surrounded by enthusiastic crowds whenever and wherever he ventured forth. There his friend Sir Gilbert Elliott, by then Lord Minto and at that time Envoy and Minister Plenipotentiary at the Court of Vienna, took the party under his wing.

Copies of an engraving of Daniel Orme's portrait of Nelson went on general sale, the composer Johann Wanhal composed a piano sonata with the title, The Great Sea-Battle of Aboukir, a Nelson fashion in clothing was hurried out, his portrait was painted by Fuger, banquets were held in his honour and visits were made to a small house near to the Hungarian Esterhazy Court at Eisenstadt where the great composer Joseph Haydn lived. There Haydn made a firm friend of Lady Hamilton.

Haydn had composed six uplifting masses to be performed in Church to commemorate Princess Martia's name days and the third of these, the *Missa in Augustiis*, or mass for times of distress, had been written in August of 1798. A mass in D minor, it had been so named because at that time it seemed to all that the French invader was everywhere triumphant. However, before the work was completed and certainly before it had ever achieved its first performance, that anxiety had abated more than a little with the news that Nelson had brought the French to battle at Aboukir Bay and had there destroyed them. It is therefore thought probable by one historian that the chorus of exultation at the end of the *Benedictus* was composed in a mood of euphoria generated by the news of that victory. And so it was that this work later came to be known in Austria and Germany as *The Nelson Mass*, although in truth the work had already been performed in Vienna almost two years before Nelson arrived there in 1800. But it is more than possible that it was then performed in his honour at the Esterhazy Palace, for much music was played under Haydn's direction during the four days of their stay. However, one eminent historian[12] who has researched the occasion in some detail considers that doubtful, although no programme survives which could identify what work was in fact in the programme for that performance.

As for Collingwood, although advanced to the rank of Rear-Admiral of the Red on New Year's day 1801 in a general promotion of flag officers to mark the Act of Union between Great Britain and Ireland, he wrote to his wife's uncle complaining that his: 'domestic comforts of life had been very much interrupted'. This he attributed to the method of command imposed on the Channel Fleet by Lord St Vincent. 'We are rather under disagreeable circumstances at the moment', he wrote.

Yet, although these times were difficult and demanding, Nelson and Collingwood still contrived to meet again as old and trusted friends, as they did in January 1801 while both were on shore waiting the order to put to sea; Nelson at Spithead and Collingwood at Plymouth. The one-armed Nelson, although not disfigured despite the myth that he wore an eye patch, had but little sight in one eye. But he was now a peer of the realm and the nation's hero on his way to the Battle of Copenhagen as second in command to Sir Hyde Parker. But all was not well for he had only very recently abandoned his wife in favour of Lady Hamilton who was pregnant with his child and several in society now condemned and shunned him for it. Indeed, in a letter to Blackett dated 25 January, Collingwood had written that:

> He gave me an account of his reception at Court, which was not very flattering, after having been the admiration of that of Naples. His Majesty merely asked him if he had recovered his health, and then, without waiting for an answer, turned to General – ,and talked to him near half an hour in great good humour. It could not have been about *his* successes.

It was an act of pettiness by a King apparently less than grateful to a commander who had served up a brilliant victory for his King and country at the Battle of the Nile. But then the King was at this stage of his life prone to bouts of passing insanity and given to erratic behaviour. And his son, the Duke of Clarence, known to be a friend of Nelson's, was also out of his favour at that moment and the explanation for his offhand treatment of Nelson may have lain in that. But one who did worship Nelson's achievements was the Irish curate, Patrick Prunty, who took the surname Bronte when Nelson received the Sicilian Dukedom of Bronte from the Naples Royal House. Prunty later fathered the three Bronte sisters. And while in the west country, the citizens of Plymouth, a town he professed to hate, granted him the freedom of the city.

But there was no such complication in Collingwood's domestic arrangements. Indeed it had been Collingwood's hope at this very time that his wife and elder daughter would make the long trip from Northumberland to be with him before he set sail on his next mission, if only for a few hours.

On 27 January, when visiting St Vincent at Tor Abbey near Plymouth, Nelson invited Collingwood to dine with him. There had been no word of Sarah's arrival, and so, at 7 p.m., the two friends sat down to dinner without them. But then soon afterwards word came that his wife and eight year old daughter Sarah had arrived at the Fountain Inn in the town, and so there the four of them came together and spent a most enjoyable and happy evening in the company of each other. Tragically the meeting was all too short for Collingwood was recalled to duty and had to leave at dawn. He was to write afterwards to his father-in-law: 'No greater happiness is human nature capable of than was mine that evening', and to Mrs Moutray, the friend of both Nelson and Collingwood, he wrote: 'How surprised you would have been to have popped into the Fountain Inn and seen Lord Nelson, my wife, and myself sitting by the fireside cosing, and little Sarah teaching Phillis, her dog, to dance.'

Collingwood's recall to duty had been prompted by an escape of French vessels from the port of Brest and an order that Sir Robert Calder should follow in pursuit, for Collingwood had been required to take over Calder's vigil at Torbay. It led Nelson to write, in a letter to Sarah Collingwood dated 8 February: 'I own I should have sent my friend after the French Squadron because I think him much fitter than the one sent, and I do not believe there are two opinions on the subject. Hoping you may soon see my dear friend.'

Two months later, the brevity of their meeting was still in the forefront of Collingwood's mind when he wrote to his father-in-law:

> ...how short our interview, and how suddenly we parted. It is grief to me to think of it now; it almost broke my heart then...no time to tell her half what my heart felt at such a proof of her affection! But I am thankful I did see her and my sweet child.

And then a month later:

> I can still talk to you of nothing but the delight I experienced in the little I have had of the company of my beloved wife and of my little Sarah. What comfort is promised to me in the affections of that child, if it should please God that we ever again return to the quiet domestic cares of peace!

A journey from Northumberland to Plymouth in those far off days was indeed an act of wifely devotion when undertaken for the sake of but a few hours with a husband. And it did not end there for she and her daughter stayed on in lodgings in Plymouth at 58 St George Street[13] through all the spring and summer months on the off chance that her husband might be granted further time ashore. Indeed Nelson, a true friend, had brought the situation to the notice of Lord St Vincent in a letter dated 28 January[14] and St Vincent, appreciating that Collingwood's home was very far distant, had then promised Collingwood that he would be allowed to visit Plymouth whenever he could be spared.

To her uncle Sarah was to write on 15 February how cold she found it in Plymouth compared with the north, reporting that:

> The weather here is very severe, I never suffered so much from cold...I have the satisfaction of knowing how much my husband is respected here by the very great kindness and attention that everyone shows me...at present I fancy I am to remain here, or in the neighbourhood of Torbay, for some time, as it is the only chance I can have of seeing my husband.

But it was not to be, for the French were preparing to put to sea and Collingwood was kept off Ushant throughout February and well into March.

Change was on the way which relaxed Collingwood's routine a little and allowed him to come on shore, for Pitt's government fell and Addington came to office, bringing with him St Vincent as First Lord of the Admiralty, to the relief of many in the Channel Fleet. But it seems to have been an appointment of which Collingwood approved despite all that had gone before. Admiral Cornwallis now took over command of the Channel Fleet, taking up his appointment on 21 February and Collingwood was able to move a little more freely and was able to spend more time with his beloved wife and daughter. Indeed on one occasion both went on board the *Barfleur* at Collingwood's invitation. But it was not a success given the storm which blew up which caused both to be very ill. The experiment was never to be repeated although it had at least given his wife some insight into the conditions her husband was required to endure day after day when on the high seas.

Collingwood was much concerned at this time at the effect which the coastal winds were having on his daughter's eyes which were often irritated and inflamed, so much so that he called in Dr Trotter, the Surgeon to the Fleet.

But good news reached him in April when reports of the great victory off Copenhagen filtered through. Such was Collingwood's joy for his friend Nelson when he heard the news, that he promptly wrote to his father-in-law asking that he send his gardener Scott: 'a guinea for me, for these hard times must pinch the poor old man, and he will miss my wife, who was very kind to him'.

From Plymouth the two Sarahs moved on to Paignton at Collingwood's suggestion in the hope that the winds might drive his ship to anchor off Torbay so that he could see a little more of them. But the elements were against him and so, towards the end of August, when off the port of Brest, he advised that they move back to the quarters they had occupied in Plymouth. This they did, which enabled Collingwood to join them for several more days during September and October before they went back to their beloved Northumberland. But not before news of the Peace of Amiens, and some prospect of respite from his labours, filtered through. In the meantime he was required to serve in January as a member of the Court in Portsmouth which tried the *Temeraire* mutineers who had refused to obey an order to sail for the West Indies, and it was not until 7 May 1802 that he was able to strike his flag and leave for home, the very last officer to do so.

He had before then, in January, sent his heavy luggage on ahead by collier, together with his beloved dog Bounce amongst the valuables.

They were never again to be parted during the dog's lifetime.

Collingwood now made his own way home, staying on the way at Egham with Sir Edward Blackett and then for a short time in London before leaving finally for Morpeth and his family. Once there he set about improving his property. By letter to Dr Carlyle in August he reported that:

> We have been jaunting about a good deal which has wearied Sarah, and she has become languid and relaxed, so that the sea bathing, she thinks, is quite necessary to set her up before the winter pinches her, and in about ten days we go down to Newbiggin...I have been very busy with the ground about our house, very much to its improvement. The old cottages that were opposite to us are removed, not a vestige of them left. In their place is a low parapet wall, with iron rails on it which opens our view to what will be a very pretty little field, at the end of which is the river and the high banks covered with wood.

Now, 200 years on, the house continues to stand in more or less its original state, although now no more than a house in a built up street of houses and surrounded by buildings on all sides. But it does of course enjoy the same location close to the lush and well wooded banks of the River Wansbeck where a bridge crosses the river. And the house across the road from Collingwood's house, with its mullioned windows and gardens running along the banks of the river towards the bend which leads to the castle, was until recent times still in the possession of the descendants of the Matheson family who were in residence when Collingwood lived there, and who were in large part responsible for the tree planting on either side of the river on the Postern Walk, much of it at Collingwood's instigation. Lord Elliott of Morpeth tells me that the Matheson family known to him, two grandsons of the Matheson neighbour of Collingwood, inherited and treasured a heavily port stained dress waistcoat of Collingwood's which they preserved in a glass case in their home.. Sadly many of the oaks were felled in later years by the descendants of Matheson to make way for a nursery market garden, and the 'quarterdeck' established by Collingwood in his garden survived but a short time. Even the house was divided later to allow for occupation by the Roman Catholic Church in one part and by a political club in the other. A plain and modest home for one of his rank, it was nevertheless a house dear to Collingwood as the only house he ever lived in apart from his parental home and a few temporary billets in the Mediterranean where he stayed on those rare occasions when he stepped on shore.

As ever he turned his mind to the education of his two daughters in the hope of persuading them that good manners, good works and charitable giving were of greater value than fashion, entertainment and the usual pleasures of life. These, he advised, would bring them much greater satisfaction and peace of mind than anything else could possibly do. The Puritan in him urged them to apply themselves to their studies.

But, however comfortable he was to be at home, Collingwood at the early age of fifty-four had begun to feel the twinges of old age after a lifetime spent at sea exposed to the elements. In a letter to Carlyle he complained of short-sightedness, and in a letter to his sister, of rheumatism in the legs, whilst at the same time his wife reported to his sister that he had suffered an attack of a nature not identified but violent enough for her to let his sister know of it.

His recall to the colours was never too far away for the Treaty of Amiens, which had been negotiated in the autumn of 1801 and then ratified in spring 1802, had clearly been no more than a temporary device to allow the French to recover and regroup. Addington had really come into office on a ticket of peace with the strong support of the merchants of the City of London who were more than anxious to re-establish their trade routes across the world, while the nation itself stood exhausted after eight years of war. His policy had, therefore, been one of peace at almost any price. But it was a peace won at a considerable price and it was obvious to all that it would only hold as long as it took the French to re-build their naval resources to a level which would enable them to compete more effectively at sea. It was a truce rather than a peace, and it gave the French a breathing space in their preparations for war. But the respite had at least allowed Nelson time enough to journey with the Hamiltons on their celebrated tour of the Midlands and the borders of Wales about which so much has been written. It enabled too, hard pressed officers such as Collingwood to pause and take breath and enjoy the comforts of home before war came again which it did on 16 March 1803 after the non-observance of so many of the treaty obligations.

In the meantime the French had used the lull profitably to rebuild and reorganize their navy and military, whereas, in Great Britain, Lord St Vincent had dismantled the dockyards in a personal war on corruption and had laid up many a warship on the altar of economy. British tourists, oblivious to the danger, roamed the streets of Paris in a freedom which they were later to discover was all too temporary. In the outcome many were caught off guard and interned as enemy aliens and, not surprisingly, the resumption of hostilities found Great Britain dangerously exposed to the French invader.

It was by letter dated 13 March that Collingwood told Dr Carlyle that

154

he had received a letter from the Secretary of the Admiralty, Sir Evan Nepean, asking if he was ready to return to the colours at very short notice. Collingwood wrote that he had confirmed that he was and that he had: 'packed up my trunk and my signal book and am now waiting for a summons to take my station wherever it may be'. The call to arms came, not immediately, but in May of that year. Then, without a moment's hesitation, he packed his bags, bade farewell to his wife and two young daughters and left home for Portsmouth and the waters of the Channel in the service of his country, taking with him his dog Bounce. He was never to set foot in England or see his home or family again.

Once at Portsmouth, Collingwood raised his flag in the frigate *Diamond* and took command of the inshore squadron standing off Brest. There he found Cornwallis off Ushant rebuilding the blockade. His arrival drew from Cornwallis the comment: 'Here comes my old friend Coll, the last to leave and the first to join me'[15]

Collingwood had much admiration for the solid and reliable Cornwallis. Two months later Collingwood moved into a flagship which had been in preparation for him, the *Venerable*, a ship which had before then carried Duncan's flag at the Battle of Camperdown. But decay had since set in, possibly caused by sham devil-bolts used by master-builders as fastenings instead of bolts which were copper through and through. Such deception could be carried off by the use of wooden plugs to which were fixed copper heads and copper tails which hid the wooden body. It enabled builders to sell the copper salvaged, to marine dealers for their own enrichment. Indeed the ship went down one stormy night in November of 1804 while lying at anchor off Torbay with considerable loss of life. Fortunately Collingwood had before then, in December, shifted his flag to the *Culloden* when the rot had been discovered at Cawsand Bay where the ship had put in for running repairs. But it caused him to write: 'We have been sailing for the last six months with only a sheet of copper between us and eternity.'

At the same time there had been compensations while in the *Venerable* for he had, it seems, on this occasion, been well served by a contingent of volunteers sent to him from his native Newcastle upon Tyne. To his father-in-law he described them as 'stout young men and a great addition to my strength'.

So too while serving on the *Culloden* he had found an officer in whom he could repose great trust, one Lieutenant John Clavell, aged twenty-five, the son of a clergyman. So much so that he kept him with him thereafter whenever he moved ship. As a very experienced and professional sailor with probably a greater knowledge of navigation and gunnery than any ever placed under his command, Collingwood found

155

it difficult when raised to flag rank not to criticize those entrusted with the sailing and running of the ship. But this was not so with Clavell. In him he found not only a friend but also a very competent officer upon whom he could rely. And the trust he reposed in Clavell was never betrayed. Indeed on many occasions the two would sit together on deck all night long, keeping watch. Collingwood valued Clavell greatly, as he did one William Landless, a lieutenant from his native north-east. Both would follow Collingwood from ship to ship whenever that was possible.

Collingwood had seven more years of life ahead of him but he was never to return home or see his wife and daughters again, or indeed 'a green leaf on a tree'. Such was the service he gave to his country. It can seldom have been equalled.

Sir T. Byam Martin was to write in his journal:

The last time I ever saw Lord Collingwood, he was on the point of stepping into his boat, never again to touch the British shore. We walked together for half an hour, and as long as I live I shall remember the words with which, in his accustomed mildness of expression, he alluded to the sacrifices our professional duties exact of us. He told me the number of years he had been married, and the number of days he had been with his family since the war commenced (then of many years duration). My family are actually strangers to me. He was greatly overcome by the feelings thus excited, and, taking me by the hand, said, What a life of privation our's is – what an abandonment of everything to our professional duty, and how little do the people of England know the sacrifices we make for them! With this he turned from me to hide the tear which ran down his manly cheek, and, saying Farewell! Walked to the boat.

Had it pleased God to spare the life of this excellent man, he would have held one of the appointments in question – he too might have lived to hear that he was enjoying a sinecure! Shame! shame upon our country!

In helping the Channel Fleet to maintain the blockade as commander of the inshore squadron, Collingwood hoisted his flag in many another ship as the months went by. These were tedious duties but, as ever, they were of the greatest importance.

The danger which France now presented began to escalate, for Napoleon devoted much of the next two years preparing for the invasion of Great Britain. This he planned with meticulous care and at enormous expense for he was ever confident of the outcome given an army which far outnumbered that of Great Britain drawn as it was from not only the much more populated land of France but also from many other of the conquered nations. 'The Channel is but a ditch,' he said,' and anyone can cross it who has but the courage to try.'

A tornado of a man with colossal energy and a massive capacity for hard work, he could survive on very few hours of sleep. And since he was not a man who could easily put pen to paper, he kept about him twenty-four hours a day a coterie of subordinates who recorded, collated, transcribed and then implemented the flow of orders and directives which poured forth from his restless and very fertile mind as he paced his study, salon or bedroom by day and by night.

Most favoured of these was Alexander Berthier, one of the few who were to remain loyal to the end. As a military commander and a chief of staff he was quite outstanding. Indeed, to Napoleon he became indispensable. He was his eyes and ears. There can be no doubt that many of Napoleon's victories in Italy and Egypt owed much to the work of Berthier. He translated his orders into action, organized the movement of troops and the provision of supplies, collected and collated intelligence and, above all, established a network of communications which enabled Napoleon to remain in control of his Army at all times, knowing that his divisions would receive his every order expeditiously and in time to respond to every turn of the battle as it developed. It was to give him a telling advantage over his opponents. Indeed, as an administrator, Berthier was a model from whom many a staff officer has since learned. It was perhaps fortunate for the British that because of his untimely death he was not available to Napoleon at Waterloo.

In a similar role was Rear Admiral Denis Decres, Minister for Marine and the Colonies. He, too, burned the candle for Napoleon from early morning until late at night, and he did so for fourteen years or more. These three were to spend many hours pacing the shores of Northern France around Boulogne from which, it had eventually been decided, the invasion was to be launched. Napoleon's daily demands now generated feverish building activity in boatyards throughout all France. Yet at every turn during that year and into the next they were met by the Channel Fleet under the command of Admiral Sir William Cornwallis who mounted a comprehensive twenty-four hour blockade off Brest which also kept a close watch on those other ports on the Atlantic coastline at Boulogne, Flushing and Rochefort. At no time did he relax his hold. The Mediterranean Fleet meanwhile guarded the French Mediterranean ports in a less defensive role. In between the two fleets stood Gibraltar from which a similar watch was kept on Ferrol, Vigo and Cadiz. In the result the French Navy was effectively sealed in port and prevented from ever sailing. The overall aim was to prevent any gathering of French ships large enough to provide escort duties to cover a crossing by Napoleon's invasion flotilla of 2,000 or more flat-bottomed craft which had been built and assembled to carry the Army of England, later renamed the Grand Armée, across the waters of the English Channel. A junction with the Brest Fleet would have provided Napoleon with all the protection he needed for a crossing of the Channel. 'If we are Masters of the Channel for six hours we shall be Masters of the World,' was his boast, although this was variously extended to twenty-four hours and then several days. The blockade was tedious, painstaking, monotonous work. But it worked and it was the saviour of Great Britain at a perilous moment in her history.

Centrepiece of the French invasion flotilla was the peniche craft which was far too flimsy to be able to withstand the waters of the English Channel save on the calmest of days. Yet Napoleon persisted with it despite what must have been a most sobering experience in July 1804, when, it was hoped, the sea would be at its most docile. It was thus on a July day that he chose to conduct a dummy run in order to test and demonstrate the utility of his flotilla, despite almost gale conditions which blew up and despite also the long-distance pounding of British guns from the sloops *Harpy* and *Autumn* and from the brigs *Bloodhound* and *Archer*. His Minister of Marine pleaded with him to postpone the experiment but Napoleon insisted that some of these flat-bottomed craft put to sea. It ended in disaster with the loss of 400 lives.

Yet, nothing daunted, Napoleon pressed on with his plans for the invasion, no doubt encouraged by St Vincent's emasculation of the British Royal Navy in the name of economy and in the hope of purging the dockyards of the corruption which undoubtedly existed and which he certainly laid bare. But his cheeseparing and surgical excision had all but destroyed the service and had left its strength at a level which would make it difficult to repulse any serious attempt at invasion. Yet he chose to ignore the most urgent warnings and pleas of William Pitt from the opposition benches that the Admiralty should turn its policy about and embark on a crash programme of restocking to match that of the French, who were committed to an intensive national campaign of ship-building. There can be no doubt that, responsible as he was for the performance of not only the four Sea Lords, but also of the Civil Lords in their superintendence of dockyard construction and indeed of the Navy Board, through them he did much good work with his meticulous and thorough investigation of dockyard production which had indeed been riddled with dishonest practices. But all of this had done little to improve the nation's capacity to withstand the threat of invasion from across the Channel. And it seems that the growing allegations of neglect, spearheaded by William Pitt, together with a gathering hatred for St

Vincent generally, began to unbalance him and he would respond to any criticism with outspoken and even abusive language whenever William Pitt was involved, outraged that anyone should have the temerity to question the word and wisdom of the Lord St Vincent, the greatest seaman of his generation.

Matters came to a head in March 1804 when, against a mounting and imminent threat of invasion, Pitt delivered a blistering attack on the Addington government in general and on Lord St Vincent in particular, accusing him roundly of criminal neglect. Eight weeks later the government fell and Pitt returned to office bringing Dundas back with him as Viscount Melville, his new First Lord of the Admiralty. He, in turn, was to become the target of a St Vincent out for revenge and was indeed eventually hounded from office, unjustifiably, before Pitt had died.

Sharing Nelson's admiration for William Pitt, Collingwood wrote to the recently widowed Dr Carlyle, off Ushant: 'This change of Ministers seems to me to have brightened all our prospects, everybody seems to be awakened to new hopes. Mr Pitt has shewn himself the greatest statesman in Europe.'

On his return to Downing Street, Pitt put the nation on a war footing. The strength of both the Army and the Navy was rapidly stepped up. Melville was able to achieve an impressive increase in the number of ships built, coastal defences were hurriedly assembled, signal beacons were built at strategic intervals along the coastline throughout the country, Martello towers were erected to act as both lookout stations and armament depots and other schemes of defence were established as a matter of urgency. There was a new spirit abroad. As William James was to write in his *Naval History*:

> At no former or subsequent time have eighty-seven ships of war been launched within the year…Nothing can better demonstrate the exertions made by the new Lord of the Admiralty…to recover the British navy from the low state into which it had previously fallen.

Ever a devotee and close friend of William Pitt, the political fortunes of Henry Dundas rode with those of Pitt himself. A product of Edinburgh High School and Edinburgh University he became successively Solicitor-General for Scotland, Lord Advocate, Dean of the Faculty of Advocates, Treasurer of the Navy and Home Secretary, before becoming First Lord. He was a loyal servant and a prodigious worker who marshalled his facts carefully and thoroughly. It made him a forceful speaker. But for some reason never explained, his broad Scots accent and unsophisticated ways seem to have irritated St Vincent beyond all measure. He regarded him as something of a wee bagpipe.

There was further change on the way for the all-important Permanent Secretary to the Admiralty was now to be William Marsden, in place of Evan Nepean who had retired due to ill health. Nepean had been made a baronet two years earlier and was later to recover enough of his health to occupy the post of Governor of Bombay.

Then, on 23 April 1804, Collingwood was promoted Vice-Admiral of the Blue in a further promotion of admirals. Sadly Sir Edward Blackett had not lived to know of it for he had died just a few weeks before the announcement came through. Lord Nelson became a Vice-Admiral of the White and Sir John Orde, still languishing at home, became a Vice-Admiral of the Red.

Nelson's now very stale action against St Vincent for his share of the prize money which St Vincent had refused to disgorge, had resolved on appeal in Nelson's favour on the ground that St Vincent had been absent when the prizes, the concern of the action, had been taken.

But events were to distance Collingwood and Nelson again until the countdown to Trafalgar the following year brought them together once more. But for the moment the Cadiz Station at the western extremity of Nelson's Mediterranean command was now detached from it. The Mediterranean command had, before then, extended as far as Cape Finisterre, beyond which it gave way to the Western Squadron. But then, in the autumn of 1804, Spain had entered the war.

For some time she had remained in uneasy neutrality, but the reality was that she had remained subservient to the wishes of France, allowing the free movement of French troops across her borders whenever that was requested and victualling and housing French soldiers as and when the need arose. But now, paradoxically, it was a decision of Lord Melville which brought her into the war as a more active ally of France for, on 18 September, he ordered Cornwallis to waylay four Spanish frigates from Rio de la Plata which were bound for Cadiz carrying a cargo of gold and silver valued at more than 1 million pounds. The order was given lest it should fall into the hands of Napoleon. Accordingly Cornwallis dispatched Captain Moore with the frigates *Indefatigable* and *Lively*, then lying off Cadiz, and commandeered also an 80-gun ship and four cruisers including the *Amphion* and the *Medusa* which were at that time under the command of Lord Nelson. And so it was on 5 October that Moore confronted the Spanish frigates and ordered them to surrender. He was met with a refusal, but a few opening shots from Moore very quickly brought the capitulation of three of the four ships without any loss of life. But with further firing the fourth exploded and went to the bottom taking 240 men, women and children with her. Women had been allowed on board, as with the British, hence the need to 'show a leg' when required to do so by the bosun on his morning round. It had been an act in violation of Spain's neutrality and it brought her into the war, thus making reality of what had until then been something of a fiction.

Melville then judged it necessary to strengthen the British presence off Cadiz if the blockade against the combined Franco-Spanish Fleet was to remain effective, for the Spanish were extremely active in their preparations. He, therefore, formed a new Cadiz Squadron consisting of half a dozen ships, some of them drawn from the Channel Fleet off Ushant and others taken from Nelson's Mediterranean command, which would no longer have jurisdiction over the waters west of Gibraltar.

For some time before this Nelson had been bombarding the Admiralty with requests that he be allowed home to rest and recuperate after months of wearisome blockade guarding British interests in the Mediterranean. It had worn him out. He had lodged his request formerly in a letter dated 15 August, but then had heard nothing, although at the same time speculating that his successor was sure to be Orde or Curtis.

In a letter to Ball dated 22 October he wrote that: 'Sir John Orde, I am told, is likely. Lord Radstock is trying; so is Sir Roger Curtis; and if a Spanish War comes, Lord Keith loves a little money... .'[16] His request was eventually granted by the Admiralty, but this was not until the day after Moore's interception of the Spanish cargo, namely on 6 October, and then on the basis that his second in command, Bickerton, would assume command of the Mediterranean Fleet in his absence. Unfortunately this news did not reach Nelson until Christmas Day by which time he had learned both of the entry of Spain into the war, but also of the detachment of the extremity of his command to that of another. These two events caused something of an insubordinate and petulant explosion, the more so since he foresaw that there was bound to be much overlapping in the administration and revictualling of the two squadrons at Gibraltar and so too the probability of friction with whoever was given command of the new Cadiz Squadron. Added to this would be the responsibility, divided, of escorting shipping through those dangerous straits.

But the main cause of Nelson's outburst when he learned that Spain had, in fact, entered the war was the thought that the prospect of rich pickings on the western fringe of his command would be denied him in favour of whoever was appointed to command the detached Cadiz Squadron, for Nelson was not a rich man.

The author C.S. Forester judged that: 'his share might have amounted to quarter of a million sterling – but actually, in view of his application for leave, he had no reason to complain. Complain he did, at first unreasonably.'

161

The flag officer chosen for this new command turned out to be none other than Sir John Orde,[17] and so it was he who was to receive the brunt of Nelson's displeasure, albeit indirectly. But it was unjust to blame Orde, for he bore Nelson no animosity personally at all and had not himself been responsible for the formation of the Cadiz Squadron, and still less for the selection of himself as its commander. This had been the work of the First Lord who did not suspect that Nelson may have thought that Sir John resented him. In fact by this time Orde was everywhere singing Nelson's praises, and the Admiralty, in any event, supposed that Nelson was coming home on leave. And so the King wrote his agreement from Weymouth on 26 October that: 'it is much safer and more prudent...to send without delay a squadron off that port under the command of Sir John Orde.'

Fearing then that command of the Mediterranean Fleet could also eventually be given to another in his absence, Nelson promptly shelved his plan to come home, sending Este back to London on 6 November with that news. By way of explanation he used the illness of Rear-Admiral Campbell as the reason for his change of plan, stating that he thought it right to remain in post until a replacement could be found for Campbell, notwithstanding that Bickerton was in place to take command of the fleet during Nelson's absence on leave.

Orde was not unaware of Nelson's growing animosity which was all the more surprising for the two had corresponded on terms which had been amicable enough in 1801. But now Nelson was much wounded, the more so when it was adjudged that Orde was entitled to £10,000 as his share of the prize money for the Spanish treasure ships captured by Moore in October, as the flag officer now commanding the squadron off Cadiz. And the naval historian Clark Russell judged that in the space of a month the Admiral and his officers were enriched for life.

His unease now manifested itself in letters written in accusatory and hysterical terms. In a letter to Lady Hamilton dated 4 December he wrote of Orde:

I have made up my mind to overwhelm him with respect and attention, and to even make an offer, as Admiral Campbell has gone home, to serve till the Admiralty can send out another flag officer...but I dare say Sir John Orde is too great a man to want my poor services, and that he will reject them; be that as it may, you will, I am sure, agree with me, that I shall shew my superiority to him by such an offer, and the World will see what a sacrifice I am ready to make for the service of my King and Country, for what greater sacrifice could I make, than serving for a moment under Sir John Orde and giving up for that moment the society of all I hold dear in that world. Many here think that he is sent out off Cadiz to take a fortune out of my mouth, that would be very curious. The late Admiralty directed Admiral Cornwallis to send Campbell to cruise at the mouth of the Straits, and he took all my sweets, and now this Admiralty sends and takes all my golden harvest; it is very odd – surely I never served faithfully, I have only dreamt I have done my duty to the advantage of my country, but I am above them, I feel it, although not one farthing richer than when I left England.

And on the following day he wrote to his old friend Ball:

I almost think that he is sent off Cadiz to reap the golden harvest, as Campbell was sent off Cadiz by Cornwallis...to reap my sugar harvest. Its very odd, two Admiralties to treat me so.

And then, with a burst of Shakespeare: 'Surely I have dreamt that "I have done the State some service".'[18]

Orde had written in civil enough terms to Nelson by letter dated 17 November soon after taking up his command, saying:

Should it be in my power, during my stay, to be useful to your lordship in promoting the King's service, or your particular views, I beg you will command me without ceremony.

Nelson had replied politely enough on 16 December,[19] the day after Orde's letter reached him, but the loss of the prospect of riches from Spain's entry into the war continued to dominate his thoughts and his correspondence. He was to write to his friend Hugh Elliott on 19 December:

...the sending an officer to such a point, to take, if it is a Spanish war, the whole harvest, after all my toils, (God knows unprofitable enough! For I am a much poorer man than when we started in the *Amphion*) seems a little hard; but patienza. I suppose Sir John, in the end, will command here.[20]

There followed two letters to Orde devoted to professional matters which were straightforward and correct enough, but then, two weeks later, in letters dated 13 January 1805, he was to complain again to Elliott that:

...he [Orde] is to wallow in wealth, whilst I am left a beggar...Sir John Orde brought my leave and many supposed that the moment I had passed the straits he would take upon him the command...[21]

And at about this time, Samuel Taylor Coleridge, the poet, then secretary to Nelson's friend Ball at Malta, and taking Nelson's part in all this, wrote in *The Friend*:

> The prizes...taken were immense. A month or two sufficed to enrich the Commander and officers of this small and highly favoured squadron...Of all the wounds which were ever inflicted on Nelson's feelings (and these were not a few) this was the deepest! This rankled most!

And so, after receiving official notice of the grant of his request for leave, which had arrived on Christmas Day 1804, Nelson firmly decided to waive the grant and remain in post.

As soon as he arrived off Cadiz, Sir John proceeded to mount a most efficient and comprehensive blockade which was to keep the Spanish Fleet in harbour throughout that winter and until the arrival of Villeneuve the following spring. Indeed *The Times* of 18 April 1805 reported that:

> The last letters by the Lisbon Mail from Cadiz state that Sir John Orde continued the blockade of that port with the utmost vigour; vessels freighted with corn only were allowed to pass unmolested.

So effective was his blockade that even British ships passing through the straits were intercepted and questioned so that intelligence could be gathered and collated. But this too led to further misunderstanding with Nelson, who assumed when a ship of his was intercepted carrying his dispatches for London, that Sir John was seeking to exercise some control over his command. So much so that on occasion he resorted to subterfuge in an attempt to deceive and circumvent Orde's squadron.

But the blockade continued successfully, thus preventing any junction of the enemy fleets and any threat of invasion throughout that winter, save for one break out by Admiral Missiessy and even this had but a very limited success.

To Collingwood Nelson wrote on 13 March:

> We are in a sad jumble with Sir John Orde off Cadiz; but let him do absurd things as he pleases about blockading the ships under my command – even to be angry at my sending ships to Lisbon with my dispatches.[22]

And to Ball on 29 March, he wrote:

> ...this cannot go on. I have, on January 17th, wrote home of what

164

would happen, and I dare say, Orde has a trimmer before this time. He will not be suffered to remain much longer; he will go to the Channel; he will be the richest Admiral that England ever had and I one of the poorest.[23]

He wrote to Radstock on 1 April:

Report says that Sir John Orde will be the richest Admiral that England ever saw...I would have made as much good use of a large fortune as Sir John Orde, or any other Admiral.[24]

And even when writing to his sister Mrs Bolton on 9 May he said:

I should have been a very rich, instead of a poor man, if Lord Melville had not given the Galleons to Sir John Orde.[25]

And so Nelson continued to smart at his deprivation in letter after letter. But there was of course no trimmer for Orde, nor any reason for one, and he was to remain in post until the onset of gout prompted him to submit a request that he be allowed to retire home. But, by then, events in the sea war with France were coming to a head, and they were to bring Nelson and Collingwood together again, supremely united in the service of their country.

Chapter 10

Collingwood and Nelson in the Countdown to Trafalgar

Collingwood and Nelson now came together again, but it was to be in tragic circumstances for it was to be the last year of Nelson's life and Collingwood would never again set foot on his native shore.

But without doubt they came together for this last time as saviours of the British nation.

The year 1805 found Collingwood still serving on the *Dreadnought* standing off Rochefort. The *Dreadnought* was a recently built ship, although, according to Collingwood, it was:

> ...ill fitted out, for it was part of Lord St Vincent's economy to employ convicts to fit out the ships, instead of the men and officers who were to sail in them. The consequence is, that they are wanting in every kind of arrangement that skilful men would have made, and most of them have been obliged to be docked since, at very great expense.

Indeed Collingwood told of a rumour that when Lord Hood had been proposed in place of St Vincent, he had replied that the paralysed state to which the Navy was reduced required superior abilities to his to restore it. Collingwood endorsed that view with the comment that:

'Such was the opinion of men capable of judging its condition.'

Raging weather in the Atlantic in the previous two months had shattered many of the ships in the fleet with *Dreadnought* one of the few able to hold her position although, even here, Collingwood had to write that so much water was pouring into her magazine that 'there is very little serviceable powder' remaining.

Although anxious enough about his own health at the close of 1804, which he put down to lack of exercise given the limited opportunities when on board ship, Collingwood was concerned too about the wellbeing of his friend Nelson as he maintained his vigil off the port of Toulon. Collingwood had written to Captain Byam Martin from the *Dreadnought* off Rochefort on 27 October 1804: 'I do not wonder that the constant anxiety attached to such a command...should have worn out his body, which was always but a flimsy case for his Herculean soul.'[1] However the detachment of the Cadiz Squadron and the appointment of Orde as its commander had persuaded Nelson to remain in post and not to seek rest and respite at home.

Not long before this Collingwood had been saddened to hear of the death of the celebrated Admiral, the Viscount Duncan of Camperdown; a giant of a man. Large in both stature and personality, he was almost as wide as he was long. A man of ample proportions his generosity of spirit had shone through as an example to all those privileged enough to serve with him. He had died on 4 August 1804 when staying overnight at an inn at Cornhill in Northumberland while making his way back home to Edinburgh.

Collingwood was concerned too at this time, as ever, about the education and upbringing of his daughters, which he could but influence from afar. On 9 April 1805 he wrote to his father-in-law:

> I am delighted with your account of my children's improvement, for it is a subject of the greatest anxiety to me. Above all things, keep novels out of their reach. They are the corrupters of tender minds: they exercise the imagination instead of the judgment: make them all desire to become the Julias and Cecilias of romance; and turn their heads before they are enabled to distinguish truth from fictions devised merely for entertainment. When they have passed their climacteric it will be time enough to begin novels.

However, now standing in the rank of vice-admiral, the minutiae of fleet duties were his main preoccupation, with the concerns of officers in his squadron to attend to, such as those of the remarkable and notorious Captain Bligh of the *Bounty*. Now in command of *Warrior* he had troubled Collingwood with a long allegation that one Lieutenant John Frazier was both lazy and a malingerer. In the subsequent court martial which Collingwood allowed, the court dismissed the charges, finding that the man had a genuine injury, and in a subsequent cross action ordered that Bligh himself be reprimanded and admonished for his use of foul language.

In the meanwhile Napoleon was devising plan after plan for the invasion of Britain. Two years before, Admiral Eustace de Bruix, who had assisted Napoleon in the *coup d'etat* of 1799, had been named commander of the invasion flotilla. The plan had been a simple one then, namely a mass breakout of the French Fleets which would make for the West Indies and rendezvous there in the hope of drawing off a significant part of the Channel and Mediterranean Fleets in pursuit, for Napoleon knew that the British would be quick to protect their sugar and other economic interests in the West Indies, such was their importance to the city merchants. Thus had Napoleon calculated that he could entice the British to relax their vigil in the English Channel long enough for the combined French Fleet to double back for escort duties and cover a crossing of the Channel by the invasion force before the British had had time to return to their watch.

It was a plan doomed to fail for it took no account of the vagaries and uncertainties of the weather, known to every sailor but not, it seems, to the soldier Napoleon. And it was a factor which even he could not control, for lack of breeze was, of course, fatal to the movement of any ship under canvas. Nor did it allow for the inadequacy and inexperience of those who manned the French Fleet. But even if the wind and the weather had been kind to him, and if too his commanders had been courageous and foolhardy enough to obey his orders, it is doubtful that the plan would ever have succeeded, for it was implicit in the standing orders issued to Admiral Cornwallis by the Admiralty that no ship was ever in any circumstance to be drawn away from the Channel Fleet. All were to remain on station at all times in protection of the channel coast of England. It was otherwise at Toulon and in the Mediterranean. There Nelson saw his role as very different. So far from keeping the French in harbour, he sought to lure them out by lying at anchor out of sight just over the horizon. By this device he strove to lull the French into a false belief that he had abandoned the vigil in the hope that they would then venture out and into confrontation with his fleet. If it worked he would then annihilate, or at least seriously cripple them and so there was the possibility that a decoy could indeed draw off his command. But not so in the Channel where a more defensive role was both required and maintained. The guard was never dropped.

All of the many plans for the invasion of Britain which Napoleon devised in the years 1804 and 1805 were but variations of that same theme.

It was his misfortune, too, that de Bruix fell seriously ill, while Vice-Admiral Ganteaume, who had been appointed to command the Brest Fleet, reported to Decres that his crews were pitifully inadequate, not only in number, experience and training, but also in resolution. It was clear that it would require all the Emperor's skill and drive to persuade the French Navy to even put to sea. And then Admiral Latouche-Treville, commander of the fleet at Toulon, suddenly died. Napoleon's choice of a successor was to have far-reaching consequences for both his own plans for the invasion of Britain and indeed for France itself, for the man appointed was Vice-Admiral Pierre Villeneuve, then forty years of age. A friend of the Minister of Marine, he was a thin-nosed aristocrat, a member of the provincial nobility and a Knight of Malta who had survived the Revolution. He was well-bred, civilized, humane, decent, intelligent and efficient.

Indeed Collingwood, who was later able to study him at close quarters when holding him prisoner at Trafalgar, was to describe him as: 'a very good officer. He has nothing in his manners of the offensive vapouring and boasting which we, perhaps too often, attribute to the Frenchman.'2 But he was ever a mild, introspective, careful and almost timid man who had lost his nerve for battle and had developed a fear of Nelson ever since the Battle of the Nile in which he had participated as a rear-admiral of two years standing. This, coupled with his own lack of belief in the fighting abilities of the men under his command, did not auger well for the French, for his pessimism was contagious and it even demoralized the officers in his own command. Clearly Napoleon was blind to these defects of character when making the appointment, and indeed still so when Villeneuve begged to be relieved of his command in the weeks which followed. And yet, whilst openly despairing of Villeneuve's inertia and failure to motivate his officers or even to respond to his countless orders to put to sea, Napoleon kept him in post as commander of the Toulon Fleet.

Throughout the winter of 1804/1805 Napoleon dissipated his energies formulating and reformulating plans for the invasion of Britain, all of which involved the squadrons at Brest, Rochefort, El Ferrol and Toulon breaking out through the blockade, forming a junction, drawing off the British Fleets by sailing for the French-held island of Martinique in the West Indies and then returning to Boulogne to give cover in the Channel for the crossing of the invasion force.

'On their successful arrival', Napoleon would say, 'hang the destinies of the World.' But at every turn he was met by the refusal of both Villeneuve and even the more robust Ganteaume to take their fleets to sea, although Villeneuve did venture out briefly on 18 January, only to creep back into harbour soon afterwards unbeknown to Nelson. But this short excursion did cause Nelson to embark on a frenzy of activity.

Napoleon's plans in March specifically ordered Villeneuve to set sail for Martinique, taking with him in support of the Toulon Squadron those ships lying at Cadiz, together with 3,140 troops under the command of General Lauriston. There he was to land the soldiers before placing his fleet under the command of Ganteaume for the return voyage to Brest and then Boulogne. He was confident that Ganteaume would, by then, have broken out and crossed to the West Indies.

On 30 March Villeneuve did at last weigh anchor when he slid out of Toulon and set sail for Cadiz and the West Indies with four 80-gun ships, seven 74-gun ships, six 40-gun frigates and two brigs together with a cargo of 3,332 troops, at a time when Nelson, unaware of the escape, was watering his fleet in Sardinia. Hugging the Spanish coast Villeneuve reached Cartagena without incident where, for reasons best known to himself, he declined the offer of six Spanish ships of the line. From there, on 9 April he slipped quietly through the Straits of Gibraltar and, again hugging the coast, sailed for Cadiz where Sir John Orde lay at anchor with a squadron of six ships.[3]

In fact, by letter to Marsden at the Admiralty dated 27 March, far from wishing to remain in post to gather the golden harvest of Spanish treasure as Nelson had assumed and asserted he did, Orde had asked to be allowed to retire home. He had found the winter policing the waters off Cadiz impossibly strenuous. Exhausted by the need for eternal vigilance and crippled with a discomforting gout,[4] he had wearied of his task, especially since there was ever the prospect of petty bickering at the Gibraltar margin of his command where it overlapped with that of the Mediterranean Fleet. He had found the dual role required of him difficult to perform, as Nelson had rightly predicted would be the case. And so he had found in a particular directive from Marsden a pretext for making his request. That had required that he should protect the trade from England all the way through to Gibraltar, which would involve both allocating part of his squadron to escort duties, which he could ill afford to spare in the emergency, while at the same time lifting the embargo which the Admiralty had themselves imposed on his employing any part of his command in the straits. This dual role he thought would be extremely difficult to discharge, and so it provided the pretext he was looking for to request permission to be allowed to retire home. By another letter of the same date he had written to Lord Melville along the same lines, ending with:

'Some other officer may possibly feel these circumstances less mor-tifying than I do;...May I then request your lordship permission to retire from a situation I owe to your goodness...In resigning my command.'[5]

But before the First Lord had had the opportunity to even consider this request, Orde was overtaken by the arrival at Cadiz of Villeneuve and his Toulon Fleet. In fact Villeneuve's passage through the straits had been spotted both by Lord Mark Kerr, captain of the frigate *Fisgard* of the Mediterranean Fleet, and also by the sloop *Beagle* of Orde's own squadron, but it was, in fact, Sir Richard Strachan in the *Renown* who brought a report of the sighting to Orde, as he lay in the Bay of Cadiz refitting his ships and taking on provisions from transports. Realizing then that Villeneuve was hard on his heels he promptly took action. According to one account written contemporaneously by an officer serving on Orde's flagship, Orde quickly ordered that the signal be made to cast off transports and prepare for battle. Both he and Sir Richard Strachan expressed themselves surprised and impressed by the coolness of Orde's reaction and by the orderliness of the withdrawal given that they had been caught unawares by a considerable force coming round Trafalgar from windward with full press of sail on a strong Levant wind. It outnumbered Orde's Squadron by at least three or four to one with a further six Spanish ships of the line lying in harbour ready to be placed at the disposal of Villeneuve. According to that same officer Orde then, at that same moment, divined that the ultimate destination of the French was probably Boulogne, with England then the target, so that his duty was to fall back, rejoin and add his strength to the depleted Channel Fleet which was standing off Ushant, mounting a defensive blockade in protection of British shores.[6] It was a decision which complied with the Cornwallis Standing Orders which governed the Channel Fleet. He decided, too, to leave the frigate *Amphion* on station to observe and report all intelligence of Villeneuve's movements and to alert any British shipping in those waters to the presence of the French and Spanish Fleets.

It was a measure of Villeneuve's timidity that despite his overwhelming superiority in numbers, he chose to slip quietly into harbour rather than confront Orde's Squadron which he obligingly allowed to withdraw unmolested. As the eminent naval historian Sir Julian Corbett was to write:

> It was a narrow escape, but there had been no panic or hurry, no cutting or slipping, but a thoroughly seamanlike retreat...it is important to note that it was not his whole fleet he was taking north, but only his battle squadron. The whole of his cruisers...were left behind with carefully framed orders for keeping touch with Villeneuve.[7]
>
> ...it will be seen that he was anticipating the intentions of the Admiralty exactly. Both he and they were following the well-known tradition, whereby ...was secured...an overwhelming concentration at the vital time and place. Boldly as the fleet was spread, it retained in the alert instinct of its squadronal commanders a reflex power of shrinking back to the centre when any rough touch gave warning that dispersal was no longer wise.[8]

Yet, back in London, Orde was castigated for not engaging the enemy, not by the Admiralty or by those who had any understanding of naval strategy, but, somewhat unfairly, by those merchants in the city who were concerned that their own commercial interests in the West Indies now stood at risk of invasion and pillaging.

In his life of Nelson, the novelist C.S. Forester opined that Orde had acted in an uninspired fashion. Of course the intrepid Nelson had left a legacy of boldness and daring in his constant determination, not just to defeat the enemy, but to annihilate him. And had he been in Orde's shoes with a force comparably small in numbers it has to be acknowledged that it is just possible that he, Nelson, would have chosen engagement rather than withdrawal, albeit with the probability, if not certainty, of glorious annihilation, but not before Villeneuve's Fleet had suffered many crippling blows. Or perhaps, given Villeneuve's timidity, of which Orde and Nelson were not then aware, had Orde confronted Villeneuve with his small detachment of ships, the French Fleet would not have sailed out of Cadiz at all.

By letter, dated 21 May, Admiral Lord Radstock wrote to his son, then serving with Nelson: 'The City people are crying out against Sir J.O., and, as usual, are equally absurd and unjust.'[9] And the much-respected historian Rear-Admiral Mahan agreed with this assessment with the comment: 'To fight eleven ships with six could only be justified by extreme circumstances.'

It is to be noted that Lord Gardner, then commanding the Channel Fleet in the absence of Cornwallis on leave, highly approved the step taken by Orde and, if Ralfe be correct, Lord Barham, then taking over as First Lord of the Admiralty, afterwards told Orde's brother, Lord Bolton, that: 'it was fully known the Admiralty approved of Sir John's conduct and expressed the hope that he might have employment again, if such a measure would be acceptable to him.'

In his masterful analysis, Orde's performance has been examined in great detail and exhaustively by Sir Julian Corbett, who did not find it wanting, and J. Steven Watson, in the Oxford History series, was to describe Orde's action as, 'prudently hurrying north'; Walder as 'the correct and impeccable one'; Bradford, in his Nelson, the Essential Hero, wrote that his withdrawal was 'in accordance with normal strategy to join the Fleet off Ushant'; and Edgar Vincent in his Nelson, Love and Fame, considered that, in failing to attack, he could not be blamed.

Kathrin Orth, in British Admirals of the Napoleonic Wars, judged that Orde who had stood up for 'a more humane treatment of the slaves' of Dominica:

...combined strict discipline with care for [his] crew...was a popular officer...[who] took the side of officers who he thought were unjustly accused...[of whom] because of Nelson, a picture...as a quarrelsome and vain man found its way into naval textbooks – whilst [his] ability was... ignored.[He had made a decision which was] considered and correct.

The Times newspaper was to write of it on 4 May: 'It appears a very wise and prudent step and best calculated to defeat the junction of the squadrons assembled from Toulon and the ports of Spain, from making a final junction with the grand fleet in that harbour.'

But perhaps the complaint then made by Nelson had greater validity for, when he learned of Villeneuve's escape, he complained bitterly that Sir John had not sent him so much as a frigate to tell him of it, thus preventing a hot pursuit. But in that criticism there may perhaps have been a note of irritation with himself for having allowed Villeneuve to slip out of Toulon in the first place without his knowing of it, for there were those in London who were currently censuring Nelson for just that. And in fact Orde had made some attempt on 11 April to get this information to Nelson and had himself spent two days in the waters to the south of Cadiz in search of Villeneuve's Fleet before finally turning north for the Channel Fleet on 18 April.

However, with hindsight, Orde could properly be criticized for not allocating one or more frigates to shadow Villeneuve's Fleet if only to discover its destination. But here again it seems that he had divined this for himself, and had done so correctly, and had quickly so informed both the commander of the Channel Fleet and the Admiralty. In a letter to Lord Robert Fitzgerald at Lisbon dated 10 April, Orde had reported the arrival of Villeneueve, together with details of his strength, and had written that:

Where their destination may be after this junction...I cannot tell, but I judge it westward...Where Lord Nelson is I cannot hear but I am told he is likely to return to Egypt on hearing of the French fleet being at sea.

Two days later he wrote a similar report to Lord Gardner, adding, 'in any case I think [the French Fleet] would not remain long in Cadiz', and he asked that Gardner should send his report on to the Admiralty without delay.[10]

The author John Terraine, in his book *Trafalgar*, cites a further letter written by Orde in which he wrote:

I think the chances are great in favour of their destination being westward where by a sudden concentration of several detachments, Bonaparte may hope to gain a temporary superiority in the Channel, and availing himself of it, strike his enemy a mortal blow.

For this prediction Terraine considered that Orde: 'deserves full credit, since no-one else had yet reached it...Orde was the first to penetrate Napoleon's plan.' And the military historian Corelli Barnett was to write that: 'the genius of Bonaparte [had] thus been rumbled at the outset by a run-of-the-mill English flag officer whose name few of his countrymen now remember.'

In fact it was not until 26 April that Gardner sent a copy of Orde's letter to Lord Robert Fitzgerald and Marsden at the Admiralty, adding that he hoped that Orde and Calder would endeavour to join him and that the Admiralty would then further augment his fleet with more ships, given the emergency.[11]

On 29 April the sloop *Sophie*, detached from Orde's squadron, delivered his own dispatches to the Admiralty, where, on 2 May, Lord Barham had succeeded Melville as First Lord. He quickly laid Orde's dispatches before William Pitt who described Orde's prediction as to Villeneuve's movements as,'of the most pressing importance', especially since a contingent of British troops under Sir James Craig had, only a few days before on 19 April, set sail from Portugal for Malta and were now on the high seas – or so they thought – with no cover but two ships of the line to escort them. In fact they had by then reached their destination and were safely on shore, but Pitt and Barham were not to know that. More information as to Villeneuve's movements then arrived on 2 May by the sloop *Beagle*, one of Orde's cruisers.

Barham now acted with speed and with the sure touch of a man with years of experience in naval strategy behind him. He immediately saw the importance of maintaining the strength of the Channel Fleet off Ushant in case of invasion and so his orders to Cornwallis were that: 'all other orders should be interpreted in terms of the necessity to keep the Western squadron in strength of not less than eighteen sail of the line'. At the same time Lord Keith's ships of the North Sea Fleet were concentrated at the Nore.

On 30 April Orde had further pressed his request to be allowed home in a letter to the First Lord which read:

When the present alarm is over should it be convenient to allow me to go into port and repair to town for a few days, I would be thankful for the indulgence, having some matters to communicate to your lordship and the Board which I cannot so well convey in writing.

174

Accordingly, on 6 May the Lords Commissioners turned their attention to his various requests, granted his permission to retire home and directed him, upon the arrival of the *Glory* at Spithead, to strike his flag and come on shore.[12] Thus ended Sir John Orde's career at sea.

There can be no doubt that, although his request for retirement had been lodged in terms which were clear and unambiguous, he was nonetheless somewhat taken aback by the speed with which it had been granted. But then he was not to know that after his requests had been written, but before they could be considered by the Lords Commissioners, Lord Melville had been succeeded as First Lord by Admiral Sir Charles Middleton, the newly created Lord Barham. And after stepping on shore at Portsmouth on 10 May, Orde soon began to regret his somewhat impetuous decision. But by then it was too late. *The Times* was to report on 15 May that Orde had asked for a court martial as a vehicle which would have enabled him to explain the wish he had expressed for retirement, but that this request had been refused. There followed an interview with Barham on 18 May which seems to have been amicable enough after which Barham wrote on 21 May that: 'If it is your wish to be re-employed, I would recommend your making it known to the Board.' There followed Barham's conversation with his brother in which he expressed the hope: 'that he might have employment again, if such a measure would be acceptable to him.'

But it was not to be, although he was in that same year raised to the rank of Admiral of the Blue in the Trafalgar promotion.

An assumption has since been made by many biographers of Nelson, amongst them C.S. Forester and the Cambridge Modern History, that Sir John Orde had been summarily ordered to return to Portsmouth and there strike his flag because of his action off Cadiz on 9 April. Such, however, was clearly not the case, as the correspondence of the time serves to confirm.[13]

At all events, after but six hours spent in Cadiz harbour, the Toulon Fleet was now at sea, and Napoleon Bonaparte waited impatiently at Boulogne for its return to home waters and for the opportunity to sail his armada of 2,000 or more invasion craft across the English Channel with the cover of naval protection. But to his amazement and to his fury Ganteaume had once again refused to break out of Brest. Napoleon resolved, nonetheless, to launch the invasion force the moment Villeneuve returned from the West Indies and was in a position to provide a naval escort and cover with or without the assistance of the fleet languishing in harbour at Brest.

The Admiralty now gave credence to the reports and predictions which they had received from Sir John Orde by appointing the reliable Collingwood, the sailor's sailor, as Orde's successor and ordering him to sail for the West Indies in pursuit of Villeneuve with a newly formed squadron of ships.

But by now it had come to the ears of Nelson that Villeneuve was at sea. Indeed it had been on 4 April that the *Phoebe* brought him intelligence to that effect as his flagship *Victory* lay in Italian waters. But there had been no indication as to Villeneuve's intentions or direction of sail. Nelson's first thought was that he must be headed east and so he scoured the Mediterranean with his frigates until, on 18 April, he was made aware that the Toulon Fleet had left the Mediterranean altogether. Yet still he regarded it as a prey that was his. The day following he wrote to Lord Gardner that he felt: 'vexed at their slipping out of the Mediterranean, as I had marked them for my own game.'

And so, although Villeneuve had had eight days start on him by then, and even though he was himself becalmed in the Mediterranean, he wrote Lord Melville that he intended to abandon the Mediterranean Station and set off in pursuit, in the hope of bringing the French to battle. His decision to do so was met with much criticism in the London press which regarded it as both an act of insubordination and an act of folly, for it meant leaving these shores unprotected in his absence. After all, Collingwood, poised with fourteen ships of the line, ready to pursue Villeneuve's Fleet, had already been given that task.

But the wise Collingwood, the moment he learned of Nelson's decision, rightly judged that it would be better to remain where he was, patrolling the waters off Cadiz which had been vacated by Sir John Orde, blocking the departure of the Spanish Fleet which still lay at anchor in Cartagena and Cadiz only waiting their moment to break out should the British ever drop their guard. At the same time he sent two of his ships to the West Indies to help there with the protection of British commercial interests. And with that same insight which Orde had demonstrated, Collingwood now read the mind of the Emperor accurately when he wrote to Dr Carlyle on 2 July 1805: 'I believe their object in the West Indies to be less conquest than to draw our force from home...they will have so much less to oppose them in their real attack, which will be at home at harvest time.'[14] But the Admiralty had the measure of Napoleon, and so all but Nelson fell back to the defence of the Channel, as had always been the plan, leaving only Nelson free to pursue Napoleon's decoy.

There followed what has come to be known as 'The Long Chase' which was perhaps more remarkable for the seamanship demonstrated by Nelson than for anything else it achieved. Putting in to Gibraltar for victualling to provide for the journey, he was impatient to be on his way the moment he detected a change in the wind. That impatience was later to be described by Doctor Scott in these terms:

Off went a gun from *Victory*, and up went the Blue Peter, whilst the Admiral paced the deck in a hurry, with anxious steps and impatient of a moment's delay. The officer said, 'Here is one of Nelson's mad pranks.' But he was nevertheless right, the wind became favourable, the linen was left on shore, the fleet cleared the gut, and away they steered for the West Indies.[15]

In fact it was not until he had reached Portugal and was anchored off Lagos Bay that he learned from the crew of ships which had been supplying Orde's Squadron, and then from a British officer serving in the Portugese Navy, Rear Admiral Donald Campbell, that it was believed that Villeneuve was headed for the West Indies. For imparting that information Campbell was dismissed his command at the insistence of the French Ambassador at Lisbon, to whom the Spanish Naval commander at Algeciras had complained.[16] The Ambassador regarded his act as a breach of Portugal's neutrality. And so it was not until 12 May that Nelson set sail for the West Indies.

Nelson crossed the Atlantic and back in record time, yet Villeneuve still managed to elude him. But for incorrect information, which he received from one General Brereton, he would have caught him. But his pursuit served British interests well, nonetheless, for the moment Villeneuve heard that Nelson was on his heels and that Ganteaume had not yet broken out of Brest and, indeed, that Misseissy had already left Martinique, he promptly disobeyed Napoleon's orders to invade British territories in the West Indies and then await the other French Fleets, and in his panic promptly landed the troops, arms and supplies which had been sent out for the protection of French-held islands, indiscriminately, and turned tail for Europe with Nelson in hot pursuit.

On 1 June Villeneuve wrote to Decres: 'The enemy is on his guard, having been warned by the *Mercury*, a ship which had been sent by Orde.'[17] In fact Nelson had also sent the brig *Curieux* on ahead to carry the news to Lord Barham at the Admiralty.

The return of Villeneuve to European waters was spotted on 22 July by Vice-Admiral Sir Robert Calder then lying some 117 miles off El Ferrol to the order of Lord Barham. An arrogant and opinionated man, he was, nonetheless, skilful, experienced and intelligent and had fifteen sail of the line under his command. The two fleets were therefore evenly matched. But, as chance would have it, fog descended on that hot July day which reduced visibility to almost zero. Ships moved silently in and out of view on a slight breeze like ghosts passing in the night. Yet Calder courageously stood towards the French, and after some two hours of hesitation, Villeneuve decided to take up the challenge.

The first shots were fired at about 5.15 p.m., and there followed an intense exchange of fire, chiefly between the British and the Spaniards who took the brunt of the fighting, although three ships of the French Fleet also played an active part. So the battle raged for three hours or more in confused and chaotic conditions until failing light, fog and the smoke of gunfire reduced visibility to almost nil which prompted Calder to discontinue the action by raising the Night Private Signal. By then two Spanish ships had surrendered and 149, mostly Spanish, seaman had been killed together with thirty-nine British officers and men.

Dawn the following day found the two fleets still confronting each other and yet, for reasons never explained adequately, no move was made by either side to renew the engagement that day, or indeed on the day following. The British in particular seemed reluctant to press home their advantage. And then, on 25 July both fleets silently withdrew, quitting the battlefield altogether, sailing off in opposite directions; Calder to join Cornwallis off Ushant and Villeneuve to Vigo Bay and then El Ferrol where the junction with two other French Squadrons raised the overall strength of the Franco-Spanish Fleet there to twenty-nine sail of the line.

In December of that year, two months after Trafalgar, a court martial, which Calder himself had demanded, was convened to enquire into what was described as 'The Humiliation'. Calder then sought to justify his decision to stand away both on the ground that he had believed that Villeneuve was about to be reinforced with a fleet coming out of El Ferrol, but also because he wished to retain and safeguard his own damaged ships together with the two he had captured. He escaped with a severe reprimand but was never employed at sea again, although it could perhaps be argued that he had, by that encounter, prevented Villeneuve from sailing to join Napoleon, and throughout his ordeal both Nelson and Collingwood had expressed a sympathy for him.

So it was that Nelson returned to the waters around Gibraltar where Collingwood was still patrolling in the *Dreadnought*. There Nelson lost no time in penning a letter to his friend from the *Victory* dated 18 July, in which he gave some account of the abortive chase across the Atlantic and in which he promised to pay Collingwood a visit as soon as may be in order to discuss tactics:

The moment the fleet is watered, and has got some refreshments, of which we are in great want, I shall come out and make you a visit...not, my dear friend, to take your command from you (for I may probably add my command to you) but to consult how we can best serve our country by detaching a part of this large force.

In reply on 21 July Collingwood wrote of Napoleon's probable targets and ended:

The summer is big with events; we may all perhaps have an active share in them; and I sincerely wish your Lordship strength of body to go through with it, and to all others your strength of mind.

He wrote too,'...how truly dear you are to my friendship'.

But, alas, events combined to prevent the meeting proposed, for Nelson, by this time exhausted, was anxious to be at home and at rest and so made post-haste for England. He wrote a parting note to Collingwood on 25 July in which he expressed his regret that he would have to: 'forego the pleasure of taking you by the hand until October next, when, if I am well enough, I shall (if the Admiralty please) resume the command.' It was on 19 August that he struck his flag, went on shore and headed for Merton, Lady Hamilton and his daughter Horatia.

It was at about this time too that Collingwood received the sad news that his faithful correspondent and relation by marriage, the Reverend Dr Alexander 'Jupiter' Carlyle, had died.

In a private letter to Decres dated 7 August, Villeneuve wrote:

I am about to set out but I do not know what I shall do. Eight line of battle ships are keeping in sight of the coast eight leagues out; they will profit by the lesson given to Admiral Orde, they will follow us; I shall not be able to close with them and they will go and join either the squadron before Brest or that of Cadiz, according as I shape my course for one or the other of these two ports.[18]

That letter, together with others, Decres sent on to the Emperor Napoleon.

The threat of invasion continued to loom large that summer as the Grand Armée stood poised on the northern coast of France waiting only for the arrival of the Combined Fleet and a fair wind to descend on these shores. Yet Villeneuve had kept his fleet in harbour at El Ferrol at the entrance to the Bay of Biscay, and although Napoleon arrived at Boulogne on 3 August for the final push and there reviewed the troops he had put on a twenty-four hour alert, it was not until 16 August that Villeneuve actually ventured out. But he then sailed south for Cadiz rather than north for Boulogne, ostensibly to take on water and supplies. And in this he was spotted by Collingwood who hurriedly wrote to Cornwallis that same day: 'This morning the combined fleet of 36 ships came down upon me when I was before Cadiz with three, and obliged me to abandon my station.'

Outnumbered as he was with now but three ships of the line and a frigate in his squadron, Collingwood, as with Orde, was in no position to take on the enemy fleet even though he had brought the gunnery of

179

the *Dreadnought* to a high proficiency in terms of both accuracy and rapidity of fire at three broadsides every 3½ minutes. Instead, beginning on 20 August, he conducted a very skilful 'cat and mouse' manoeuvre before Cadiz by successfully drawing off towards the Straits of Gibraltar the sixteen or so ships of the Franco-Spanish Fleet which had, by then, been detached by Villeneuve to follow him in the hope of breaking the blockade. Collingwood managed to outrun them notwithstanding that the *Dreadnought* was slow in the water, and each time the enemy turned from the pursuit, Collingwood tacked about and doggedly followed them back, only to be chased again until they finally abandoned the mission altogether and returned to Cadiz. There, with his three ships of the line reinforced by a fourth under Captain Duff, he resumed his watch on the harbour using a deception which had served Admiral Duncan so well at Camperdown when his force had been reduced to but a very few by mutiny in the face of the enemy. This was to position two of his ships on the horizon and have them signal constantly to an imaginary fleet out of sight of those on watch in Cadiz. In this way, and with but four ships at his disposal, Collingwood effectively bottled up thirty-six or more of the enemy fleet until reinforcements arrived under the command of Sir Richard Bickerton. A further detachment under the command of Sir Robert Calder,[19] then provided Collingwood with an additional twenty-one or so ships. Small wonder that his friend Nelson was later to write: 'Everybody in England admired your adroitness in not being forced unnecessarily into the Straits', and the *Naval Chronicle* described it as: 'an instance of genius and address that is scarcely to be paralleled in the pages of our naval history.' It was remarkable, wrote the editor, that he should have blocked up the port of Cadiz with only four ships at his disposal. Certainly in this Collingwood had shown greater initiative than Orde had shown earlier.

In a letter to one of his sisters written on 26 August Collingwood gave a detailed account of this courageous manoeuvre, describing, with some pride and with some justification, how he had managed to cling to the skirts of the enemy ships throughout this whole episode. It is surprising therefore that he should then have tarnished this account a little by ending his letter with an uncharacteristic and rather gratuitous attack on the Flag Captain of his own ship, Edward Rotherham:

I have a diligent young man for my secretary and Clavell, my Lieutenant is the spirit of the ship; but such a Captain, such a stick, I wonder very much how such people get forward. I should (I firmly believe) with his nautical ability and knowledge and exertion, have been a bad lieutenant at this day. Was he brought up in the Navy?

For he has very much the stile of the Coal trade about him, except that they are good seamen.

In later years Admiral Hercules Robinson, who had served under Collingwood's command as a midshipman, wrote that:

Collingwood's dry, caustic mind lives before me in the recollection of his calling across the deck his fat, stupid Captain – long since dead – when he had seen him commit some monstrous blunder, and after the usual bowing and formality – which the excellent old chief never omitted – he said: 'Captain, I have been thinking, whilst I looked at you, how strange it is that a man should *grow* so big, and *know* so little. That's all Sir; that's all.'

Rotherham had been born in 1753 in the delightful abbey town of Hexham in the lush Tyne Valley, where his father was in practice as a doctor, some twenty-three miles west of Collingwood's native Newcastle upon Tyne. A memorial tablet placed in the abbey commemorates Dr Rotherham's life. And so Edward Rotherham was a near contemporary of Collingwood. His father later succeeded one Dr Askew as senior physician at the infirmary in Newcastle, later renamed the Royal Victoria Infirmary, and became also a founder member and first President of the Literary and Philosophical Society in that City, which continues to flourish to this day. A strong opponent of the Jacobites, he attached a pasquinade to a statue of Charles II when it was erected in the Exchange at Newcastle which ran to forty nine lines, and began:

> Sacred to the Memory of Charles Stuart,
> Of a justly detested race,
> And the most detestable rascal that ever disgraced the British throne,
> Ungrateful to his friends,
> Treacherous to his country,
> To humanity a stranger,
> He prostituted the best gifts of nature.

But his younger son Edward, after several years at the Head School in Newcastle upon Tyne, chose to go to sea rather than enter the medical profession, and he had indeed ended up serving in a collier. Perhaps it was this which gave Collingwood the impression that he had the style of the coal trade about him. But when Collingwood wrote as he did, Rotherham had long since been a naval officer. Indeed, after seven years service he had transferred across from the merchant service as a seaman when a young man of twenty-four in 1777. He later won promotion to the ranks of midshipman and master's mate, and then, in 1783, lieutenant, before serving on *Culloden* at the Battle of the Glorious First of June, as a senior naval first lieutenant. In that battle he had been instrumental in rescuing many of the crew of the French ship *Vengeur*. His reward had been promotion to the rank of commander.[20]

It was in 1800, and so five years before this time, that he had been advanced to the rank of post captain with command of the *Lapwing*. It had been an unconventional route into the service, for an officer usually arrived on the back of patronage or, failing that, perhaps following nomination as a King's Letter Volunteer under a scheme introduced by Samuel Pepys as a sort of sea-going apprenticeship which led to the quarterdeck. But it may be significant that in 1803, when not employed, Francis, Lord Elibo MP, had promoted Rotherham's cause in correspondence with Lord St Vincent which was followed in December of 1804 by his appointment as flag-captain to Collingwood. And in truth Collingwood must have placed some value on the man for when, before Trafalgar, Collingwood transferred over to the *Royal Sovereign* he was careful to take Rotherham with him as his Flag Captain along with Clavell and several other officers upon whom he knew he could rely. Indeed the *Royal Sovereign* was manned for the most part by men from his native Northumberland, labelled by him 'Tars of the Tyne' and, as it turned out, Rotherham was to demonstrate extremely cool judgment and commendable courage when under fire during the battle itself. So much so that Collingwood then gave him command of the *Bellerophon*, which was a good deal less successful.

In the ensuing weeks while under Collingwood's command, training for the emergency was given priority over entertainment and fraternization, and there were some in the fleet such as the newly-married Captain Codrington who resented it. He was to label Collingwood as another Stay-on Board Admiral and later turned out to be his severest critic. The judgment of William Hoste was that Collingwood liked quiet people.

On 22 August Napoleon once again ordered Villeneuve to: 'Put to sea and sail here. We will avenge 6 centuries of insults and shame.' And it was on 2 September that Captain Blackwood, bringing home dispatches for the Admiralty from Collingwood, brought word to Nelson from Collingwood that the Combined Fleet had assembled at Cadiz.

Now, with a series of masterful strokes, Barham set the stage for the Battle of Trafalgar by relaxing the blockade at both Brest and Cadiz in order to entice the French Fleet out and into battle with the Mediterranean Fleet while, at the same time, maintaining the strength of the Channel Fleet lest the southern shores of England should stand unprotected. Thus was the Squadron off Rochefort sent to reinforce Calder off El Ferrol while Cornwallis was ordered to draw back from

182

Brest where he had been keeping watch on Ganteaume.

Although Barham had been in office no more than thirteen weeks and was in his seventy-ninth year, he was by then a very seasoned campaigner. His predecessor, Melville, even though the enemy was at the door and much to the delight of Napoleon Bonaparte, had been hounded from office by St Vincent with accusations of corruption and embezzlement, committed by a subordinate for whom he maintained Melville was responsible, when holding as a sinecure the office of Treasurer of the Navy when also Home Secretary very many years before. In those difficult early months of 1805, while Melville and Pitt were exhausting every effort and every waking hour prosecuting the war with France, at their back was always the figure of St Vincent, who eventually moved the impeachment of Melville for Gross Malversation and breach of duty. At his trial Melville was eventually acquitted on all counts but that did not take place until the following year by which time he had been driven from office by a Vote of Censure carried by but one vote, the casting vote of the Speaker, and his resignation had followed on 9 April 1805. Melville, a just and honourable man and recognized to be the greatest man in Scotland in his day, then retired to his estates north of the border where he lived out the five or six years of life which remained to him. It was no more than appropriate that the statue erected in his memory and mounted on a column raised in the very heart of St Andrew's Square in Edinburgh, should have been presented by officers and men of His Majesty's Royal Navy, for his contribution towards rebuilding the strength of the Navy to meet the growing emergency after it had been so sadly decimated by the Earl St Vincent, had been immense. Not surprisingly, Napoleon had lost no time in exploiting the government's embarrassment, ordering his Finance Minister to: 'Have a little pamphlet prepared on the Melville affair to show the immorality of the English Government.'[21]

But then Pitt remembered Charles Middleton who had gone to the Navy Office as comptroller back in 1778. There he had won much praise as an immensely hardworking and efficient professional with responsibility for dockyard production. So much so that Pitt had brought him back as a Lord Commissioner on the outbreak of war in 1793, and there he had remained until he had fallen foul of St Vincent, who seemed to harbour a surprising dislike for all Scotsmen, and for Middleton in particular, whom he described as 'a Scotch Packhorse'. It was to Middleton, by this time nearly eighty years of age, that Pitt had turned when Melville departed, as a man known to have a safe pair of hands. And it turned out to be an inspired choice for, with remarkable industry for a man of his age, and at all times calm and in control, it was he who deployed the fleets, masterminded the countdown to the battle itself and supported the appointment of Nelson as Commander-in-Chief. Indeed, as Lord Barham, he was to be one of the few ministers who could be counted a success in Pitt's administration apart from Pitt himself, for it was Pitt who largely carried the government with his brilliant debating skills and prodigious hard work. Barham was to live on until 1813 when, at the age of eighty-seven, he died in his bed.

So, in September 1805, the stage was set and all England now put their trust in Horatio Nelson and looked to him for deliverance.

On 20 August he had ordered from Lock's the hatters of St James's Street, London, a cocked hat with cockade and green shade, and on 7 September he had taken delivery, at Merton, of no less than three pipes, the equivalent of 375 gallons, of best quality port which had cost him £308 at Lavell of St.Martin's Lane, clearly hoping to live long enough to drink that enormous quantity of wine, perhaps in celebration of victory.[22]

In the few days which remained to him on shore, he found his way to Downing Street, not just to Lord Castlereagh's Colonial Office where the celebrated first and only encounter with Wellington took place, but to Number 10, there to spend many a long hour with the politician both he and Collingwood admired most in this world, William Pitt.

A proud, reserved, aloof, lonely but articulate patrician of a man, he stood in stark contrast to the flamboyant, excitable and desperately ambitious Nelson. But there was much that united them – an integrity, an openness, a warmth, a generosity of spirit and a humanity, coupled with an underlying genius, and each was prepared, in his own way, to lay down his life for his country. Sadly, too, both were in their mid-forties with but a few more weeks to live. At least Nelson of the two had the reassurance of faith. The son of a clergyman he got down on his knees and knelt in prayer every day of his life, both when he rose in the morning and before going to bed.

Inevitably command of the fleet fell for discussion. Nelson immediately suggested that Collingwood was the obvious choice, saying, according to George Matcham, claiming to quote Nelson: 'You cannot have a better man than the present one.'

But Pitt had before then made up his mind that it must be Nelson, and so it was that he warned him to be ready at any moment to rejoin the Mediterranean Fleet as its commander. Pitt had not before this time troubled to know Nelson at all well, but now, after this last briefing with him on 6 September, he paid him a compliment he had accorded precious few others, for he escorted him out to his carriage which stood at the door and there bid him a farewell he seemed to know would be final.[23]

That same day Nelson wrote to his friend and treasurer Alexander Davison:

I much fear that I shall not have the pleasure of seeing you before my departure, and to thank you for all your kind attentions. I wish you would name anyone to settle my long term Account; for, although I may not be able to pay off at this moment the balance due to you, still it would be a satisfaction to me to have it settled; and then I could give you a bond for the amount, until I may be able to pay it, which I still hope to be able to do in spite of Sir John Orde.

The following day, 7 September, Nelson wrote a note to Collingwood from the Admiralty in London: 'I shall be with you in a very few days, and I hope you will remain second in command. You will change the *Dreadnought* for the *Royal Sovereign*, which I hope you will like.'

The *Royal Sovereign* had earned the label 'West Country Wagon' because she was slow in the water, but now, newly coppered, she was transformed. Although Nelson had obviously written in order to soften the blow, since Collingwood was senior to him in years, such was the character of the man and such was their friendship that Collingwood harboured no possible resentment that Nelson should have been put in over his head.

Then, after leaving instructions in London with his upholsterers to prepare and engrave the coffin which had earlier been made from wood salvaged from the mast of the French admiral's flagship at the Battle of the Nile and then presented to him by Captain Hallowell, and after kneeling in prayer by the bedside of his sleeping infant daughter, Nelson left Merton on the evening of Friday 13 September for the George at Portsmouth, traditionally the resort of senior officers in that very crowded town.

Then, in the early hours of the following day he walked from that hostelry down a back lane to the seafront in the hope of avoiding the crowd, which had assembled to see him off. There he stepped through the short tunnel which survives to this day, before crossing the moat which leads onto the front where his barge lay waiting his arrival. And so Horatio Nelson left England for the very last time, seen off by George Canning, then Treasurer of the Navy, together with George Rose, another minister in the government. A large crowd of well-wishers had assembled in the hope of catching a glimpse of their hero, many of whom cheered him to the echo and wished him God speed, others of them sinking to their knees in silent prayer.

It was on 15 September that *Victory* set sail for Cadiz and the Cape of Trafalgar.

In fact, and unbeknown to the British, the immediate danger of invasion had, by now, passed, for Napoleon, despairing of both the timid Villeneuve and indeed the hesitant Ganteaume, who was likewise still refusing to leave harbour and asking to be relieved of his command, had finally accepted that naval cover for a crossing of his naval force was unlikely to materialize. His patience now exhausted and faced with a mounting bill for the cost of the flotilla which had been built at great expense, coupled with the exorbitant expense of provisioning the Grand Armée daily on the shores of northern France, which was in any case rapidly becoming demoralized with sure inactivity, he had decided to abandon the whole enterprise. On 26 August he ordered Marshal Soult to break camp at Montreuil, St Omer and Bruges and to force march the Grand Armée east to the Danube as General Mack advanced into Bavaria and as the Czar moved down through Poland.

He himself quit his own headquarters at Boulogne on 2 September to take command of the Army and with a series of lightning strokes won great victories at Ulm in October, where Mack surrendered 27,000 Austrian soldiers, and at Austerlitz on 2 December where the Russian and Austrian Armies were both routed. It was probably the greatest victory of his career. These and other victories elsewhere gave France full-scale territorial expansion on the mainland of Europe and resulted in the dissolution of the Holy Roman Empire and the creation of the Confederation of the Rhine. Then, in the months which followed, as a substitute for an invasion of Britain, he established the Continental System which was designed to exclude Great Britain from all European trade. And to a large extent and for a time, it worked. But the greater loss in the long run was to be to Europe itself which lost not only a lucrative market in Britain but also trade elsewhere in the world as the British continued to blockade European ports and so prevent exporters from sailing, while at the same time developing new markets of their own overseas.

Meanwhile, in an exercise of saving face, for Napoleon had boasted of victory over the British for so long, he lost no time dressing up the presence of the Grand Armée on the northern shores of France for two long years between 1803 and 1805 as no more than a charade played out simply in order to deceive and frighten the British, claiming that he had never had any real intention of mounting an invasion. If in truth a pretence, it must have been one of the most costly pieces of play-acting known to history.

Corbett was, therefore, to write of the battle which was to follow, that although:

By universal assent, Trafalgar is ranked as one of the decisive battles of the world,...yet of all the great victories there is not one which to all appearances was so barren of immediate result. It had brought to a triumphant conclusion one of the most masterly and complex sea campaigns in history, but in so far as it was an integral part of the combined campaign its results are scarcely to be discerned. It gave to England finally the dominion of the seas, but it left Napoleon dictator of the Continent. So incomprehensible was its apparent sterility that to fill the void a legend grew up that it saved England from invasion...why did Pitt die believing himself defeated?

Nonetheless, so long as the Franco-Spanish Fleet remained in being, the possibility of invasion and the threat to British commercial interests in the West Indies and the East, would remain. The nation therefore had much to thank Nelson for in the weeks that followed which culminated in the Battle of Trafalgar and the virtual annihilation of the Franco-Spanish Fleet.

To some extent it was chance that persuaded the Combined Fleet out of harbour. Having, by now, lost all interest in his Navy, as a parting shot before moving east with his Army, on 16 September Napoleon ordered the Navy to return to the Mediterranean, to Genoa and to Toulon where they might be of more use in support of his campaigns on land. And then, at last, on 17 September he ordered that Villeneuve be removed from supreme command to be replaced by Admiral Rosily. Ominously, he directed that Villeneuve should return to Paris to explain himself. Paradoxically it was this last order and the prospect of the impending humiliation and disgrace which would inevitably follow, which was to finally stir Villeneuve into action and drive him out into the Atlantic, albeit on a pointless voyage and by then far too late to be of any assistance to his Emperor.

Thus did Napoleon's own order make possible the Battle of Trafalgar and the destruction of the French Fleet, for Villeneuve found himself trapped uncomfortably between the wrath and displeasure of his Emperor inland and the ferocity of Horatio Nelson lying out at sea! In fact Napoleon's orders did not reach Villeneuve until the end of September and Rosily had not by then arrived at Cadiz to take over the command. But even when they did arrive, Villeneuve and several of his officers still refused to sail for the Mediterranean, pleading lack of trained men and shortage of supplies. But in truth the real obstacle was Nelson's Fleet lying offshore, even though the French now outnumbered the British in both ships and guns.

It was not until 18 October that news of his successor did reach Villeneuve, when he was told that Rosily had set out from Madrid four days earlier on his journey to Cadiz to take over his command. Then, rather than await his arrival, followed by the inevitable loss of face, Villeneuve at last ordered the fleet to weigh anchor and set sail for the Mediterranean, believing, wrongly, that some of Nelson's ships had, by then, been detached to Gibraltar, thus giving him an even greater numerical advantage.

Long before that moment Nelson had returned to his post. On 26 September he had sent the frigate *Euryalus* on ahead to let Collingwood know of his imminent arrival and to ask that no salute should be fired or colours hoisted, lest this should warn the enemy fleet of the build up of strength in the fleet.

In the meantime, despite the promise of action suggested in Nelson's correspondence, Collingwood wrote to his father-in-law on 21 September that he was: 'fully determined, if I can get home and manage it properly, to go on shore next spring for the rest of my life; for I am very weary.' In that same letter he wrote 'How happy should I be could I but hear from home, and know how my dear girls are getting on! Bounce is my only pet now, and he is indeed a good fellow: he sleeps by the side of my cot, whenever I lie in one, until near the time of tacking, and then marches off to be out of the hearing of the guns, for he is not reconciled to them yet'. Indeed there were some in the fleet who thought that Collingwood preferred his company to theirs.

On 7 October Nelson placed their friendship on record yet again with a letter to Collingwood which finished: 'Telegraph on all occasions without ceremony. We are one and hope ever shall be.'

Then, by letter dated 9 October, Nelson sent Collingwood his plan of attack for the forthcoming encounter with the combined fleet which he judged and hoped was now inevitable:

> ...my dear friend, it is to place you perfectly at ease respecting my intentions, and to give full scope to your judgment for carrying them into effect. We can, my dear Coll., have no little jealousies: we have only one great object in view – that of annihilating our enemies and getting a glorious peace for our country. No man has more confidence in another than I have in you; and no man will render your services more justice than your very old friend, Nelson and Bronte.[24]

Collingwood's wish to be able to return home was therefore shelved yet again and this time for ever. By a letter of that same date Collingwood thanked Nelson for the confidence he had reposed in him.

On 14 October Nelson invited Collingwood over to the *Victory* for a third time since his return, on this occasion to tell him what he had in mind, and in a letter written after Trafalgar on 2 November Collingwood was to claim that at a meeting with Nelson to discuss tactics before the battle: 'We made our line of battle together, and concerted the mode of attack, which was put in execution in the most admirable style '

The General Order for the battle which Nelson produced on 18 October provided his captains with a fixed order of sailing but left some discretion to himself, leading the weather column and to his second in command, Collingwood, leading the lee column, albeit within Nelson's overall concept. It was to allow either of them to respond to any unforeseen development as it occurred. In his tactical memorandum he ordained that:

> ...the entire management of the Lee Line after the intentions of the commander in chief are signified is intended to be left to the Admiral commanding that Line. The remainder of the Enemy's fleet ...are to be left to the management of the commander in chief, who will endeavour to take care that the movements of the second in command are as little interrupted as possible.[25]

In short, Nelson deliberately left much to Collingwood's own initiative, courage and skill, and rightly so.

As ever, the wind and the weather, upon which the speed and direction of sail so much depended, was unpredictable and, in the confusion of battle, the plan devised was, in fact, little adhered to in its later stages. Countless attempts have been made over the years, including one made by the commission set up by the Admiralty in 1813, to discover some underlying fact which would explain the reason for the victory which followed, but no universal truth has ever been discovered for much of the battle was fought in a state of confusion. But it was a plan with but one object, the total destruction of the enemy fleet, for Nelson realized full well that unless that was achieved the constant threat of invasion would for ever continue. And it was to be achieved by firm, swift and decisive blows.

As Howe had intended it to be at the Battle of the First of June, and as the attack turned out to be at Cape St Vincent, and as Nelson had applied it to be at Aboukir Bay, it was to be a simple case of divide and conquer with the weight of the British Fleet under Collingwood thrown at the enemy line to the rear of centre. If successful this would mean that those enemy ships which lay isolated to the windward of the line, where it had been broken and haemorrhaged, could then be prevented from coming to the rescue of those to the leeward and could themselves be targeted and picked off by all the might and greater numbers of the

British line under Nelson advancing towards the centre. It was reckoned that it would take the rest of the ships of the combined fleet several hours to turn about if any attempt was made to assist their severed compatriots. And so the numerical advantage would remain with the British for a critical period of time. But the real hope and intention was that the enemy rear division would be subdued, rendered impotent and be driven from the battle altogether which would enable the British to concentrate upon the untouched main enemy fleet, by then reduced in number, and therefore nearer parity with the British. This then was the plan labelled by Nelson himself 'The Nelson Touch'.

In planning to drive a wedge through the enemy line it abandoned the tradition of sailing alongside enemy ships, which had recognized the fact that gunfire only became at all accurate in the last few hundred yards. But the strategy adopted by Nelson was not, in fact, new. Indeed it had been employed by Napoleon Bonaparte in many a land battle before this time. But it did involve risk for the old convention that a fleet should sail into battle in one line and that each vessel should lie alongside the enemy ship targeted and then conduct a war of attrition, did reduce the risk of being caught in friendly crossfire.

It followed that, under Nelson's plan, the leading ships of the van heading to break the enemy line at the outset of the battle would, once they came within range, be required to run the gauntlet of punishing broadsides directed across their bows without any ability to reply, for there was, at that time, no equivalent of the modern rotating gun turret. For a time, therefore, they would be at the mercy of the enemy. And since the invariable French tactic was to seek to dismast enemy ships with fire directed at their rigging where British gunners went for the hull, but with the additional assistance of small carronades which were lethal at close range to any exposed on deck, the risk of sustaining disabling fire damage running through the length of a ship before it had ever reached the enemy line was present in the plan devised by Nelson.[26]

But then he had scant regard for the gunnery and navigational skills of the untried French and Spanish sailors who lacked much in the way of operational battle or seagoing experience. It was true that they did not lack courage and had at their disposal some of the most newly commissioned and largest, albeit top-heavy, ships in the world, but they had by then very little experience on the open seas thanks to the efficiency of the blockade which had kept them cooped up in harbour for weeks and sometimes months at a time. Added to that much of the trained French officer corps had been decimated in the Revolution, whilst many of their Spanish brethren were infantrymen, fishermen, and men who had been pressed into service for a temporary spell of duty led by officers, many of whom had been born of noble families and were little more than

190

novices at sea. The British sailor on the other hand, in his well-ordered ship crewed by highly-trained officers, although to some extent worn out by months and, in many cases, years spent at sea, was for the most part very much more experienced in warfare at sea and supremely confident of success. And, as before, the ships themselves were lighter, copper-bottomed and crewed by professionals which gave them much greater manoeuvrability than their counterparts, whilst the rate of fire achieved was far superior to that of the enemy.

Nelson therefore considered that it was a risk worth taking. He would not have been so confident had he been pitched up against an enemy fleet of a fighting efficiency comparable to his own.

In this way Nelson left the direction of the line to Collingwood and it is clear from his directives that he intended that Collingwood should both lead the attack towards the rear of the crescent of the enemy fleet with what turned out to be fifteen ships under his command and then bear the brunt of the fighting, while Nelson led a second column to break the enemy line towards the centre, which in fact gave him command of the remaining twelve ships. And it was his parting directive that: 'In case signals can neither be seen or perfectly understood, no captain can do very wrong if he places his ship alongside that of an enemy.' In other words his plan was to give his captains free rein.

Nelson was careful then to bring all his captains together so that all would know of his plan of campaign, a concept of leadership far in advance of its time and one which was to be applied with such success by General Montgomery in the Second World War. Not only did he seek to lure the enemy fleet out of port so that he could destroy it, in contrast to Collingwood's blockade which sought to keep it in, but his policy too was to encourage fraternization between his ships' captains, which Collingwood had not encouraged. Thus had Hoste made the observation that 'Old Collingwood likes quiet people', adding, 'he seems to prefer the company of his beloved dog Bounce'.

On one such occasion he noted that Collingwood's Flag Captain, Rotherham, was absent, and when he asked where he was, one of those present suggested that all may not have been well between he and Collingwood. Somewhat alarmed that that may have been so when so close to a battle of such importance, Nelson promptly dispatched a boat to collect Rotherham and then led him over to Collingwood with the words: 'Look yonder at the enemy and shake hands,' and both were then glad to do just that.[27] Nelson had rightly considered that all should be brothers in the face of the enemy.

On 19 October Nelson invited his friend to join him yet again in a letter which read: 'What a beautiful day! Will you be tempted out of your ship?'

But a note written on that letter by Collingwood indicates that before his reply ever reached Nelson the balloon had gone up, for the signal was made that the enemy fleet was coming out of Cadiz, and, as Collingwood noted, 'we chased immediately'.

And so at last, and much to the undisguised astonishment and delight of Horatio Nelson, the Combined Fleet came out and battle was joined. And those two dear friends were never to meet again.

Chapter 11

Nelson and Collingwood at Trafalgar

As the mist lifted at first light in the early hours of the morning of 21 October and the curtain went up on Trafalgar, it revealed a veritable forest of ships bobbing on the horizon, poised, assembled and ready for battle, albeit in no proper formation. Collingwood described the enemy disposition in his dispatch as, 'Forming a crescent to leeward, it stretched from North to South.'[1]

Many in the British Fleet who saw it and realized the enormity of the task which lay ahead, sank to their knees in solemn prayer and made peace with their Maker before attending to the business of war. For every man knew full well both what had to be done and the chance of surviving it.

All then was frenzied activity on the flag-bedecked ships of the British Fleet as ports were hauled open, decks were cleared, canvass was run up and guns were rolled out by gunners stripped to the waist. And throughout all this and as the two fleets closed the gap of two miles which separated them, so the bands played on.

For one last time Nelson went down to his cabin and there at almost 11 o' clock committed to his diary the now famous prayer which is still read out on *Victory* every Trafalgar Day:

> May the Great God, whom I worship, Grant to my Country and for the benefit of Europe in General a great and Glorious Victory, and may no misconduct in any one tarnish it, and may humanity after Victory be the predominant feature in the British Fleet. For myself individually I commit my life to Him who made me, and may his blessing light upon my endeavours for serving My Country faithfully, to Him I resign myself and the Just cause which is entrusted to me to defend. Amen. Amen. Amen.'[2]

And it was on his knees that his Signals Lieutenant John Pasco found

193

him, quickly withdrawing before he had spoken the message he had come to deliver lest he should disturb his commander at prayer. Nelson then applied his mind to the famous codicil to his will which left Lady Hamilton as a legacy to his King and Country, before going up on deck.

Collingwood, in the 100-gun *Royal Sovereign*, cool and composed as ever, carefully shaved and slowly dressed before going up on deck. As he did so he casually asked Smith, who had succeeded William Ireland as his servant, if he had yet seen the enemy, only to carry on with his ablutions when told that a crowd of great ships could now be seen through the mist. Ready to perform the leading role which had been allocated to him which was to head and orchestrate the first attack, like both Nelson and Villeneuve that morning, Collingwood then put on his silk stockings and full gold epauletted dress uniform, medals resplendent. And then, while making his rounds as any good officer would before a battle to comfort and encourage the men who were to do the fighting that day, it is said that he advised Lieutenant Clavell to change his boots and put on shoes and silk stockings as he had himself to make it more manageable for the surgeon should he be shot in the leg. It is doubtful that Clavell was much comforted by that advice. And then, addressing his officers, he said: 'Now, gentlemen, let us do something today which the world may talk of hereafter.'

Morale on his ship was high for many under his command, and Collingwood himself, hailed from that same distant town, Newcastle upon Tyne.[3] And so a pride and a loyalty bound them all together in their exile. Midshipman Thomas Aikenhead wrote of Collingwood to his sister at home: 'Our old Admiral is quite young with the thoughts of it.'

When Rotherham made his appearance on deck it was seen that he wore a cocked hat which was disproportionately large and colourfully embroidered with gold lace which more than capped his ample frame. It presented a prominent and noticeable target for any enemy sniper who might care to exercise his trigger finger. Yet when this was pointed out to him he responded with: 'Let me alone, I have always fought in a cocked hat and I always will.'[4]

Gun crews were ordered to lie flat in an attempt to minimize casualties as they withstood enemy fire on the approach.

It was at 11.48 a.m. and under a grey Trafalgar sky that the signal 'England expects that every man will do his duty' was hoisted aloft by *Victory*. And it drew cheers from the crew, several of them not even English. But from Collingwood came the laconic: 'What is Nelson signalling about? We all know what we have to do', as indeed they did. But then he too expressed to all around him his delight at the signal, for it joined them all together in a common cause and was at last the starting gun for their encounter with the enemy that day.

There is great disparity between times recorded in the ships' logs for the next few hours, but it was about twelve midday,[5] and without a moment's hesitation and with a courage which can only be marvelled at, Collingwood, at the head of his column of fifteen ships and with full spread of canvass, sailed forthright into the very belly of the enemy fleet of thirty-three ships. He hit it between the 18th and 19th of the line and not at the 13th as had been intended, having outsailed the rest of his squadron and put a good twenty minutes of sailing time between himself and the nearest British ship astern. The plan had been to outnumber those to the rear of the combined fleet but a bunching had produced a partially double line so that he was outnumbered by seventeen. It is oft said that Nelson, watching this manoeuvre with amazement and delight, cried to his captain, Hardy: 'See how that noble fellow Collingwood takes his ship into action!', and it as often said too that at about that same moment Collingwood was heard to say to Rotherham: 'What would Nelson give to be here!'.[6]

Small wonder that Admiral Hercules Robinson, who was then a midshipman and a witness to this event, should have written later in his book *Seadrift*:

How I see at this moment glorious old Collingwood a quarter of a mile ahead of his second astern, and opening the battle with the magnificent black *Santa Ana*...and extinguishing one ship of the thirty-three we had to deal with...I see before me ...dear old Cuddie (as we called Collingwood), walking the break of the poop with his little triangular gold-laced cocked hat, tights, silk stockings and buckles, musing over the progress of the fight and munching an apple.

Quarterdecks, and poops when provided, lay in the aftermost part of a ship. As areas reserved for officers from which they could direct and control a ship's activities, they must have been fertile grounds for enemy marksman nestling in the tops of ships lying alongside, as Nelson was to discover all too soon. Yet there both he and Collingwood and most of the captains stood their ground, exposed as they were.

It was reported too that at this critical moment Collingwood was seen to be calmly folding up a studding sail which had fallen out of place so that it might be used another day. And, as Robinson was to write: 'looking himself along the guns to see that they were properly pointed...[he] had a single-handed coolness that he showed all day.'

Inevitably as he sailed into the thick of the combined fleet at 12.10,

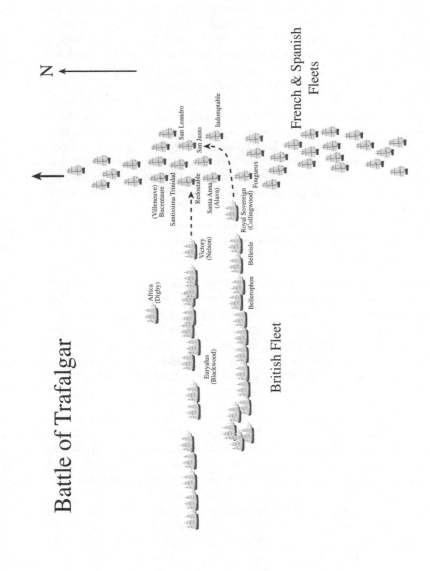

Battle of Trafalgar

N

French & Spanish
Fleets

British Fleet

Africa
(Digby)

Euryalus
(Blackwood)

Victory
(Nelson)

Belleisle

Bellerophon

Royal Sovereign
(Collingwood)

Fougueux

Santa Anna
(Alava)

Redoutable

Santissima Trinidad

(Villeneuve)
Bucentaure

San Justo

San Leandro

Indomptable

some fifteen or twenty minutes before *Victory* had hit the line, he came within range of sighting rounds from the enemy's guns. And then, within seconds, he drew down upon himself a merciless fire from the towering Spaniards ranged around him. Although he then pierced the line to some extent, far from cutting through it and then coming round behind the enemy, which had been Nelson's plan, the wind had carried five ships abreast of him which surrounded him, barred his way and effectively halted all further progress. These included the *Fougueux* which first attempted to close the gap until Collingwood made to ram her, but also the 112-gun *Santa Ana,* the second largest ship afloat, both of which opened fire as he approached, while the *San Leandro, Indomptable* and *San Justo* added to the onslaught which then came in from all sides, so much so that some of their salvos collided mid-air. But, although outnumbered five to one, alone in the midst of the enemy and under heavy albeit inaccurate bombardment, Collingwood, with great courage, discipline and astonishing restraint held his fire until within very close range. Only then did the *Royal Sovereign* respond with the first shots of the battle from the British side in order to send up a pro-tective screen of smoke. He then released a murderous raking fire which belched out and swept the decks of the 112-gun *Santa Ana* followed by a barrage of unremitting hot-iron broadsides as he drew alongside. The first blows are always the most telling, better aimed and more carefully prepared than those delivered in the heat of battle. It had a deadly effect, causing wholesale slaughter on the deck. It crippled her fire power, put fourteen guns out of action and killed several hundred terrified men. *Fougueux* too was driven off course by the sure enormity of it.

Meanwhile, *Victory*, to windward, leading a column of sixteen with Captain Eliab Harvey in the *Temeraire* next astern, had met with oppo-sition from the *Bucentaure, Neptune* and *Redoutable* which had brought Nelson to a standstill. He, too, had failed to penetrate the line to any extent and had been left stranded at the mercy of murderous crossfire until *Temeraire* had come to his aid. But in the chaos, confusion and heat of unplanned battle which followed, and using their own ini-tiative and following the example of each other as Nelson had intended they should, it was to be the vastly superior gunnery skills of the British sailors which tipped the balance in their favour. In their handling of their ordinary rated firepower, but augmented now by 32-pound short-range carronades from the Glasgow yard of Carron which were lighter, more easily manipulated and more deadly than their predecessors, their greater skill began to tell. In Collingwood's judgment: 'A battle planned by officers but won by sailors'.

As ever the French, in the main, aimed at masts and rigging where the British concentrated upon the hulls. And as the battle raged so a gap in the enemy line did in fact open up, but not by severance or design. The *Santa Ana* now stood at the head of the rear column of nineteen ships and the *Redoutable* was the last of the remaining fourteen.

Although he had taken command of the *Royal Sovereign* but ten days before, the famous Collingwood firepower now came into its own and as she ranged up against the *Santa Ana*, so the *Santa Ana* responded and there followed one of the most epic sea battles in all naval history and the most violent, destructive and longest of the many encounters of that day. It was to last for two hours or more with both ships mercilessly intent on annihilation. The fighting was undoubtedly fierce, for the French and Spanish Fleet, once brought to action, fought tenaciously and with great courage. This is evidenced in a letter written after the battle by Collingwood to his wife, in which he, not a man to exaggerate, tells of supporting on his shoulder the head of the master of the *Royal Sovereign*, William Chalmers, who had fallen mortally wounded close to his side. And it recalls too a moment on the quarterdeck when all around him were either killed or wounded save for himself, his secretary Cosway and Captain Edward Rotherham.

Indeed Collingwood was, himself, fortunate to escape serious injury for he had calmly remained on the poop in full uniform and in an exposed position throughout the battle and dangerously long after he had ordered the Captain of Marines and his men to evacuate that hazardous area and go below. But he did not emerge entirely unscathed for a flying splinter struck one of his legs and caused a flesh wound which, fortunately, was superficial. Yet still he stuck to his post, stemming the flow of blood with a pocket handkerchief applied as a tourniquet and carrying on.

A typical eyewitness account was that of a Durham midshipman, one George Castle, who wrote of the Spanish that: 'it was shocking to see the many brave seamen mangled so, some with their heads half shot away.'

Mercifully the time came when in the confusion of the moment the Spaniards realized they were inflicting as much damage to their own vessels with their crossfire as they were causing to Collingwood, and this, together with the timely arrival of three British ships of the line, the *Belleisle, Mars* and *Tonnant*, persuaded the Spaniards to withdraw and leave the *Santa Ana* to continue the battle alone. But it was only after a further hour or so of hard pounding that the Spaniard finally submitted to Collingwood's superior gunnery and eventually struck her colours at 2.15 p.m. By this time the *Santa Ana* had lost almost 300 men killed or wounded, whilst the *Royal Sovereign* had lost forty-seven men killed, including three officers and two midshipmen, and ninety-four wounded,[7] amongst whom Clavell and Thompson were numbered. Lost too were both her main and mizzen masts, with only her foremast remaining, and so, unable to carry sail, she was of no further use in the battle. It was then that the frigate *Euryalus*, commanded by Captain Blackwood, came to the rescue and took the *Royal Sovereign* in tow and it was from there, as the battle raged, that Collingwood continued to lead and command the four groups of his lee column and indeed the fleet itself after the death of Nelson. Small wonder that the Trafalgar Roll was to record of the *Royal Sovereign* that: 'no ship covered herself with greater distinction.'

In the heat of battle Collingwood was to show a magnanimity which was his nature when Blackwood, who had been sent over to the *Santa Ana* to take Admiral Alava prisoner, returned with his captain instead. He then proffered the Admiral's sword with the explanation that his admiral was at death's door. Hearing this Collingwood promptly sent the man back to care for him.

Although it was fifteen minutes or so after 1 p.m.[8] that a French marine in the mizzen top of the *Redoutable*, firing at random at figures moving in and out of the smoke and tumult at close range, put a musket ball into Nelson's left shoulder which lodged in his spine as he paced the quarterdeck, at a spot where his secretary Scott had been felled but a little while before, it was not until about 2.30 p.m. that Collingwood received the news. It came from Captain Hardy and was delivered by Lieutenant Hills of the *Victory* after his sailors had managed to row him the half a mile or so which separated the two ships, through smoke, debris and scorching gunfire. The fact that they had troubled to run such a gauntlet to bring Hardy's message to him told Collingwood that the wound must have been severe indeed and he immediately feared the worst. But then Nelson lay dying down below for two hours or more with Dr Beatty, his surgeon, and Dr Scott, his chaplain never leaving his side, lying in the surgeon's shallow cockpit deck, which passed for a makeshift dispensary below the lowest gun deck, in the absence of any hospital quarters. Amongst reports of 'Kiss me Hardy' and 'Thank God I have done my duty', it is said that when the tall and large Dorset man, Captain Hardy, feared as a fierce disciplinarian, suggested that Collingwood would now take upon himself the direction of affairs, his response was 'Not while I live, I hope', and 'if I live I'll anchor.' With him, too, were some of his officers, including Collingwood's kinsman, Midshipman Francis Collingwood; all of them gathered around him, and it was not until shortly after 4 p.m. that all life left him. And when the news of his friend's death was then brought to Collingwood, this time by Captain Hardy himself, tears coursed down his old ruddy, weather-beaten cheeks.

But the two fleets were still locked in battle and duty called and so it was Collingwood who now directed and continued the British attack. Eventually it was the explosion of the *Achille* which effectively marked the end of the Battle of Trafalgar as those 100 or so members of her crew still alive of the 600 who had manned her, struggled to keep afloat in the now dark waters of Trafalgar, many of them only saved thanks to the Herculean efforts of mercy crews sent out from Captain Grindall's *Prince*. Soon afterward the wounded Don Frederico Gravina, commander of the enemy rear division which had taken the full brunt of Collingwood's initial onslaught, finally surrendered and signalled for the Spanish Fleet to withdraw. The guns on both sides then fell mercifully silent in a deadly hush, and so ended the greatest victory at sea in the whole of British naval history.

And so it was on the *Euryalus* after the battle was over, that Collingwood, in place of Nelson, received Villeneuve, the tall, thin, patrician commander-in-chief of the combined Franco-Spanish Fleet, dressed in a long-tailed uniform coat and sporting green coloured corduroy pantaloons. Despite Villeneuve's earlier hesitation and clear misgivings, once in action he had met the British attack with commendable courage.

Despite the carnage and devastation which had been caused to the combined Franco-Spanish Fleet, Gravina managed to shepherd eleven of his ships back to the safety of Cadiz, but he was to die of his wounds but a few months later, then aged forty-nine years. Perhaps only eight of the British Fleet, four in Nelson's column and four in Collingwood's, had been at the heart of the battle all day as the higher casualty figures for *Victory, Royal Sovereign, Temeraire* and *Colossus* show. But in three hours of fighting, seventeen of the thirty-three sail of the line in the enemy fleet, which had engaged the British, had been captured, and one had been destroyed, whilst a further four of the fifteen which had escaped were taken by the British fifteen days later and hauled off to Gibraltar as prizes. But, of those taken, all but four were to be lost to the high seas before they could be brought into harbour and of the eleven led back to Cadiz by Gravina, several were badly damaged. Almost 7,000 Spaniards and Frenchmen had been killed or wounded and many more taken prisoner, two thirds of them Frenchmen. In contrast, the British did not lose a single ship but of the 17,000 men who had been engaged, 1,700 were lost as casualties, including almost 449 killed. They, like Nelson, had not lived to celebrate the victory. The presence of death all around and the loss of many a comrade cast a long shadow over those who had, only a few hours before, rejoiced at the prospect of battle. But they now set to work with a will in the hope of restoring order to the dreadful chaos. To Collingwood's annoyance, his own capture, the *Santa Ana*, was one of those which escaped back to

Cadiz, carrying with it its flag commander and Collingwood's prisoner, Admiral Alava, who, thanks to Collingwood, had been allowed to remain on board on his captain's protestation that he was a dying man. His claim now was that as an escapee he was no longer a prisoner of war. With a remarkable recovery he was able ,the following year to take over command of the fleet from Gravina, subsequently became Governor of Havana, was later promoted Captain-General at Cadiz and finally became Captain General of the Fleet.

Collingwood's column had captured or disabled no less than nine ships of the enemy's rear and effectively destroyed it.

Although very relieved at the sure magnitude of the victory which had delivered the combined fleet a mortal blow, and although an immense task now faced him in trying to secure the prizes taken in a rising sea where there was no opportunity to anchor, Collingwood's abiding thought now was for his friend Nelson, who was no more. The inescapable reality was that a friendship of thirty years was now at an end. Indeed this dreadful thought dominated every report of the battle that he was afterwards required to make. For him it was the end of an era.

He wrote to his father-in-law by letter dated 2 November of the moment when he learned of Nelson's death:

> When my dear friend received his wound, he immediately sent an officer to me to tell me of it, and give his love to me. Though the officer was directed to say the wound was not dangerous, I read in his countenance what I had to fear, and before the action was over, Captain Hardy came to inform me of his death. I cannot tell you how deeply I was affected; my friendship for him was unlike anything that I have left in the Navy – a brotherhood of more than thirty years. In this affair he did nothing without my counsel, we made our line of battle together, and concerted the mode of attack, which was put in execution in the most admirable style.

He was to write to the same effect to the Duke of Clarence. And to Spencer-Stanhope, in a letter dated 6 March 1806, he wrote:

> I have indeed had a severe loss in the death of my excellent friend Lord Nelson...since the year 73 we have been on the terms of the greatest intimacy, chance has thrown us very much together in service, and on many occasions we have acted in concert; there is scarce a naval subject that has not been the subject of our discussion, so that his opinions were familiar to me, and so firmly founded on principles of honour, of justice, of attachment to his Country, at the

same time so entirely divested of every thing interested to himself, that it was impossible to consider him but with admiration. He liked fame, and was open to flattery, so that people sometimes got about him who were unworthy of him: he is a loss to his country that cannot easily be replaced.[9]

Looked at in the round, the contribution which Collingwood had made to the success of the day had been massive. His command and training of the fleet in preparation for the battle, before Nelson ever sailed out to take command, had been meticulous. The firepower which he had wrung from his own crew had been awesome and pre-eminent. His command of the lee column during the action itself had been impeccable, and he had led it from the front as the first to break the enemy line, taking on without hesitation the mightiest of the ships of the line of the combined Franco-Spanish Fleet. And after the death of Nelson he had carried the British Fleet through to victory. The nation had much to thank him for.

In fact, by a curious twist of circumstance, the second vessel to strike the enemy's line had been the smallest ship in the fleet, the *Africa* of 64 guns, commanded by the youngest captain in the fleet, the same, now wealthy, Captain Henry Digby, aged thirty-five, of whom Collingwood had written in such flattering terms six years before in the autumn of 1799. In that letter to Sir Edward Blackett he had described him as 'a Fine Young Man'.

The *Africa* had come out from home and joined Nelson's Weather Column on 14 October only seven days before. But then, the night before the battle itself and, at a moment when she had lost touch with the *Victory*, unbeknown to Digby the fleet had turned south leaving the *Africa* out of touch and straying on a course which took her northward and away from the rest of the fleet. However a further twist the following day had brought her back into the very heart of the action when the enemy fleet had gone about and turned into the path of the now isolated and bewildered *Africa*. The moment he saw this Nelson had put up an urgent signal to Digby to immediately: 'Make all sail possible with safety to the masts.'[10]

But instead of reading this to mean,'Rejoin the Fleet without delay', as it undoubtedly did, the intrepid Digby had chosen to interpret that signal otherwise as an order to 'Engage the Enemy'. And this he had then proceeded to do, and with gusto. First, according to his own journal, he jettisoned overboard all stores of bread, beef, drink and other cargo which was surplus to requirement in order to lighten his vessel and improve its speed and manoeuvrability in preparation for the engagement which lay ahead. And then, as he ran the gauntlet of the enemy line to regain his position with Nelson's column, he let fly with broadsides at every enemy ship he encountered on the way, until he ended up confronting the vast, magnificent and forbidding 130-gun 4-decker monster, *Santissima Trinidad*, the largest ship afloat. It towered like Goliath over his diminutive vessel, the smallest ship in the fleet.

But by then the battle-worn *Santissima* was motionless and limping in the water with all her masts collapsed and with the 74-gun *Conqueror* pounding her from the lee quarter. And so Digby, understandably, sent a boarding party over, under the command of Lieutenant John Smith to take the surrender of a ship he assumed was out of the battle. But Smith was met by an affronted but courteous officer on the quarterdeck who told him that he had no intention of striking. With commendable chivalry the boarding party had then been allowed to withdraw unmolested. In his own journal Digby afterwards claimed he had actively engaged the *Santissima* in support of Captain Fremantle's 3-decker *Neptune*, but it is not at all clear how long Fremantle's engagement had been ongoing by the time he came on the scene. In a letter to his uncle, Admiral Robert Digby, to be found at Minterne and dated 1 November, he wrote that he had brought down the foremast of the *Santissama*.

Whatever be the true position, the *Africa* then turned its attention to the 74-gun *Intrepide*, the next ship which had come into its sights, which by then had got the better of Henry Bayntun in the *Leviathan*. There followed more than forty minutes of thunderous exchange which eventually silenced *Africa*'s guns and shattered her masts but yet still failed to conquer her captain who steadfastly refused to capitulate. Mercifully Sir Edward Codrington in the 74-gun *Orion* then came to the rescue. Closing in on the *Leviathan* and placing his ship between her and the *Africa* and with a withering bombardment he blasted away her main and mizzen masts and pounded her into surrender. And so, by 5 p.m. that day, Digby and Codrington had forced the *Intrepide* to haul down her colours. It was only then that the admiral flying his flag in the *Santissima* was taken prisoner, but now by Captain Grindall of the *Prince*. And no shot had been fired by her since Digby had left her.

In the service of their country, eighteen men on the *Africa* were killed and thirty-seven or more were wounded.[11] The casualties on *Intrepide* were 320. And so, without doubt, many courageous men contributed to the victory that day, but first amongst these had been Nelson and his friend Collingwood.

After the battle Captain Blackwood wrote of Collingwood to his wife. Collingwood was not really a man known to him well, but he wrote:

I hope it is not injustice to the Second in Command,...who fought like a hero, to say that the Fleet under any other, never would have performed what they did under Lord N. But under Lord N. it seemed like inspiration to most of them...

Admiral Collingwood,...is a very reserved, though a very pleasing good man, and as he fought like an angel, I take the more to him.[12]

At Trafalgar the will of the French Navy was broken irrevocably and Napoleon's plans for the invasion of Britain could never again be resurrected. The British Navy was to reign invincible and supreme on the high seas for a century or more. Thus ended eight of the most glorious years in the long history of the British Royal Navy.

Although Napoleon's thirst for territorial expansion continued apace for a decade or more until the defeat of his armies at Waterloo, it was in the years 1803, 1804 and 1805 that Great Britain had been most at risk of invasion. Nelson had appreciated this well enough, as had William Pitt who was woken at 3 a.m. on the morning of 6 November to be told of the great victory off Trafalgar, but also of the sad death of Horatio Nelson; news delivered by the captain of the frigate *Pickle*, Lieutenant John Richard Lapenotiere, who had been nominated by Collingwood to carry his Trafalgar dispatch to the Admiralty. It was dated 22 October and was in the form of two letters amounting to more than 1,000 words. Pitt was to say that it was the one occasion in the whole of his prime ministerial career on which he had been unable to go back to sleep after being woken with urgent news.

Quite why the thirty-five year old Devonian John Lapenotiere of French descent had been chosen for this prestigious mission was never explained. But the probability is that it was because Collingwood knew that the schooner *Pickle*, rather than the usual frigate, was quicker than most in the water. And so it proved for, after farming out his prisoners and casting four of the ship's carronades overboard to lighten her load, she had then, with her ensign at half mast, made sail on 26 October, and although hostile weather was encountered on the voyage, Lapenotiere came ashore at Falmouth only eight days later on the morning of 4 November. His expenses sheet survives to corroborate his account of the journey. Then, without pause, he travelled post haste by coach for London and the Admiralty in Whitehall which, after several changes of horse, he reached at 1 a.m. on 6 November, a date which has ever since been celebrated by officers of the Royal Navy attending Pickle Night dinners. And in doing so he had out sailed Captain Sykes of the *Nautilus* who had met up with the *Pickle* on the high seas and who had himself made for Lisbon and then raced to the Admiralty in London with the news, arriving there but a short time after Lapenotiere. There the breathless Lapenotiere reported to Marsden, Secretary to the Board, who was just rising from his desk: 'Sir,we have gained a great victory; but we have lost Lord Nelson', news which Marsden then conveyed to the First Lord, Lord Barham, who calmly rose from his bed to make the necessary arrangements for its dissemination.

The King, too, recognized full well that a great danger had passed when he was woken at 7 a.m. at Windsor and read aloud the noble dispatch written by Cuthbert Collingwood, modest of the part which he had played himself:

> The ever to be lamented death of Vice-Admiral Lord Viscount Nelson, who, in the late conflict with the enemy, fell in the hour of victory...the loss of a hero whose name will be immortal...I beg to congratulate their lordships on a victory which I hope will add a ray to the sun of His Majesty's Crown, and be attended with public benefit to our country.

These were the words of a man who had suffered personal loss.[13] Visibly moved by the tragic news of Nelson's death, and by, also, the exquisite grace and elegance of Collingwood's majestic and masterly language, the King was unable to find words for more than a while as the tears rolled down his old care-worn cheeks. He then slowly led his family into St George's Chapel to give thanks to Almighty God for the victory of his countrymen at sea.[14]

Later he was to ask his Lord Chancellor Eldon: 'Where did this sea-Captain get his admirable English?', before going on, 'Oh I remember he was educated by Moises', recalling what Eldon had earlier told him that the two had sat together at the feet of Moises some forty-five years before. Indeed Eldon was to report this with some pride to Moises himself in a letter written shortly after the event.[15]

The dispatch was an impressive piece of work, the more so since it had been written hurriedly by Collingwood soon after the battle and in cramped conditions while in the small cabin of his temporary quarters on board the *Euryalus* as it rode on very rough and turbulent seas, graphically captured by John Thomas Serres in his painting *Storm After The Battle of Trafalgar* which is at Minterne.

Official news of the victory was then quickly published in the *London Gazette* and rushed to Lady Nelson and Lady Hamilton by Sir Andrew Snape Hamond,[16] Sir John Orde's friend and mentor in the service, and Comptroller of the Navy at that time. The Lord Mayor was then informed so that the message should be conveyed to Lloyds of London. Bells then rang out across the rooftops of the city and the roar of cannon in Windsor Great Park heralded the victory. The following morning *The Times* newspaper carried the full momentous story which echoed

205

through the nation and became the talking point on every street corner, although rumours of it had in fact reached Penzance the day before, carried there by Cornish fishermen who had met up with the *Pickle*. Indeed the mayor, one Giddes, had interrupted a banquet, over which he was presiding at the Union Hotel, to broadcast the news to those assembled there.[17] Hence the claim that the *Royal Cornwall Gazette* and not the *London Gazette* was the first to carry the news,[18] although it seems that the *Gibraltar Chronicle Extraordinary* may have had that honour, for it had, on 24 October, already published Collingwood's dispatch of 22 October.[19]

As for Collingwood's wife Sarah, it was said that she fainted when she first heard the news on 8 November[20] for she was at the moment in a shop in Newcastle upon Tyne and heard it from a coachman bringing mail, who foolishly said also that not only Nelson but all the admirals in the fleet had been killed in the action.

On the night of 9 November Pitt was toasted at a banquet at the Guildhall as 'The saviour of Europe'. In reply he chose his words with care and caution:

> I return you my thanks for the honour you have done me; but Europe is not to be saved by any single man. England has saved herself by her exertions, and will, I trust, save Europe by her example.

With but a weak team of ministers to rely on, he had himself taken much of the burden of the exchequer, foreign affairs and war upon his own frail shoulders and he was now all but spent.

The nation now started to dismantle its coastal defences and stand down the voluntary militia in preparation for a return to normal life and for the return also of HMS *Victory* and the body of its hero. It was to be a long delay, for the crew of *Victory*, devoted to the memory of their commander, as they were, rightly insisted that he be brought home in his own battle-damaged ship and by his own crew. Nelson had expressed a wish, as he lay dying, that he should not be thrown overboard, as was the norm, and this was respected.

Although they had met but seldom, that good old man, King George III, saw Collingwood's worth and goodness immediately and so, almost by return of post, he sat down and dictated a letter to his personal secretary to be sent without delay to Collingwood out in the Mediterranean. It was fulsome in its praise with a generosity he had never shown to Nelson and it was to become Collingwood's most treasured possession, as he was to tell his wife in a letter home dated 16 December 1805:

...as the King's personal compliment I value it above everything. I am told that when my letter was carried to him he could not read it for tears, joy, and gratitude to heaven for our success so entirely overcame him...but I will tell you what I feel nearest to my heart after the honour which His Majesty has done me, and that is the praise of every officer of the fleet.

It read:

Windsor, Nov. 7th, 1805.

Every tribute of praise appears to His Majesty due to Lord Nelson, whose loss he can never sufficiently regret; but His Majesty considers it very fortunate that the command, under circumstances so critical, should have devolved upon an officer of such consummate valour, judgement and skill as Admiral Collingwood has proved himself to be, every part of whose conduct he considers deserving his entire approbation and admiration. The feeling manner in which he has described the events of that great day and those subsequent, and the modesty with which he speaks of himself, whilst he does justice, in terms so elegant and so ample, to the meritorious exertions of the gallant officers and men under his command, have also proved extremely gratifying to the King.

In due course, at the insistence of his sovereign and not surprisingly, Collingwood was appointed to supreme command of the Mediterranean Fleet in succession to Horatio Nelson, and the King continued to support him for the rest of his life.

His General Order, commending the role played in the battle by every officer and man, was written in terms equally moving, and indeed the whole body of his correspondence with the Admiralty accounting for every last detail of the battle was written in prose which would have done credit to any of the foremost writers of the day.

To the Admiralty he had written:

I have not only to lament in common with the British Navy and the British Nation in the fall of the Commander-in-Chief, the loss of a Hero whose name will be immortal, and his memory ever dear to his country; but my heart is rent with the most poignant grief for the death of a friend to whom by many years intimacy, and the perfect knowledge of the virtues of his mind, which inspired ideas superior to the common race of men, I was bound by the strongest ties of affection; a grief to which even the glorious occasion on which he fell does not bring that consolation which perhaps it ought.[21]

207

Collingwood's wife referred again to her husband's grief at the loss of his friend when she wrote to her own friend, Miss Woodman, on 10 November 1805:

> The list of congratulations on the safety of My dear Husband and of his great and glorious Victory tho it has cost us dear in the death of the gallant and brave Nelson whose fate I lament not only as a public loss but being the intimate and beloved friend of My Husband, who was in great affliction at the event.[22]

And amidst all this Collingwood made time to write of Nelson's death to Mrs Moutray who had been such a friend to both of them.

A few days after the battle Collingwood shifted his blue flag as a Vice-Admiral of the Blue from the *Euryalus* to the *Queen*. It was from that ship on 1 November that he penned a letter giving an account of the battle to old Admiral Sir Peter Parker who had been such a good patron to both Nelson and Collingwood in their early years, a thing they had never forgotten when finding positions for friends and relatives he sent out to them:

> ...had it not been for the fall of our noble friend, who was indeed the glory of England, and the admiration of all who ever saw him in Battle, your pleasure would have been perfect – that two of your own pupils, raised under your eye, and cherished by your kindness, should render such service to their Country as I hope this Battle, in its effect, will be...Our Ships were fought with a degree of gallantry that would have warmed your heart. Everybody exerted themselves, and a glorious day they made of it...all did admirably well; and the conclusion was grand beyond description; eighteen hulks of the Enemy lying among the British Fleet without a stick standing, and the French *Achille* burning...The storm being violent and many of our own Ships in most perilous situations, I found it necessary to order the captures, all without masts, some without rudders, to be destroyed, and many half full of water, to be destroyed, except such as were in better plight; for my object was their ruin, and not what might be made of them.
> God bless you my dear Sir Peter! May you ever be happy.
> Your affectionate and faithful servant, C. Collingwood. [23]

Sir Peter was pleased beyond measure to receive such a letter of gratitude and took it with him to show the King. And he, in turn, was so taken by it that he had a copy of the letter made for himself.

In fact, at the final count, sixteen of the thirty-three ships of the

208

Franco-Spanish Fleet had been destroyed, either during or immediately after the battle, four were hauled off to Gibraltar as prizes, eleven escaped, two were taken back by the enemy, albeit at a cost, and of those which had escaped, several were damaged, and four others were afterwards soon recaptured by Sir Richard Strachan's squadron and later brought into Plymouth.

Initially there had been criticism in some quarters of the fleet under Collingwood's command because he had failed to anchor as Hardy told him had been Nelson's wish, and because he had then scuttled so many of the prizes won. It had been hoped that those captured would be bought for repair to be restored for use in the British Fleet, thus raising substantial prize money.. But, in truth, it had been the weather at sea which had dictated that decision. A strong south-westerly had built up shortly after the battle and then changed direction towards midnight which had threatened to drive the captures onto the sharp reefs of Cape Trafalgar a few miles to the leeward. This had made it impossible, over the next two days as the sea ran high, to hold the battered prizes in tow or to anchor with a view to salvage, as Nelson had directed in his dying moments, and as Collingwood had at first ordered himself, for many had lost their stability together with their anchors or cables in the battle.[24] Indeed four of the captured ships ran against the rocky shore in the gale and sank with considerable loss of life, and the mighty *Santissima Trinidad* went to the bottom before her battle damage could be plugged. Collingwood rightly thought it better that the remainder should be destroyed rather than that they should be allowed to endanger those ships towing them or that they should be left to drift back into the hands of the enemy. It had been a hard decision to make since it meant for all concerned, and most of all for Collingwood, the sacrifice of a fortune in prize money but, as ever, Collingwood had put the interests of his country first, and not one of his own ships was lost. All had been able to ride out the storm which raged for four long days, albeit with great difficulty. As Collingwood himself wrote, he 'would rather fight another battle than pass through such a week as followed it', and, 'I never saw such exertions as were made to save those ships'. For all that, there were some naval historians who afterwards blamed him for it, although St Vincent was to tell Lord Eldon that Collingwood's conduct after Trafalgar was beyond all praise. The Serres painting at Minterne shows the flag signal flown to captains, namely 'Prepare to quit and withdraw men from Prizes after having destroyed or disabled if time permits'.

Indeed, two days after the battle a small squadron of French ships had emerged from Cadiz and had attempted to salvage some of the prizes but, fortunately, the British Fleet was able to stand between the prizes and the French, although they did succeed in towing the *Santa Ana* and the *Algeciras* back to port. But a similar attempt with the *Neptuno* failed when the ship sank before reaching Cadiz.

In Digby's letter to his uncle dated 1 November 1805, he wrote that: 'Out of so many prizes , it has pleased God that the elements should destroy most, perhaps to lessen the vanity of man after so great a victory.'

Afterwards parliament voted a special award of £300,000 to those who had fought at Trafalgar to compensate to some extent for the loss of those prizes which had had to be abandoned and this, together with the money raised on the four captures brought home successfully, gave each captain more than £3,000, although more junior officers would receive only about a tenth of that figure, and other personnel and ordinary seamen a good deal less than that.

The question whether more prizes could have been saved by ordering the ships to anchor, is a question which has been debated ever since and is not now capable of resolution but the probability is that it would have made very little difference.

After the battle Collingwood put to one side the conqueror's pride and demonstrated magnanimity by offering, in a letter to the Governor of Cadiz, the Marquis de Solano, to repatriate all wounded Spanish prisoners.[25] It was an act of humanity which won over the Spaniards completely for they then reciprocated fulsomely with generous offers of hospital care, accommodation, food and wine and with loud applause for the British.

Collingwood was, obviously and understandably, very pleased and flattered to receive the plaudits of all and sundry for the part he had played at Trafalgar but, as events turned out, he was never able to taste or enjoy the fruits of his success back at home amongst his own family, friends and those who knew him, for he was destined to spend all of what remained of his life at sea in the service of his country. But for his wife it was otherwise. Now the wife of one of the nation's heroes, every door was opened to her. She was guest of honour at a Victory Ball held in the Mansion House by the City and Corporation of Collingwood's native Newcastle upon Tyne, the mayor's official residence, then fronting the Tyne, and it seems clear from letters written by her to her friends at the time that she then entered into the social round with con-siderable enthusiasm.

It is doubtful that Collingwood himself would have obtained the same degree of pleasure from such a programme of entertainment, but no doubt he drew satisfaction vicariously from the honour done to his wife.

Although treated less generously than Nelson's family, he was now showered with honours by a grateful nation. These were announced on 9 November. Raised to the peerage as Baron Collingwood of Caldburne and Hethpool – Hethpool after an estate in which his wife had inherited a half interest, Caldburne being land owned by Carlyle's wife – he was made a Freeman of the Cities of London, Bath, Bristol, Exeter, Cork, Portsmouth and Southampton, and also of Trinity House at Newcastle upon Tyne. He was granted a pension of £2,000 a year for life, with a reversion of £1,000 to his wife and £500 each to his two daughters on his death, and he was raised to the rank of Vice-Admiral of the Red in the general Trafalgar promotion of 9 November 1805. In his letter to his wife on 16 December, to which reference has already been made, he wrote:

> I never dreamed that I was to be a Peer of the Realm. How are my darlings? I hope they will take pains to make themselves wise and good, and fit for the station to which they are raised.[26]

And with that same letter he sent her a copy of the letter he had received from the King. He later received a commemorative silver vase to the value of £500 from the Patriotic Fund, as did Nelson's widow and his brother.

In the House of Lords, the Duke of Clarence and future King secured an amendment to Lord Hawkesbury's Resolution of general thanks in order to single out the crucial contribution which had been made by Collingwood at Trafalgar in forcing the enemy to action and in his decision to destroy the prizes when he saw that they could not be retained. Old Admiral Lord Hood spoke of:

> ...the very high opinion I have long entertained of that truly meritorious officer, Lord Collingwood...I will venture to presage that the noble lord, now in command of His Majesty's Fleet in the Mediterranean, wants only an opportunity to prove himself another Nelson in judgment as well as valour.

And in his letter of thanks to Collingwood, the magnanimous and warm-hearted Duke of Clarence wrote as a fellow sailor:

> Earl St Vincent and Lord Nelson, both, in the hour of victory, accepted from me a sword, and I hope you will now confer on me the same pleasure.

In contrast, to mark the great heroism of its own Newcastle born hero, the Common Council of Newcastle upon Tyne Corporation voted no more than the token sum of 150 guineas for the purchase of a silver kettle, whilst the Newcastle Associated Volunteer Infantry presented a piece of plate at a cost of 125 guineas and the promise of a portrait.

One who was present at the battle yet received no medal or honour at all was Collingwood's dog, Bounce. And he must have suffered as much as any for he had a great fear of gunfire and sought cover whenever the barrage commenced.. However, it seems that he was able to bask in reflected glory, for his Master wrote of him to his wife, in a letter dated 20 December:

> The consequential airs he gives himself since he became a Right Honourable dog are insufferable. He considers it beneath his dignity to play with commoner's dogs, and truly thinks he does them grace when he condescends to lift up his leg against them. This, I think, is carrying the insolence of rank to the extreme, but he is a dog that does it.

For his part, Lord Eldon wrote his congratulations and thanks, not only to Collingwood, but also to their old headmaster, the Revd Moises, congratulating him upon Collingwood's conduct and describing the great impression which both his modesty and command of the English language had made upon the King. His twin persuasions of birch and bible had clearly left their mark on these two former pupils, for Eldon wrote: 'I cannot forbear congratulating you, whilst we are all congratulating our country, upon the services which your former scholar and my old schoolfellow, Lord Collingwood, has done the country, and the honour he has done himself.'

But Moises too was to depart this life on 5 July of the year following, still then able to enjoy the *Mens Sana In Corpore Sana* in his eighty-fifth year. Indeed he was found by a visiting cleric shortly before his death reading, without spectacles, the homilies of Chrysostom in the original language.[27]

Of the elevation of Nelson's clergyman brother, William, to an earldom together with the generous grant of monies which went with it, Collingwood wrote cryptically what many others felt and said:

> I suppose all the public reward of money will go to the parson, who of all the dull stupid fellows you ever saw, perhaps he is the most so. Nothing in him like a gentleman. Nature never intended him for anything superior to a village curate and here has Fortune, in one of her frisks, raised him, without his body and mind having anything to do with it, to the highest dignity.

A later request that his daughters be allowed to inherit his title was to be denied Collingwood and so it is not at all surprising that, like most of his contemporaries, he should have so resented it. By special remainder it was ordained that the earldom conferred on William, together with the barony of the Nile and Hilsborough, be allowed to descend to the male heirs of Nelson's Bolton or Matcham sisters failing male issue to William. On the death of William's only son from typhus, followed by William's own death later on, both of whom lie buried in St Paul's Cathedral, the titles therefore went to Thomas Bolton upon his taking the name Nelson as a condition of the inheritance. But then he died but eight months later. No such special remainder was granted to Collingwood to allow that his title could pass to his daughters, which was often the case in Scotland, still less that his younger brother and his heirs be allowed to inherit, and his title was therefore to die with him.

It was on 4 December that *Victory* arrived home. Five weeks later, on 9 January 1806, following a complete autopsy of a body which had been placed in a barrel and preserved in brandy, and then, at Gibraltar, in a coffin in vinegar wine, a better preservative for the journey back to England, and after it had lain in state at Greenwich Hospital for two whole days so that the British public, in deep mourning for the little admiral, could pay its last respects, the funeral procession set out from Whitehall bound for St Paul's Cathedral and Nelson's last resting place. Unrivalled though the British may be in mounting grand processions on great occasions, the sure grandeur of this occasion was matched only by the terrible grief felt by those who watched it, for here was the quintessential and much-loved hero who had died in the moment of victory.

Led by General Sir David Dundas with detachments of Light Dragoons, Light Infantry, Royal Artillery and Grenadiers, the procession, which contained all the great and the good including the chief mourner, old Admiral of the Fleet Sir Peter Parker, now eighty-four years of age, with Captain Blackwood as his train-bearer and Admirals Lord Hood and Lord Radstock as his supporters, set off at midday to the beat of Handel's *Dead March in Saul* and to the distant tolling of the great bell at St Paul's. As General Dundas ascended the steps of the cathedral and entered by the great west door, so the tail of the procession was still leaving the Admiralty, such was its length and the congestion of the crowds. It was not until almost 4 p.m. that all had assembled at the cathedral. From all contemporary accounts, as the column moved down the Strand and up Fleet Street to Ludgate Hill, streets densely packed with silent mourners, heads bared in silent homage, it was the contingent of sailors from *Victory* who most caught the public eye as they bore their Union Jacks and the St George's Ensign brought from the ship, perforated and torn as it was by enemy shot. It was a tangible and direct link with the battle itself and a moving reminder that as well as Nelson, many others had fallen for their country at Trafalgar. And as he entered the cathedral behind his brother, the Prince of Wales, and with the other Dukes of the Blood Royal, the Duke of Clarence wept uncontrollably.

Amongst the congregation sat the commander of the French Fleet, Admiral Villeneuve together with Captain Magendie of the *Bucentaur*, both brought to England by Blackwood in the *Euralyus* and now in captivity but paroled for the day by the Admiralty. War at this time was indeed conducted according to a more chivalrous code. Three months later Villeneuve was to be released by the British, and was then found dead in a hotel room in Rennes, stabbed by his own hand or that of another to the order of Napoleon; it was never discovered which.[28] Present too was Captain Rotherham carrying the banner or Guidon.[29] Although he had received no mention by Collingwood for his part in the battle, he had been awarded his gold medal and had been given command of the *Bellerophon* by Collingwood, and it was in that ship that he returned home for the funeral.[30] But it was to be a mixed blessing for he was afterwards, in that same year, to be held responsible by the Admiralty for negligent loss of her topmasts, and in the year following for unofficerlike conduct towards his officers and chaplain. But he did provide a survey of his crews, which left the historian with a mine of information. After three times seeking a knighthood, he was awarded a CB in 1815 and lived on until 1830 when he died at Bildeston in Suffolk at the age of seventy-six. But it wasn't until 1906 that a headstone was erected in his memory and a memorial tablet installed in the nearby chancel recording his service to Collingwood at Trafalgar, thanks to one Admiral Woollcombe and the then rector of the church.[31]

Absent, tragically, was William Pitt, worn out by his exertions, who had but days to live. The French victory at Austerlitz and so the end of the third coalition had taken away his will to live just as surely as a sniper's bullet had put an end to Horatio Nelson. So changed, now, were the boundaries of Europe after Napoleon's expansion, that he had said of a map lying on his desk: 'Roll up that map, it will not be wanted these ten years.'

But he had indeed been a great prime minister. Had he known it when he died on 27 January, he had by this time guided his country through the worst of its storms and steered it on a course which was to end in the defeat of the French at Waterloo.

Absent too were those who had been closest to Nelson. Lady Hamilton, for this was an all male affair, and his friend Cuthbert Collingwood, required to remain on the high seas keeping watch for his country off Cadiz. As for the ever-dutiful Cornwallis, he too was at sea, lying off Torbay, watching the Channel, not invited to the funeral. But the Earl St Vincent, who *had* been invited, and who had claimed for himself so much of what had been achieved by Nelson and the Royal Navy in years past, was absent that day, his seventy-second birthday, pleading ill-health. The true reason for his absence was never to be explained, for it was seen that he was able to ride off on his horse the following day.

But the final irony was that, of the four admirals appointed as pall-bearers, and who therefore rode in the procession closest to the body of Nelson and then sat and stood nearest to him in the cathedral in the final moments before his body was laid to rest, chief of these was Admiral Sir John Orde.

And so, half a minute after 5.33 p.m., and in failing light with candles lit, when the coffin was finally carried by the admirals from the choir to the centre of the great dome and, as the thin and emaciated Bishop of Lincoln and Dean of St Paul's, Sir George Pretyman Tomline, who had been Pitt's tutor at Pembroke College, Cambridge and had been appointed to that office by Pitt himself, raised his arms aloft to the heavens and gave voice to the final rites: 'We therefore commit this body to the ground, earth to earth, ashes to ashes, dust to dust.'

In the presence of these four officers it was lowered through the door immediately below the great dome of the cathedral to the crypt below. And there the body of Horatio Nelson lies in a coffin of his choosing, enclosed in a black marble sarcophagus, ornate in its design which had been constructed for Cardinal Wolsey's tomb by the Florentine sculptor Benedetto da Rovezzano. Confiscated by Henry VIII it had then lain in Wolsey's Chapel at Windsor over the centuries until space had been required by the Royal family.

In fact, in spite of their differences, Sir John Orde had never spoken an ill word of Nelson personally. It had been the manner of his appointment which had rankled with him. Indeed he had continued to demonstrate his admiration for him, although in fact his presence at his funeral as chief pall-bearer had come about quite by chance when one of the four originally nominated, Vice-Admiral Henry Savage, had pleaded indisposition. Although already invited to attend, Sir John had then been invited to stand in his place as chief pall-bearer.[32]

He too had been unwell, but such was his regard for Nelson by this time, that he rose from his sickbed in order to be at Nelson's side in his very last moments and, indeed, in the procession up river the day before, for it was reported that, such was the wind that blew that day, that his hat was blown into the Thames, much to the amusement of the crowd.[33]

Although his naval career was by now over, he was raised to the rank of full Admiral of the Blue in the Trafalgar promotion. And he became for five years an unremarkable member of parliament for the Yarmouth Division of the Isle of Wight, succeeding in that constituency his nephew who had gone to the House of Lords as Lord Bolton on the death of Sir John's brother Thomas at his home at Hackwood Park, Basingstoke in 1807.[34]

Thomas had been raised to the peerage in October 1797 after a career in parliament, in the service of William Pitt, which had been industrious rather than spectacular, especially so in Ireland as Chief Secretary to the Lord Lieutenant. There he became The First Instrument of Administration and its main spokesman in the Irish parliament until the pressure of work broke his health and ended his political career.[35] Married to the illegitimate daughter of the Duke of Bolton, he had served on at Fernhill House and then at Carisbrooke Castle as Governor and Vice-Admiral of the Isle of Wight and also as Lord Lieutenant of Hampshire in succession to his father-in-law, drawing from Jane Austen the comment in a letter written by her on 19 December 1798:

> My father is glad to hear so good an account of Edward's pigs, and desires it may be told, as encouragement to his taste for them, that Lord Bolton is particularly curious in his pigs, has had pigstyes of a most elegant construction built for them, and visits them every morning as soon as he rises.[36]

In another letter dated 24th of that same month, she set out a list of those who had partnered her at a ball, including one:

> William Orde (Cousin of the Kingsclere Man), reckoned to be William Orde of Nunnykirk in Northumberland, the older half brother of Thomas and John, and cousin of the Reverend John Orde of Weetwood Hall, Northumberland, then vicar of Kingsclere in Hampshire.

But on 9 January 1799 she was to write that:

> ...one of my gayest actions was sitting down two Dances in prefer- ence to having Lord Bolton's eldest son for my partner, who danced too ill to be endeared.

Twelve years later she was to write in approving terms when her cousin, Margaret Beckford, married Lieutenant Colonel Orde of Weetwood Hall.[37]

216

A talented artist and caricaturist and a friend of Romney, Thomas Orde had himself been painted by Pompeo Batoni while on his travels in Rome, and was in fact an able and efficient second minister so that the words written of him in the *Rolliad* were a little cruel and unfair where it began with:

> Tall and erect, unmeaning, mute and pale,
> O'er his blank face no gleams of thought prevail.

The more so where it ended with:

> But fruitless all-for what was Caesar's sword
> To thy all-conquering speeches, mighty Orde!
> Amphion's lyre, they say, could raise a town:
> Orde's elocution pulls a nation down.[38]

As for Sir John, he was later advanced to the rank of Admiral of the White in 1809[96] and was finally raised to the rank of Admiral of the Red on 4 June 1814. He devoted much of his time in his final years to the promotion of naval and other charities,[39] and then, having made his peace with the world, he died at his home in Gloucester Place, London, on 19 February 1824 after a long and painful illness, reportedly borne with great courage and composure. He was then in his seventy-third year and stood eighth in the list of naval officers. It was reported that shortly before his death he took stock of his life with the words:

> I have had a great many political enemies, few men more; but those who have gone before me, and those whom I may not outlive, I have long, long ago forgiven; and in private life, I do believe none ever wished to shove me off the stage.[40]

Thus implicitly did Sir John finally withdraw the challenge he had issued to St Vincent some twenty-five years before, for a decision which had been high-handed and made with little thought for the career and embarrassment of its victim, albeit St Vincent had died an Admiral of the Fleet some thirteen months before Sir John. There can be little peace in the world until we learn to suffer through the flesh of others.

Work was soon begun on a biography of Nelson, written by Admiral Lord Hood's former secretary, John M'Arthur, in collaboration with the chaplain to the Prince of Wales, Revd James Clarke. And, inevitably, there was a scramble for the lucrative position of agent to captains entitled to any money which the four prizes salvaged from Trafalgar might generate. Captains Durham and Digby supported the claim of

Nelson's friend Davison, but the remainder left the decision to Collingwood. He considered that he could not be involved in captains' business and so returned it to them. They in turn chose Collingwood's secretary, Cosway. This provoked a strong letter from Davison who claimed that Nelson had always promised the post to him, to which Collingwood replied that it was for the captains to decide, and that although he had seen Nelson almost every day, he had never heard him name Davison for that position. This was perhaps an echo of a letter included in Pettigrew which had been sent by Orde to Davison after the Battle of the Nile which had advanced the claims of one George Purvis as agent in preference to Davison. In that letter, with some prescience, he had questioned the suitability of Davison to be Nelson's agent.

The long and enduring friendship of Collingwood for Nelson and of Nelson for Collingwood had now ended, but in his prediction contained and hallmarked in his Trafalgar dispatch that the memory of Nelson would remain immortal, the phrase 'the immortal memory' was thereafter repeated at the funeral itself when the titles of the deceased were proclaimed by Sir Isaac Heard, and then in countless newspaper reports, stage productions and historical tracts which followed. And *The Immortal Memory* is toasted every Trafalgar Day by naval officers high and low up and down the land to this day, especially so on board HMS *Victory*, now the flagship of the commander-in-chief of the Home Fleet and Second Sea Lord, who hosts a dinner on Trafalgar Night for a few chosen guests in Nelson's own small cabin, which the author has been privileged to attend.

On 4 July 1807 the foundation stone for a granite obelisk monument to Nelson was laid on the Portsdown Hills on the road leading to Borchurst some eight or nine miles from Portsmouth.[41] This was done at Collingwood's instigation and at the squadron's expense for, at his suggestion contained in a letter which he circulated on 2 November 1805 to all captains, £2,000 of the prize money obtained was applied to that end with the agreement of every ship's company. It was the equivalent of two days pay for every man and boy who had fought in the action. The first monument to be raised to Nelson, the location of it had a utility too for it was so sited that it could be used as a sea mark to help vessels avoid the shoal of St Helens as they entered Portsmouth harbour in the days when St Helens Roads and not Spithead was used as the route in and out. And when the need for cross-marks disappeared the mark still had a use when testing and adjusting the compasses of ships. Attempts made later to re-site the monument in the city itself when its original use had gone, were resisted and there the monument stands to this day. A relief bust of Nelson is set in a niche at its top standing a modest 150 feet in height overlooking the harbour, the Solent and the Isle of Wight as a tribute by Collingwood and his men to the memory of his friend, although he never saw it himself for he was never to return to England until carried home in a coffin. It is no rival to the work of John Flaxman in St Paul's Cathedral which has Nelson in his peer's robes with Britannia to his left and a British lion to his right, but the Portsdown Monument stands as a tribute from those survivors who had, in fact, secured the victory at Trafalgar. In due time the column raised to Nelson in Trafalgar Square was to dwarf all others as it reached to the sky in adulation, but it was the statue at Portsmouth which had a closer place in the heart of those sailors who survived Trafalgar.

Chapter 12

Collingwood as Commander-in-Chief
of the Mediterranean Fleet

Although the four years of life which now remained to Collingwood
were crowned with great professional and diplomatic success, in reality
he derived little happiness from them for, in the wake of Trafalgar, there
was, in truth, very little opportunity left for naval activity or distinction.
The British Navy now reigned supreme, as did Collingwood as
commander of its principal fleet; at that time the largest ever to put to
sea from the shores of England.

By the same token there was little prospect of prize money either.
Collingwood, ever careful with money, was to complain of this in his
letters home, for he had won very little in that way to supplement his
salary over the past three years although, as probate revealed after his
death, he was by now, with his pension, far from poor.

However, although never much interested in rank or status, he *was*
concerned about the survival of his hard-won title. It troubled him that
this would die with him. It had been arranged otherwise for Nelson so
that memory of *his* achievements might be carried on down through the
years. And so he now wrote several letters to the Admiralty asking that,
by Act of Parliament, one of his daughters be allowed to succeed to his
title. He reminded them that as long as they kept him in the
Mediterranean he was really in no position to father a male heir. The
pension granted, he pointed out, was of less importance to him than that
his title be allowed to pass to his daughters with remainder to their heirs.
But sadly his pleas fell on deaf ears, perhaps because it was thought that
the grant of pensions to his daughters was reward enough.

His elevation to the chief command in the principle theatre of war had
been a clear recognition of, and confidence in, his masterly fighting and
diplomatic skills. So much so that nearly all matters in the
Mediterranean were now left for him to decide with really very little

interference from London. It is true that this was in part because of the departure of the busy First Lord of the Admiralty, the octogenarian Lord Barham, and the arrival of his Whig replacement, Charles Grey, now Lord Howick as son of the newly created Earl Grey. Grey, although an able man and a fellow Northumbrian, really had no experience of naval affairs and so very wisely deferred to Collingwood's judgment whenever decisions affecting the Mediterranean had to be made. There he allowed him almost plenipotentiary powers. And those who succeeded Grey did likewise. And so the burden on Collingwood steadily increased and, in the course of time, it was to break him.

But in the meanwhile he conducted his new diplomatic role with meticulous application and skill. Although he had had no training or experience in international diplomacy and had only come to the rank of vice-admiral less than two years before, his judgment and integrity were such that his performance won him the full support of the government back in England.

Indeed he made himself indispensable to the Admiralty. So much so that his many requests to be relieved of his duties and allowed home when failing health began to dog him, were each of them refused until it was too late. He made himself a slave to his ever increasing fleet and diplomatic responsibilities and was never to see his family or homeland again. His cabin became his office and his ship became his home, and there he spent the rest of his days, dealing with diplomatic demands and all those administrative duties involved in keeping a fleet at sea. Desk-bound for much of the time, the sedentary and lonely quality of his existence did little for his health and wellbeing. And now, in the isolation of high command at sea and without Horatio Nelson, he had but few friends with whom he could talk, save perhaps for his faithful dog Bounce. And even he was beginning to put on weight and suffer from sailor's boredom, or so Collingwood reported to his father-in-law.

Indeed, such was the burden of his duties that he seldom had time to converse even with the officers under his own command. A lonely man, he had been able to unbend with Nelson and converse with him freely as with no other officer in the service. But now there was no-one.

Confident of his own abilities Collingwood was never a man to delegate. He had no wish to see others less capable than he making mistakes which could have been avoided had decisions been left in his hands. He spurned the custom of appointing a Captain of the Fleet who could have taken some of the burden, but placed his trust in perhaps no more than two or three of his more loyal subordinates, the officer he had promoted to be his Flag Captain, Richard Thomas, who had been with him for eleven years and who was to remain with him for the rest of his life, and Cosway, his trusted secretary who also remained faithful to him to the end. But supreme control he kept in his own hands.

Never a man for the frivolity of social occasions, he now really had little appetite for entertaining. It was an intensely lonely existence and the dull and frustrating routine of blockade was relieved only by the ever increasing burden of diplomatic correspondence which he was required to conduct with ambassadors and court officials the length and breadth of the Mediterranean. Almost inevitably the overall weight of his duties began to take its toll on his eyesight and his mobility and a nagging pain in his abdomen was sapping his energy. Indeed it was eventually to destroy him. He began to lose his zest for life which he felt was slowly ebbing away. Much of this he attributed to lack of exercise, held by his duties as he was to the confines of the ship.

But at least his wife was able to bask in the glory of her husband's achievements. Indeed she and her daughters were presented at Court at an event held on 15 May 1806 to honour Queen Charlotte's birthday.[1]

At the same time, during those long periods of tedium when there was no hope of action, still less of prize money, and although it was not admiral's work, Collingwood endeavoured to occupy his ship's company of 800 or so officers and men by encouraging them to promote theatrical entertainments. These were staged each Thursday night to the accompaniment of the ship's band. At the same time he made sure of their health by insisting that the ship was kept well-aired and dry and that they were fed a healthy diet.

But, sadly for him, there really was very little opportunity to exercise his battle skills in the years following Trafalgar. Before then the French had been more than able to match the British in naval resources. Although the British had possessed almost twice as many ships with 158 at their disposal, half of these had been in dock or unseaworthy, and so there had been little disparity. And when Spain and Holland came into the war in support of France, Britain had then been opposed by no less than 295 ships of the same class so that she had then been outnumbered greatly. But, immediately after Trafalgar, the British found themselves with an overwhelming numerical advantage, for their overall strength of 128 ships was then opposed by but nineteen French, fifty-seven Spanish and sixteen Dutch. And many in the British Fleet were those which had been captured from the enemy and so were free of those devil bolts so often fitted negligently in British dockyards. They tended to be faster and better designed than their British counterparts. Only five French ships of the line had remained at the port of Cadiz when Admiral Rosily had arrived to take over Villeneuve's command and each of these was damaged almost beyond repair. Spain was soon to quit the war as an ally of France. The crippled French Fleet, severely disabled, then seldom ventured out. However France had, in fact, lost less than one-fifth of her overall fleet of ships of the line at Trafalgar, and those they had lost were then soon to be replaced in a crash building programme quickly launched as a matter of urgency.

And so, although they seldom put to sea, Collingwood could but mount a constant blockade to contain what amounted to a very real and growing threat that the French might at any moment break out in pursuit of Napoleon's ambitions for Malta, Sicily, the eastern states and the route to India, even though the psychological blow of Trafalgar had been such that they were ever after reluctant to do so, for fear of meeting ships of the Royal Navy manned by skilled, intrepid, experienced and now confident sailors. Such was the damage which had been done to the morale of the French navy. And so Collingwood had no choice but to maintain the vigil at Toulon, Brest and Cartagena, exacting from his captains and men the same high standards as before.

Some naval historians were later to attribute this period of comparative inactivity to caution and even timidity on the part of Collingwood, despite his record of lion courage in the face of the enemy on so many occasions before. Others harboured the suspicion that he actually preferred his desk work to more active pursuits and lacked the will to seek out the enemy when not led by the example of Nelson. But this was to misunderstand totally the climate of naval warfare in the wake of Trafalgar, which had been a true landmark in British naval history.

In a sense Collingwood and the British Navy were victims of their own success. Their essential role now became to watch Cadiz and keep the French out of the Mediterranean. And in this they succeeded for the most part. Indeed Napoleon had encouraged the adoption of a defensive policy himself, for he had eventually come to accept that an invasion of Britain was out of the question. He realized now that he could expect little from his timid, demoralized and impotent naval officer corps. And so he opted instead to keep his ships in harbour ready and equipped to sail at a moment's notice while all the while adding to their numbers. In this way his strategy was to force the British to remain at sea inactive and ever on watch. And by this device he hoped as well to exhaust their patience and reduce their ability to confront the French in battle. But it did indeed mean that the days of major naval engagements and the prospect of action and glory at sea had gone for ever.

Thus was Collingwood to write: 'It is lamentable to see what a desert the waters are become.'

And to Mrs Stead he wrote:

Fourteen or sixteen hours of every day I am employed. I have eighty ships of war under my orders, and the direction of naval affairs from

Constantinople to Cadiz, with an active and powerful enemy always threatening, and though he seldom moves, keeps us constantly on the alert.

At the same time it is clear from his letters home that Collingwood was not himself content with pure containment. Although now a veteran of three of the five most significant naval battles of the Napoleonic Wars, he still hoped daily for yet a further major confrontation with the French so that whatever menace they might still possess at sea could be eradicated completely.

In February of 1806 a small opportunity for an engagement at sea did arise when the French Admiral le Marre, under the watchful eye of Collingwood's fleet, left Cadiz and put to sea on a troop carrying expedition with a modest squadron of four frigates and the brig *Furet*. But he was careful to choose a moment when a strong easterly wind was holding Collingwood at bay over the horizon to the westward and so escaped unmolested save for the brig which was caught by the *Hydra* and taken into captivity. But then not even Nelson could have controlled the elements.

In this appointment Collingwood inherited from Nelson not only the Mediterranean Command but also the problems which went with it, not least the plight of Naples and its Queen, Maria Carolina, for the King of the Two Sicilies, Ferdinand I, her husband, took little part in affairs of state. When not hunting or shooting, the hours of that amiable man were spent languishing at sea sailing the Bay of Naples in his yacht

Although the legacy of Nelson had included the protection of this Royal couple and defence of their Sicilian Empire against the French invader after their second expulsion from Naples, despite the assistance given by General Craig, Collingwood's more cautious and more pragmatic northern temperament was less susceptible to the flattery and entertainment served up for him by this rampant Queen for whom he privately developed a considerable distrust and dislike. Her way of life was anathema to his more straightforward northern character and it troubled him that he was being asked to bolster and support a corrupt, depraved and ineffective regime composed for the most part of feckless and pleasure-loving officials led by a cunning and scheming Queen, the sister of the unfortunate Queen Marie Antoinette. The more so when he learned that she was secretly making similar overtures to the French while all the while enjoying the protection of the British.

Nonetheless, and ever the slave to duty, in reply to one of their many requests for help, Collingwood assured the King that he would serve his country as best he could. And he sought to honour the commitment which his friend Nelson had made by sending a squadron of ships to patrol the waters around the Sicilian coast, which he later reinforced, although the Kingdom of Naples was soon to be firmly under the yoke of the French invader.

And then, in April 1806, he dispatched further reinforcements to Palermo in the shape of an inshore squadron under the command of the outspoken, outrageous and often irritating Sir Sidney Smith, famous for his defence of Acre, who had, on 9 November 1805, been promoted to the rank of rear admiral. The ship assigned to him by Collingwood bore the name *Pompee*, perhaps not inappropriately, and with him he sent the *Eagle* in support. His orders were to redeem Nelson's promise to assist in the expulsion of Napoleon's brother, Joseph Bonaparte, from the throne of Naples, and to help in the liberation of the kingdom of Naples and its territories in Calabria so that it might be restored to its legitimate King and Queen. This was their true wish, rather than simply that Sicily be defended.

Collingwood had doubts about the suitability of Sir Sidney Smith for this task, with all his preposterous ideas. This, after all, was the officer he had so criticized to his father-in-law for his ineptitude at Toulon when entrusted by Lord Hood with the destruction of those French ships which had to be left behind when the British were forced to withdraw from that port. That assignment he had bungled with enthusiasm. So much so that many of the abandoned French ships lived to fight another day.

But in fact, although Smith was a vain, excitable and garrulous man who was undoubtedly desperate for fame, he was also without doubt intelligent, courageous, energetic, kind and generous and he did have the advantage of fluent French, acquired when living for more than two years at Caen, in Normandy. And he had by then acquired a great deal of battle experience both in the American War and at the Battle of St Vincent and indeed when serving in the Swedish Navy which had won him a knighthood from the King of Sweden whose life he had contrived to save on at least one occasion. And his defence at Acre in 1799 had been inspired in that it had involved the capture of artillery, ammunition and stores from Napoleon's transports which he had then proceeded to use against Napoleon himself to great and destructive effect. Not surprisingly, that had made him a hero in the eyes of the British nation and a rival to Nelson for its affections. But then Collingwood seldom warmed to the loud and the ostentatious.

Yet, faithful to the instructions which Collingwood gave him, there followed the Battle of Maida, largely inspired by Smith. And it was in many respects extremely successful in the sense that many thousands of French troops were slaughtered by British infantry muskets and artillery broadsides. Collingwood was fair and objective enough to recognize this, describing the action as a most gallant thing:

> ...but, as we could not keep an army there, I am afraid that the suffering of the Calabrians will be increased by our having made them take a part against their enemy, which we are not in a position to maintain.

And so it proved to be since the ground taken was very soon recovered by the French. It turned out to be a pyrrhic victory of short-term duration.

In any event, Collingwood rightly considered that probably the greatest service he could render the kingdom of Naples would be to keep French warships off the high seas in the Mediterranean.

Like Nelson before him, Smith had, in this campaign, won the friendship of the Queen of Naples and indeed a Calabrian title from the King which prompted Collingwood to write to his wife that:

> He [Collingwood] would receive no such honours from any sovereign but his own.

And to his brother John, Collingwood wrote:

> I am sadly off with this Sir S. Smith at Sicily; the man's head is full of strange vapours and I am convinced Lord Barham sent him here to be clear of a tormentor, but, he annoys me more than the French or Spanish Fleet.

In a letter to Admiral Markham at the Admiralty, dated 16 April 1806, Collingwood referred to Sir Sidney as:

> I dare say a very clever man – bold and enterprising – but I confess I wish you could have found employment for him in the Channel; his talent (from the little conversation I have had with him) seems to turn more on boats and bombs, and fire-vessels, than on the arrangement of a squadron of men-of-war – and in such employment I shall have the ships unmanned and unfit for service; but I have given him my sentiments very fully on those subjects.[2]

Then, on 28 June, in a further letter to Markham, he described Sir Sidney as:

> ...the Knight of the Sword. I hope he is going on well, but since he went into the Mediterranean I am totally ignorant of everything going on there.

And yet Smith succeeded in harrying the French at every turn in the Bay of Naples during the summer of 1806 and he managed to take the island of Capri. Notwithstanding, his recall to home waters later that year came as a relief and was welcomed by all and sundry in the Mediterranean Fleet where his popularity rating had sunk to an extremely low ebb. He was to live on until 1840 by which time he had acquired a KCB and a GCB and the rank of full admiral.

Otherwise the French and the Spanish lay low throughout that year, fully engaged with the repair and restoration of their broken fleets, until, by the end of the year, their combined fleet at Cadiz included twelve or so ships of the line, all restored to a seaworthy state.

Further wealth was bestowed on Collingwood in March 1806 when he profited from a legacy which made him a much richer man, drawing incomes from not only his salary and pension, but now also from a small estate. This had belonged to the Roddams. The last daughter of that family had earlier married Edward Collingwood's father who had died in 1792.[3] Collingwood was very touched that he should have been remembered in this way. Indeed this was the second time the Edward Collingwoods had come to the aid of the Cuthbert Collingwoods for, many years before, Edward Collingwood senior, then Recorder of Newcastle, had given Cuthbert Collingwood's father financial assistance in his moment of need. But Collingwood was to write: 'I'm sorry the possessor of it is gone, for I have lost a friend who I believe sincerely loved me and have got an Estate which I could have done very well without.'[4]

But it could not of course do anything to relieve the monotony of the blockade and it really brought him little pleasure, marooned as he was at sea and totally unable to expand his own way of life. And so, when he received the news that his cousin Edward Collingwood had died suddenly and unexpectedly and had left him a life interest *in tail male* with the remainder to his brother John in that estate at Chirton near North Shields, some fifteen or so miles from Newcastle upon Tyne, after which it would go to his brother John, Collingwood asked his wife to take care of the dog left behind and expressed the hope that his cousin's servants had been properly provided for. When he learned that coal was to be mined on the land, which would involve increasing the rents of many of those living there, to his father-in-law he wrote:

I do not think it would be common justice to turn out those already established; nor would I consent to it for any increase of rent, however great.

He wrote further:

> Whatever establishment may be found there for the comfort of the poor, or the education and improvement of their children, I would have continued and increased. I want to make no great occasion of wealth from it, nor will I have anybody put to the smallest inconvenience for me. I shall never live there; nor were it as many thousands as it is hundreds would I quit my present situation to regulate it.

However, although Collingwood, who ever preferred the simple way of life, had no intention of abandoning his unpretentious Morpeth home and the beautiful gardens there which he had planned and nurtured with such meticulous care, in favour of residence in an area which was to be turned over to coalmining and industrial activity, his wife clearly had other ideas for the much grander house at Chirton would obviously be more appropriate for a peer of the realm.

Indeed Collingwood clearly feared as much, for he was to write in June of that summer, not only, as always, of the education of his daughters, but also that if they were to move to Chirton, he would:

> ...be forever regretting those beautiful views which are nowhere to be exceeded; and even the rattling of that old wagon that used to pass our door at 6 o clock in a winter's morning had its charms. The fact is, whenever I think how I am to be happy again, my thoughts carry me back to Morpeth.

In September, he wrote of Chirton to his brother that:

> It is a place I should dislike exceedingly as a residence...Had I been fortunate in prizes I would have bought a more suitable residence, but as it is I fancy I must make Chirton my home, in a neighbourhood very disagreeable and in the smoke of coal engines and every kind of filth...

And then, a little later, to one of his sisters he wrote:

> ...since Sarah has resolved on Chirton, she very cunningly has left off talking of those old beauties of Morpeth....

Of course, had he but known it, these concerns were really of mere academic importance since he himself was never to return to either address again.

This legacy brought with it other problems too, for there were many matters relating to the upkeep of the property which required

Collingwood's attention. These he had to deal with at a distance which added to the volume of his correspondence. But there were compensations too, for questions relating to the right of access to a colliery in which he now had an interest led to negotiations and a correspondence with the Duke of Northumberland who owned land in the area which was affected. The Duke was an old soldier and a veteran of Minden and the American War of Independence who took a keen interest in the progress of the war in Europe, and an active and very friendly correspondence developed between the two of them as to events in the Mediterranean. It led also to a further friendship for Collingwood's wife.

Had he lived for another fifty years, royalties from coal mined on the Chirton land would probably have made Collingwood a very wealthy man indeed. As it was, his total annual income now stood at more than £10,000, once his service pay of £1,000, his Trafalgar Pension of £2,000, his income from the Chirton properties of £6,000 – £7,000 and the income to be drawn from accumulated prize money was taken into account.[5]

Although there was no opportunity to apply his new found riches to the betterment of his own way of life, without doubt they liberated his wife, for her correspondence in that year is sprinkled with references to social events for which her new status and affluence had made her eligible. And, inevitably, in the spring of 1807 she moved into Chirton as Collingwood had predicted she would.

In July of 1806 Collingwood was saddened to be told that his old headmaster, the Reverend Moises, had died. But Moises had lived just long enough to be able to bask in the glow of his former pupil's success. Unable to attend the funeral, Collingwood instructed his bankers to draw the sum of £100 on his behalf, £20 of which was to go towards a mural monument to be erected in St Nicholas Cathedral in Newcastle by Stowell, Eldon and others of his grateful pupils, the balance to be donated to certain hospitals in Newcastle upon Tyne.

Howick was succeeded at the Admiralty as First Lord that September by Thomas Grenville, older brother of the Prime Minister, although Grenville was destined to remain in office for no more than six months before departing with his brother's 'Ministry of All the Talents' when it was dismissed by the King over the question of Catholic commissions. His replacement as First Lord was to be Henry Phipps, third Lord and first Earl Mulgrave.

That same year Collingwood's diplomatic skills were put to the test when he was drawn into a squabble caused by the insistence of the French Ambassador, Major-General the Count Sebastiani, that the French should have sole use of the canal of Constantinople to the exclusion of the Russians and the British. This arose when Mustapha succeeded the Sultan Salim. The British minister at Constantinople, Charles Arbuthnot, fearing that the Turkish Ottoman Court, The Sublime Porte, were in danger of breaking with the Russians, their allies, in favour of the French, now sought the help of Collingwood. And Collingwood, also anticipating trouble, promptly dispatched a squadron of three ships to the area under Rear-Admiral Sir Thomas Louis in the *Canopus*.[6] This restored calm which won for Collingwood the approval of Grenville.

But then further success by Napoleon's armies in Europe encouraged further demands by the French in Constantinople. More concessions were then made by the frightened Turkish authorities. And so, with the prospect of a local war with the Turks looming, Collingwood, now sailing in the *Ocean*, a three-decker, was ordered by the government to send the hesitant and over-cautious yet indiscreet Sir John Duckworth to the Dardanelles with a small squadron of ships to reconnoitre fort protection in the area. It was unusual for London to dictate policy to Collingwood and Duckworth would not have been Collingwood's choice. Indeed the force, already inadequate for the task required, was then further depleted when a fire and explosion broke out on one of Duckworth's ships, the 74-gun *Ajax*, commanded by Captain Blackwood, when off the Dardanelles. Two hundred and fifty officers, men and boys perished in that tragedy, although Blackwood himself, after an hour in the water, managed to survive. But to his credit, Sir Sidney Smith, who, because of his standing with the Turks who remembered his defence of Acre, had been sent out to assist Duckworth and given command of the rear squadron, carried out with considerable success Duckworth's orders to destroy several Turkish ships which, along with shore batteries, had opened fire as they had entered the narrows. And his support afterwards won fulsome praise from Duckworth himself in his report of the action.

But tragically, Duckworth's inadequacy soon became all too apparent. It had been Collingwood's clear directive that if the Turks, who were still in name the allies of Russia and Great Britain although in fact at war with Russia and openly hostile to Great Britain failed, within a specified time, to respond to Duckworth's negotiations for a surrender together with restoration of the triple alliance guaranteed by the Anglo-Turkish Treaty and removal of the French ambassador, they should be broken off. He was, in that circumstance, to withdraw without delay, bombarding the city as he left. Regrettably, and although there was never any hope of success, Duckworth, cleverly egged on by the Sultan at the instance of General Sebastiani, prolonged his negotiations with the ambassador well beyond the appointed time and over a considerable number of days. And, in the time bought, the Turks were able to strengthen their fortifications, so that when Duckworth eventually did withdraw empty-handed on 3 March, his squadron had to run a gauntlet of punishing fire from onshore batteries of artillery as it retreated through the narrowest section of the channel. And in that withdrawal forty-six men were killed and 235 were wounded. So, too, his attempt at winning the friendship and support of the Russian admiral had failed *in limine*, as Collingwood had predicted it would.

And so, on 9 August 1807, the Admiralty ordered Collingwood to sail for the Dardanelles himself in order, with the support of the Russians, to negotiate peace with the Turks and compose the differences which now existed between those two nations. There he was met with hospitality and friendliness, but it very quickly became apparent that the Russian vice-admiral, Dmitri Nicolaievitch Siniavin, who had been trained by a British naval academy in his youth, had not the slightest intention of negotiating peace with Turkey, a nation the Russians despised. At the same time overtures by Collingwood himself were met with evasion and procrastination by the Turkish Lord High Admiral, Capita Pasha. So much so that Collingwood withdrew to Corfu rather than waste further time on pointless discussion which was destined to lead nowhere. In any event, on 24 August, their negotiations were overtaken by the Peace of Tilsit by which Russia became an ally of France. Russia then promptly withdrew from the Mediterranean and any possible encounter with the British Navy, staying just long enough to negotiate an armistice with Constantinople. This then caused Collingwood to withdraw to Syracuse, a port which received him with ceremony and great hospitality.

In fact, unbeknown to Collingwood, the order of 9 August to seek the support of the Russians was already otiose before he ever set sail, for the Treaty of Tilsit made between Napoleon and Czar Alexander, following the defeat of the Prussians at Jena and the Russians at Friedland, had already been signed the month before on 8 July. But such was the aristocratic Siniavin's friendship of Collingwood that Siniavin had still accepted the invitation to enter into talks with him and had not broken the news of the treaty or the fact that the third coalition was over, until the end of August. Siniavin had no love for the excesses of the French Revolution and he shared with Collingwood a hatred of Napoleon. It was therefore with some reluctance that he withdrew from the Mediterranean for the Baltic, taking with him all Collingwood's good wishes. In fact it was then Siniavin's good fortune to encounter bad weather in the Tagus which allowed the British to detain his ships for the duration of the hostilities. He arrived at a moment when Smith was evacuating the Portuguese Royal family and British personnel from

Portugal as Napoleon's army marched across Spain. Siniavin was then able to spend a convivial year in England renewing old friendships and contacts.[7]

That summer Collingwood was to report in a letter to his father-in-law that he was: 'worn to a thread'; his eyes were weak, his body was swollen and his legs were shrunk to tapers. 'I hardly ever see the face of an officer, except when they dine with me, and am seldom on deck above an hour in the day, when I go in the twilight to breathe the fresh air.'

Indeed, a portrait of him painted for his wife in Syracuse by one Guiseppe Polite, described by Collingwood as the most eminent painter in Sicily and signed 18 December 1807, pictured a rather bowed and drawn figure of a man. Not surprisingly, when shipped home it caused his wife great distress when she saw it for her last memory of her husband had been of a tall, upright, slender and strong man in the prime of life.

It seems that his dog Bounce, also deskbound, was suffering from boredom too, for in a New Year's message to his children the previous winter, Collingwood had asked his wife to tell them that:

> Bounce is very well and very fat, yet he seems not to be content, and sighs so piteously these long evenings that I am obliged to sing him to sleep.

It was not until January 1808 that a real opportunity to bring the French Navy to battle presented itself. Sicily was a base of crucial importance to the British as the key to the central Mediterranean. Malta, with inadequate resources to support both an army and the fleet, was no substitute. This Napoleon appreciated full well. Hence there was a constant threat of invasion of an island from which Napoleon realized it would be possible both to prey on all shipping passing down the Mediterranean through the Sicilian Channel, and also to mount a second invasion of Egypt. Therefore, the moment Napoleon learned that the British, under the command of General Moore, had evacuated some of their troops from the island, his brother Joseph was ordered to take the British fortresses at Scylla and Reggio on the toe of Italy where it overlooks the Straits of Messina on the north-western tip of the island, in order to clear the way for an invasion force to cross the two mile gap which separates the island from the mainland.

And then, on 12 December, he ordered Allemand and Ganteaume to put to sea along with squadrons lying at Lorient, Brest and Cartagena, in the hope of providing substantial cover and protection for the invasion force.

On this occasion, Allemand did manage to slip out of Rochefort while Sir Richard Strachan was away provisioning. And after overcoming a number of weather hazards and other mishaps at sea he then joined forces on 10 February with Vice-Admiral Ganteaume who had emerged from Toulon unnoticed by Captain Fellowes of the *Apollo* who was there keeping vigil but had been blown out to sea by turbulent weather. But in the outcome these were the only squadrons able to slip the blockade. And although the British presence on the island had been reduced to a mere 9,000 soldiers under the command of General Sherbrooke, for some reason never explained, Napoleon suddenly abandoned his plan for the invasion and ordered the two fleets to sail instead to reinforce the island of Corfu which lies between Albania and the heel of Italy, even though it already lay in French hands. It is just possible that he had realized that his navy would be no match for Collingwood's fleet, given the memory of Trafalgar.

And so the combined French Fleet with ten ships of the line accompanied by frigates, corvettes and transports then set sail, not for the Sicilian Straits, but for Corfu.

That they were at sea at all had been reported to Collingwood in early February by Rear-Admiral John Child Purvis who was policing the straits off Gibraltar, but their destination was unknown. Collingwood therefore collected his fleet of fifteen ships in the waters to the west of Sicily in the hope of intercepting them and bringing them to battle, for it was his belief that Sicily must be their target, little knowing that they were, by then, to the east of Sicily. But their arrival at Corfu on the 23rd was spotted by Captain T. Harvey[8] in the *Standard* and he promptly set sail for Collingwood who was by then at Syracuse on the south-eastern corner of Sicily, guarding against a possible attack from the Adriatic.[9]

Vice-Admiral Edward Thornborough, meanwhile, had command of a squadron at Palermo on the north-western coast of the island, keeping watch to the north and north-west. But it was then Collingwood's ill-luck that Captain Harvey missed him by no more than a few hours for the *Standard* had sailed into Syracuse on the evening of the very day that Collingwood sailed for Palermo, namely 24 February, and so the opportunity to intercept the French was lost.

When word of Ganteaume's latest movements did reach Collingwood on 6 March as he lay off Cape St Vito, close to Palermo, he lost no time in putting out frigates to trawl the sea around Naples in the hope of running him to ground, while at the same time sailing for the west coast of Sicily in the belief that Ganteaume's manoeuvres had been no more than a ploy to draw the British Fleet away from the protection of Sicily which was so vital to the British interest. And he was confirmed in this belief when reports reached him that Captain Jahleel Brenton in the

Spartan had watched Ganteaume leave Corfu on 16 March and sail for the waters around Sicily and Sardinia, and, from Hudson Lowe, that a French squadron had assembled in the Gulf of Taranto at the heel of Italy and was preparing for an invasion of Sicily. So desperate now was Collingwood for a second Trafalgar, he lost no time in trawling the Gulf of Taranto and then getting out a detailed General Order which set out his plan for the deployment of his ships in battle formation. But, alas, he had no occasion to implement it, for, unbeknown to him, Ganteaume was by then far west of Sicily and safely on his way back to Toulon, although the famous General Order or Fighting Instructions were to be retained as standing instructions in the fleet throughout the two years which followed, with appropriate amendment as circumstances required.

When eventually he did learn of Ganteaume's departure, Collingwood knew then that the now refurbished French Fleet had escaped unharmed and that the need for unremitting and tedious blockade would continue.

Inevitably unfavourable comparisons were drawn with the fighting success of Nelson and, predictably, accusations of timidity were levelled at Collingwood. But in truth a combination of unfortunate circumstances had dictated the outcome, for he could but rely on whatever information was brought in by his frigates, tied as he was to the shores of Sicily in its defence, such was its priority and strategic importance. And in that policy he was successful for, once again, Napoleon had been forced to abandon his plans for an invasion and Ganteaume had returned to Toulon with nothing achieved. As ever the shortage of frigates had been critical. Nelson had suffered the same handicap back in 1798 when scouring the Mediterranean for Napoleon before the Battle of the Nile.

Hence the letter to his wife dated 15 May already quoted:,

> At sea there is no getting intelligence as there used to be on former occasions, for now there is not a trading ship upon the seas – nothing but ourselves. It is lamentable to see what a desert the waters are become.[10]

Before Trafalgar much of the intelligence on the high seas had been gathered by intercepting and interrogating neutral commercial traffic. But this was now a rarity. And so Collingwood was to write to William Waldegrave, Lord Radstock, on 18 June:

> I never got intelligence, where they really were until they were out of reach...Their escape was by chance; for at one time we were very near them without knowing it.

But Collingwood had read Napoleon's mind correctly when anticipating that he may have had such an expedition in mind when asking the Admiralty in the previous month for more ships and for Captain Hoste so that the coast of Sicily might be better protected. And it was his own close watch on Sicily which had made a crossing impossible, for Ganteaume would have to have defeated the British navy first. But the need for constant watch and tedious blockade continued, the more so since the Russians had abandoned their bases in the Mediterranean to the French under the terms of the Treaty of Tilsit, and Napoleon had, by this time, extended his control of the coastline from Spain in the west all the way down the Adriatic and to Corfu in the east. He now had a plethora of naval ports at his disposal.

And so, for all the monotony and burden of his duty, Collingwood stuck faithfully to his task and continued as before, maintaining a tight and efficient vigil and blockade in the Mediterranean day after day, week after week and month after month. And it was totally successful, for Ganteaume's abortive sally to Corfu was the very last time the French ventured out into the Mediterranean while Collingwood was there. And at no time during his tenure of command did the British bases at Sicily and Malta ever fall to the enemy.

However, the burden of Collingwood's responsibilities lessened dramatically in the year 1807 when the need to continue the watch on Cadiz and Cartagena abated, for it was at this time that Napoleon invaded Portugal as the last door open to British trade on the continent of Europe. Soon afterwards and in response to public demand the unpopular Spanish King, Charles IV, was forced to abdicate in favour of Ferdinand VII, his equally unpopular rival, son and heir, and then, taking advantage of the political fragmentation, Napoleon quickly dismissed Prime Minister Godoy, placed his brother Joseph on the throne and took both Charles and Ferdinand into captivity. Not surprisingly the Spanish people, already in revolt, rose in protest, and on 4 June 1808 the Supreme Junta at Seville declared war on France.

Collingwood was then ordered by the Admiralty to sail immediately for Cadiz, not this time to mount a blockade but rather now to lend what support he could to the Spanish people in their struggle to recover their country from the French invader. And so Collingwood delegated to Vice-Admiral Thornborough the responsibility for the blockade at Toulon and he himself lost no time in setting sail for Cadiz.

When on the high seas news was communicated to him that the French Admiral Rosilly, now the enemy of Spain, was seeking from General Thomas de Morda, the Captain-General of Andalusia, a guarantee of safe passage out of Cadiz with his ships and it seemed that the Spaniards were disposed to grant this in their reluctance to join battle with the French, who had been their allies until but a few days before. But the moment Collingwood learned of it he immediately advised the Spanish General that Rosilly's request was unacceptable and that no such amnesty would ever be granted by the British. He reminded him that the French occupied their country as their enemies and were holding their Royal family captive. An exchange of fire followed but even then Rosily sought to extract a guarantee of safe conduct if only for himself and his men. And it was only when the British turned down all his requests that he finally surrendered.

At Cadiz, where he was remembered and revered for his humanity and magnanimity after the Battle of Trafalgar, Collingwood received a hero's welcome the moment he, Purvis and other officers stepped on shore and again when he attended the opera. A gala and lavish entertainments were mounted in his honour.

The work he then did in organizing military supplies for their struggle was vital in its importance. The more so when Sir Arthur Wellesley landed in Spain with the British Army and the six year fight for Spanish independence began, although much of this work at Cadiz was delegated to his friend Rear-Admiral Purvis who commanded the squadron there and who had been brought out to that command at Collingwood's request. His younger brother George, one-time secretary to St Vincent and a successful prize agent to many captains, had had the agency of many after the Nile until the intervention of Nelson who wanted Davison for that work. His protest at that turn of events had at that time received strong support from Orde.

Although Collingwood had little faith in the ability of the Spanish to set aside local differences and govern themselves should they ever regain their freedom, when Prince Leopold, son of the Queen of Sicily, arrived in Gibraltar with his mentor, the Duke of Orleans, and offered himself as Regent of Spain, Collingwood advised Orleans very firmly that affairs of government were best left to the Spaniards themselves, and that they should go back home. And so, when it was requested, he refused to grant the party permission to step ashore. They turned about and made their way back to Sicily.

Collingwood's future son-in-law, Newnham Collingwood was to tell of an occasion when the Spaniards fired off ammunition, which the British had gifted from their ships, in honour of a saint whose festival they were celebrating. He claims that when Collingwood heard of this he cautioned them that no more ammunition would be spared unless they promised to reserve it for sinners, and not for saints.[11]

But Collingwood's duties lay at sea to which he soon returned, leaving Purvis at Cadiz as the French advance continued. And Collingwood was given the assistance that year of the courageous and able but volatile, tactless and unpredictable adventurer, Lord Cochrane, son of the Earl of Dundonnell.

Cochrane had entered the Navy under the wing of an uncle at the advanced age of seventeen years at the outset of the war in 1793. But that same uncle had had the foresight to place his name on a ship's register when he was but a boy, and so, within eighteen months of joining, Cochrane had been advanced to the rank of lieutenant. Needless to say, very soon afterwards his total lack of tact and diplomacy became apparent when he was admonished at court martial for showing disrespect to the ship's lieutenant. But when himself in command in the years 1800 and 1801 there had followed enormous success along the coast of Spain in the capture of privateers, merchant shipping and Spanish frigates alike which made his name a legend as a daring and dashing commander. He was duly raised to the rank of post captain in August 1801 when only twenty-five years of age and after only eight years service in the Navy.

But then, like Sir John Orde and like so many others in the service, he fell foul of the Lord St Vincent, who was by then First Lord of the Admiralty. St Vincent had refused to promote Cochrane's lieutenant on the *Speedy* despite Cochrane's recommendation that he should do so in recognition of distinguished service in his latest capture. St Vincent gave as his reason that it was not warranted since very few had been killed in the action. Cochrane was then foolish enough to argue that there had been more casualties on the *Speedy* on that occasion than had been suffered on board St Vincent's flagship at St Vincent in the whole of that battle, yet he, St Vincent, had received an earldom for it and his flag-captain a knighthood. Not surprisingly, when hostilities were resumed after the Peace of Amiens, Cochrane, like Sir John Orde and several others, had then been banished from any theatre of action until the departure of St Vincent from the Admiralty in 1804. He was relegated to serving as commander of an old collier at Plymouth, and then in the Orkneys protecting non-existent fisheries.

And so it was not until 1804 before Cochrane, like Sir John Orde, was brought back to the colours by the new First Lord, Lord Melville. Then the rate of his captures resumed on much the same scale as before.

In 1806 and 1807 he served as a member of parliament for the divisions of Honiton and Westminster before, in November 1807, joining Collingwood in the Mediterranean as commander of the *Impererieuse*. And in the fifteen months which followed before returning home, his activity in the Mediterranean was immense.

The first assignment he received from Collingwood was to relieve the senior officer at Corfu, Captain Patrick Campbell. But within a short time he had made so many enemies there that, on the advice of Captain

Campbell, Collingwood was forced to recall him, reporting that he was: 'Wanting in discretion.'

In this Collingwood had perhaps forgotten the stand he and Nelson had taken in the West Indies some twenty-three years before when upholding the enforcement of the Navigation Acts, for Cochrane's only crime on this occasion had been to place an embargo on the grant of passes to merchant ships which were raising the blockade, which his predecessor had permitted.

But then Collingwood was soon to make amends, recognizing from his long friendship with Nelson that an officer who showed initiative and individual brilliance, should, if anything, be encouraged. For this same reason he had helped the career of Captain Hoste after that officer had lost the support and patronage of Nelson at Trafalgar. And so now, in January 1808, he gave Captain Cochrane his head too, by appointing him to a roving commission to harass the French and the Spanish along the Mediterranean coast as and when the opportunity arose. In the four months which followed, very many enemy merchant vessels fell prey to Cochrane's activities and many was the battery and shore installation destroyed by fire until Collingwood transferred him to the Spanish front to assist Spain in her struggle for independence.

There he was just as active in the destruction of highways essential to the French for the transport of troops. And, in particular, he led officers and men from his own ship in the defence of the Spanish castle of Trinidad at Rosas on the Costa Brava when it had been on the point of capitulation to the French. In the result the garrison held out for a further two weeks or more before Cochrane withdrew without any loss of life, blowing up the fortifications as he went.

In the round, while under Collingwood's command, Cochrane left a trail of devastation and destruction along the entire Mediterranean coast of France where his activities forced the French to commit troops in defence of their installations at a time when they were sorely needed on the Spanish front. His contribution to the war against Spain was therefore of enormous value to the British cause. Blowing up signal stations had been his particular speciality, and by letter to Collingwood dated 28 September of 1808, Cochrane wrote:

> With varying opposition, but with unvaried success, the newly con-structed Semaphonic Telegraphs, which are of the utmost consequence to the safety of the numerous convoys that pass along the coast of France...have been blown up and completely demol-ished, together with their telegraph houses, fourteen barracks of gendarmes, one battery and the strong tower on the lake of Frontignan.

Collingwood replied:

> Nothing can exceed the zeal and activity with which his lordship
> pursues the enemy. The success which attends his enterprises clearly
> indicates with what skill and ability they are conducted, besides
> keeping the coast in constant alarm, causing a general suspension of
> the trade and harassing a body of troops employed in opposing him.

Collingwood had supported Cochrane throughout. But for its part the
Admiralty had been a good deal more critical, complaining that
Cochrane had overworked his ship's crew unnecessarily and had
expended ammunition in defence of Fort Trinidad too extravagantly.

Cochrane's buccaneering career was to continue in this same way for
many a year more, both at sea and at home as a member of parliament,
long after Collingwood had departed this life. Imprisoned for fraud and
cashiered the service at one point, he nonetheless died an Admiral of the
Fleet and a hero, following reinstatement in the Royal Navy after years
spent at sea commanding the navies of Chile, Brazil and Greece. He was
then buried at Westminster Abbey, where his grave is visited each year
by representatives of the Chilean Navy.

Anthony Price was to write in his book, *The Eyes of the Fleet*, that:

> Cochrane was the greatest and most daring frigate Captain of them
> all who must have presented many a writer of naval fiction as his
> role model....In the next World War...his qualities required the
> opportunities of a T.E. Lawrence. In the World War after that one,
> he might have been another Orde Wingate in Burma...Winston
> Churchill would have recognized Cochrane's qualities... .

Curiously Wingate was distantly related to Lawrence by marriage.

In August of that year Collingwood became all too aware that undi-
agnosed illness was sapping his strength for he was otherwise still a
comparatively young man, and so he once again pleaded with the
Admiralty to be allowed to relinquish his command and come home. But
Lord Mulgrave's reply was that:

> It is a justice which I owe you and the country to tell you candidly
> that I know not how I should be able to supply all that would be lost
> to the service of the country, and to the general interests of Europe,
> by your absence from the Mediterranean.

And so he wrote to his wife:

> The conduct of the fleet alone would be easy; but the political

correspondence which I have to carry on with the Spaniards, the Turks, the Albanians, the Egyptians and all the states of Barbary gives me such constant occupation that I really often feel my spirits quite exhausted, and of course my health is much impaired; but if I must go on I will do the best I can.

Although it would indeed have been extremely difficult to replace Collingwood with another who could have matched his professional and diplomatic skills and experience, Admiral Sir Thomas Byam Martin suggested many years later that there was a further reason for refusing Collingwood's application and that was that the government were more than well aware that the Duke of Clarence was taking a close interest in the succession. Alive to the state of Collingwood's health, it seems that he was very keen to succeed to the command himself if Collingwood should ever decide to relinquish it, while at the same time the Admiralty realized that if that situation arose it could then be difficult to refuse him the command, given his exalted rank. Yet as a commander it was felt that to appoint him would be to court disaster, for he lacked both the professional skill necessary for the work but also the sort of common-sense and sensitivity which was necessary for the conduct of delicate diplomacy. In short they felt that he was wholly unfit for the work.

As it was, in Byam Martin's opinion:

Old Cuddy, as we always called Lord Collingwood, who had worked all his life with greater diligence for professional applause than any other man, was flattered to be urged to stay on, and replied that if the good of the service required that he should remain, he was content to wait and die at his post, for he felt his days were numbered, and this proved too true.

But in Collingwood's own mind it was his sense of duty which left him no choice but to soldier on, and it was indeed to cost him his life. It was a noble sacrifice and it was made for his country.

And so, his work done in Cadiz, in September of that year he resumed his command in the Mediterranean, hoisted his flag in the *Ocean* and from there continued to both watch the French and direct aid operations in Spain, while all the while writing privately to his wife of his longing to be back at home amongst his family and friends.

In September Lord Mulgrave again wrote that it would be difficult to replace him and again asked him to remain in post unless further ill-health really made that impossible in which case a command at Plymouth might be considered.

Convinced by this that the Admiralty regarded him as indispensable, by letter dated 10 January 1809, Collingwood replied:

My long continuance at sea has made me very feeble; and the fear of my unfitness, which I know people are often the last to discover in themselves, induced me to make the application. My situation requires the most vigorous mind, which is seldom possessed at the same time with great debility of body...I have nothing to add to what was said in that letter. I have no object in the world that I put in competition with my public duty; and so long as your lordship thinks it proper to continue me in this command, my utmost efforts shall be made to strengthen the impression which you now have. But I still hope that whenever it may be done with convenience your lordship will bear in mind my request. On the subject of Plymouth I have only to say that wherever I can best render my service I shall be at your lordship's command...but with the little I have ever had to do with ports I shall enter on that field with great diffidence.

At such a distance from home Collingwood was troubled too that he was unable to exert a greater control over the running of Chirton, for reports were reaching him from his sister Mary that expenditure was beginning to run out of control.

And, very surprisingly, his now aged father-in-law, who seems to have received a deal of extravagant hospitality at Chirton from his daughter when he found himself in financial difficulties, now involved Collingwood in a commercial transaction which irritated and embarrassed Collingwood beyond measure. Blackett appears to have made over to Collingwood a stake he had in a fire office without so much as telling him of it. And he had done it, it seems, in order to compensate him for a pledge he himself had made of Collingwood's credit to cover a debt of £2,200 which Blackett had himself incurred, all of this unbeknown to Collingwood. It seems that Sarah had been prevailed upon, against her wishes, to draw on Collingwood's bankers for just that sum.

This led Collingwood to write three letters to one of his sisters, the first in March of 1809 in which he stated that he was:

...determined to sell [his] property at Morpeth immediately...You may suppose my affairs are in a very unsettled state. In short I know nothing of them...

And then, in July:

I am sorry for the derangement, for I call it derangement when there is no order, of my house. It is what gives me great pain. I have endeavoured to restrain it. My wife would gladly confine herself to what I prescribe, but the gaiety, the vanity, and the love of feeding of her father, there is no bounds to. It has been the habit of his life, and the means I am afraid, has never been of much consideration...I have been exceedingly plain with Mr B on the liberties taken with my fortune, and told him that if he wished his daughter to have elegancies beyond my convenience he should have provided her with a fortune.

And again in October:

I have never heard from Mr B. since I wrote him a sharp letter on the subject.

This very ungenerous outburst was no doubt born of illness coupled with an awareness of the very unfavourable comparison which his own very frugal and simple way of life made with that which his income was purchasing for his family at home.. But it was certainly most uncharacteristic of Collingwood and was very soon forgotten for it is clear from their correspondence that harmony was very soon restored.

Clearly what had really irritated him most about this whole episode was that he should have been linked against his wishes with a fire office which was keen to use his name to solicit custom. Indeed, although making it clear that he did not blame Blackett for it, in the October letter to his sister he told her that he had written to Newton, his Newcastle agent:

...to go to the Fire Office and if the share is not sold (which Mr B told my wife was to fetch £2500 any day) to inform the gentlemen that my name has been added to their Society without my authority and desire that it may be immediately erased, for that I am not, nor ever was, of the company. It is an undertaking for speculators and adventurers who have nothing to lose... .

It continued to rankle with him, for when a general promotion of flag officers that autumn was restricted to flag officers below the rank of vice-admiral, Collingwood foolishly, unreasonably and erroneously convinced himself that it must have been at the insistence of the King in order to deprive him of promotion to the rank of full admiral because of his supposed connection with trade and commerce. And so, to his sister he wrote:

...they say the King has expressed his desire that I may not be recalled. His Majesty knows everything about everybody and I dare say having read the advertisement in the Newcastle paper (for he reads all provincial papers) is unwilling that an insurance broker should sit in the house of peers.

There is the cause of my illness and broken spirit...and now my character is established as a mercantile jobber, without me even knowing about it. Everybody expresses surprise that the promotion did not give a flag at the main top. I am not surprised at all, but am ashamed to tell them why. The King jealous of the dignity of his flag cannot be very anxious to have it an insurance beacon.

In truth the promotion had been restricted by the Admiralty to the lower echelon simply in order to bring on younger blood. It had not in any way been pitched at that level to prevent Collingwood from advancing to the rank of full admiral, a rank which would assuredly have been his had he but lived a little longer. As it was, like Nelson, he was to end his days in the rank of vice-admiral, a rank thought by Lord Howe to be superior to all other ranks in the Navy except that of Lord High Admiral, although this was a view expressed when required to relinquish the rank of Vice-Admiral of England in order to become the Admiral of the Fleet in 1796.

At all events, in March of that same year, Collingwood was cheered a little and very flattered to be appointed by the King, Major-General of Marines, a post which had fallen vacant on the death of Admiral Lord Gardner.

And then, despite his dislike of the Queen of Naples and although still weak in health, he accepted her invitation to attend a grand ball and supper to be held in Palermo for the nobility on Ash Wednesday, the last night of a carnival. There he was placed next to the Queen and the following day dined with the King at his country house. Although received in style and with great civility during this visit, for they were beholden to him for their security, it is clear from accounts of the occasion that his dignified but reserved northern temperament and penetrating, disapproving gaze had disconcerted the Queen more than a little. In a long letter to his wife describing the occasion, he ended with: 'They never desire, I am sure, to see my face again.' And, to Admiral Purvis, he wrote: 'God protect them: I wish you had seen that Court. I consider it as a sort of curiosity, and how such a one can exist in civilized Europe is a matter of great astonishment.'

During the autumn, acting on his own iniative, Collingwood achieved the liberation of the islands of Zante, Cephalonia, Ithaca, and Cerigo employing troops commanded by Lieutenant General Sir John Stuart accompanied by a naval escort. It was the product of a surprise attack which had therefore met with little opposition and it led to the recovery of Corfu from the French, as Collingwood had predicted that it would. And it brought with it too, applause from the Admiralty at home.

But his real hope, still, was that he might encounter the French Fleet at sea. Alas, in this he suffered yet another disappointment in April when Rear-Admiral Baudin in the *Robuste* slipped out of Toulon with a small force including four sail of the line, two frigates, one corvette and sixteen brigs and settees carrying troops and supplies for the relief of Barcelona. It was Collingwood's misfortune that he was at this moment far away with the blockading fleet at Port Mahon in the *Ville de Paris* of 110 guns to which he had shifted his flag in April 1809 when the *Ocean* returned home for repairs. He, therefore, remained unaware that there was prey on the high seas until Baudin had been able to land his cargo unmolested and had started to creep back to Toulon.

Collingwood only learned of this expedition when intelligence reached him four days after the French had embarked from Barcelona on their return journey and although he set off in hot pursuit and was at one stage but a few hours behind them, Baudin encountered favourable winds and was safely back in port by the time Collingwood reached Toulon. For his pains Collingwood collected no more than two French ships found in the seas off Barcelona and they were on no more than a mission of mercy carrying wounded soldiers back home.

But Collingwood did taste some success in October of that year when Baudin slipped out of Toulon again with more troops and supplies to be landed at Barcelona. Coincidentally, chancing fate, Baudin had chosen to set sail on 21 October, not because it was the anniversary of Trafalgar, but because a strong gale had blown out to sea the British ships which had been blockading Toulon during the previous several weeks, or so he thought. In fact, knowing that the French were desperate to supply their hard-pressed troops in Barcelona, Collingwood had foreseen that Baudin would see it as an opportunity to put to sea if he withdrew his ships out of sight in the face of the wind. It was a ruse to lure them out. And so, when the gale blew up he quickly weighed anchor and took the fleet to Minorca leaving the port of Toulon clear of British ships while, at the same time, posting frigates to watch Baudin's every move. He then let it be known in Toulon that the British Fleet were settled in Minorca before sailing for the waters around Cape Sebastian where he hoped to intercept Baudin's convoy mid-journey. Baudin duly obliged and was spotted by Collingwood's outlying frigates on the 23rd, although Collingwood, fully ready for battle with fifteen sail of the line, was disappointed to see that the French convoy numbered no more than three line of battle ships, two frigates and several store ships and transports, all of which then turned tail and fled on sight of the British with Rear-Admiral Martin and a squadron of eight ships in hot pursuit. But then, in their flight, the three line of battle ships and the two frigates abandoned the convoy and sailed off in different directions leaving a few of the small ships in the convoy to the mercy of the British. These were then easily destroyed while the rest made their escape.

However, Martin, now with six ships at his disposal, rightly judged that the French would make for the mainland and, the following day, he found them there, running along the coast. After a chase of several hours, the French, in desperation, ran two of their liners ashore, landed their crews and then set fire to the ships, while the third liner and one frigate managed to achieve the safety of Cette Harbour. But the remainder of Baudin's convoy was not so fortunate for when they were discovered in the Bay of Roses by Captain Hallowell, with a squadron of ships which had been detached by Collingwood on 1 November, all were either fired or captured, but not without a fight and the loss of many British lives.

Although the whole action had really been very one-sided with the French very much outnumbered, the success of it did prompt the Duke of Clarence to write Collingwood a warm letter of congratulations which Collingwood much appreciated. He received a similar letter from the Prime Minister of the Kingdom of Sicily which had been written at the request of his King.

The editor of a selection of Collingwood's letters in Volume VI of *The Naval Miscellany* published in 2003, Captain C.H.H. Owen, rightly opined that:

> To the surrounding states he was indeed the embodiment of British power in the Mediterranean, and it was largely due to his skills as both admiral and diplomat that Napoleon's Mediterranean designs were defeated.

And he there cited the view expressed by Thomas Creevey in 1828 in a letter to Miss Ord that:

> ...Collingwood alone...sustained the interests of England and eternally defeated the projects of France. He was, in truth, the prime and sole minister of England, acting upon the seas, corresponding himself with all surrounding States, and ordering and executing everything upon his own responsibility.[12]

It was a fair summary of Collingwood's command even though it has to be allowed that Creevey was there writing to his stepdaughter, a lady who had been born to another son of Newcastle upon Tyne, one William Ord, one time member of parliament for that city, and a grand-daughter of Charles Brandling MP of Gosforth in Northumberland.[13]

Chapter 13

The End

By this time, sadly, Collingwood's life was drawing to a close.
   To his wife he wrote:

> The Admiralty have been exceedingly kind and attentive to me; they
> have sent me the best ship in the Navy and have reinforced my
> squadron; but what I most want is a new pair of legs and a new pair
> of eyes...

In the summer of 1809 Collingwood had written prophetically to his
wife:

> Tough as I am, I cannot last much longer. I have seen all the ships
> and men out two or three times. Bounce and I seem to be the only
> personages who stand our ground. Many about me are yielding to
> the fatigue and confinement of a life which is certainly not natural
> to man.

But then, in August, even the elderly and Honourable Bounce
Collingwood left him, no doubt as worn out as his old master.
Collingwood reported the death to one of his sisters:

> You will be sorry to hear my poor dog Bounce is dead. I am afraid
> he fell overboard in the night. He is a great loss to me. I have few
> comforts, but he was one, for he loved me. Everybody sorrows for
> him. He was wiser than [many] who hold their heads higher, and
> was grateful [to those] who were kind to him.

At least, with his great fright at the roar of the guns, there had been little
need in his closing years to seek cover below decks for there had been
precious few occasions since Trafalgar when the cannons had been run
out on Collingwood's ship. Quite how he had survived the punishment

taken by the *Royal Sovereign* at Trafalgar will never be known. And although at the end he was both grossly overweight and extremely bored, Collingwood missed him greatly for he had been his constant, faithful and often his only companion for twenty years or more, ever since he had gone with him in the *Mermaid*. And just as Collingwood in his last years had been held captive by his duties to the curtilage of the ship, so too, Bounce at his side had suffered like deprivation. Not for him those country walks and the comforts of home which are the ordinary right of any respectable dog, and seldom did he see another animal with which he could fraternize save when at Morpeth for the duration of the Peace of Amiens when shipped home by sea with the valuables.

The two had been devoted to each other and inseparable in their lone-liness. It had been reported often enough that whenever standing on the weather gangway breathing the midnight air, scanning the horizon with his night glass, Bounce would be at his feet. And on those occasions when Collingwood was at rest in his cot, the faithful Bounce would be there, asleep by his side. And he became a firm favourite with many a sailor who sailed with Collingwood. As Robert Hay noted in his memoirs, referring to his service with Collingwood on the *Culloden* in 1804: 'He and his favourite dog Bounce were known to every member of the crew.'

Indeed the future Admiral Hercules Robinson, when a midshipman, attributed his advance under Collingwood to his practice of making a fuss of Bounce. And the place Bounce held in Collingwood's own affections was demonstrated often enough for he was accorded frequent mention in Collingwood's many letters home.

Shortly before Trafalgar Collingwood had written to his father-in-law in a letter dated 21 September of 1805:

Bounce is my only pet now, and he is indeed a good fellow; he sleeps by the side of my cot, whenever I lie on one, until near the time of tacking, and then marches off to be out of hearing of the guns, for he is not reconciled to them yet.

After Trafalgar there had been the report to his wife, mentioned earlier, of:

The consequential airs he gives himself since he became a Right Honourable dog are insufferable. He considers it beneath his dignity to play with commoners dogs, and truly thinks he does them grace when he condescends to lift up his leg against them.

And, on another occasion, when writing to his sister, Mrs Stead, in a letter dated 1 July 1807, while complaining of the shortcomings of another, he wrote:

> ...tis like teaching a rook to sing, or Bounce to play the fiddle – long labour lost – for though Bounce is a dog of talents, I suspect he wou'd make but a discordant fiddler.

His New Year's message to his daughters in 1807 had contained a further report as to his welfare, noting that: 'Bounce sighs so piteously these long evenings that I am obliged to sing him to sleep.'

And then, in a letter to his elder daughter dated 12 August 1808, he wrote of Bounce growing old, and that: 'I once thought of having his picture taken, but he had the good fortune to escape that.' But sadly there was now little time left to Collingwood for grieving.

On New Year's Day he attempted to explain his illness in a letter to his father-in-law saying that his doctors attributed it to lack of exercise and a sedentary way of life, confined as he was to the boundaries of the ship. But modern medical diagnosis would probably have recognized it as something a good deal more serious which no amount of exercise could have cured.

And then, on 10 February 1810, he wrote to his friend Clavell, now a captain, complaining of a very severe complaint in his stomach and that:

> It is high time I should return to England, and I hope that I shall be allowed to do so before long. It will otherwise be too late.

These were prophetic words. To his sister he wrote:

> I have been very ill ever since I came here and the physician has much difficulty in determining on the nature of my complaint, which is in my stomach, and they say entirely the consequence of the sedentary life I must have. I have lost digestion and I have a constant pain, and my spirits are so bad, and so low, that I am become indifferent to everything.

A tentative diagnosis was made, which was 'a contraction of the pylorus', namely of the lower outlet of the stomach between the stomach and the intestine, thought to have been caused by months of crouching over a desk. But modern X-Ray procedures would no doubt have exposed scarring as a legacy of ulcer trouble as the cause of the contraction, or perhaps even an undetected growth.

But whatever the cause he was physically unable to go on and so, on 22 February, he tendered his resignation to Lord Mulgrave, requesting that he be allowed to return to England, writing that:

...this, I can assure your Lordship, I have not done until I am past service, being at present totally incapable of applying to the duties of my office. My complaint is of a nature to which I apprehend it is difficult to apply a remedy, for I have hitherto received no benefit from medical advice. Since November it has been daily increasing, so that I am now almost past walking across my cabin; and as it is attributed to my long service in a ship, I have little hope of amendment until I can land.

On 25 February, Collingwood, attended by the loyal and trusted Captain Hallowell, stepped on shore at Port Mahon on doctor's orders in the hope that gentle exercise, perhaps taken on horseback, would effect an improvement. But it was all to no avail for strength continued to drain from his body until, on 3 March, when really no longer able to attend to any of his duties, he finally accepted that the end was nigh.

By letter to the Admiralty of that same date he finally handed over command of the fleet to Purvis, now a vice-admiral, who became acting commander-in-chief. For some reason some were later to assume, wrongly, that it was Rear-Admiral Martin, in command of a squadron in the Mediterranean, who had taken over, perhaps because Purvis had, by then, requested retirement home, which was duly granted. It was not until 9 April that Sir Charles Cotton was appointed to the full command.

After the handover on 3 March Collingwood retreated to his cabin and the sanctuary of his cot and the *Ville de Paris* then set sail for home.

But it was two days before the ship eventually got under way, and it was said that when it did and eventually cleared the harbour, he rallied a little, long enough to say when it was reported to him that they were at sea again: 'Then I may yet live to meet the French once more.' But, ever a realist, Collingwood knew that the end was near and he prepared himself accordingly.

It was said also that when Captain Thomas asked if the motion of the ship disturbed him, his reply was:

No Thomas, I am now in a state in which nothing in this world can disturb me more. I am dying; and I am sure it must be consolatory to you, and all who love me, to see how comfortably I am coming to my end.

Indeed he met death on the evening of 7 March 1810 with a composure, resignation and dignity which was quite remarkable. After bidding sad farewells to his staff and making his peace with the Almighty, he gave himself up without a struggle. According to the doctor present, Mr Macanst, who watched:

...in wonder and admiration...In no part of his lordship's brilliant life did his character appear with greater lustre than when he was approaching his end. It was dignified in the extreme. If it be on the bed of sickness, and at the approach of death – when ambition, the love of glory, and the interests of the world are over – that the true character is to be discovered surely never did any man's appear to greater advantage than did that of my Lord Collingwood.

For my own part I did not believe it possible that any one, on such an occasion, could have behaved so nobly. Cruelly harassed by a most afflicting disease, obtaining no relief from the means employed, and perceiving his death to be inevitable, he suffered no sigh of regret to escape, no murmuring at his past life, no apprehension of the future. He met death as became him, with a composure and fortitude which have seldom been equalled and never surpassed.

And these were the words of one who must have witnessed death in battle on countless occasions. Perhaps it was for this same reason that Collingwood was able to face his end with such remarkable equanimity, for he too must have witnessed death all around him often enough, and usually of men much younger than was he.

To his sister, Mrs Stead, Collingwood had written the year before:

I have lived long enough in the world to know that there is no sense in lamenting the death of people; indeed, to consider it not as a subject of lamentation. I do not know any thing the mind can dwell upon with more pleasure than the idea of dying comfortably. I think it has got all its horror in weak minds, by the same sort of operation that the soul shrinks at the story of a ghost. In infancy we get the impression that death is horrible, but I believe if the same pains were taken to combine the ideas of death and delight, we should wait as impatiently for it as they do for a Guild ball, or a Lord Mayor's feast, or any other of those great events which make people perfectly happy.

Thus strengthened by his faith, it was perhaps such as he that Psalm cvii 23, 24 had in mind: 'They that go down to the sea in ships, and occupy their business in great waters, these men see the works of the Lord, and his wonders in the deep.'

The tragedy of it was that but for the disease of his stomach Collingwood was still a fit, healthy and strong figure of a man, or so the autopsy found. However, whether an earlier return home for surgery or convalescence would have saved him, as his doctors fondly believed, is open to doubt, for it may well be that modern science would have diagnosed his condition as incurable in the year 1810 when medical knowledge was still in its infancy.

And so, four and a half years on, Collingwood followed his friend Nelson for one last time and on one last journey, both of them when in the rank of vice-admiral. But whereas Nelson had departed this life in a blaze of glory with the noise of battle which he so loved still ringing in his ears, Collingwood slipped away calmly, quietly and in peace. As in life so in death they each of them died as they had lived and, in death, it is to be hoped that each found his own tranquillity.

But where on so many occasions in his much shorter life Nelson had been able to return to his homeland to parade the rank to which he had been so rapidly elevated, and to taste the fruits of victory and enjoy the adulation of his fellow countrymen, Collingwood had been condemned to celebrate the fame, recognition and many honours which came his way, in the isolation of foreign waters. Never allowed home, he had never taken his seat in the House of Lords, and now the title, so recently conferred upon him, became extinct. Perhaps more so than of most men it can truly be said of Collingwood that his entire life had been given over to the service of his country. He was perhaps the noblest sailor of them all.

It had been Collingwood's wish that he be buried at sea or, failing that, at the very least that his funeral be kept private. But it was not to be. As Sarah Collingwood's friend Miss Woodman was to write on 20 April of that year, when staying at the Blackett's house in Charlotte Square:

> We had just returned from church when Mr C. Blackett himself brought up a letter from Lord Mulgrave with the melancholy account of his having died at sea on 7 March…It was his particular request that he might be buried where he died; but as he died at sea, they think it proper for his remains to be brought down. Lady C., Mr J. Collingwood and Mr John Davison are left executors. Poor Lady C was put to bed immediately and given a good deal of laudanum…Poor Mr Blackett!!! My heart bled for him yesterday; but like most old people he is today very much composed.[1]

The body was carried off in the frigate *Nereus* captained by Peter Heywood, an officer with an unusual career behind him including a sentence of death. When a midshipman of sixteen years he had found himself serving on the infamous *Bounty* when it had gone into mutiny in the year 1789. He had then been one of the non-mutinous elements left behind by the captain, Lieutenant Bligh, his patron, quite simply because the launch which carried him off was too small to be able to safely carry all those who had remained loyal, or so Heywood main-

251

tained. And so, rather than add to the burden by taking his chance in the launch he, young and inexperienced as he was, had chosen the safety of the ship. But he had not supported the mutineers. Then, of the two parties which split up on the island of Tahiti, Heywood had joined that which had remained on the island and so surrendered to the *Pandora* when it came looking for the mutineers in 1791. His reward had been to be held captive, naked, in handcuffs and chained to thirteen others in a cage eleven feet long on the quarterdeck of the ship until the armourer's mate had released all thirteen after the *Pandora* struck a reef and only moments before it went down with all hands. Heywood was one of those then able to swim clear. But having escaped death by drowning he had then been sentenced to death by hanging at a court martial of the mutineers presided over by Lord Hood, for Bligh had written home stating that Heywood had in fact been one of the ring-leaders. Heywood himself had run a contradictory story at trial to the effect that he had tried to join the launch but had been prevented by the mutineers, a defence which the court rejected. But the court had recommended mercy in his case[2] and it was his good fortune that the Earl of Chatham was then persuaded of his innocence and a pardon followed. Indeed Lord Hood himself, together with Lord Howe, a distant relative by marriage, and probably the Earl Spencer too, later backed his advancement. And so, by then something of a celebrity, his naval career had flourished and he had reached post rank in April of the year 1803.

At Gibraltar Collingwood's body was transferred to the frigate *Nereide* for the journey home and on 26 April it was received at Greenwich Hospital. There it was placed in a plain stone coffin donated by the King which, like the sarcophagus in which Nelson's coffin had been placed, had been commissioned by Cardinal Wolsey for his own funeral, but this too had been confiscated by Henry VIII and had then lain unused those many years in a room adjoining St George's Chapel at Windsor.[3] Here the body lay in state until 11 May when it was carried in procession to St Paul's Cathedral along roads lined with spectators, transported in the self same funeral car which had carried Nelson on that identical journey but a few years before; drummers of the hospital beating out the solemn lament of the *Dead March* in Handel's *Saul*,[4] always guaranteed to awaken the soul. And so Collingwood followed in Nelson's car, still in his shadow on this, his very last journey.

In the cathedral a large congregation had gathered. The *Naval Chronicle* was to report that:

The spectators were...numerous and the greatest confusion prevailed in St Paul's in consequence of the pressure of the crowd.

252

His old commanding officer, the Earl St Vincent, now seventy-four years of age, who had not found it convenient to attend the funeral of Horatio Nelson, made a point of finding his way to the cathedral for Collingwood's funeral, as did old Sir Peter Parker, now the Admiral of the Fleet at the age of eighty-seven. He had been a father to each of them yet had managed to outlive both of them, albeit by no more than twelve months or so. Present too was Lord Hood, and Collingwood's fellow Northumbrian, Lord Grey, and, prominent among the many distinguished mourners that day, his old schoolfellow, Lord Eldon the Lord Chancellor, almost uncontrollable with grief. He was to report afterwards that:

> It was very affecting – his sailors crowded so around all anxious to see the last of their commander. One sailor seized me by the arm, and entreated that I would take him in with me that he might be there at the end. I told him to stick fast to me, and I did take him in; but when it came to throwing some earth on the coffin (you know the part of the service 'dust to dust') he burst past me and threw himself into the vault.[5]

Lord Mulgrave, who had been such a contact at the Admiralty in the last four years of Collingwood's life, attended the occasion with his predecessor as First Lord, Thomas Grenville. So, too, did the celebrated Lord Cochrane and many other admirals, captains, officers and sailors who had served with Collingwood over the years.

Chief mourner was Collingwood's surviving brother John, supported by Spencer Stanhope MP as second mourner.

At the conclusion of the service, Smith, his loyal servant of eleven years or more, placed Collingwood's coronet upon the coffin positioned under the very centre of the Dome, and it was then lowered to the vault below to lie next to that of Nelson. And so, fittingly, the two friends finally came together again to rest alongside one another, Collingwood at peace nestling in the shadow of Nelson's more flamboyant tomb. As in life so in death. And there they have remained.

Tributes continued to flow. The Duke of Clarence, later King William IV, placed on a finger of his hand which already carried a ring in memory of Nelson, a mourning ring in memory of Collingwood which Lady Collingwood had sent him. In a letter to her he wrote:

> I feel great concern in having been prevented from attending his funeral. I was informed that the internment was to be quite private or else I should have made a point of attending the remains of my departed friend to the grave. No one could have had a more sincere

regard for the public character and abilities of Lord Collingwood than myself; indeed, with me it is enough to have been the friend of Nelson to possess my estimation. The Hero of the Nile was a man of great mind, but self-taught; Lord Collingwood, the old companion in arms of the immortal Nelson, was equally great in judgment and abilities, and had also the advantage of an excellent education. Pardon me, madam, for having said so much on this melancholy occasion; but my feelings as a brother officer, and my admiration of the late Lord Collingwood, have dictated this expression of my sentiments. I will now conclude, and shall place on the same finger the ring which your ladyship has sent me with the gold bust of Lord Nelson. Lord Collingwood's must ever be prized by me as coming from his family; the bust of Lord Nelson I received from an unknown hand on the day the event of his death reached this country. To me the two rings are invaluable; and the sight of them must ever give me sensations of grief and admiration.

A gold ring with a brass locket set into the top of a heavily engraved band and allegedly containing a lock of Collingwood's hair, turned up at Phillips, auctioneers, in London in May 2000. Inscribed on the inside was: 'Lord Collingwood, Obt. 7 March 1810, aged 59.'

Clearly the engraver had neglected to check Collingwood's true date of birth. It was sold for the sum of £1,350.[6]

Parliament voted that a monument by Richard Westmacott RA be erected in St Paul's Cathedral in the east bay of the south transept, close to that of Nelson. It was to be joined there in the fullness of time by another in memory of Wellington. The monument, which shows Collingwood recumbent in a funeral barge protected by an angel, has been described by Peter Burman in his book *St Paul's Cathedral* as 'superbly carved', and: 'One of the most striking and memorable monuments in the Cathedral.'

However, and surprisingly, the citizens of his native Newcastle upon Tyne opted for no more than a single medallion mounted on a cenotaph to be placed in St Nicholas's Church in that city, later St Nicholas Cathedral, the scene of both his baptism and his marriage. But it was then left to his widow and his two daughters to erect it which they did in 1819 with a marble bust of Collingwood by Rossi placed on a pedestal.[7] A more elaborate memory than Collingwood would have wished [8] it was sited in the nave of the church and the inscription, composed by Sarah herself, records his age and the year of his birth as 1750, incorrectly. Later that same year her daughters added Sarah's name to the inscription when she too died, unexpectedly, and then, in more recent times, it was moved near to the entrance of what is now the cathedral.

Apart from the drawing done of Collingwood by Nelson, so treasured by Mrs Moutray, which is now in the National Maritime Museum, a self-portrait of Collingwood had appeared in 1783 and a head and shoulders likeness in print form attributed to one Henry R. Cook after Robert Bowyer had been published in the *Naval Chronicle* in 1806. In 1807 Collingwood had had his portrait painted by Guiseppe Polite at Syracuse which was the last portrait painted of him in life and was probably therefore the nearest likeness. Indeed he was to write to Sarah: 'The painter represented me as I am, not as I once was.' A mezzotint of it is now in the Royal Naval Museum at Portsmouth. In 1812 the promised whole-length portrait of Collingwood by J. Lonsdale was presented to the mayor and corporation of his native city by the Newcastle Volunteers to be hung in the Guildhall. The presentation was made on 6 August by Lieutenant Colonel Clennel of Harbottle, after which the regiment fired three volleys, and the guns on the castle fired a salute. It now hangs in the City's Laing Art Gallery.

A half-length print based upon the Lonsdale portrait was published by William Greatbach in 1836. The celebrated full-length portrait by Henry Howard of Collingwood resplendent in his full dress clothes, hand to chin, clutching a telescope and wearing, incorrectly, a small, and not his fighting, sword, was not in fact painted until the year 1827. And in all probability it was then painted from a miniature, in turn based on Politi's portrait in life.[9]

It was later presented by the family to the Painted Hall at Greenwich and is now to be found in the Greenwich Maritime Museum.

Other likenesses were later got out based upon the Politi painting, including a miniature by the renowned artist Henry Bone, which was sold at auction in 2004 for the sum of £ 38,050, and a head and shoulders portrait published in 1823 as a mezzotint by Charles Turner.

And still later, in 1835, he was to achieve immortality as one of the heroes of Alfred de Vigny's *Servitude et Grandeur Militaires*.[10]

In his will Collingwood left estate worth £163,743, a not inconsiderable sum for a man who had started out with very little and who had enjoyed little good fortune with prize money. £40,000 of this he left to his daughter Sarah and £40,000 he left to his daughter Mary.[11]

Sarah, his wife, born on 16 June 1762, was then only forty-seven years of age. She was to live on for a further nine years, just long enough to enjoy some of the fruits of Collingwood's success.

A property was purchased at 9, York Place off Portman Square in the city of London, but a few yards from the front door of Admiral Sir John

Orde's London house in Gloucester Place. And there she entertained lavishly in between return visits to her home at Charlotte Square in Newcastle and to holiday houses which she took at Whitburn and Tynemouth on the Newcastle coast, firm in the belief that sea bathing brought with it therapeutic benefit.

She lost the companionship of her father, John Erasmus Blackett, on 11 June 1814 when he died aged eighty-six years.[12] His name was then inscribed on the floorstone dedicated to the Blackett family in the Cathedral Church of St Nicholas, and he too was later given immortality when a street in the city was named Blackett Street after him.

But Collingwood's secretary Cosway proved to be a great support to her, as her letters of 9 January 1811 and 10 May 1812 bear witness.[13] In those same letters she wrote that she had been presented at the Drawing Room at Court and that she had sent out about 400 invitations for a party to be held at York Place. There is mention too of taking a box at Covent Garden and of dining at Lady de Crespigny's where she had: 'met Lord and Lady Nelson...Lord Nelson', she wrote, 'is a most vulgar and disagreeable man...The widow Viscountess Nelson has been in town, and we saw a great deal of her. She is a most pleasing woman...'.

Later letters speak of further visits to Covent Garden and Drury Lane and of what was clearly an intense social round. But from a letter written in Tynemouth to her friend Miss Woodman on 29 August 1819, it is clear that all was not well for she wrote that she had, 'great deficiency in walking', and that one of her legs was, 'swollen so much that it makes me quite feeble and weak'

Less than three weeks later she suffered a stroke and died unexpectedly aged fifty-seven on 16 or 17 September, although an addition to the inscription on the cenotaph added by her daughters, records that it was the 17th.[14]

By then Collingwood's elder daughter Sarah had married a barrister, George Lewis Newnham. The marriage had taken place at St George's, Hanover Square on 30 May 1816, after which they lived at Hawkhurst in Kent until his death on 8 July 1837, when aged fifty-five. Lady Collingwood had reported him to be:

> ...an, ...amiable pleasing young man...lately...appointed one of the Commissioners at Paris for settling the English claims on the funds there...My dear Sarah might have married more advantageously in point of fortune...but his father has acted most liberally towards him on the occasion... .[15]

At another time she wrote of him as:

> ...very good looking with very fine teeth and a fine open good humoured countenance...rather tall but his manners are still superior to his looks... .

Although he had never known Collingwood, Newnham was so captivated by accounts of the great man's life that he assumed the surname Collingwood himself, and painstakingly compiled the valuable, if in many places, doctored and favourably selective, *Memoir and Correspondence of Collingwood* which contained and so preserved for posterity extracts from much of Collingwood's private correspondence. This he dedicated to the Duke of Clarence, clearly in the forlorn hope that Collingwood's many requests that his title be allowed to pass through his elder daughter, would be reconsidered.

A son was born, but died in infancy. But then a daughter, Sarah Newnham Collingwood, was born in Paris on 4 October 1817, and, if Lady Collingwood be correct, Newnham's father died in the month following, a very rich man. A second daughter, Mary, was born in 1821 but died unmarried in or about the year 1840.

When Collingwood's daughter Sarah died at the comparatively early age of sixty in November 1851, she was a lady of marked eccentricity.

By then she had given away the Trafalgar kettle which had been presented to her mother, to her maid's husband, and it ended up in Alderman Hart's pawnbroker's shop in Canterbury. Fortunately it surfaced again many years later and ended up in the Laing Art Gallery.

True to the end Mrs Moutray, who had died in 1841, was faithful to her friend Collingwood and long after his death had written Sarah a letter extolling his fine qualities.

Sarah Newnham Collingwood married in 1841 Cuthbert Collingwood Hall of Paddington Green, and then, after his death in 1859, John Richard Howell of Cardigan in 1861, but then died without issue on 27 November 1872. Her Hethpool bequest was sold on by Howell in 1879.

As for Collingwood's younger daughter, Mary, Collingwood's secretary Cosway had turned his attention her way while visiting and staying with her mother and, in the course of time, Lady Collingwood was to write to her friend Miss Woodman on 1 July 1813 that: 'The marriage of my dear Mary and Mr Cosway will take place about the middle or end of August.'

But then tragically Cosway met with an accident while driving through Temple Bar in London and remained so disabled for several years that his marriage to Mary never took place. And, soon after that mishap, she became engaged to Anthony Denny instead, son of the Reverend Maynard Denny of Tralee, and a young man of whom, according to Lady Collingwood writing in 1817: 'everybody speaks well...They have really been two fortunate young women and dear Mary has had such a lucky escape.'

After the marriage on 12 June of that year, she was to write that Denny was: 'everything I could wish for in a son-in-law'. A son was born to Mary on 9 September 1818 and named Anthony Cuthbert Collingwood Denny. And then a daughter, Sarah Blackett Denny, arrived in December of 1819. She was, in due time, to marry Sir John Stephen Robinson Bt of Rokeby, County Louth and to produce issue before her death in 1875.

Sadly a second daughter born to Mary in 1822 and named after her was to die in 1839 when only seventeen years of age. Another son was born in 1823, named Arthur Maynard Denny, who later married a cousin who was resident in County Cork where they set up home.

Sadly, Collingwood's daughter Mary, died young in that same year. But her descendants continue in direct descent. Her share of the interest in Hethpool was also sold in 1879 by her grandson Cuthbert Collingwood Denny.

At Collingwood's death his brother John succeeded to the Chirton estates under the terms of the reversion which had been set up by Edward Collingwood, and there he lived on until his death in 1841.[16] But by then the area had been overtaken by industrial development, so much so that John Collingwood had started to build as his new home, Dissington Hall in Northumberland, there replacing a house which had been inherited by Winifred Collingwood, a third cousin of Collingwood. That property he then left to Edmund Spencer Stanhope, Walter Spencer-Stanhope's youngest son who later took the name Collingwood as a condition of the inheritance, with provision enough to ensure that the work of construction would in due time be completed.

When sixty-two years of age, John Collingwood married Sarah Fenwicke of Earsdon and a son, Edward John Collingwood, Collingwood's nephew, was born in the year of Waterloo – 1815. So the Collingwood name lived on through Collingwood's brother. For the same reason he quit Chirton and then purchased the large and imposing Lilburn Tower in north Northumberland, then in the course of erection under the watchful eye of the celebrated architect John Dobson, on the site of an older house which had been demolished. Although the purchase of the site in 1841 was from yet another Collingwood, there is no traceable connection between those two families.[17]

Mary Winifred Pulleine, daughter of Thomas Babington Pulleine and his wife Winifred Collingwood and, therefore, a niece of Edward

Collingwood, had married Walter Spencer-Stanhope of Cannon Hall in Yorkshire, father of the Edmund Spencer Stanhope who inherited Dissington. Walter was the Spencer Stanhope who had stood at Collingwood's funeral as second mourner to Collingwood's brother John. Indeed, one of Walter's sons, William, who afterwards took the name Roddam when inheriting the estate of Admiral Roddam as a condition of his inheritance, was the Stanhope who had served with Collingwood in the ship *Ocean*.

A member of the House of Commons for forty years or more, twice for the city of Carlisle, Walter had become known for the great hospitality he dispensed from his house in Grosvenor Square and, as one of the group of members of the Dilettanti Club, was captured in the notable picture painted by Sir Joshua Reynolds.[18]

John Collingwood's descendants lived on at Lilburn Tower for more than 100 years. During the extensive post Second World War expansion of its campus, Durham University named one of its new colleges Collingwood College, often supposed to have been in memory of Cuthbert Collingwood. But in fact it was named after Sir Edward Collingwood the distinguished mathematician and medical administrator of Lilburn Tower, one of four brothers who were the descendants of Collingwood's younger brother, and himself a graduate of Dartmouth, a Cambridge don and an acting captain in the RNVR during the Second World War. An able man, short in stature, he was one of the few to spot the talent of Frances Crick early on, and so employed him on several technical projects and allied missions in the later stages of the war, long before Crick discovered the secret of the genetic code, to become, in the judgement of the distinguished science writer and fellow Northumbrian, Dr Matt Ridley, one of the greatest scientists of all time.[19] Like his youngest brother, Lieutenant General Sir George Collingwood, Sir Edward died a bachelor without issue after which Lilburn Tower was sold on by another of his brothers, Group Captain Cuthbert Collingwood.

And so two branches of Collingwood's family survived, one direct through his younger daughter Mary and living in Ireland which did not carry his surname, and one indirect through his brother and living at Lilburn Tower in Northumberland, which did. But alas, although John had produced a son and two daughters, and his son fathered three sons, only the youngest of them left issue, and of his four sons two died unmarried and the others died without leaving male issue. And so, as with the title more than 170 years before, when the last of the four brothers died, so too did the surname, although the brother's family lives on through the married daughter of one of the married brothers, and through the four daughters of the other married brother.

As for Cosway, wounded at Trafalgar and the son of a baker in Devonport who had risen by merit alone and who had been held in such high regard by Collingwood as his first lieutenant and secretary, it was reported that he was to marry Miss Dennet in 1821. And a friend of Lady Collingwood's was to write of Miss Dennet that she: 'has a fortune of three thousand per annum...but I understand the Dennets cannot boast of rank.'

But again, for reasons not disclosed, that marriage never took place, but he did later marry the daughter of one Halliday, a banker. And when he died in 1834 in an accident involving the Brighton coach, it was as Sir William Richard Cosway.[20] A monument at Bilsington near Hythe stands in his memory.

At a much later date his old school, by then the Royal Grammar School, named one of its school houses after Collingwood and a full-length copy by Harry Fogan, an old boy, of the Mansion House portrait of him,[21] was hung in the school Chapel Hall alongside those of his schoolfellows, Lord Eldon, the Lord Chancellor, and Lord Stowell, the Admiralty Judge, although similar portraits had been hung long before in the Exchange Building on Sandhill in Newcastle.[22] This was no more than appropriate for, as the Duke of Clarence had written, he had at that school received an excellent education.

In due time the street along which he had trudged when making his way past the cathedral from home to school as a boy, was given Collingwood's name, while the place of his birth was marked by a bust placed in a niche on the wall of Milburn House, a building erected 100 years after his death on the site of the Collingwood home. To this has now been added a plaque. And in the year 1905 an inscription was mounted on the wall of the house where he lived in Morpeth, now a Roman Catholic presbytery.[23]

Still five years further on, in March 1910, a ceremony was staged at the cathedral by the Lord Mayor and City Council of Newcastle upon Tyne to commemorate the death of Collingwood 100 years before, attended by local dignitaries, the band and sailors of the Tyne Training Ship HMS *Calliope* and the headmaster, masters and boys of his old school.[24]

The following year a Collingwood prize was established in perpetuity by A. B. Collingwood, to be awarded each year to that boy about to leave that same school who, in the opinion of the masters there and of the boys themselves, had exhibited the most honourable and upright character in the school[25] and had given the most worthwhile all-round service to the community. And each year too Collingwood has been remembered by his school which lays flowers below his portrait on the anniversary of his death and then follows this ceremony with a visit to the cathedral where its headmaster and head boy, escorted by the naval section of its Officer Training Corps, more recently renamed the Combined Cadet Force, lay a wreath in his memory.

A training ship in Portsmouth still carries the name of *Collingwood* and a mural painted in oil on wood by Ralph Gillies Cole and measuring 8 feet by 4 feet, depicting the different stages of his life, hangs on the walls of the base for naval electricians at Fareham in Hampshire which bears Collingwood's name. It portrays his parents, his old headmaster Moises, his uncle Admiral Braithwaite, his gunnery expertise, the battles in which he took part, Collingwood scattering acorns, Howe, St Vincent, Nelson and St Paul's Cathedral where he lies.

But perhaps most appropriate of all the name 'Excellent' was given to a Royal Naval School of Gunnery in Portsmouth, now a naval shore training establishment, in recognition of the skills displayed by Collingwood's ship at the Battle of St Vincent.

There is also a library and museum which are named after Collingwood, albeit they are dedicated to an appreciation of the American heritage rather than to the exploits of Cuthbert Collingwood. They lie on the banks of the Potomac River in what was once George Washington's River Farm which had been built for Sam Johnson and his family, the deputy overseer of Washington's farm. One of Johnson's duties had been to operate the ferry which plied across the Potomac at that point and in so doing he met up with many a ship's captain who had broken off his journey up river near a ferry dock, to draw fresh water for his barrels from a spring which rose near the banks of the river, all for a fee payable to Johnson on behalf of Washington.

There is no record to evidence that Collingwood had so stopped when serving on the American station during the War of Independence, but the foundation which acquired the property in 1927 do report that he was on terms of friendship with one Tobias Lear who inherited a life tenancy of the farm under the will of George Washington.

And near Port Mahon there is a house which has been named after the Admiral in the belief that he stayed there when standing off Menorca. Although never mentioned by Collingwood in any document or letter, there is apparently strong local rumour handed down over the generations to that effect.

Each year the Admiral is remembered in a pageant held in the grounds of Tynemouth Priory.

So the memory of Collingwood lives on.

But it was not until thirty-five years had gone by after his death at Port

Mahon that a statue was raised to Collingwood after much feuding. Unveiled on 30 August 1845,[26] it was the work of the Northumbrian sculptor John Gordon Lough then living in London and shipped up in thirteen pieces by the ship *Halcyon*. It had been funded by public subscription raised by the citizens of his native city. Even then it was of no more than modest proportions, standing twenty-three feet high and mounted on a stone pedestal or plinth some forty-five feet in height, banished to a location ten miles east of the city at the mouth of the River Tyne, built on a site which had been donated by the Duke of Northumberland. At least on this particular memorial the year of his birth is correctly stated as 1748. Three years later, in 1848, four 35-pounder guns, salvaged from his old Trafalgar ship, the *Royal Sovereign*, were shipped up from Woolwich and placed around the plinth of the monument under the direction of John Dobson, the architect of the monument itself, as he had been of Sir John Orde's father's Nunnykirk, Edward John Collingwood's Lilburn Tower, the author's more modest Chollerton, and many other Georgian country houses.

A Grade II listed building, restoration work was carried out on the monument in 2001 at a cost of £170,000 and there he stands to this day, all alone and wistfully looking out to sea, still on guard for England, watching out for the enemy.

In contrast, the statue of another great Northumbrian, Earl Grey of the Reform Bill, was mounted in 1838 soon after his death, and in the very heart of the city on a column almost as tall as that which supports Collingwood's friend, Horatio, Lord Nelson, in Trafalgar Square, which had been erected in 1843. Yet this good and modest man had given his entire life to the defence of his country and his contribution to eventual victory over Napoleon Bonaparte, five years after his death, had been immense. And so, although so often in the shadow of Nelson, he was perhaps the noblest sailor of them all. And it is this which stands as his true and everlasting monument.

Notes

Chapter 1
1. Letter from Collingwood to J.E. Blackett, 2 November 1805.
2. Letter to Walter Spencer-Stanhope dated 6 March 1806 in British Museum Add. MSS 52780 reproduced in full in *Naval Miscellany VI* at pp.189-92 together with a footnote in which the editor suggests that Collingwood and Nelson may have met in November of that year, 1793, when both were at Portsmouth, Collingwood in the *Lenox* and Nelson in the *Seahorse*.

Chapter 2
1. *Naval Miscellany Vol. VI* p.188 letter dated 20 January 1806.
2. *Naval Miscellany Vol. VI* p.197 letter dated 1 July 1807.
3. *Naval Miscellany Vol. VI* p. 202 letter dated 16 May 1808.
4. *The Youth's Instructor and Guardian, Vol. xii*i, No. 145, Jan. 1829; *Mariner's Mirror Vol. 53* (1967), G.W.R. Nicholl at p.98.
5. *The Youth's Instructor and Guardian, Vol. xiii,* No. 145, Jan. 1829; *Mariner's Mirror Vol. 53* (1967), G.W.R. Nicholl at p.98.
6. Ralfe's *Naval Biography of Great Britain* (1824) Vol. II at p. 350; also *Naval Chronicle Obituary Vol. xxiii* p.351 cited at pp. 98 and 102 of *Mariner's Mirror Vol. 41*(1955)
7. p. 161 of *The Life and Literary Remains of Charles Reece Pemberton,* who served under Collingwood. Cited by Clark Russell at p. 128.
8. *Naval Miscellany Vol. VI* p.216 letter dated 18 December 1909.
9. *Mariner's Mirror Vol. 35* (1949) at p.424 in an article by Rear-Admiral A.H. Taylor.
10. *Mariner's Mirror Vol. 53* (1967), G.W.R. Nicholl at p.98.
11. *Letters of .Sir T. Byam Martin Vol. I* pp 72-3; *Naval Chronicle Vol. XV* 1806 at p.371.

Chapter 3
1. *Naval Chronicle Vol. xxiii* for 1810 pp.379-82; *Consolidated Edition Vol. IV* 328-330.
2. *Naval Chronicle Vol. xxiii* for 1810 p.380; Consolidated Edition Vol. IV p.329.

3. *Naval Chronicle Vol. xxiii* for 1810 p.380.
4. *Ralfe's Naval Biography of Great Britain (1824) Vol. II* p.339.

Chapter 4
1. *Naval Chronicle Vol. xv* for 1806 at p.360, citing John Charnock's *Biographia Navalis 1794-8; Nelson's Letters* ed. by Rawson p.42.
2. *Letters of Sir T. Byam Martin Vol. 1* p.72.
3. *Mariner's Mirror Vol. 75* for 1989, Brian S. Kirby at p.137-9.
4. National Archives CO 152/64.
5. *Dictionary of National Biography* (1917 ed.) Vol. 10, pp.186-7, and Vol. 13 p. 1113, both by J. Knox Laughton citing Charnock's *Biographia Navalis 1794-8* and Nicolas's *Letters of Lord Nelson.*
6. *A Fine Old English Gentleman* by William Davies (1875) pp16-17.
7. J de Raigersfeld.(1830) pp. xi-xvii.
8. *Mariner's Mirror Vol. 68* (1982) Victoria Howard-Vyse p.45.
9. *Letters of Nelson* ed. by Nicolas (1844-46) Vol. I pp. 109, 110,113.
10. *The Later Correspondence of George III Vol. 1* para. 341 at pp 266-8. Orde pp. 76-7.
11. *Nelson's Letters to his Wife* ed. by Naish, letter 17 p.38.

Chapter 5
1. Gooch pp 65 and 124.
2. Hepple pp 85-8 and Gooch 103.
3. Davies p.7.
4. Welford Vol.1 p. 608; J.C. Hodgson in *Archeologia Ael. 3rd Series Vol. 2* at p.150 et seq.
5. Welford Vol. 1 p.608; also J. Clayton in *Archeolog. Ael. 2nd Series Vol. 13* p. 174.
6. *Autobiography of Dr. Alexander Carlyle* (1860) p.437.
7. J.Clayton in *Archeolog.Ael. 2nd. Series Vol. 13* for 1889, p.175.
8. *Letters of Nelson* ed. by Nicolas Vol. 1 pp. 230-1.
9. The Family Tree of Lord and Lady Collingwood set out in *Archeolog. Ael. 4th Series, Vol. 32,* drawn from an earlier article in the same publication and from the *Northumberland County Histories Volumes XI and XIV,* indicates that her maternal grandfather was also a Robert Roddam, but he died in the year 1744. Admiral Robert Roddam (1720-1808) was not, therefore, Sarah Blackett's father, and so not Lady Collingwood's maternal grandfather, as Clark Russell at p.21 and as Oliver Warner at p.30, assert. But, although Robert Roddam was not the postmaster at Berwick (*Naval Miscellany VI* p.161), he was the son of the postmaster at Berwick, which is a town which lies close to the hamlet of Roddam, and most local historians accept that he and the Admiral were related, albeit distantly, although Collingwood always referred to him as 'friend' rather than 'uncle' or 'cousin' (by marriage) in his correspondence. He thus described him as 'a kind friend' when writing of his death in a letter dated 20 August 1808 (*Naval Miscellany VI*).

10. Welford Vol. I, p. 317.
11. *Arch. A. ,Series IV, Vol. 32*, Dodds and Hall, at p.31.
12. Welford Vol. 1, p.317.
13. *Dr. Carlyle Autobiography,* p.435.
14. *A History of Northumberland*, 1935, ed., by Hope-Dodds, Vol. XIV, p. 289; Welford Vol. III at p.326.
15. Welford Vol. I, pp.618-19; *Dr. Carlyle Autobiography* p.437.
16. In a note sent by Cowan to Clark Russell .See also the *Memoirs of Moises* by Revd. John Brewster (1823), cited at pp. 32-5 of Vol. 1 of *The Life of Lord Eldon* by Twiss.
17. *Dictionary of National Biography* (1917 ed.) Vol. 1 pp. 208-9; Welford Vol. I, p. 26-31.
18. *Life of Lord Eldon* by Twiss Vol. II p.118.
19. *Tyneside Celebrities* by Lawson (1873) pp. 30-8.
20. Hill p.15 citing Henry J. Bourguignon's *Sir William Scott*, Lord Stowell (Cambridge Univ. Press 1987).

Chapter 6
1. Hughes letter 3 at p.7.
2. *Fighting Sail* by Warner p.121.
3. Letter from Orde in the Spencer Papers p.208 complaining of lack of signalling code. Howe's code of 1794 was for use in the Home Fleets only, and a general signal book did not appear until 1799.
4. Boyd p. 15; Warner, *The Glorious First of June* p. 93.
5. Extract provided by Sir Patrick Nairne from a book about the Nairne family published privately; Pope pp. 369-70 and p.380.
6. Nairne p.18.
7. Letter dated 21 June in *Naval Chronicle* for 1806 at p. 362; Warner, *The Glorious First of June* pp 97-8.
8. And see *Mariner's Mirror Vol. 55* for 1969 at pp. 415-16.
9. *Mariner's Mirror Vol. 37* for 1951, Commander W.B. Rowbotham RN at pp. 258-68.
10. *Mariner's Mirror Vol. 37* for 1951, Commander W.B. Rowbotham RN at p 261.

Chapter 7
1. Letter to *Daily Telegraph* from Revd. Alan Cliff, grandson of the Chairman, dated 10 July 1999.
2. Ronald Shadbolt to *Daily Telegraph*, 18 November 2001.
3. *Westminster Abbey* by Smith, p. 350; *Westminster Abbey* by Stanley p.325.
4. M.A.J. Palmer in *Mariner's Mirror Vol. 77* No. 1 for February 1991 at p.32.
5. Moorhouse *New Letters* p.630.
6. Vincent p.198.
7. Moorhouse *New Letters* p.630.
8. Tucker's *Memoirs of St. Vincent* p. 262n.

9. M.A.J. Palmer in *Mariner's Mirror Vol. 77* for February 1991 at p.38.
10. Ralfe Vol. I at p.309.
11. Orde p. 34; Marriott p.22.
12. Orde p. 34; Bradford p.142.
13. Vincent p. 191; Bradford p. 143; Orde p.34.
14. Ralfe Vol. II p.340.

Chapter 8
1. *Mariner's Mirror Vol. 45* for 1959, J.D. Spinney at p.207.
2. Brenton (1838) Vol. 1 pp. 425-6; Orde pp. 126-7.
3. Ralfe Vol.II p.55; *Dictionary of National Biography* (1917 ed.) Vol. 15 pp. 287-8; Orde p.101.
4. Bell's Pedigrees; also entry by the author at pp. 920-21 of Vol. 41 of the *Oxford Dictionary of National Biography* (2004).
5. *Naval Chronicle Vol. xi* for 1810 p.185; Ralfe Vol. II pp. 59-60; Orde pp. 60-62.
6. Arbuthnot's *Despatch of 14 May 1780* cited at pp. 139-42 of Vol. 1 of the Keith Papers.
7. *American Naval History* by Sweetman p.12.
8. The Priest de Rochefort, 1658.
9. *The Orde Papers; Naval Chronicle Vol. xi* pp. 188-9; *The Times* 4 July, 2 September, 13 October, 14 October and 21 October 1789; Orde pp. 73-81.
10. *Letters of Nelson* ed. By Nicolas Vol. 1 at pp. 109, 110 and 113; Mahan Vol. 1 p.81.
11. *Later Letters of George III* letter. 341 at pp. 266-7; *Nelson's letters to his Wife* ed. by Naish p. 38; Nicolas Vol. I p. 203.
12. *Lloyd's Nelson Collection* p. 91; *Letters from the Lower Deck* (Navy Records Society) p.353.
13. The Orde Papers; *Lloyd's Nelson Collection* p.91.
14. Berckman pp. 160-161..
15. Dillon's *Narrative* p.194.
16. *The Orde Papers.*
17. *The Spencer Papers Vol. II* pp. 208-9.
18. *The Orde Papers.*
19. *The Orde Papers; Later Letters of George III Vol. III* paras 1584 and 1591; Ralfe p.64.
20. *Lloyd's Nelson Collection* p.70.
21. *Lloyd's Nelson Collection* p.91.
22. *Naval Miscellany Vol. 1* p.271.
23. *Nelson's Letters to his Wife* ed. By Naish p. 395; *Letters of Nelson* ed. by Nicolas Vol. III p.12.
24. *Letters of Nelson* ed. by Nicolas Vol. III p.24 citing Spencer's letter.
25. *Churchill's Life Vol. 1914-1916* by Gilbert pp. 14-16.
26. Clarke & MacArthur; Holme p.126.
27. Nicolas, *Letters of Nelson Vol. III* p.84
28. Nicolas, *Letters of Nelson Vol. III* p.25.

29. *The Orde Papers.*
30. Pettigrew Vol. II p.112.
31. *The Spencer Papers Vol. III p.27.*
32. Ralfe Vol. II p.56.
33. *Lloyds' Nelson Collection p.73.*
34. *The Orde Papers.*
35. *The Orde Papers; The Spencer Papers Vol. III pp. 450-52;* Brenton Vol. I pp.397-8.
36. Brenton Vol. 1 pp. 402-3; *The Orde Papers.*
37. *The Orde Papers; Lloyds' Nelson Collection p.94.*
38. The letter in full is set out in Tucker at pp. 353-4.
39. *Lloyd's Nelson Collection p.112.*
40. *The Naval Chronicle Vol. ii,* p. 440.
41. *Later Letters of George III Vol. III* pp. 275 and 280; *Spencer Papers* Vol. III pp. 25-6.
42. *Letters of Nelson to his Wife* ed. by Naish pp. 534.
43. The most thorough analysis of St. Vincent's decision is to be found in Orde's 'Mediterranean Command', wrote Hayward at p. 212 of his very thoughtful new study of Nelson.

Chapter 9
1. *The Daily Telegraph* 8 October 1999, Paul Stokes; *Glorious Victory* (Dundee Council 1997).
2. Keith Papers Vol. II pp. 395-7; Hill p.16.
3. *Naval Chronicle Vol. x* p. 432 (Consolidated Ed. Vol. II p.351).
4. Orde pp. 149 and 151.
5. Ogden p. 23
6. *Burke's Peerage 106th ed.* p. 972.
7. Guinness p. 213.
8. Private letter in the possession of Tom Bowles.
9. Note to Hughes letter 194 at p. 306.
10. Letter dated 28 January 1801 at p. ccxxviii in the Addenda to Vol. VII of the *Letters of Nelson* ed. by Nicolas.
11. *Medicana Nautica (1804)* reproduced at p. 288 of *The Health of Seamen* ed. by C. Lloyd (Navy Records Society 1965)
12. Otto Erich Deutsch p. 61.
13. *Archeolog. Ael. Vol. 32* at p. 59.
14. *Letters of Nelson* by Nicolas, Addenda to Vol. VII at p. ccxxix.
15. Ralfe Vol. II p.341.
16. Nicolas *Letters of Nelson Vol. VI* p. 250.
17. *Later letters of George III, Vol. III* Para. 2959; *Blockade of Brest Vol. II* p. 114; Orde pp. 152-4.
18. Nicolas *Letters of Nelson Vol. VI* p. 285.
19. Nicolas Vol. VI p. 288.
20. Nicolas Vol. VI p. 289.
21. Nicolas Vol. VI pp. 319 and 320.
22. Nicolas Vol. VI p. 359.

23. Nicolas Vol. VI p. 383.
24. Nicolas Vol. VI p. 391-2.
25. Nicolas Vol. VI p. 429.

Chapter 10
1. Letters of Sir T. Byam Martin Vol. I pp. 306-7.
2. *Mariner's Mirror* report of lecture by D. Howarth 5 December 1970, Vol. 57 for 1971 pp. 361-70;
3. *Blockade of Brest Vol. II* p. 225; Orde pp. 164-5.
4. *Letters of Nelson* ed. by Nicolas Vol. VI p. 258.
5. *The Barham Papers Vol. III* p. 301-4; *Letters of Nelson* ed. by Nicolas Vol. VI p.383-4n.
6. Ralfe Vol. II pp. 75-7.
7. Sir Julian Corbett pp. 63-4, who adds at pp. 66-7, 'With a decision founded on so well reasoned an appreciation there seems little fault to find', and, at p. 84, 'his action was approved by Barham'.
8. Corbett p. 84.
9. Mahan Vol. II p. 290.
10. *Blockade of Brest Vol. II* letters 475 and 476 at p. 225; Orde pp. 164-76.
11. *Blockade of Brest Vol. II* letters 489 and 490 at p. 240. Orde pp. 164-76.
12. *The Barham Papers Vol. III* p. 304.
13. See *Nelson's Mediterranean Command* by the author pp. 166-75 for a more detailed analysis of this episode.
14. Moorhouse *New Letters* p. 635.
15. Captain Mahan p. 293; Bradford at p. 318 citing p. 171 of *The Life of Revd. A.J. Scott*. The Blue Peter was the signal flag for a vessel about to sail.
16. Clarke and MacArthur Vol. II p. 406; *The Durable Monument* by James p. 264.
17. Schom p. 226.
18. p. 22 of *The Naval Campaign of 1805* by Edourd Desbriere citing the reports of Decres.
19. *Naval Chronicle Consolidated ed. Vol. III* p. 173.
20. *Archeolog. Ael. 4th Series Vol. 43* p. 307-9; Trafalgar Roll; Welford Vol. III 328-36; Orde p 199.
21. Schom p. 151
22. *The Times* 22 September 1997 based on a letter and a receipt discovered.
23. Ehrman Vol. III p. 790.
24. *Letters of Nelson* by Nicolas Vol. VII p. 95.
25. British Museum Add. MSS. 33963f.104.
26. *The Price of Admiralty* by Keegan p. 66.
27. *Archeolog. Ael. 4th Series Vol. 43* for 1965 at p. 307, citing Southey.

Chapter 11

1. Mordal pp. 196-7.
2. *Naval Chronicle Vol. xv* p. 190; *Consolidated Edition Vol. III* p.207.
3. *Newcastle Chronicle* 4 November 1876, cited by Clark Russell at p. 142, although the list of officers named in the Trafalgar Roll does not suggest that most came from the north-east of England.
4. *Archeolog. Ael. 4th Series Vol. 43* for 1965 p. 312, citing Edward Fraser's *The Bellerophon* 1909.
5. *Naval Chronicle Vol. xv* for 1806 p. 371; *Naval Miscellany VI* p. 182.
6. *Letters of Sir Byam Martin Vol. I* pp. 72-3; *Naval Chronicle Vol. xv* for 1806 at p. 371(*Consolidated ed. Vol. III* p. 210).
7. Welford Vol. III p. 331. Numbers in the *Naval Chronicle Vol. xv* for 1806 at p. 371, and the Trafalgar Roll, differ.
8. According to Victory's logbook cited in *Naval Chronicle Vol. xv* for 1806 p. 371.
9. British Museum Add.MSS.52780; *Naval Miscellany VI* pp.189-192.
10. *Trafalgar* by Oliver Warner p. 99.
11. *Trafalgar* by Oliver Warner p.178.
12. *Letters of Nelson* by Nicolas Vol. VII, pp. 225-6.
13. *Naval Chronicle Vol. xiv* pp. 420-40; *Consolidated Edition Vol. III* pp. 212-15.
14. Hibbert p. 381 citing the account of James Harrison, which he considers improbable.
15. *Naval Chronicle Vol. xv* for 1806 at pp. 379-80; *Life of Lord Eldon* by Twiss Vol. II pp. 118-19.
16. Hibbert p. 379.
17. Harris p. 157.
18. Letter to the *Daily Telegraph* from David Mann dated 21 November 1999.
19. Letter to the *Daily Telegraph* from F.L. Galliano, Vice-Chairman of the Gibraltar Heritage Trust in Gibraltar dated November 1999.
20. *Archeolog. Ael. 4th Series Vol. 32* p, 60; Oliver Warner p. 154, citing *The Letter Bag of Lady Elizabeth Spencer-Stanhope* by A.M.W. Stirling (1913) Vol. I p. 69.
21. *Naval Chronicle Vol. xv* for 1806 at p. 372.
22. *Archeolog. Ael. 4th Series Vol. 32* p. 35 Dodds and Hall letters.
23. *Letters of Nelson* by Nicolas Vol. VII pp. 233-4; pp. 183-6 of the *Naval Miscellany Vol. VI*.
24. *Naval Chronicle Vol. xv* for 1806 p. 373.
25. *Naval Chronicle Vol. xv* for 1806 pp. 375-.6; Collingwood wrote of this in his letter to Sir Peter Parker noted at 23 above, and in a letter to his father-in-law, included in Newnham Collingwood p. 137.
26. Without land to go with his title, Collingwood, who enjoyed a pun, was to write to Mary Moutray that 'all the world knew I was no Land-Lord'!-*Naval Miscellany VI* p. 187.
27. *Naval Chronicle Vol. xv* for 1806 p. 380.
28. Lecture by David Howarth reported in *Mariner's Mirror 1971 Vol.*

LVII pp. 369-70; Orde p. 198.

29. Trafalgar Roll p. 30.
30. In his letters at the National Maritime Museum LBK/58, cited at p. 337 of Cordingly. They contain a very comprehensive survey of his ship's company compiled by Rotherham himself which has proved useful to the naval historian. See too the note at p. 181 of Naval Miscellany VI.
31. *Archeolog. Ael. 4th Series Vol. 43* for 1965 at pp. 306-7.
32. *Naval Chronicle Vol. xv* for 1806 p. 143 citing the London Gazette for 18 January 1806.
33. Coleman p. 332 citing the National Archives/Admiralty 1/158, the *Morning Chronicle* for 7 November 1805 and for 11 January 1806 and the *Morning Herald* for 9 January 1806.
34. Thorne p. 696; Orde pp. 208-10.
35. Namier p.232-4; Ashbourne p. 78; Orde pp. 204-5.
36. *Austen Letters 3rd ed.* p. 25.
37. *Austen Letters 3rd ed.* pp. 29, 35 ,187 (letter of 29 May 1811), 207 and 559 and Index.
38. Welford Vol. III pp. 243-4.
39. Welford Vol. III p. 243. Young p.72 and notes to his book in Bognor Regis Library.
40. Ralfe Vol. II p. 81.
41. *Mariner's Mirror 1926 Vol. 12* at p. 341 citing *Naval Chronicle* 1807 Vol. xviii.

Chapter 12

1. *Archeolog. Ael. 4th Series Vol. 32* Dodds and Hall letters p. 60.
2. Markham Correspondence p. 71.
3. *Archeolog. Ael. 4th Series Vol. 32* p. 61, Dodds and Hall.
4. *Archeolog. Ael. 4th Series Vol. 32* p. 61; the letter quoted was addressed to Spencer-Stanhope dated 21 April 1806, pp. 193-4 of the *Naval Miscellany Vol. VI*.
5. *Archeolog. Ael. 4th Series Vol. 32* p. 61n.
6. Markham Correspondence p. 96. Sebastiani was to end his career thirty-five years later as Ambassador to London and a Marshal of France.
7. *Mariner's Mirror* 1948 Vol. 34 p. 177.
8. Ralfe p. 346.
9. *Mariner's Mirror* 1955 Vol. 41,Piers Mackesy p. 138.
10. Collingwood wrote again that 'the sea is a desert' in a letter to Spencer-Stanhope dated 16 May 1808 – *Naval Miscellany VI* pp. 202-3.
11. Collingwood was to write to Spencer-Stanhope on 20 August 1808 that 'We have ever since gone on with the greatest harmony and I am sure I ought to be much flattered with the reception I have met with. The first day I went on shore the multitude of people was immense

that came to receive me, and I received from high and low every mark of respect and of hospitality that could be devised...'*Naval Miscellany VI* pp. 206-9.

12. *The Creevey Papers* (The Sir H. Maxwell ed., London 1904) letter dated 11 August 1828 at II, p.161.

13. *The Creevey Papers* (The John Gore ed., B.T. Batsford Ltd, 1902 and revised 1963) at pp. 1 and 3.

Chapter 13

1. *Archeolog. Ael. 4th Series Vol. 32* p. 39. Dodds and Hall letters.
2. Barrow, Chapter VI p. 244.
3. *Naval Chronicle Vol. xxiii* for 1810 p. 448; *Naval Chronicle Consolidated Edition Vol. IV* p. 330.
4. *Naval Chronicle Vol. xxiii* for 1810 p. 383.
5. *Life of Lord Eldon* by Twiss Vol. II pp. 118-9.
6. *The Journal* newspaper for 9 May 2000.
7. The inscription itself so records.
8. *Table Book Vol. III* Chapter V p. 97.
9. *Mariner's Mirror Vol. 51* for 1965, p. 17. The presentation of the Lonsdale portrait was reported in the *Tyne Mercury* for 11 August 1812.
10. Price p. 132.
11. Note to Hughes letter 194.
12. Welford Vol. 1 p. 319.
13. *Archeolog. Ael. 4th Series Vol. 32* pp. 41, 42, 49, 56, 57; Dodds and Hall letters.
14. *Archeolog. Ael. 4th Series Vol. 32* p. 64, Dodds and Hall letters.
15. *Archeolog. Ael. 4th Series Vol. 32* p. 48, Dodds and Hall letters.
16. *Archeolog. Ael. 3rd Series Vol. 2* pp. 157-8.
17. *History of Northumberland* (1935) ed. by Hope Dodds Vol. XIV at p. 438.
18. Correspondence of Markham p.72.
19. *Francis Crick* by Matt Ridley pp. 15-16.
20. *Gentleman's Magazine* for 1834, New Series II p. 316 cited in *Archeolog. Ael. Vol. 32* pp. 63-4 by Dodds and Hall as the same Cosway, although in official ship letters written on Collingwood's behalf, Cosway signed his name with the initials J.R. Cosway.' See for example *Lloyd's Nelson Collection* p. 210.
21. Mains and Tuck p. 165.
22. *Newcastle Chronicle* 28 November 1885, cited by Clark Russell p. 268.
23. *The Nelson Dispatch Vol. 5* Part 7 for July 1995 at p. 7.
24. The programme for this event can be found at the Newcastle City Library.
25. Mains and Tuck p. 165.
26. *The Nelson Dispatch Vol. 5* Part 7 for July 1995 (Jim Saunders).

Bibliography

Manuscript Collections,Newspapers and Periodicals:

The Public and Private Correspondence of Vice-Admiral Lord Collingwood selected by G.L. Newnham
Collingwood (first published by James Ridgway, London, 1828. The 5th ed published in 1837 in two Vols. Contains 34 additional letters)
The letters of Lord Collingwood, Navy Records Society, 1914
The Private Correspondence of Admiral Lord Collingwood ed. by Edward Hughes, Navy Records Society, 1957
The Barham Papers, Navy Records Society, 1907
The Spencer Papers, (Navy Records Society
The Keith Papers, (Navy Records Society, 1927
The Orde Papers at The National Maritime Museum, Greenwich
The Dillon Narrative, Navy Records Society
Naval Miscellany in 3 vols. Navy Records Society, 1902
Naval Miscellany Vol. VI ed. by Michael Duffy, Chapter IV by Captain C H H Owen, Navy Records Society, 2003
The Blockade of Brest, Navy Records Society
The Letters and Papers of Sir Thomas Byam Martin, Navy Records Society, 1901
The Correspondence of Admiral John Markham, Navy Records Society, 1904
The Creevey Papers, The Sir H. Maxwell ed. London, 1904
The Creevey Papers, The John Gore ed. B T Batsford Ltd, 1902 and revised 1963
National Archives Documents.
British Museum Additional MS.
The Mariner's Mirror
The Naval Chronicle, 40 vols, 1799-1819.
The Naval Chronicle Consolidated Edition prepared by Nicholas Tracy, Chatham Publishing, 1999
Archaeologia Aeliana, Society of Antiquaries of Newcastle upon Tyne
The Times newspaper

The Newcastle Courant newspaper, taken over by the 1832 *Newcastle Journal* in 1876
The Evening Chronicle newspaper
The Gentleman's Magazine.
The Nelson Dispatch

Published Collingwood biographies in date order

A Fine Old English Gentleman by William Davies (Sampson Low, Marston, Low & Searle 1875)
The Life of Admiral Lord Collingwood by W. Clark Russell, Methuen, 1891.
The Life of Admiral Lord Collingwood by Geoffrey Murray, Hutchinson, 1936
Admiral Collingwood and the Problems of the Naval Blockade after Trafalgar by D.F Stephenson, Northumberland Press Ltd, 1948
The Life and Letters of Vice-Admiral Lord Collingwood by Oliver Warner, Oxford University Press, 1968
Lord Howe and the Case of Captain Collingwood by Oliver Warner
New letters from Admiral Collingwood ed. by E. Hallam Moorhouse (Deposited in the Newcastle City Library and published in the *Cornhill Magazine*)
Admiral Collingwood, Nelson's Own Hero by Max Adams [Weidenfeld & Nicolson, 2005]

Published Nelson biographies in date order

The Life of Admiral Lord Nelson ed. by Revd James Stainer Clarke and John MacArthur, Cadell & W. Davis, 1809
The Life of Horatio Lord Nelson by Robert Southey, 1813
The Dispatches and Letters of Vice-Admiral Lord Nelson ed. by Sir Nicholas Harris Nicolas, 7 Vols 1844-1846.
The Memoirs and Life of Vice-Admiral Lord Nelson by Dr Thomas James Pettigrew, T & W Boone, 1849
The Letters and Dispatches of Horatio Viscount Nelson selected and arranged by J.K. Laughton, 1886
The Nelson Memorial :Nelson and his Companions in Arms by Sir John Knox Laughton, George Allen, 1896
Horatio Nelson and the Naval Supremacy of England by W. Clark Russell, G.P Putnam & Sons, 1896)
The Life of Nelson: The Embodiment of the Sea Power of Great Britain by Alfred Thayer Mahan, in 2 Vols., Sampson Low, Marston & Co., 1897
Nelson and His Times by Lord Charles Beresford and H.W. Wilson, Eyre and Spottiswoode, 1897-8)
Nelson and His Captains by W.H Fitchett, Smith Elder, 1902
Horatio Nelson by Richard H. Holme, Sir Walter Scott Publishing, 1905

The Last of Nelson's Captains by Sir Augustus Phillimore, 1906

Trafalgar, la campagne maritime de 1805 by Edouard Desbriere, Paris, 1907

The Campaign of Trafalgar by Sir Julian S. Corbett, Longmans, Green & Co., 1910

The Trafalgar Roll, the Ships and Officials by R.H. Mackenzie, George Allen & Co. Ltd, 1913, republished by Greenhill Books, 1989

Nelson by C.S. Forester, Cassette Productions, 1929

Horatio Nelson by George Edinger and E.J.C. Neep, Jonathan Cape, 1931

Nelson by Clennel Wilkinson, George G. Harrap, 1931

Lloyds Nelson Collection ed. by Warren R. Dawson, MacMillan, 1932

The Sailor's Nelson by Admiral Mark Kerr CB MVO, Hurst & Blackett, 1932

Nelson by Carola Oman, Hodder & Stoughton, 1947

The Durable Monument – Horatio Nelson by Admiral Sir W.M. James, Longmans Green, 1948

Nelson the Sailor by Captain Russell Grenfell, Faber & Faber, 1953

Nelson's Letters to his Wife by G.P.B. Naish, Routledge and Keegan Paul, 1958

Trafalgar by Oliver Warner, Batsford Ltd, 1959

Nelson's letters selected and edited by Geoffrey Rawson, J.M. Dent & Sons Ltd, 1960

Trafalgar, The Nelson Touch by David Howarth, Collins, 1969

Nelson and the Hamiltons by Jack Russell, Anthony Blond, 1969

Nelson by Arthur Bryant, Collins, 1970

Nelson The Commander by Geoffrey Bennett, Batsford Ltd, 1972

The Great Gamble: Nelson at Copenhagen by Dudley Pope, 1972, reprinted by Chatham Publishing, 2001

Nelson by Oliver Warner, Weidenfeld & Nicolson, 1975

Trafalgar by John Terraine, Sidgwick & Jackson; Purnell, 1976

Nelson's War by Peter Padfield, Book Club Associates, 1976

Nelson – The Essential Hero by Ernle Bradford, MacMillan, 1977

Remember Nelson by Tom Pocock, Collins, 1977

Nelson by David Walder, Hamish Hamilton, 1978

The Young Nelson in the Americas by Tom Pocock, Collins, 1980

Horatio Nelson by Thomas Pocock, Bodley Head, 1987

Nelson:The Immortal Memory by David and Stephen Howarth, Dent, 1988

Trafalgar by Alan Schom, Michael Joseph, 1990

Nelson: A Personal History by Christopher Hibbert, Viking, 1994

Nelson, An Illustrated History, Laurence King and the National Maritime Museum, 1995

The Nelson Companion ed. by Colin White, Royal Naval Museum, Alan Sutton Publishing Ltd, Naval Institute Press, 1995

What's Left of Nelson by Leo Marriot, Dial House, 1995

Nelson's Mediterranean Command by Denis Orde, Pentland Press, 1997

1797, Nelson's Year of Destiny by Colin White, Royal Naval Museum Publications, Sutton Publishing, 1998

The Nelson Almanac ed. by David Harris, Warwick Leadlay Gallery, Conway, 1998

Nelson's Women by Tom Pocock, Andre Deutsch, 1999

Admiral Nelson and Joseph Haydn by Otto Erich Deutsch, The Nelson Society, 2000

Nelson: The Man and the Legend by Terry Coleman, Bloomsbury, 2001

Nelson Speaks by Joseph F. Callo, Chatham Publishing, 2001

The Nelson Encyclopaedia by Colin White, Chatham Publishing, 2002

Nelson: Love and Fame by Edgar Vincent, Yale University Press, 2003

For God and Glory by Joel Hayward, Naval Institute Press, 2003

Nelson by Andrew Lambert, Faber & Faber, 2004

Nelson's Purse by Martyn Downer, The Bantam Press, 2004

Nelson – A Dream Of Glory by John Sugden, Jonathan Cape, 2004

Nelson, The New Letters ed. by Colin White, The Boydell Press, 2005

Nelson – The Pursuit of Victory by Roger Knight, Allen Lane, 2005

Published Jervis biographies in date order

Life of Earl St Vincent by Edward Pelham Brenton in 2 Vols., Henry Colburn, 1838

Memoir of Admiral The Rt Hon the Earl of St Vincent by J. Tucker, 1844.

Life of John Jervis, Admiral Lord St. Vincent by Captain W.V. Anson, John Murray, 1913

Life of Lord St Vincent by O.A. Sherrard, Allen and Unwin, 1933

Old Oak: The Life of John Jervis, Earl of St Vincent by Sir W.L. James, 1950

Nelson's Dear Lord by Evelyn Berckman, MacMillan, 1962

Miscellaneous Published in date order

The Naval Biography of Great Britain by James Ralfe, 1828.

Life of a Sea Officer by Jeffrey Baron de Raigersfeld, Printed privately in 1830, and by the Seafarers Library in 1929

A History of Morpeth by Revd John Hodgson, Chamley & Ackenhead, Newcastle, 1832

Royal Naval Biography by Lieutenant John Marshall, Longman 1823-1835

The Local Historian's Table Book, Newcastle upon Tyne, Historical Division, written and published by M.A. Richardson of Newcastle, 1843.

The Public and Private Life of Lord Chancellor Eldon by Horace Twiss in 3 Vols., John Murray, London, 1844

History of North Durham by Revd James Raine, John Bowyer Nichols & Son and George Andrew, 1852

Sea Drift by Rear-Admiral Hercules Robinson, 1858
Autobiography of Dr Alexander Carlyle, New edition 1910 T.N. Foulis, reprinted from earlier edition of 1860
Tyneside Celebrities by William D. Lawson, 1873
Bell's Pedigrees
Historical Memorials of Westminster Abbey by Dean Arthur Penrhyn Stanley DD, John Murray, 1882
A History of The Four Georges by Justin McCarthy in 4 Vols., Chatto & Windus, 1884
The Dictionary of National Biography, Smith, Elder 1887, then Oxford University Press
Men of Mark 'twixt Tyne and Tweed in 3 Vols. by Richard Welford, Walter Scott Ltd, 1895
Pitt: Some Chapters of his Life and Times by Lord Ashbourne, Longman's Green, 1898
The Roll Call of Westminster Abbey by Mrs A. Murray Smith, Smith, Elder, 1903
Sea Law and Sea Power by T. Gibson Bowles MP, 1910
The Letter Bag of Lady Elizabeth Spencer-Stanhope by A.M.W. Stirling, 1913
My Early Life by Winston S. Churchill, MacMillan, 1930
Royal Dukes by Roger Fulford, Collins, 1933
A History of Northumberland, 1935 edition by Madeleine Hope-Dodds
Janes Naval History, Ed. Charnier
The History of Radley College 1847-1947 by A.K. Boyd, Basil Blackwell, 1948
Nelson's Band of Brothers by Ludovic Kennedy, Odhams Press, 1951
Landsman Hay;The Memoirs of Robert Hay 1789-1847 ed. by M.D. Hay, 1953
The War In The Mediterranean 1803-1810 by Piers Mackesy, 1957
25 Centuries of Sea Warfare by Jacques Mordal, Abbey Library, first published in France by Editions Robert Laffont, 1959
Lord Eldon's Anecdote Book, ed. by Anthony L.J. Lincoln and Robert Lindley McEwan, Stevens & Son, London, 1960
The Reign of George III by J. Steven Watson, Oxford At The Clarendon Press, 1960
The Glorious First of June by Oliver Warner, B. T. Batsford Ltd, 1961
The Later Correspondence of George III edited by A. Aspinall in 5 Vols., Cambridge University Press, 1963
The British Admiralty by Leslie Gardiner, William Blackwood & Sons, 1968
Command at Sea by Oliver Warner, Cassell, nd
A Northumbrian Remembers by Nancy Ridley, Robert Hale, 1970
Royal Sailors by A. Cecil Hampshire, William Kimber, 1971
Winston Churchill 1914-1916 by Martin Gilbert, Heinemann, 1971
Heart of Oak by G.J. Marcus, Oxford, 1975

The American War of Independence published for the British Library, 1975

Beware of Heroes by Peter Shankland, William Kimber, 1975

A History of Northumberland and Newcastle upon Tyne by Leslie W. Hepple, Phillimore, 1976

Britannia Rules by C. Northcote Parkinson, Weidenfeld & Nicolson, 1977

Bonaparte by Corelli Barnett, Allen & Unwin, 1978

Fighting Sail by Oliver Warner, Cassell Ltd, 1979

The Life and Times of William IV by Anne Somerset, (Weidenfeld & Nicolson, 1980

Britain's Naval Heritage by Gregory Clarke, HMSO, 1981

The Complete Peerage by GEC in 13 Vols., Sutton Publishing, 1982 edition

A History of Bognor Regis by Gerard Young, Phillimore, 1983

History of the Royal Navy by Antony Preston, Hamlyn Bison, 1983

Navy and Empire by James L. Stokesbury, Robert Hale, 1984

The House of Mitford by Jonathan Guiness, Hutchinson, 1984

The History of Parliament by R.G. Thorne, Secker & Warburg, 1986

History of the Royal Grammar School by Brian Mains and Anthony Tuck, Oriel Press, 1986

The Wooden World by N.A.M. Rodger, Collins, 1986

St Paul's Cathedral by Peter Burman, Bell & Hyman, 1987

The Price of Admiralty by John Keegan, Hutchinson, 1988

The Mutiny of the Bounty by Sir John Barrow, reprinted by Oxford University Press, 1989

The Eyes of the Fleet by Anthony Price, Hutchinson, 1990

Sailor King; the Life of King William IV by Tom Pocock, Sinclair Stevenson, 1991

American Naval History by Jack Sweetman, Naval Institute Press, 1991

The Oxford Companion to Ships and the Sea ed. by Paul, 1993

The American Revolution ed. by Jack P. Greene and J.R. Pole, Blackwell, 1994

Life of The Party by Christopher Ogden, Little, Brown & Co., 1994

The Desperate Faction? The Jacobites of North-East England 1688-1745 by Leo Gooch, University of Hull Press, 1995

The Scandalous Life by Mary Lovell, Richard Cohen Books, 1995

The Younger Pitt by John Ehrman in 3 Vols., Constable 1969-1996

Jane Austen's Letters .3rd ed., Oxford University Press, 1995, 1997

Thirst For Glory by Tom Pocock, Aurum Press, 1996

Glorious Victory, Dundee Council, 1997

The Prizes of War by Richard Hill, Royal Naval Museum Publications, Sutton Publishing, 1998

Burke's Peerage and Baronetage 106th Edition, Genealogical Books Ltd, 1999

Cochrane by Donald Thomas, Deutsch 1978, Cassell 1999

Billy Ruffian by David Cordingly, Bloomsbury, 2003

The Bounty by Caroline Alexander, Harper Collins, 2003
Cassells Biographical Dictionary of the American War of Independence
The History of Parliament by Namier and Brooke, HMSO
The Command of the Ocean by N.A.M. Rodger, Allen Lane, 2004
The Ship That came Home by A.W. Purdue, Third Millennium
   Publishers, 2004
British Admirals of the Napoleonic Wars ed. by Peter Le Fevre and
   Richard Harding, Chatham Publishing, 2005
Francis Crick by Matt Ridley, Harper Press, 2006

Index

Elliott, Sir Gilbert, 1st Earl of Minto, 97, 118, 148
Elliot, Admiral the Hon. Sir George, 11
Elliott, Hugh, 163
Ellis, Sir Henry, 59
Elphinstone, Admiral Sir George Keith, Viscount Keith, 138, 161, 174
El Thetis, 138, 139
Este, 162
Esterhazy, Prince Nicholas, 148
Esterhazy, Princess Maria, 148, 149
Ethalion, 138
Euryalus, 188, 199, 200, 205, 214
Excellent, 4, 75, 78, 81, 87, 88, 91, 92, 93, 94, 98, 99, 105, 132, 135, 261

Fearney, William, 93
Fellowes, Captain, 233
Fenwick, Robert, 54
Fenwicke, Sarah, *see* Collingwood
Ferdinand I of the Two Sicilies and Ferdinand IV of Naples, 67, 224, 226, 343
Ferdinand VII of Spain, 235
Fisgard, 170
Fisher, Admiral of the Fleet John Arbuthnot, 1st Lord, 120
Fitzgerald, Lord Robert, 173, 174
Flaxman, John, 219
Fogan, Henry, 260
Forbes, Admiral of the Fleet, the Hon. John, 76
Ford, Sir Richard, 130, 131
Foudroyant, 111
Fougeux, 197
Frazier, Lieutenant John, 167
Frederick, Rear-Admiral Thomas, 99, 117
Fremantle, Vice-Admiral Sir Thomas Francis, 203
Frere, John, 113
Fryers, Mrs, 118
Fuger, Friedrich Heinrich, 149
Furet, 224

Gage, General Thomas, 21, 22, 23
Gambier, Admiral James, 1st Lord, 111,
Ganteaume, Vice-Admiral Honore, 168, 169, 175, 177, 186, 232-5

Gardner, Admiral Sir Alan, 1st Lord, 116, 172-4, 176, 243
Garlies, Captain Lord, 98
General Kyd, 72
George III, 3, 18, 19, 23, 45, 56, 61, 65, 70, 71, 75, 77, 100, 112, 116, 118, 119, 123, 131, 138, 150, 162, 205, 206, 207, 208, 211, 242, 243, 252
George IV, 214
George V, 144
Germain, Lord George, 1st Viscount Sackville, 23, 26
Gibraltar, 55
Glasgow, 22
Glory, 175
Glover, Captain Bonovier, 29
Goschen, George Joachim, 1st Viscount, 113
Graves, Admiral Samuel, 22, 23, 24
Graves, Admiral Thomas, 1st Lord, 23, 69, 111
Gravina, Admiral Don Frederico, 200, 201
Grenville, Thomas, 229, 230, 253
Grey, General Charles, 1st Earl, 125
Grey, Charles, Viscount Howick and 2nd Earl Grey, 125, 221, 229, 243, 262
Grey, Admiral Sir George, 95, 125
Grindall, Captain, 200, 203
Gutierrez, General Don Antonio, 104

Hall, Cuthbert Collingwood, 257
Hallowell, Admiral Sir Benjamin Carew, 96, 185, 245, 249
Halcyon, 262
Hamilton, Emma, Lady, 42, 67, 119, 148, 149, 150, 154, 162, 179, 194, 205, 214
Hamilton, Sir William, 67, 148, 154
Hamond, Captain Sir Andrew Snape, 205
Hardy, Vice-Admiral Sir Thomas Masterman, 124, 195, 199, 201, 209,
Harpy, 158
Harvey, Admiral Eliab, 197
Harvey, Captain T., 233
Haswell, Captain, 24, 25, 26
Hay, Robert, 10, 247

283

285

Pitt, William, the Younger, 2, 3, 65, 113, 118, 121, 131, 132, 152, 158, 159, 174, 183-5, 204, 206, 214-16
Polite, Guiseppe, 232, 255
Polson, Major John, 27-9,
Polyphemus, 70
Pompee, 225
Pope, Alexander, 9
Popham, Rear-Admiral Sir Home Riggs, 68
Portland, Duke of, *see* Cavendish
Portland, 18
Preston, 21, 22
Preston, Colonel William, 22
Prince, 65, 66, 67, 200, 203
Prince George, 93, 98, 108, 113, 114, 115, 116, 121
Princess Royal, 117, 125, 127
Purvis, George, 218, 236
Purvis, Vice Admiral John Child, 233, 236, 243, 249

Queen, 116, 208
Queen Charlotte, 68, 69, 70, 74

Radcliffe, James, Earl Derwentwater, 46
Radstock, Lord, *see* Waldegrave
Raisonnable, 107
Raleigh, Sir Walter, 141
Ramillies, 40
Rattler, 35
Ravensworth, Lord, *see* Liddell
Redesdale, Algernon Bertram Mitford, Lord, *see* Mitford
Redoubtable, 197, 198, 199
Renown, 171
Resource, 30
Revolutionnaire, 107
Reynolds, Sir Joshua, 259
Robespierre, Maximilien, 64
Robinson, Admiral Hercules, 181, 195, 247
Robinson, Sir John Stephenson, 258
Roddam, Edward, 52
Roddam, Mary, *see* Carlyle
Roddam, Admiral Robert, 50, 52, 53, 73
Roddam, Robert, 51
Roddam, Sarah, *see* Blackett
Rodney, Admiral George Brydges, 1st Lord, 65, 110, 111
Roebuck, 110, 111

Romney, George, 217
Rose, George, 121, 185
Rosily, Vice-Admiral Francois, 187, 222, 235, 236
Rotherham, Captain Edward, 15, 180-2, 191, 194, 195, 198, 214
Rotherham, Dr. John, 181,
Da Rovezzano, Benedetto, 215
Royal George, 87
Royal Sovereign, 182, 185, 194, 197, 198, 199, 200, 247, 262
Rylands, Mrs John, 113

St. Vincent, Earl of, *see* John Jervis
Salim, Sultan, 230
Salvador del Mundo, 91, 92, 93
Sampson, 33
Sandwich, John Montagu, 4th Earl of, *see* Montagu
San Josef, 91, 93, 94, 98
San Justo, 197
San Leandro, 197
San Nicolas, 91, 92, 93, 94, 98, 99
Santa Ana, 195, 197, 198, 199, 200, 210
Santa Brigida, 138
Santissima Trinidad, 86, 91, 93, 100, 203, 209
San-Ysidro, 92, 93, 97
Savage, Vice-Admiral Henry, 215
Schwarzenberg, Prince Felix, 142
Scott, Revd. Dr Alexander, 176, 199
Scott, John, 199
Scott, John, 1st Earl of Eldon, 10, 58-61, 205, 209, 212, 229, 243, 260
Scott, Sir Walter, 53
Scott, William, 1st Lord Stowell, 58, 59, 60, 145, 229, 260
Seahorse, 18
Sebastiani, General, 229, 230
Serres, Thomas, 205, 209
Seymour, Vice-Admiral Lord Hugh, 70, 117
Shannon, 55
Shelbourne, Lord, *see* Lansdowne
Sherbrooke, General Sir John, 233
Sherbrooke, Rear-Admiral Robert St. Vincent, 143
Shirley, General Sir Thomas, 37
Simpson, John, 51
Siniavin, Vice-Admiral Dmitri Nicolaievitch, 231, 232